JOHN CHRYSOSTOM, THEOLOGIAN OF THE EUCHARIST

PATRISTIC THEOLOGY

John Chrysostom, Theologian of the Eucharist

KENNETH J. HOWELL

The Catholic University of America Press
Washington, D.C.

Portions of chapters 1, 2, and 3 have been previously published
in Kenneth J. Howell, "The Eucharist and the Life of Christ in the Preaching
of John Chrysostom," *Nova et Vetera* 19, no. 3 (2021): 791–824. Used with permission.

The paper used in this publication meets the minimum requirements
of American National Standards for Information Science—
Permanence of Paper for Printed Library Materials, ANSI Z39.48-1992.

Nihil Obstat:
Very Reverend John J. Dillon, S.T.B., Ph.D.
Censor Deputatus

Imprimatur:
Most Reverend Juan Esposito, J.C.D.
Vicar General and Moderator of the Curia

The Roman Catholic Archdiocese of Washington
May 13, 2024

The *nihil obstat* and *imprimatur* are official declarations that a book or
pamphlet is free of doctrinal or moral error. There is no implication that
those who have granted the *nihil obstat* and the *imprimatur* agree
with the content, opinions or statements expressed therein.

Cataloging-in-Publication Data is available from the Library of Congress

ISBN: 978-0-8132-3842-5 | eISBN: 978-0-8132-3843-2

Interior design by Burt&Burt
The text is set in Minion Pro and Meta Sans

To Sharon
My Beloved Companion

✠ ✠ ✠

Sharoni mulieri meae
amantissimae quae iuxta me semper
stabat et me amabat et amat,
qua tanto indignus sum.

✠ ✠ ✠

οὐδεμία δόξα, μικρὰ ἢ μακρά,
ἧς ἀξία πρὸς τὸν ἔρωτα τῆς γυναικός.
πάσα δόξα γίνεται κενοδοξία
ἐνώπιον τοῦ ὑπερβάλλοντος ἔρωτος
οὗ ἡ ἀρχὴ ἔστιν ἀπὸ τοῦ θεοῦ.

CONTENTS

Preface

St. John Chrysostom is a Church Father who deserves to be better known. Although he has been revered in both the Eastern and Western Church, his wisdom has not always been appreciated and has sometimes been misjudged, even by those who have read his writings. That many have had only a minimal acquaintance with his homilies is understandable because he wrote more than any other Greek-speaking Church Father that we know of. The size of his corpus rivals that of Augustine's 5.3 million words, the largest in the Latin-speaking Church. There has never been a complete edition of all Chrysostom's works in English, while there were at least two French bilingual editions done in the nineteenth century.

His writings on the Eucharist are even less known than other aspects of his pastoral and theological teaching. Those writings consist not of treatises but passages scattered throughout his homilies, over eighty of which I quote or cite in this volume. It took the monumental labors of the Spanish Jesuit Jesus Solano, around the mid-twentieth century, to cull through the entire *Patrologia Graeca* and *Patrologia Latina* to uncover the eucharistic passages in the Fathers for the first eight centuries of the Church. He showed that John wrote more about the Eucharist than any other Greek Father of the Church. Even more impressive than the amount of John's eucharistic passages is the depth and scope of his insights.

The knowledge of Chrysostom's eucharistic teachings has also been limited by the questions that scholars have posed to his texts. In the modern era since the sixteenth century, Western scholars have largely asked whether John believed in the *real presence*, a term neither he nor any Church Father ever used. I will argue that John did indeed believe in what would later be called the real presence and in the sacrificial nature of the Eucharist, but these beliefs were not the main focus of his concern. For the most part, he assumed their truth as he sought to elevate the liturgy of the Church and to apply the moral implications of the sacrament to his audience.

John was of course primarily a shepherd, not an academic theologian, and so his homilies reflect that pastoral situation. He was preeminently concerned with how his people would lead their lives in the light of Christ and the Eucharist. This orientation led him to look in two directions simultaneously. He read the Scriptures to see how the mysteries revealed there could shape the lives of Christians, and he read the struggles, both interior and exterior, which his people faced. This double vision gave him keen insights into one of the most persistent problems facing Christians. I explore this problem of "the remembrance of evil" or *mnesikakia* in chapter 8 because John wrote more about this than any other Church Father. He concentrated on the unforgiveness, bitterness, anger, and hatred that can linger in a Christian soul and thereby destroy divine life in it. John knew well what may surprise many about him. Only divine love could heal the soul. And above all, John embraced God's love for the human race, his *philanthropia*.

This realization may be one of his reasons for becoming a priest in the first place. As one trained in the school of Libanius, John was familiar with all the attempts of ancient philosophers to make human beings more virtuous. Platonists, Stoics, Epicureans, and teachers of a plethora of mixed philosophies were circulating in Chrysostom's society. They promised a better world if people would only follow their prescriptions. Even his teacher Libanius lamented John's abandonment of the noble aspirations of Greco-Roman paganism. John shared his teacher's desire for better morality, but he became convinced that it was only in Christ that such could be achieved. And the power to become virtuous was accessible only through the liturgy of the Church and the Eucharist that lay at its center.

This book has been several years in the making, and my reading of John's works extends back fifteen to twenty years. Yet it has only been in the last five years that an adequate picture of John's thinking has come into focus. This has been a labor of love, but not in the usual sense of that phrase. As any author knows, months and years of reading, writing, editing, and compiling are only repaid by the hope that readers will benefit from the author's work. The painstaking work of translating the Greek texts of John Chrysostom into coherent English can only be rewarded by placing the wisdom of the Golden Mouth in front of those who need it most. None of these efforts can match the pleasure and sense of joy that comes from encountering a man who was deeply in love with God, a man who sought to dangle the faith he professed as a love-charm to entice others into the same. As was said of Abel, being dead, he still speaks.

I have always tried to keep in mind a wider scope of readers than patristic scholars. Because I hope that Christians of both the East and the West will appreciate this homiletic and pastoral giant, I have decided to use transliterations of certain key Greek words to make them easier to pronounce (see the technical note). If a wide swath of Christians can profit from this book, I have no doubt that they will discover, as I have, that John Chrysostom is a man who can still be of great benefit today. The universal Church in all its geographical and liturgical diversity can find in this Church Father a renewed love of God manifested in Scripture and in sacrament. His teachings on the Eucharist are needed today as much as they were in his own day. If Christians today can find in John's writings a fresh love of the Eucharist as a divine gift, my labors will have been more than rewarded.

Acknowledgements

The debts I owe in the writing this book are so enormous that a complete list would exceed its pages. My interest in John Chrysostom was kindled by the sheer size of his corpus, but my grasp of his eucharistic teaching began with reading Jesus Solano's excerpts in *Textos Eucaristicos Primitivos*. I have profited from the many Chrysostom scholars of the past and the present. Chrysostomos Baur, Bertrand de Margerie, Bradley Nassif, and David Rylaarsdam are just a few who stand out for their scholarship. It is Wendy Mayer, perhaps the most preeminent living Chrysostom scholar, who has gone out of her way to help me when I needed it most. The anonymous reviewers from The Catholic University of America Press have also been very helpful.

Others who have made this work possible include Mathew Levering and Andrew Hofer, both of whom evidence the highest standards of scholarship. Thomas J. Kronholz did much in helping this book come to conclusion. Daniel Toma's knowledge of the Byzantine traditions has been a sounding board for me. The Rev. Stuart Swetland has long been a valued spiritual presence in my life and work. Without his encouragement I would not have brought this project to conclusion. Melissa Marquart was kind enough to create the graphics, Rebekah Bambenek helped with the Indices, and John Martino's professionalism has also been crucial in bringing this manuscript to light.

Abbreviations

CCC	*Catechism of the Catholic Church.*
FC	*Fathers of the Church: A New Translation* series. The Catholic University of America Press.
PG	*Patrologia Graeca.* Edited by J.-P. Migne. 162 vols. Paris, 1857–86.
PL	*Patrologia Latina.* Edited by J.-P. Migne. 217 vols. Paris, 1844–64.
SC	*Sources Chrétiennes.* Paris: Editions du Cerf.
ST	*Summa Theologiae* (Thomas Aquinas).
LXX	The Septuagint, Greek translation of the Old Testament Hebrew text originating in Alexandria around 250 BC.
MT	Masoretic Text, the standard Hebrew text of the Old Testament.

Technical Note

Chrysostom's works are typically cited in abbreviated Latin titles. In consideration of readers who are not familiar with Latin or Greek, I have used English titles of Chrysostom's homilies to aid them. If the English title is not close to the Latin title, I have occasionally inserted the standard Latin title to help scholars identify the proper homily under discussion. An index of Chrysostom's homilies used is attached.

I have also decided to transliterate certain Greek words into the Roman alphabet to ease their pronunciation for a wider audience. Therefore commonly used words like *oikonomia* (οἰκονομία), *sugkatabasis* (συγκατάβασις), and even *mnesikakia* (μνησικακία) are always placed in italics to indicate that they are foreign words whose range of meaning is not always equivalent to one English word.

The Thesaurus Linguae Graecae (TLG) housed at the University of California, Irvine, is a gold mine for scholars working in ancient Greek. It has been my daily companion, a kind of *vade mecum*. The Greek texts used here, however, are from the *Patrologia Graeca* and *Sources Chretiennes*. All translations from ancient and modern languages are my own unless otherwise noted.

JOHN CHRYSOSTOM, THEOLOGIAN OF THE EUCHARIST

Introduction

Golden Mouth, Golden Chalice

On a Good Friday in a cemetery outside Antioch, John Chrysostom stood beside a makeshift altar to celebrate the death of Jesus Christ some four centuries earlier. Although John had probably been ordained a priest only a few years earlier, he was already drawing attention as one of the most effective preachers in the Greek-speaking Church. He owed his eloquence in part to his study under one of the finest orators of the East, Libanius, who would later lament John's becoming a Christian. Within a century after his own death, John would be dubbed by Pope Vigilius "The Golden Mouth" (Χρυσόστομος). His eloquence would allow him to rise to the most prominent See of the Eastern Church, Constantinople, in a little more than a dozen years.

His concern that Good Friday evening was not for himself, however, but for his flock, whom he had brought from the city to remember the death of the Lord he served. That he and his congregation should have gathered in a cemetery rather than in a church or shrine in the city provoked him to explain that Christ was present there on the altar no less than when he walked the earth. As he would many times, John referred to the liturgy and the Eucharist in his homily as the entry of earth into heaven. In poignant terms, he proclaimed, "Where Christ is, there too is heaven."[1] Nothing better expresses the teaching of John Chrysostom on the Eucharist than this pithy statement, but the breadth of his teaching transcends almost anything found in other Church Fathers. The acclaimed preacher of Antioch, and later the Patriarch of Constantinople, has left more material on the Eucharist than any other Father of the Greek-speaking Church.

John never wrote a treatise devoted to the Eucharist—no Church Father ever did—but his homilies contain hundreds of references to and explanations of the liturgy and the central player in that liturgy, the eucharistic Christ. We shall see in the pages that follow that the Eucharist with its home in the liturgy of the Church embodies and extends the presence and ministry of Christ within space and time. The reality of Christ's presence in the world is the unifying force between heaven and earth and between the members of Christ's mystical body. It stands at the crossroads of good and evil, of love and hate, calling all believers to holiness and charity. It is what underlies the use of Scripture in worship, what unites the disparate concerns Christians have, and what provides hope for their future. It is what offers strength and sustenance for living a Christian life. This means that the presence of Christ is multifaceted, bearing the appearance of a diamond that must be examined from various angles to be appreciated and received. The Eucharist is the highest expression of the presence of Jesus Christ and, as such, is the source and summit of the Christian life. The Eucharist stands front and center in the liturgy of the Church, in the reading of Scripture, and in private prayer, which is why its presence in the life of the Church is so important. For John, "Where Christ is, there is heaven."

As important as the Eucharist was for John Chrysostom, the Eucharist made no sense apart from the Incarnation of the Eternal Logos into the world.[2] For John, as for so many other Church Fathers, the descent of the Son of God was the central truth of Christianity, the central truth of his death and resurrection. The French theologian Jean Daniélou, himself a student of the Fathers, summarized this well when he said that the Christian faith has only one subject, the mystery of Christ dead and risen, but John knew, that there were many modes in which this one truth was understood and lived in

1 *The Cemetery and the Cross*, PG 49:395.

2 August Naegle, *Die Eucharistielehre des Heiligen Johannes Chrysostomus* (Freiburg, Germany, 1900), 65, writes, "For the Incarnation and Eucharist stand in the closest connection with one another. This is a truth that Chrysostom never tires of expressing."

ancient Christianity. For John, the various venues of truth are all manifestations of one underlying reality, that of the Incarnate Christ. The old covenant anticipates it; the life of Jesus reveals it fully; the liturgy celebrates it; and the Eucharist embodies it. Under all these guises the same divine presence exerts its influence and beckons earthly dwellers to a heavenly destination. So when John said that heaven was where Christ is, he consciously drew attention to the liturgy as the source of grace.[3]

Although the focus of this volume is not on John's biography, it may be helpful to give some sense of his life and context. John was born in Antioch of Syria sometime between 345 and 349. He was a younger contemporary of Basil the Great (330–79), and Ambrose of Milan (340–97) while being slightly younger than Basil's brother Gregory of Nyssa (335–95). He was an older contemporary of Augustine of Hippo (354–430) and almost an exact contemporary of Jerome (347–420), Paulinus of Nola (345–431), and Prudentius (348–405), although he probably knew none of them personally. This list, however partial, illustrates that he lived during one of the most theologically productive periods of the Church's history and became a leader of gigantic proportions amid many trials and sufferings. Neither the rigors of Antioch nor the intrigues of Constantinople ever diminished the power of his preaching. Although the honorific title of "Golden Mouth" was probably not bestowed because of the amount of his preaching, that honor reflects both its quality and its voluminous proportions.

John was born into a Christian family of some standing, although his father died when he was young. His mother wanted him to have the best education possible and so John was sent to the leading orator (rhetor) of Antioch, Libanius. Although Libanius was a self-conscious pagan, he had among his students several from Christian backgrounds. Acquiring a rhetorical education in most major cities of the empire would open doors to important positions and privileges. Augustine had a similar experience in Carthage, which gave him an opportunity to take the position of court orator in Milan. John's choice of life, however, did not follow the standard trajectory.

The Antioch into which John was ordained was much more diverse than moderns might suppose. Robert Wilken rendered an invaluable service to Church history when he revealed that the relations between Jews and Christians in fourth-century Antioch were much more complex than previously

3 The full quotation from Jean Daniélou appears later in this introduction.

believed.[4] Not only was there a sizable community of Jews and prominent non-Christians like Libanius, there were also various Christian factions in the city. John belonged to the Meletian faction named after Bishop Meletius, who groomed him, first as a lector in 371 and then as a personal assistant. In that same year, John abandoned Antioch for the caves in the mountains around the city to which ascetics had retreated. This withdrawal was the fulfillment of a wish he had been nurturing since leaving Libanius's school some years earlier, but it may have been precipitated at that moment by the troubles in the Church of Antioch. In any case, we know very little of John's solitary life for the next four years. We can easily imagine, however, that John devoted a considerable amount of time to memorizing the Scriptures, both because the full utilization of the memory was something he developed well under Libanius and because of the intrinsic value of such an effort. We often hear John quoting extensively from Scripture in his homilies preached later.

After John's return from the solitary caves outside Antioch, he was ordained a deacon by Meletius in 381. During his time as a deacon, John was not allowed to preach, but he was employed in the instruction of catechumens and in service to the poor. This latter duty no doubt left an impression on him, for thereafter he was always a vocal advocate of the underprivileged.[5] John's ordination to the priesthood took place in January of 386 at the hands of the new bishop of Antioch, Flavian, who had been elected by the Council of Constantinople in 381. We have two important writings (homilies) from this early period: *On the Priesthood* and his *Homilies on the Incomprehensibility of God.* Over the next eleven or twelve years, John expended much energy on expounding the meaning of the Scriptures in homilies on various biblical books.

Life changed rather dramatically for Chrysostom once he was elevated as the Patriarch of Constantinople in 397. His life became a series of conflicts due to intrigues in the royal court and his being a constant thorn in the side of the imperial family. He suffered two exiles from his See, the last of which ended in his death September 14, 407, in Comana in Pontus near the Black

4 "In the fourth century, Christians lived in a pluralistic world and it could not be assumed without argument that Christian beliefs were true or that the Christian way of relating scriptural prophecies to historical events was manifest. It was not enough simply to assert one's beliefs" (Robert Wilken, *John Chrysostom and the Jews: Rhetoric and Reality in the Late 4th Century* [Eugene, OR: Wipf and Stock, 1983], 159).

5 J. N. D. Kelly, *Golden Mouth: The Story of John Chrysostom; Ascetic, Preacher, Bishop* (London: Duckworth, 1995), 39.

Sea. In his troubles both outward and inward, he continued to show pastoral solicitude for his beloved flock. And we still benefit from his last writing, *On the Providence of God*, which he apparently sent to his favored friend Olympias back in Constantinople.

The Western Church has recognized John Chrysostom as the Doctor of the Eucharist partially because of how much he wrote about this sacrament but, strangely enough, there has been a relative paucity of research on John's doctrine of the Eucharist.[6] Through the centuries the occasional study of his sacramental thought has taken a back seat to his biblical hermeneutics and his use of rhetoric. The most extensive survey of scholarly literature up to 1906 only included a few studies on Chrysostom's eucharistic doctrine.[7] And as Wendy Mayer, Chrysostom's preeminent bibliographer, has noted, the twentieth century was not particularly kind to John in general. Explorations of his sacramental teaching were few and far between. This contrasts with a veritable explosion of research in the twenty-first century, which includes two doctoral theses on the Eucharist in French. Both of these, however, were limited to a select range of Chrysostom's texts.[8]

What might account for this lack of attention to the variety of John's eucharistic doctrine? The answer may lie in the questions asked by scholars in the modern period. Since the Reformation, Catholic and Protestant scholars have debated long and hard over the real presence and the Eucharist as sacrifice, both bones of contention in the sixteenth century, the dynamics of which influenced scholars for centuries. At the turn of the twentieth century the problematics of that framing of the question influenced Pierre Batiffol as he focused his history on conversion of the eucharistic elements.[9] August Naegle likewise asked similar questions of Chrysostom's eucharistic passages.

6 Benedict XVI offered some salient reflections on the importance of Chrysostom for the present-day Church that are balanced and instructive. See Benedict XVI (Joseph Ratzinger), "Letter of His Holiness Benedict XVI on the Occasion of the 16th Centenary of the Death of St. John Chrysostom," https://www.vatican.va/content/benedict-xvi/en/letters/2007/documents/hf_ben-xvi_let_20070810_giovanni-crisostomo.html.

7 Chrysostomos Baur, OSB, *S. Jean Chrysostome et ses oeuvres dans l'histoire littéraire: Essai présenté à l'occasion de XV centenaire* (Louvain: Bureaux de recueil, 1907), 290–93.

8 Jacky Marsaux, "La Théologie de l'Eucharistie selon Jean Chrysostome: Étude du schéma sacrificiel" (doctoral diss., Université Paris-IV et Institut Catholique de Paris, 2008), and Pierre Molinié, *Jean Chrysostome, exégète: Le commentaire de la deuxième épître aux Corinthiens*, Orientalia Christiana Analecta 305 (Rome: Pontificio Istituto Orientale, 2019).

9 Pierre Batiffol, *L'Eucharistie: La Presence Réele et la Transubstantiation*, 10th ed., Études d'histoire et de théologie positive (Paris: Libraire Victor Lecoffre, 1930), 407–21.

While Naegle recognized other strains of thought in Chrysostom's corpus, he nevertheless zeroed in on the issue of real presence while passing by the other connections.[10] Both these works were careful and detailed, but they lacked a comprehensive examination of Chrysostom's texts. More recent histories of the Eucharist have enlarged the questions asked but there is still much to be explored. Christoph Markschies recounts how more recent scholars have supposed that a kind of transformation in eucharistic faith took place in the fourth century.[11] Paul Bradshaw also emphasizes this change as an instance of the liturgy becoming an instrument of catechesis.[12] In this framework the practice and theology of the Eucharist moved from a sacred meal to a conception of the liturgy as mystery. And certainly John Chrysostom sees both liturgy and Eucharist as a mystery but how that played out in a wider theological context still remains to be understood. Rudolf Brändle shows how John was intent on the moral application of the sacrament to his congregants both on individual and societal levels, themes we will explore in chapters 7-9.[13] Brändle's study implies, and some extent demonstrates, there is much more to be explored in the Chrysostom corpus. At times he cites John's homilies without much plumbing of their meaning.[14]

There remains a plethora of virtually untouched homilies that can lead the modern reader to a much profounder understanding of John's doctrine. The abundance of those eucharistic texts is in evidence in the bilingual collection *Textos Eucaristicos Primitivos* by Jesus Solano, SJ, which excerpted and translated a wide range of patristic texts from the first eight centuries of the Church.[15] Solano's monumental work showed that there were more

10 Naegle, *Die Eucharistielehre des Heiligen Johannes Chrysostomus*.

11 Markschies, Christoph "Current Research on the Eucharist in Ancient Christianity" *Early Christianity* 7 (2016) 417-446.

12 Paul Bradshaw *Eucharistic Origins* (Oxford: Oxford University Press, 2004), 139-157.

13 Brändle, Rudolf "Eucharistie und christliches Leben" in D. Hellholm and D. Sänger (eds.), *The Eucharist – Its Origins and Contexts: Sacred Meal, Communal Meal, Table Fellowship in Late Antiquity, Early Judaism, and Early Christianity* (Tubingen: Mohr Siebeck. 2017), 1191-1215. Because Brändle's study encompassed both John and his fellow Antiochene Theodore of Mopsuestia, his treatment, he necessarily had to remain at a more superficial level.

14 Brändle does argue that the Epiclesis is the most important element in the liturgy since it is by the Spirit's descent that the transmutation of the bread and wine takes place. I mildly challenge this interpretation in chapter four.

15 Jesus Solano, *Textos Eucaristicos Primitivos, edicion bilingue de los contenidos en la Sagrada Escritura y los Santos Padres*, vol 1, *Hasta fines del siglo IV* (Madrid: Biblioteca de Autores Cristianos, 1952); vol. 2, *Hasta el fin de la epoca patristica (s. VII-VIII)* (1954).

passages on the Eucharist in Chrysostom's corpus than in any other Greek Father. It was not until the 1990s that a similar work appeared in Italian.[16] No comparable work has ever appeared in English. In what follows, I will draw on these passages and more to demonstrate that John was not a superficial thinker in regard to the sacraments but in fact possessed a profundity worthy of admiration.[17] In this volume, I explore a much wider range of texts that bear on John's eucharistic doctrine. That exploration shows quite adequately that posing a limited number of doctrinal questions can severely restrict understanding of the wealth of eucharistic wisdom in John's preaching.

In earlier generations John Chrysostom was sometimes thought to be a moralizing preacher who did not have a deep theology to contribute to the Church. Unlike the spiritual depth of a Gregory of Nyssa or the theological acumen of a Gregory Nazianzen, Chrysostom's thinking might appear superficial in many of his running scriptural homilies where he limits himself to direct commentary on biblical texts. However, I believe this is a misjudgment that is based on an incomplete reading. In recent years, a number of scholars have argued that Chrysostom's theology is both coherent and more profound than previously recognized. David Rylaarsdam's study of Chrysostom's use of divine pedagogy and adaptability has shown a more perceptive and profound theology underlying John's many sermons. His work deepened our understanding of what scholars had long noticed about the Antiochene's use of *sugkatabasis* (συγκατάβασις = *condescensio*).[18] We will observe many times how John sees God's lowering of himself to the level of human beings as operative in the Eucharist and the liturgy of the Church.

A second perspective has also opened new windows on the Golden Mouth. Recasting John as a Christian philosopher who sought to use classic methods of *paideia* in the service of Christian truth has shown that *philosophia*, so different from modern connotations of its English derivative, was

16 Gerardo di Nola, *Bibliotheca Patristica Eucharistica*. Volume 3 is devoted exclusively to John Chrysostom: *La Dottrina Eucharistica de Giovanni Crisostomo* (Vatican City: Libreria Editrice Vaticana, 1997).

17 George D. Dragas gives a helpful summary of modern Greek theologians who have done work on Chrysostom's theology. See Dragas, "Perceptions of John Chrysostom in Contemporary Greek Orthodoxy," in *Chrysostomosbilder in 1600 Jahren Facetten der Wirkungsgeschichte eines Kirchenvaters*, ed. Martin Wallraff and Rudolf Brändle (Berlin: Walter de Gruyter, 2008), 373–409.

18 David Rylaarsdam, *John Chrysostom on Divine Pedagogy: The Coherence of His Theology and Preaching* (Oxford: Oxford University Press, 2014).

a preeminent concern of his. This approach is based on the groundbreaking work of Pierre Hadot, who more than any other scholar elucidated the spiritual goals of personal and moral formation underlying Hellenistic philosophy.[19] Ancient philosophers of many stripes shared a common goal of making human life better by engagement with *philosophia*, and so their work was not (only) theoretical but practical. It was designed to help people live more productive and meaningful lives. The Epicurean dictum "Vain is the word of that philosopher which does not heal the sufferings of man" was shared widely by both Christian and pagan thinkers in Chrysostom's day.[20] John's own teacher, Libanius, displays such concerns in his letters when he glossed his own words "near to philosophy" by enumerating "freedom of speech, a life of despising evil, love of noble things, . . . and contempt for gold [i.e., money]."[21] Chrysostom shared the concerns of his teacher even though he had come to believe that a different *philosophia* would lead to such virtues. The practical implication for Chrysostom scholars becomes evident because the line between philosopher and pastoral guide was simply not that clear. The Neoplatonists, the Stoics, and even the Epicureans engaged in activities and teaching that today might be seen as religious or pastoral. And certainly, Christian pastors presented their teaching as *philosophia*, a way of living superior to other alternatives present in late antiquity. One example, among many, of this medico-philosophical approach (or motivation) may be found in Chrysostom's homilies on the Gospel of John, where he understands that "the condition of his listeners requires a kind of medical care" that can transform their lives into a better art of living.[22]

John Chrysostom has also been viewed through the lens of hermeneutics and exegesis. A classic distinction said that the Antiochene (literal)

19 Pierre Hadot, *Philosophy as a Way of Life: Spiritual Exercises from Socrates to Foucault*, ed. Arnold I. Davidson, trans. Michael Chase (Oxford: Blackwell Publishing, 1995).

20 Hadot, *Philosophy as a Way of Life*, 267. The application of Hadot's approach to Chrysostom can be observed in a number of publications. For a survey of the relevant literature see Wendy Mayer, "John Chrysostom: Moral Philosopher and Physician of the Soul," in *John Chrysostom Past, Present, Future*, ed. Doru Costache and Merio Baghos (Sydney: AIOOS Press, 2017), 193–215.

21 Libanius, *Letter to Thalassius*, in *Libanius: Autobiography and Selected Letters*, trans. and ed. A. F. Norman, LCL 478 (Cambridge, MA: Harvard University Press, 1992), 341–42.

22 Athanasios Despotis, "The Philosophical-Religious Hybridity in John 6 and Its Reception in the Commentaries of Origen and Chrysostom," in *Drawing and Transcending Boundaries in the New Testament and Early Christianity*, ed. Jacobus Kok, Martin Webber, and Jermo van Nes (Münster: LIT Verlag, 2020), 59–60. Most recently the theme of the healing of the soul has been explored in Junghun Bae, *John Chrysostom on Almsgiving and the Therapy of the Soul* (Leiden: Brill, 2021).

method of interpretation was in sharp contrast with the Alexandrian (allegorical) method, which played fast and footloose with the biblical text. And there is no doubt that the Antiochenes, such as Diodore of Tarsus (John's teacher), saw figures like Origen of Alexandria as engaging in flights of fancy that moved too far away from the biblical text. John was indeed a careful observer of the biblical text as seen in the way he often invokes the notion of ἀκρίβεια (accuracy, precision) explicitly to attend to the particulars of a text. He certainly does not engage in what is typically called allegorical interpretation, characteristic of the Alexandrians like Origen or Clement, but neither is he opposed to seeing deeper or higher meanings in the text. Furthermore, recent scholarship has rightly maintained that the reputed opposition between Alexandrian allegorism and Antiochene literalism is less than an adequate characterization. Frances Young captures this new perspective accurately: "The traditional categories of 'literal,' 'typological,' and 'allegorical' are quite simply inadequate as descriptive tools, let alone analytical tools. Nor is the Antiochene reaction against Alexandrian allegory correctly described as an appeal to literal or historical meaning."[23] Hans Boersma has elaborated on Young's theme by laying bare what he calls a sacramental reading of Scripture that characterized many Church Fathers.[24] I shall return to this theme later, but it is certain that John's literal interpretation by no means excluded a reading of both the Scriptures and the liturgy that involved higher dimensions than the historical.[25]

I leave aside the judgment as to what it might mean to call John Chrysostom a literal interpreter of the Bible, primarily because of the inherent ambiguity in what constitutes literal interpretation.[26] Yet his homilies

23 Frances Young, *Biblical Exegesis and the Formation of Christian Culture* (Cambridge: Cambridge University Press, 1997; reprint, Peabody, MA: Hendrickson, 2002), 2.

24 Hans Boersma, *Scripture as Real Presence: Sacramental Exegesis in the Early Church* (Grand Rapids, MI: Baker Academic, 2017), 1–26.

25 The hermeneutics of Chrysostom has recently been explored in Andrew Hofer, *The Power of Patristic Preaching: The Word in Our Flesh* (Washington, DC: The Catholic University of America Press, 2023); Guillaume Bady, *La Source sans fin: La Bible chez Jean Chrysostome*, Cahiers de Biblia Patristica 23 (Turnhout: Brepols, 2021).

26 The notion of literal interpretation may refer to the *sensus litteralis*, used by Augustine as a near equivalent to *sensus historicus*, or to the more modern idea that it entails a one-to-one correspondence with the historical events. The *sensus historicus* meant only that the biblical narrative was relating a historical event, not that every detail in the narrative was in a one-to-one correspondence with the actual history. Thus, Augustine saw his interpretation of Genesis chapter one as literal even though he did not see the days as describing twelve- or twenty-four-hour periods. For further analysis of this see Kenneth J. Howell, "Natural Knowledge and Textual

display several notable patterns that are certainly not pedantic or pedestrian. Most homilies range from four to five thousand words and sometimes cover a wide range of topics. He is very attentive to the rhetorical nature of the biblical text in that he sees certain wording as being significant. He sometimes says that the biblical author used a certain phrase or word with deliberate contrast to another possible choice of speech ("he did not say this but said that"). John also leaves his outside standpoint at times and enters into the story itself by way of a dialogue with the participants in the scriptural narrative. "Why did you say . . . , O Elijah?" or "What were you thinking, O Peter?" becomes a method to elucidate an aspect of meaning which may be easily missed if one remains in an external viewpoint. He even ventures to take on the voice of Christ in more than simple quotation. He paraphrases and expands Christ's voice and actions so as to draw out meaning or to connect aspects of truth that seem to be separate. These interpretative strategies show that John desires his congregants to experience the realities recounted in the text rather than just be informed about them. As Margaret Mitchell observed, the Antiochene preacher seeks to go beyond mere description of Paul, John's favorite saint: "The purpose of Chrysostom's portraiture was to bring the saint to life in the presence of his congregational audience so that they, too, might experience the living encounter with Paul that John describes himself having when reading Paul's letter, and most importantly, by hearing these portraits, might become like the apostle."[27] Other scholars concur. Bradley Nassif and David Rylaarsdam have both arrived at the same conclusion.[28] John is more than a descriptive pedagogue. His preaching attempted to bring Christ and his salvific work to the present so that his hearers might enjoy the fruits of redemption.[29] For John this bringing the past into the present

Meaning in Augustine's Interpretation of Genesis: The Three Functions of Natural Philosophy," in *Interpreting Nature and Scripture: History of a Dialogue in the Abrahamic Religions*, ed. Jitse M. van der Meer and Scott M. Mandelbrote (Leiden: Brill, 2008), 117–45.

27 Margaret Mitchell, *The Heavenly Trumpet: John Chrysostom and the Art of Pauline Interpretation* (London: Westminster John Knox Press, 2002), xxi.

28 Bradley Nassif, "Theoria in St. John Chrysostom's Exegesis: A Study in Biblical Hermeneutics and the Spiritual Life" (PhD diss., Fordham University, 1991), and Rylaarsdam, *John Chrysostom on Divine Pedagogy*.

29 Robert Hill, the most extensive translator of Chrysostom's homilies, contends that John's preaching had the multidimensional purpose of proclaiming and instantiating saving truth. Chrysostom's doctrine of scriptural inspiration was more than inerrancy, though it included that. See Robert Hill, introduction to *St. John Chrysostom: Homilies on Genesis*, FC 74 (Washington, DC: The Catholic University of America Press, 1986), 19.

and the eternal into time had a twofold manifestation: word and sacrament. Proclamation and sacramental embodiment were two complimentary ways of the Church encountering the same divine reality.[30]

KEY CONCEPTS AND TERMS

Throughout this book I shall invite my readers into the world of John Chrysostom and further into the things he would want us to encounter with the hope that we may be transported back in time but upward in spirit. Being so transported is the primary function of the liturgy of the Church. For John, as for many Eastern Christians still today, the liturgy is the centerpiece of the Christian life because it affords the unparalleled opportunity to enter into heaven and to make of earth a heaven. In *Homily 24 on 1 Corinthians* Chrysostom captures the essence of the liturgy in a pithy but compelling statement, "Here this mystery makes earth a heaven for you."[31] The context makes it clear that the mystery is the eucharistic table where "hope, salvation, light, and life" can be found.[32] In Chrysostom we encounter the stark realism in which faith and moral virtue are not manufactured by human invention. They are engendered by contact with celestial realities. For the encounter with this reality, I choose the term *actualization* to express what many Eastern writers speak of as "entrance into the kingdom," a phrase that expresses aptly John's view of the liturgy and the Eucharist as advancing into another world through the divine gifts present in the liturgy. Alexander Schmemann expressed this well when he spoke of the liturgy as an entry into something much greater than this world: "Our entrance into the presence of Christ is an entrance into a fourth dimension which allows us to see the ultimate reality of life. It is not an escape from the world, rather it is the arrival at the vantage point from which we can see more deeply into the reality of the world."[33]

30 Craig Satterlee explicated the sacramental nature of preaching in Ambrose of Milan. See *Ambrose of Milan's Method of Mystagogical Preaching* (Collegeville, MN: Liturgical Press, 2002).

31 *Homily 24 on 1 Corinthians*, PG 61:205. Ἐνταῦθα γάρ σοι τὴν γῆν οὐρανὸν ποιεῖ τουτὶ τὸ μυστήριον.

32 *Homily 24 on 1 Corinthians*, PG 61:205.

33 Alexander Schmemann, *For the Life of the World* (Crestwood, NY: St. Vladimir's Press, 1973), 27.

This entry is an entry into "the joy of the Lord" (cf. Mt 25:21). It represents the whole life of the Christian, not simply one part among many. In this view, all of life becomes eucharistic, a thanksgiving rendered back to God. This entrance into and dwelling in the presence of Christ is so essential that it is what makes the Church what it is, "For they [worshipers] are now on their way to constitute the Church, or to be more exact, to be transformed into the Church of God."[34] And Schmemann sees every aspect of liturgy as sacramental: "The proclamation of the Word is a sacramental act par excellence because it is a transforming act. It transforms the human words of the Gospel into the Word of God and the manifestation of the Kingdom."[35] This reflects accurately the way in which actualization was at play both in John's preaching and in the liturgy as a whole. Preaching Christ and his redemption from the Scriptures made those things present to the worshiper, and this presence was strengthened by the eucharistic liturgy. Both word and sacrament were visibly human, but the deeper spiritual reality came from the world above, "For the church is forged not in a gold or silver shop but in the festal assembly of angels."[36] This task of actualization in preaching was not unique to Chrysostom since it was common to the Fathers in both the East and the West, but John did engage in certain readings of the biblical text which highlighted actualization.

Liturgy then is the temporal uniting of the celestial arrangement and the earthly events of salvation (*oikonomia*) in anticipation of the eschaton at which the two will converge and merge into one. Then eternity becomes history and history is swallowed up in eternity. This is why the liturgy was for John "awe-inspiring" or even "frightful." One of his favorite family of words to capture the liturgy is φρικτός, φρικώδης, and φρίκη, words that bear both strong negative ("frightful," "shudder") and positive ("awe-inspiring") connotations. In many contexts he combines these adjectives with other significant liturgical terms: "What are you doing, O man? As Christ is present and angels attending, do you turn away from this awe-inspiring table lying in abandonment as your brothers are being led into the mysteries?"[37] The awe-inspiring nature of the liturgy derives from its contact with heavenly

34 Schmemann, *For the Life of the World*, 27.

35 Schmemann, *For the Life of the World*, 33.

36 *Homily 50 on Matthew*, PG 58:508.

37 *On the Baptism of Christ*, PG 49:370. Similar expressions occur in *The Betrayal of Judas*, PG 49:380, and *On the Birth of Christ*, PG 49:360, where he adds, "awesome and divine table."

realities. This view of liturgy survives down to today in the Eastern Churches, and it has not been lost on liturgical scholars in the West. Robert Taft, the dean of Eastern liturgical studies, once captured it thus: "In a very real sense the whole life of the Church in the patristic period was liturgical."[38] Speaking of the integral union of parts in Eastern liturgies Taft also laid bare what we will observe in John Chrysostom's view of liturgy: "This [union of parts] may be because of the *iconographic* nature of worship in the East: the liturgical action is not just a "ceremony"; it is an object of contemplation, an awesome vision, full of mystery, before which one prostrates in reverential fear."[39] The liturgy of the Church is a mirror and reflects the hierarchical structure of the angels as it joins in their lauding of the Creator and Redeemer.

The liturgy is glorious to be sure, but what of the goal or *telos* of this liturgy? On one level it is to extend the life of Jesus Christ beyond the limitations of his time and place in Palestine. We will often see in the following pages that what modern theologians call the real presence—a term unknown among the ancients—amounts to something simple and profound. The Eucharist is simply an extension of the earthly life of Jesus Christ, but this reality is also beyond human comprehension; it defies rational explanation. In short, it is a mystery. But even that fact is not enough because we can and should ask why this arrangement was chosen. Why did God want Christ's life extended into the life of the Church? There are many ways that John answers this question implicitly, but one that strikes at the core of the eucharistic mystery is when he contrasts the Israelites coming out of Egypt with the Christians in liturgy. The eucharistic altar was an implicit call to follow the example of the ancient Hebrews: "They were about to enter Palestine and so they walked with a roadmap; but we are about to go on a journey to heaven."[40] The goal or *telos* of communion in the Eucharist is nothing less than food for the journey to heaven. The earthly liturgy is the only key to open the door to heaven and so John exults and glories in it to the greatest degree. For John the liturgy is in effect an actualization of heaven for earthbound creatures.

God ultimately lies so shrouded in mystery that the liturgy had to be a kind of lowering and adapting of himself that was based on a plan or arrangement (οἰκονομία). The liturgy of the Church is a kind of condescension

38 Robert F. Taft, "The Spirit of Eastern Christian Worship," in *Beyond East and West: Problems in Liturgical Understanding* (Rome: Edizioni Orientalia Christiana, 2001), 145.

39 Taft, "Spirit of Eastern Christian Worship," 153.

40 *Homily 82 on Matthew*, PG 58:743.

because it is an extension of the *oikonomia* found in Scripture. The patterns of salvation history evident in the Old Testament included strict regulations of Israel's cult or worship of the Lord. Those regulations were not an afterthought to the plan of redemption; they were part and parcel of that salvific plan. For John, as for the entire ancient Church, the liturgy of the new covenant Church was also an essential component of the divine *oikonomia*. At the center of that new covenant plan was the Eucharist because it was considered the consummate means by which the redemption accomplished by Christ would be communicated to the Church.

While many modern theologians immersed in the Fathers have seen the divine *oikonomia* as central to their conception of the faith and their interpretation of the Bible, few have captured this notion as succinctly as Jean Daniélou. Appearing as the opening sentence of an article in a rather obscure French journal, this Jesuit could probably never have anticipated how often and appreciatively his words would be quoted:

> The Christian faith has only one object, the mystery of Christ died and risen. But this unique mystery subsists under different modes. It is prefigured in the Old Testament, it is accomplished historically in the earthly life of Christ, it is contained in mystery in the sacraments, it is lived mystically in souls, it is accomplished socially in the Church, it is consummated eschatologically in the heavenly kingdom. Thus, the Christian has at his disposal several registers, a multi-dimensional symbolism, to express this unique reality. The whole of Christian culture consists in grasping the links that exist between Bible and liturgy, Gospel and eschatology, mysticism and liturgy. The application of this method to scripture is called spiritual exegesis, applied to liturgy it is called mystagogy. This consists in reading in the rites the mystery of Christ, and in contemplating beneath the symbols the invisible reality.[41]

Daniélou here captures the essence of Christianity in as poignant a fashion as one might imagine. The underlying question seems to be what unites all the disparate aspects of a truly Christian theology. As a systematic thinker as well as a detailed historian, Daniélou reflected much on the question of continuity and discontinuity across the spectrum of Christian doctrines. Amid the diversity of biblical texts and genres, amongst the diversity of

41 Jean Daniélou, "Le symbolisme des rites baptismaux," *Dieu vivant* 1 (1945): 15–43, as quoted in Robert F. Taft, "Toward a Theology of the Christian Feast," in *Beyond East and West*, 28–29.

patristic authors, what unified all doctrine and devotion? Daniélou saw *the* unifying factor in Christ's redemptive work and its diverse manifestations in Scripture and in the life of the Church. How was he able to see that unity and diversity all at once? Because he saw this unique reality underneath the diversity of forms and expressions. In other words, he looked at the Christian faith in terms of substance and appearances. All the appearances in redemptive history and in the life of the Church were but manifestations of one singular substantial reality.

I suggest in this volume that Daniélou's words capture perfectly how John Chrysostom viewed both the *oikonomia* of God and the life of the Church centered around its liturgical celebration of the Eucharist. John's view of Christ's death and resurrection shaped his view of the Bible and the Church. Reading his homilies, especially his running commentaries on biblical books, confirms the impression that he does approach the biblical text "literally," but there is a deeper underlying mentality shared by most, if not all, of the Eastern Fathers, including those under the influence of Antioch. In due course, we shall see a striking feature of John's handling of scriptural texts and stories, a mark shared by other Fathers both East and West. The Fathers tended to see the events recorded in the Bible and especially in the life of Christ not only as historical events to be explained but as mysteries to be entered into. This perspective can also be observed in Augustine of Hippo and Peter Chrysologus of Ravenna in the early fifth century.[42] And like Peter, when John treats the story of the woman healed of a hemorrhage after twelve years, he makes an application to the Eucharist for his audience. The Eucharist gives the same healing power that anonymous woman experienced by touching Jesus's garment.[43] This all implies that the *oikonomia* established by God through Israel and then through the Church has a profound content that shapes the patristic conception of the Church and life.

What then is the content or substance of the *oikonomia*? What is that divine reality being actualized? The answer highlights the divine arrangement of redemptive history that has its center in Christ and the Paschal

42 See Kenneth J. Howell, "The Eucharist as a Hermeneutical Lens in the Preaching of Peter Chrysologus," *Toronto Journal of Theology* 35, no. 2 (2020): 199–207. See also Caroline Tolton, "From Memory to Topology: The Architecture of Persuasion in the Sermons of Peter Chrysologus" (PhD diss., University of Chicago Divinity School, 2005), 149. For a very insightful essay on Peter's life and theology, see David Vincent Meconi, *Peter Chrysologus*, The Early Church Fathers (New York: Routledge, 2021).

43 See Mk 5:25–34 and John's commentary on this event in PG 57:371 and PG 61:708.

mystery. Chrysostom's treatment of the *oikonomia* underscores his conceptual dependence on Paul. In the New Testament, *oikonomia* means "administration" (e.g., Lk 16:3) or arrangement. This term is used by Paul six times but his most significant usage is found three times in Ephesians. There Paul speaks of "the *oikonomia* of the fullness of times" (Eph 1:10), "the *oikonomia* of God's grace" (Eph 3:2), and "the *oikonomia* of the mystery hidden from the ages in God" (Eph 3:9). Paul glosses "the *oikonomia* of the fullness of times" with a phrase that will later be used as a centerpiece of Irenaeus's theology, "the summing up or recapitulation (ἀνακεφαλαιώσασθαι) of all things in Christ, things in heaven and things on earth." A central part of this "summing up" is no doubt the reconciliation of things on earth with those of heaven. Thus, the arrangement or *oikonomia* of God's redemptive plan had a universal scope, a point not lost on John Chrysostom later. An even clearer delineation of this *oikonomia* is given by Paul in chapter three of Ephesians. There Paul calls the divine plan "the *oikonomia* of the mystery hidden from the ages in God." The genitive "of the mystery" could be read in two ways. One would be the explicative genitive with the meaning "the *oikonomia*, that is, the mystery." The other is to read the genitive as meaning that the arrangement or distribution reveals the mystery. This second seems to fit better with the words "hidden in God" in Eph 3:9. The *oikonomia* is not the same as the mystery, but it is the concrete acts of history which unveil something supernatural, something no one could know without the *oikonomia*. The context of Eph 3:9 in Eph 3:1–10 is chock full of revelatory terms which point to Christ and his advent as the final and most complete revelation of the divine mystery.

Clearly for Paul, as for John his heir, Christ is the center and meaning of the divine *oikonomia*. But Paul's texts do not seem to introduce any note of condescension, whereas John expounds God's plan by heavy reliance on the notion of *sugkatabasis*. God has lowered and adapted himself to human limitations. And so two closely related concepts, *sugkatabasis* and *oikonomia*, act as organizing categories, the former assuming the infinite distance between God and humanity while the latter traces the lineaments of divine love in the concrete acts of redemption. We shall return to these two concepts in later chapters as they are central to John's eucharistic theology. He was profoundly aware of the incomprehensibility of God, which he sought to defend against the Anomoeans, but his emphasis may have run the risk of making God so remote from the human race that he could not be known. John's answer is *sugkatabasis*, the idea that without God's condescension there would be no salvation, no knowledge of God. But because the Logos became flesh in his profound lowering of himself (cf. Phil 2:6–9) human knowledge of God is possible.

The etymological breakdown of the Greek word *sugkatabasis* may be instructive since most modern English speakers don't usually contemplate the etymology of the Latinate term "condescension." Although "condescension" carries connotations of disdain and contempt in the twenty-first century that it did not have in the nineteenth when a number of Chrysostom's homilies were brought into English, it nevertheless does have some important theological significance. Both the Greek and Latin words mean "a coming down to be with," not simply a coming down or descent, but a descent that joins itself to a lower thing.[44] Out of the fullness of divine love, the Eternal Son came to live with and among the human family and thereby raise humanity up to God. John will expand on this idea in a number of homilies, but in doing so his emphasis falls on the union or companionship of Christ with the human race. A number of ancient religions, the Greeks' included, could imagine the gods descending to the lower realms where humans dwell. They could even imagine the gods consorting with humans, but only Christianity could proclaim the Eternal God descending to be with humanity while remaining fully God. This truth makes John's emphasis on the cross of Christ all the more astonishing, and yet he glories in the cross like Paul. For John the cross is the apex and ultimate reference point for the Church.[45]

The greatest and most significant divide in the *oikonomia* of salvation history is of course before and after the advent of Christ. The Old Testament is a period of prefiguration, an extended pedagogy in which God was preparing the world for the fullness of revelation. Through images, events, and words, God gave hints of the later manifestation of Christ. In this regard, of course, Chrysostom was not in any way unique. From the authors of the New Testament through second-century figures like Irenaeus of Lyons and Melito of Sardis, and into John's time, Christian interpreters had long been accustomed to read the Old Testament through the lens of promise and fulfillment. Yet because of his strong attention and attachment to the specificity of the

44 Robert Hill suggested "considerateness" for *sugkatabasis*, arguing against "condescension." I am comfortable retaining the latter term with the understanding expressed above that *sugkatabasis* has a much richer meaning in Chrysostom than our current connotations of condescension imply. See Hill, *Chrysostom: Homilies on Genesis*, 17–18.

45 For the centrality of the cross in Eastern Christian thought in general see Khaled Anatolios, *Deification through the Cross: An Eastern Christian Theology of Salvation* (Grand Rapids, MI: Eerdmans, 2020).

biblical text, John perhaps emphasized these anticipations even more than his predecessors. This is why in chapter 2 I propose that John has an invisible line or axis running through his reading of the Old Testament stories. This Axis of Anticipation is one side of a twofold picture that captures John's theological reading of biblical history, and if that were the only salient aspect, his reading would differ little from that of other patristic authors. However, in the Old Testament events, words, and stories John sees anticipations not only of later redemptive history but of the liturgy of the Church itself with the Eucharist as its focal point. For example, John not only sees the Passover story as a contrastive harbinger of the grace that was to come, he also sees the prophet Elijah as a sure sign of continuity and discontinuity.[46]

The complement to the Axis of Anticipation is that which lies on the other side of Christ's passion, death, and resurrection. While the Church still anticipates the consummation of all things in the eschaton, it does so in a fundamentally different manner than did the Old Testament people of God. In the Axis of Participation the members of Christ's body, the Church, not only remember the death of the Lord (cf. 1 Cor 11:26), they engage in the *anamnesis* of redemptive history through a process of participation or interiorization of those saving events.[47] As we will see in later chapters, John employs a range of terminology to describe this process of participation. He speaks of μέθεξις, μετοχή, κοινωνία, and a few others to describe this unique mode of being for the new covenant people of God. This participation can legitimately be called an axis because it runs like a invisible line through the ordinances and ceremonies of the new covenant. All those aspects of the life of the Church and of the individual Christian revolve around the liturgy of the Church as that which provides this Axis of Participation. Through the actualization present in and provided by the liturgical celebrations of the Church, the process of deification can proceed. Actualization is a way of capturing the biblical concept of *anamnesis*, customarily translated "remembrance" or "memory," but carrying a far more significant connotation than those English words suggest. In due course we will see how *anamnesis* as a liturgical reality is rooted deeply in biblical history and theology. The Christian then shares in the life of Christ by way of a kind of liturgical mysticism that carries profound implications of a moral and social nature. Those implications are explored in considerable detail in chapters 7 through 9.

46 See chapter 2 below.

47 See the diagram in chapter 2.

John Chrysostom also reflected much on the deepest divine motivations for the *oikonomia* of God. Why did God so order the plan of salvation that it proved to be such an apparently confused morass of sin, repentance, promise, and failure? And why did salvation involve the Word-Become-Flesh? John believed that God was forever beyond human comprehension not only in his essence but also in his providential guidance of the human family. However, he was convinced of something even greater. God loves humanity with a love beyond the wildest human imaginings. The failures and foibles of humanity, the hardships and bitter sufferings of many individuals—including his own—never caused John to waver about the love of God. Although the New Testament authors preferred the word *agape* (ἀγάπη) to designate God's love, the Greek Fathers used a wider range of terms. One that was especially loved by John was *philanthropia* (φιλανθρωπία) or the love of the human race. In one form or another, John uses *philanthropia* over three thousand times to describe the attitudes and actions of God toward humanity.[48] I judge the choice of this term to be significant because the etymological breakdown of *philanthropia* seems to reflect Chrysostom's awareness of a fundamental disposition of God toward the human race as a whole. In his third *Homily on the Ascension of Christ*, John says, "Learn what kind of nature ascended [into heaven] or what it was like before [this event]. I gladly spend time meditating on the lowliness of our race that I may learn the exceeding honor bestowed on it by the Master's love of humanity" (*philanthropia*).[49] Christ dignified human nature by his Incarnation, which culminated in taking that nature back into heaven. What greater honor could Christ bestow on the human race than to bring it into heaven with himself on his return there? This one example reflects a broader pattern of John's preaching when at times he boldly calls the Master "the humanity-loving God" or conjoins mercy and love of humanity as God's response to human contrition.[50] In John's profound awareness of the incomprehensibility of God, he marvels at

48 *Philanthropia* is used only twice in the New Testament and only once applied to God. See Ti 3:4 and Acts 28:2. John uses it over seven hundred times in a formula at the end of homilies, but this does not exhaust John's rich use of the word. Here and elsewhere the term carries a profound significance. Interestingly, the Greek Fathers in general use *philanthropia* more than *agape*. It is worth further exploration whether they intend *philanthropia* as a means of explicating the meaning of *agape*.

49 *Homily 3 on the Ascension of Christ*, SC 562, 174, lines 52–55.

50 The expression "the humanity-loving God" (τον φιλανθρωπον θεον) occurs in *The Incomprehensibility of God*, Homily 2, line 533. For God's mercy and love (ἠλέησε καὶ ἐφιλανθρωπεύσατο) see Homily 5, line 548.

the inexpressible love of humanity shown by Christ. Michael Sherwin has recently captured this aspect of Chrysostom's theology again by emphasizing the relation of patron-client in late antiquity. He argues that John is using this cultural custom to speak about God's relation as a divine patron to a human client.[51] So strong is God's love that not even human sin can obstruct it, as seen, for example, in God's relation to Adam. Chrysostom speaks in persuasive tones, not authoritarian ones: "God treats Adam . . . wishing by means of this honor to persuade him to obey his instructions." Sherwin comments, "God did not treat Adam as a slave. . . . Adam sinned and God continues to act as a patient patron."[52]

While Adam stands at the commencement of salvation history, the entire *oikonomia* is ordered according to the *philanthropia* of God, which is the motivation and underlying impetus behind it all. Liturgy is an essential part because the goal of the plan, as John often says, is to join heaven and earth together in the final eschaton once and for all. The conjoining of *oikonomia* and *philanthropia* is found in a number of John's homilies; one of the more meaningful of these instances is in *Homily 2 on 2 Timothy*:

> Look at Marcion, Mani, and Valentinus and all the other heresies and damnable dogmas they introduced into the church of God that they may be ashamed for trying to measure divine matters about the *oikonomia* by human reasonings. What may be worthy not of shame but of great boasting, I tell you, is the cross of Christ. For there is no greater proof of his love for the human race [*philanthropia*]. Not the sky nor the sea nor land, not the bringing all things into existence out of nothing. There is nothing else like the cross. So Paul says that he boasts in it, "May it never be that I boast in anything except in the cross of our Lord Jesus Christ."[53]

John is commenting on Paul's exhortation to Timothy, "Do not be ashamed of the testimony of the Lord nor of me his prisoner" (2 Tim 1:8). The temptation to be ashamed of God's plan of salvation shows up in those who reject Christ's teachings (e.g., Marcion et al.). John pierces to the root cause of their rejection by tracing it back to "judging divine things by human reasonings." John's rejection of heresy on the grounds that one should not judge God's

51 Michael Sherwin, *On Love and Virtue: Theological Essays* (Steubenville, OH: Emmaus Press, 2018).

52 Sherwin, *On Love and Virtue*, 130.

53 *Homily 2 on 2 Timothy*, PG 62:607. See Gal 6:14.

oikonomia by human standards picks up on Paul's words about the foolishness of secular wisdom in 1 Cor 1:18–25. The cross was Paul's boast, and it is John's no less. None of the powerful acts of God can demonstrate God's *philanthropia* like the cross. To be ashamed of the cross entails a rejection of God's divine plan of salvation enacted in history. To reject God's *oikonomia* is to reject his love for the human race. The mutually reinforcing union of God's salvific arrangement and his love for humanity shows up again in John's consideration of Is 7:14 and 9:6. That the promised Redeemer would be born as a child rather than a powerful ruler from the beginning is not an occasion for looking down on God's plan but one for amazement: "When you hear of a child, do not despise the word. Rather stand in amazement of God's *philanthropia* and be astounded at the salvation in the *oikonomia* that you may become worthy of hearing the words of the gospel, following by faith, struggling with perseverance, agonizing with devotion, being perfected by love, and becoming whole in Christ Jesus our Lord through all these."[54]

Though John does not quote Is 55:8 at this juncture, the thought of God's ways being above and beyond human comprehension seem to underlie this exhortation. The salvation in the *oikonomia* (τῆς οἰκονομίας τὴν σωτηρίαν) surprises and overturns human expectations. John is anxious that above all Christian people would see God's love for humanity (θαύμασον τοῦ Θεοῦ τὴν φιλανθρωπίαν).

John has other ways of expressing God's love for the human race, but one of the most delightful is "love-charm" (φίλτρον). This word has a rather consistent meaning of its 147 occurrences in the Chrysostom corpus; it signifies a love-potion or love-charm. We gain a hint of its meaning when John quotes Gn 3:9, where God questions Adam after his sin, "Where are you?" and adds that God did this "to show his love-charm and great care." He then glosses φίλτρον by the "evidence of his genuine love" (φιλίας γνησίας).[55] Further insight into φίλτρον is afforded by its use in a homily after he returned from his first exile. Commending his flock for the courage they displayed in his absence, John implicitly rebukes the authorities: "They kept such things away because they feared your courage and the love-charm of your love [τῆς ἀγάπης τὸ φίλτρον] and your longing for me."[56] The people's love for their shepherd acted as a powerful draw for John and a warning for the authorities

54 *On the Saying: The Edict Went Out*, PG 50:800.

55 *Homily 7 To the People of Antioch*, PG 49:95.

56 *Homily 2 After His Return from the First Exile*, PG 52:443–44.

who had exiled him. John here seems to suggest that he had internalized their love, but the term *love-charm* tends to be used with external objects rather than ingested liquid.

This appears to be true in one of its most enchanting occurrences found in his homily *On Blessed Philogonius*, where he shows his desire to make his hearers "partakers of this love-charm" (ἵνα κοινωνοὺς ὑμᾶς ποιήσω τοῦ φίλτρου).[57] As we will see in chapter 3, this term is used of Jesus's manger and/or the eucharistic table that extends the manger into the Church's liturgy. God's love-charms are dangled before the eyes of believers to entice them into worship and love of God. A love-charm then is a concrete and tangible way of making God's love apparent. As this last instance indicates, the *oikonomia* of God is full of love-charms by which God draws erring humanity back to himself. The most powerful love-charm is Christ's sufferings: "I will display this love-charm not only with these but also with the things I suffered. It was for your sake I was spit on and beaten with a cudgel. I emptied myself of glory. I left my Father and came to you who hated me and turned away and who cannot bear to hear my name."[58] Because the Eucharist embodies the sufferings of Christ, it too is just such a love-charm.

God's love for the human race is revealed in Scripture. The events recorded there are mysteries that are extended in the sacramental mysteries of the Church. Those mysteries were not mysteries or secrets in our modern sense, mysteries that could be banished by gathering more information. The mysteries of which John often speaks are embodiments of Divine Presence, are gifts to convey grace to their partakers, and are signs of heaven and the world to come. The following chapters then seek to flesh out John's understanding of these mysteries, of their nature, of what they embody, and of the differences they make in the lives of believing Christians. Reading his homilies reveals how he thought of the mysteries almost in passing, as it were, because he never spoke about them as unto themselves, but always in the context of some other subject. Yet, precisely because he spoke so often of them, we will see that every subject he addresses tends to circle back to the central mystery of Christian life and worship, the Eucharist.

John Chrysostom was no theoretician, not at least in the modern sense, but certainly he did possess a *theoria*, a vision of something greater than himself, more eternal than this world. Jesus Christ was the center of that

57 *On Blessed Philogonius*, PG 48:753–56.

58 *Homily 15 on 1 Timothy*, PG 62:586.

vision, and his earthly life accomplished the redemption that was foretold in the prophets of Israel and celebrated in the liturgy of the Church. Since Christ stood at the core of John's vision, he also considered the Eucharist as the principal sacramental means by which Christians could know and love God. The presence of Christ in the Eucharist was for John a living presence of the resurrected Jesus, but all that Christ accomplished for the salvation of the world in his earthly sojourn was also there. That explains why for John the cross of Christ was his preeminent glory. Like Paul, John had a deep pastoral concern for his people that always circled back to the cross. And it was the Eucharist that conveyed the realities of the cross to believers in his own day. This glorious story was celebrated by John with deep reverence and great joy. Although it would be a century after his death that the Patriarch of Constantinople would be dubbed "The Golden Mouth," he sought with a heart attuned to the Spirit's harp to bring his fellow Christians the gold of salvation given by Christ. As John would once say, God was interested in golden souls, not golden vessels.[59] Yet the Golden Mouth knew and believed with unwavering conviction that it was the Golden Chalice, brimming over with the blood of Christ, that would produce those golden souls.

✠ ✠ ✠

The reader will find four kinds of writing contained in this volume: presentation, exposition, exegesis, and explanation. Presentation consists of quotations from Chrysostom's own writings, many of which have never seen the light of day in English, or are hidden away in little-known and dated academic works. The occasional long quotations are designed to allow John to speak in his own voice and thereby to afford the reader the ability to interact with Chrysostom directly and to arrive at his or her own conclusions about John's meaning.[60] These quotations then provide the material for exposition that attempts to draw out the meaning of the quotations further, because many of John's homilies state, but do not explain, his eucharistic teaching. Although there are well over eighty different homilies from which I

59 *Homily 50 on Matthew*, PG 58:508.

60 It may strike the reader as strange, as it once did me, that sixteen hundred years after the death of this great preacher, some of his homilies and writings have never been translated into English.

quote, there are a few that resurface repeatedly as markers of John's theology because these are simply richer than others.

My expositions are analogous to biblical commentary and may be thought of as concentric circles. They begin by placing John's specific words in the wider context of each homily and by locating the ideas under consideration in his wider theology as a whole. A further step is to see his teachings, especially with regard to liturgy, within Eastern history and traditions. Thus, I occasionally quote from other ancient authors to supplement Chrysostom's reflections. I sometimes also refer to Western Church Fathers to demonstrate continuity with the wider Church of which John certainly saw himself a part.

Exegesis surfaces at crucial points when certain key sentences, concepts, or vocabulary require a more thorough analysis. Such analysis draws in other uses of the same words or ideas to lay bare a meaning that may not be evident on a superficial reading. Careful exegesis also permits me to interact with other scholarly translations and interpretations with which I demur at times. As will become clear, many pithy sayings in John's corpus have escaped the notice of other scholars who have concentrated on different aspects of his theology.

Lastly, I offer explanations that attempt to combine different aspects of John's thinking in giving an account of his underlying eucharistic theology. Although these explanations are properly less frequent, they nevertheless elucidate John's thinking in a manner heretofore left undone.[61] In the end, I continue a sound methodology already evident in recent scholarship of tying together seemingly disparate parts of Chrysostom's theology.

This volume explicates John Chrysostom's theology of the Eucharist by placing it in relation to many other aspects of his larger worldview, from the plan of salvation in the Old Testament to events in the life of Jesus Christ, and to virtues and vices resident in the lives of Christians. It shows how he believed deeply in Christ's bodily presence in the Eucharist, how that presence was sacrificial, and how the liturgy manifested that presence to the world. All this John Chrysostom put at the service of moral admonition leading to spiritual transformation. However, John's most profound wisdom is based on a simple truth that the Eucharist is the continuation of the earthly life of Jesus Christ embodied in the liturgy of the Church.

61 The explanation of *mnesikakia* (μνησικακία) in chapter 8 is a prime example.

Part I

Anticipation

1

The Eucharistic Liturgy as the Union of Heaven and Earth

In the tenth century visitors on a mission from Prince Vladimir of Kiev arrived in Constantinople to investigate the various forms of Christianity then present in the world. When the emissaries visited the churches of the city, they reported back to their sovereign in words quoted many times, "The Greeks led us to the edifices where they worship their God, and we knew not whether we were in heaven or on earth. For on earth there is no such splendor or such beauty, and we are at a loss how to describe it. We know only that God dwells there among men, and their liturgy is fairer than the ceremonies of other nations. For we cannot forget that beauty. Every man, after tasting something sweet, is afterward unwilling to accept that which is bitter, and therefore we cannot dwell longer here."[1] Although this account may be apocryphal, it illustrates something about the world in which John Chrysostom lived. The visitors no doubt saw one of the most magnificent churches in the world, Hagia

1 The story comes from the *Chronicle of Nestor* for 987. For an enlightening discussion of the importance of liturgy in Eastern Christianity, see Robert F. Taft, "The Spirit of Eastern Christian Worship," in *Beyond East and West: Problems in Liturgical Understanding*, 2nd ed. (Rome: Edizioni Orientalia Christiana, 2001), 143–60.

Sophia, which was built under the Emperor Justinian in the sixth century. Though John Chrysostom had died over a century before the construction of Hagia Sophia, the spirit of beauty, wonder, and awe which this edifice evoked was reflected in the ministry of one who was often acclaimed the greatest preacher since apostolic times. Yet no visual beauty of any building could match the beauty of the liturgy that John considered to be a gift from God.

This chapter explores the inseparable link between the liturgy and the Eucharist. Every aspect of John Chrysostom's teaching on the Eucharist derives its meaning and significance from its home in the divine liturgy. He often expressed his sense of awe and wonder by circling back to the divine liturgy as the source and summit of the human obligation to God. That obligation was also the highest human privilege because the liturgy was first and foremost a union of heaven and earth. For him, not only is heaven where Christ is but heaven touches earth through the liturgy for, as he says in a homily on the Gospel of John, "it is into heaven itself that we enter when we enter here," that is, the liturgy.[2] In this respect, John represents the entire Eastern (Greek-speaking) side of the ancient Church. For the East, entrance into the presence of the heavenly Christ is to join angels and heavenly hosts. Running like a thread through John Chrysostom's writings, the worship of the Church is a reflection of and a union with the eternal and perpetual worship of heaven.[3] The liturgy is an *actualization* on earth of heavenly realities. As John comments on various biblical texts or events, he glosses the scriptural meanings from a perspective of one fully immersed in the Bible as read and understood within the context of Christian worship.

According to John Chrysostom, the liturgy of the Church is not created by the Church but is given to it by God. The Church enters into an already existing worship of the Creator and Redeemer. While most Eastern theologians prefer to speak of the liturgy as an entrance into the kingdom,[4] my use of the term *actualization* encompasses the idea of entrance with

2 *Homily 2 on the Gospel of John*, PG 59:35.

3 Jacky Marsaux affirms the central place of the liturgy as an act of encounter with God. "Through the celebration [of the liturgy] the participants are made present to a unique event of salvation which in turn does not cease to transform them" (Jacky Marsaux, "La théologie de l'Eucharistie selon Jean Chrysostome: Étude du schéma sacrificiel" [doctoral diss., Université Paris-IV et Institut Catholique de Paris, 2008]).

4 See Vassilios Papavassiliou, *Journey to the Kingdom: An Insider's Look at the Liturgy and Beliefs of the Eastern Orthodox Church* (Brewster, MA: Paraclete Press, 2012), 9; see also Alexander Schmemann, *For the Life of the World* (Crestwood, NY: St. Vladimir's Press, 1973), 27.

the nuance that all of God's redemptive acts in history are made present to the worshiping community. That is why it is important to understand how the salvation portrayed and promised in the old covenant played into the new covenant mysteries. The understanding of liturgy as the actualizing of a heavenly gift comes to expression on the pages of the Old Testament, especially in that passage which most captured John's imagination, Is 6:1–7:

> In the year that King Uzziah died, I saw the Lord seated on a high and exalted throne. The house was full of his glory. The Seraphim were standing around him, six wings for one and six wings for the other. With two they covered their face and with two their feet, and with two they flew. They each cried out to the other and said, "Holy, holy, holy, Lord of Sabaoth, the whole earth is full of his glory." And the entry of the door was shaken by the voice with which they cried and the house was filled with smoke. And then I said, "Woe is me. I am undone because I am a man and have unclean lips and I dwell in the midst of a people having unclean lips. I have seen the King, the Lord of Sabaoth, with my own eyes." One of the Seraphim was sent to me and he had a coal in his hand that he had taken with tongs from the altar. And he touched my mouth and said, "Behold, this has touched your lips and taken away your iniquity and cleansed away your sin."[5]

There are several striking features of this text that make it almost unique in the Old Testament. The vision of God that Isaiah has occurs in the context of his prophetic call. In the verses following those just translated (8–13), he hears God's call to proclaim to Judah that judgment is coming. Isaiah's prophetic ministry will suffer many setbacks because of the hardheartedness of the chosen people. In light of this call, the vision the prophet experiences is intended to sustain him, a vision that, according to John Chrysostom, exceeds anything a human being can imagine:

> And what a wonder it is if you stand with the Seraphim in that place where the Seraphim dare not touch. God gave you these things with freedom from fear. He says, "He sent one of the Seraphim to me and he had a ember of fire which he took from the altar with tongs." That altar [in the church] is a type and icon of this altar [heavenly], that fire a type and icon of spiritual fire. The Seraphim did not dare to touch it with their hands but with tongs. But you receive in the hand. So when you see the dignity of the gifts offered

5 I have chosen to translate this text from the Septuagint (LXX) since that is the form in which Chrysostom knew it. There are some points at which the LXX differs from the Masoretic text. The Hebrew has "his train was filling the temple" instead of "the house was full of his glory."

> here, these things are much greater than the Seraphim's touch. When you fix upon your Master's love for humanity, [then you realize that] he is not ashamed to descend to our lowliness by the grace of the gifts.[6]

The altar of the Church and the fire of the sacrament represent the heavenly altar and the celestial fire of God's love and presence. The earthly worship of the Church is derived from, dependent on, and directed toward that heavenly worship. It is not only modeled on heaven; it is heaven on earth. This is the theme common to all John's reflections on the Eucharist. For him nothing could be more wonderful than the realization that "he [Christ] is not ashamed to descend to our lowliness by the grace of the gifts." We may infer from the biblical text that Isaiah does not see the Lord directly. The smoke that fills the temple obscures the prophet's vision, but it leaves him with an overwhelming sense of his utter unworthiness ("Woe is me. I am undone"). This theme of the transcendence of God will also deeply inform John's sense of the liturgy. For Chrysostom, participation in liturgy is grace from God because, in the end, God is utterly beyond all human concepts of him.

THE GOD ABOVE AND THE LITURGY BELOW

John's doctrine of the incomprehensibility of God highlights the profound love of God for humanity. The gift of God's love for the human race in the Eucharist stands out in bold relief when it is seen against the inability of the human mind to comprehend the essence of God. John did not bring up this contrast between God's being and human knowledge out of the blue; it arose out of a controversy that shook the Eastern Church in the person of Eunomius of Cyzicus. Eunomius was born in Cappadocia but studied under Aetius in Alexandria. In time he became the most vocal advocate of the extreme Arian position of the Anomoeans. This deviant bishop contended that the human mind was able to know the essence of God as certainly as God knows himself. Other Greek Fathers had countered Eunomius by stressing a biblical text that spoke of God "dwelling in unapproachable light" (1 Tim 6:16). None offered a more scathing critique of Eunomius than

6 *I Saw the Lord: Homily 6,3*, Jean Dumortier, *Jean Chrysostome: Homélies sur Ozias*, SC 277 (Paris: Editions du Cerf, 1981).

Gregory of Nyssa.[7] Eunomius had attacked Gregory's older brother Basil and accused him of heresy. Defending Nicaea, Basil had reaffirmed that God is one nature in three persons.

Contrary to Nicaea, Eunomius affirmed three distinct beings, not persons, in the godhead. Basil had also adamantly defended the Nicaean formula of *homoousia* (the same nature) which Eunomius and all followers of Arius had rejected. In twelve books Gregory of Nyssa offers a devasting critique of Eunomius. The tenth book treats the knowledge of God possible for human beings. Gregory contends that it is difficult for human beings to understand even creatures such as the ant in a theoretical sense. If human beings have such a difficult time understanding what in principle can be understood by them, how could Eunomius claim that the essence of God is comprehensible to the human mind? Gregory is not arguing against the pursuit of true knowledge, only arguing that the human mind is limited in its ability to understand God's essence.[8]

John Chrysostom adopted Gregory's style of argumentation in homilies preached at Antioch in the 380s in response to the followers of Eunomius. The Anomoeans derived their name from the word meaning "unlike" (ἀνόμοιος = unlike) because they contended that the divine nature or being of the Son (the *Logos*) was different from that of the Father. Like Gregory of Nyssa, John argues that the essence of God is inaccessible to human comprehension. His argumentation underscores his faith in the transcendence of God. Referring to Paul's words in 1 Tim 6:16, John says,

> But he [Paul] did not say "dwelling as incomprehensible light" but "inaccessible," which is something greater than incomprehensible. Incomprehensible is used when something sought and explored is not grasped by those who seek to know it. Inaccessible, on the other hand, is used when the beginning of the search has not even begun and when someone is not able to do so. A sea is called incomprehensible when divers let themselves down into the great deep but they are unable to find the ocean floor. Something is said to be inaccessible when the beginning cannot be sought or explored.[9]

7 Gregory of Nyssa, *Against Eunomius*, 10.

8 For a more detailed exposition of Gregory's critique, see David Rylaarsdam, *John Chrysostom on Divine Pedagogy: The Coherence of His Theology and Preaching* (Oxford: Oxford University Press, 2014), 102–3.

9 *Homily 3 on the Incomprehensibility of God*, SC 28 (bis), 196, lines 124–33. My translation in based on this critical edition. All twelve homilies have been translated into English with excellent commentary by Paul Harkins in the Fathers of the Church series, vol. 72, *Homilies on the*

The human mind not only cannot comprehend the divine essence; it cannot even approach understanding it. John takes the argument a step further to show that the divine being is not even accessible to the angels. To accomplish this, he returns to the text in Isaiah chapter 6. Since no biblical text explicitly affirms that angels cannot comprehend God's essence, John admits the possibility for the sake of argument. If human beings could understand the divine essence, surely angels could. But this is impossible. John takes the Isaiah passage as clear evidence that not even angels can understand God's nature. How much less human beings! His quotation of Is 6:2 focuses on the Seraphim covering their eyes with their wings. Why must the Seraphim, the highest in the angelic hierarchy, cover their eyes? Because the presence of God is too blinding, even for the angels. If these preternatural beings cannot bear to look directly at God, how can the human mind know the Divine Essence?[10]

It is clear that this belief in God as the Incomprehensible One, even as the Unapproachable One, was pervasive and compelling in Chrysostom's life. The first five homilies against the Anomoeans were preached within the first year of John's priesthood (386–87) at Antioch, but the theme stuck with him until the end of his life.[11] In his last work *On the Providence of God*, written while he was in his last exile (404–07), John returns to this theme of how incomprehensible God is not only to human beings but to angels and the hosts above: "He about whom you are so anxious to investigate is indestructible, unchangeable, eternally the same, without beginning, without end, incomprehensible, transcending understanding, conquering human reason, inexpressible, ineffable, incomprehensible not only to you and to me, to prophets and apostles, but also to the powers above that are pure and invisible, incorporeal in their life in heaven."[12]

Here the distinction between Creator and creature stands out as Chrysostom contemplated his own end. Under the harsh conditions of exile he learned to accept God's providence as beyond his human reason because

---

Incomprehensible Nature of God by St. John Chrysostom (Washington, DC: The Catholic University of America Press, 1984).

10 *Homily 3 on the Incomprehensibility of God*, SC 28 (bis), 198–200, lines 147–66.

11 On John's ordination in 386, see Harkins, introduction to *Homilies on the Incomprehensible Nature of God*, 22.

12 *On the Providence of God*, SC 79, 70, no line numbers.

God himself is beyond human imaginations.[13] Yet John believed firmly that while God can never be understood by men, they can know God. But how?

For John the liturgy is exactly what brings human beings into the presence of the Incomprehensible and Unapproachable One.[14] The songs of the Seraphim, those holy and mystical hymns of heaven, allow the believing soul to participate in the celestial choir:

> Think on whose presence you stand near, with whom you are about to invoke God, with the Cherubim. Consider carefully your fellow choir members and sobriety will be pleasing to you when you take to heart that though you are beset with a body and entangled with flesh, you have been counted worthy to sing the hymn to the common Lord of all along with the incorporeal powers. So, let no one whose desire has dissipated participate in those holy and mystical hymns. At that moment [*kairos*], let no one have earthbound thoughts. Rather cordon off all earthly things from your mind, having oriented your whole self toward heaven. Standing near the throne of glory and flying with the Seraphim, let [everyone] offer up the all-holy hymn to the God of glory and majesty.[15]

Here we observe a theme that will reoccur many times in John's preaching. The liturgy is God's *kairos*, his chosen moment and means to unite the angelic and human choirs in unison to praise the Creator and Redeemer of humanity. Entering into this *kairos* will require moving beyond an earthly perspective while remaining on earth. To join the angelic refrain is only possible because of the descent of the Eternal Word who brought the music of heaven to earth:

> Did you recognize this sound? Is it ours or the Seraphim's? It is in fact ours and the Seraphim's. This is because Christ destroyed the dividing wall of partition when he made peace between the things in heaven and on earth.

13 This theme of the incomprehensibility of God and his ways will echo down through the centuries in Byzantine writers, among whom are Maximus the Confessor, John Damascene, Symeon the New Theologian, Gregory Palamas, and Nicholas Cabasilas.

14 The Eunomian/Anomoean controversy plays into the determination of the Liturgy of St. John Chrysostom as well because some of the language used in that anaphora almost surely derives from John himself although he is by no means the author of that liturgy in the modern sense. He probably modified what we now call the lost Antiochene Greek Liturgy of the Apostles which then became the basis for the liturgy that bears his name. For the complicated history of that liturgy see Robert Taft, "The Authenticity of the Chrysostom Anaphora Revisited: Determining the Authorship of Liturgical Texts by Computer," *Orientalia Christiana Periodica* 56 (1990): 5–51.

15 *Homily 4 on the Incomprehensibility of God*, SC 428 (bis), 260–62, lines 408–20.

> It is because he made them both one. At first, this hymn was known only in heaven, but the Master deemed it right to descend to the earth and to bring down this melody to us. Therefore, this great high priest, when he stands upon this holy table offering rational worship and lifting up the bloodless sacrifice, he is not simply calling on us for this praise. First, when he spoke to the Cherubim and reminded the Seraphim, he commanded everyone to send up this most awesome sound, thereby drawing back from earth our understanding by the memory of this united chorus and all but crying out to each of us, "You sing with the Seraphim, you stand with the Seraphim, flap your wings of the mind with them, and with them fly around the royal throne."[16]

Chrysostom interprets the vision of Isaiah through a Pauline lens with his adaptation of Eph 2:14–15 ("the dividing wall and making peace"), but he has rotated the Pauline expressions ninety degrees. Instead of the dividing wall being between Jew and Gentile, John applies the same language to the barrier between heaven and earth. The peace of Christ's reconciliation of Jew and Gentile in Eph 2:15 becomes in Chrysostom the peace between heaven and earth more generally. Christ has accomplished this reconciliation of heaven and earth by his offering of rational worship. The expression "rational worship" (τὴν λογικὴν λατρείαν), taken from Rom 12:1, occurs twelve times in the Chrysostom corpus. Only here in the homily on Isaiah is Christ the subject of the verb "offer" with rational worship being the object. Elsewhere Chrysostom explains τὴν λογικὴν λατρείαν as "through the soul, through the Spirit," quoting Jn 4:24, and he contrasts it with the corporeal nature of worship in the old covenant.

Rational worship is the kind that is appropriate for rational creatures such as human beings. Christ as man offers worship to the Father by lifting up his own sacrifice embodied in the Eucharist. This is the reason why human beings can be drawn into the worship of heaven. Because Christ is acting as the great high priest, in and through the liturgy, the sound of the Seraphim becomes the praise of the Church. The fact that "the Master deemed it right to descend to the earth and to bring down this melody to us" results in all the praises of earth being drawn back to heaven. The Church stands with the heavenly court, singing and bowing down before the royal throne. Heaven and earth with their combined melody are no longer distinguishable in the liturgy.

16 *I Saw the Lord: Homily 6,3*, Dumortier, *Jean Chrysostome: Homélies sur Ozias*, 42–228.

Given John's lofty view of the liturgy and even loftier view of God, it is reasonable to ask which influenced which. Did John view the liturgy of the Church as he did because he knew the truth of the incomprehensibility of God or did he view God as incomprehensible because he had experienced the liturgy of the Church? Those experienced in the divine liturgy of the Byzantine East may promptly reply that John was no doubt led to his view of God as incomprehensible because he had been so immersed in the experience of liturgy. And that may be the case, but it may also be profitable to consider that John saw the liturgy as so exalted because he had sunk his mind deeply into the vision of God as he committed vast portions of Scripture to memory. Recall that the first five homilies on the incomprehensibility of God were preached in John's first year of priesthood, not very long after he had returned from the caves outside Antioch where his mind had been absorbed with memorizing Scripture. Perhaps it was then in the solitude of the caves that John came to understand how incomprehensible God was. When he returned to the city and participated in public liturgy, first as one of the faithful, then as celebrant, perhaps he saw the liturgy as expressing divine incomprehensibility with fresh eyes enlightened by his intake of Scripture. Or it could be that his participation in the liturgy of the Church spoke to him of God's transcendence in such a manner that he began to see God as the Inexpressible One, the Incomprehensible One whose existence was beyond every human's grasp? Perhaps it was his experience of the liturgy which made him realize how those liturgies obliquely pointed to a God beyond human comprehension.

It is probably impossible to answer this question with any certainty, but considering it illumines an important aspect of John's preaching and theology. There can be no doubt that John saw the liturgy of the Church as revolving around two poles: word and sacrament. As God spoke definitively in his written word, so he meets with his people to heal them of their sins in and through the liturgy. The same presence of God is encountered in Scripture and in the Eucharist in the privileged context of public worship. Yet the homilies on divine incomprehensibility were a vivid reminder that the God so encountered is forever beyond our human comprehension. Were it not for his condescending love, there could be no knowledge of God. The most appropriate response is prostration before the Divine Presence out of a sense of awe, an awe unlike any other a human being can know.

FIRE FROM THE HEAVENLY ALTAR

John seems to have reflected much on the text of Isaiah chapter 6 and used its imagery to develop his theology of the liturgy. For John, the liturgy partook of that seraphic fire that the prophet speaks about: "One of the Seraphim . . . had a coal in his hand that was taken with tongs from the altar. And he touched my mouth and said, 'Behold, this has touched your lips and taken away your iniquity and cleansed away your sin'" (Is 6:6–7). The earthly Church shares in this seraphic fire because the liturgy is an icon of the celestial celebration.[17] The union of heaven and earth, as the references to the seraphic fire in the *Homily on Isaiah* indicate, is based on the inviting and repelling effects of fire. The liturgy is off-putting and enticing all at once. Such an awe-inspiring liturgy provides Chrysostom with a basis for his moral exhortations to his congregation. The faithful must not, like all too many outside, "despise God, consider the sayings of the Spirit as common, [and] emit disordered voices" but should be "sending up an angelic doxology with fear and trembling, and making confession to your Creator with reverence." This invitation to join the heavenly throng while still on earth focuses all the complexities of the Church's worship on the simple fact that "the Master himself is present invisibly and measures the movement of each one, and searches the conscience." The call of worship is at once also a call away from the disturbing cacophony of the world.[18]

Whether John knew any Hebrew or not, his invoking the imagery of fire was consistent with the meaning of the Hebrew root. "Seraphim" derives from a Hebrew root (*s r f*) meaning "burning" or "fire." The imagery of fire is not incidental to Chrysostom's preaching. The reasons for this usage may be numerous but one is certainly his conviction that nowhere else can one find a comparable source of spiritual grace. As the Scriptures employed fire as an image of the Spirit, so John sees the Eucharist as the fullness of that same Spirit made manifest. As we shall see later, John brings out important implications of this conviction in his personalized exhortations to his hearers, but

17 Later Byzantine theology develops the iconic nature of the liturgy more fully, as does Germanos of Constantinople in the early eighth century. See the Greek text and translation in Paul Meyendorff, *On the Divine Liturgy: Germanus of Constantinople* (Crestwood, NY: St. Vladimir's Press, 1999).

18 "Don't you know that the angels are standing at this awesome table and are diligently caring for it in reverence? But you don't recognize these things because your mind has been darkened by the sights and sounds of the theater." All the quotations in this paragraph come from *I Saw the Lord: Homily 1*; Dumortier, *Jean Chrysostome: Homélies sur Ozias*, 42–228.

such hortatory language means little without his prior faith in the unique character of the mystical table. The Eucharist burns deep in the human soul because it holds the fire of heaven:

> Don't you know that this table is full of spiritual fire? As springs gush forth the nature of water, so it has a certain inexplicable flame. So, don't come with straw or wood and grass so as to bring about a greater conflagration and to burn up the receiving soul. But come with precious stones, gold, and silver that you may make a purer forest so that you may depart with much gain.[19]

As frightful and enticing as Isaiah's experience of the presence of God may have been, John sees in the new covenant two differences beyond what the prophet could know. What only one prophet could experience in the older dispensation, every believer can experience in the new, the very fire of heaven. Isaiah's encounter with the heavenly fire could only be a foretaste of the fullness of spiritual fire on the altar of the Church. The greater spiritual fire in the Church then provides John with the grounds for his moral exhortation, "Does anyone have an enemy? Has he been wronged in a great way? Let him banish the enmity; let him keep in check his mind full of disorder that no one may be distracted or troubled."[20] What will be the result of encountering and ingesting such fire from the Church's mystical table? The spiritual fire emanating from the sacred table will leave the communicant "in much tranquility, much silence, deep peace of thoughts."[21] Here then is the effect of participation in the liturgy and the Eucharist. The believer is cleansed of hate and filled with a peaceful spirit.

This glorious vision of the liturgy and the Eucharist begs for an explanation. Why did God choose this way to communicate himself to humanity? What motivated the undivided Trinity to offer this gift to the human race? If we were looking for one word to capture the answer given by the Greek

19 *On Blessed Philogonius*, PG 48:756. This homily was preached five days before Christmas in 386 at Antioch in honor of the fourth-century bishop of the city, about whom nothing else is known. It was sometimes designated no. 6 because in a certain manuscript tradition it was inserted as the sixth in the series on the incomprehensibility of God. There are two existing English translations: Paul Harkins, *Homilies on the Incomprehensible Nature of God*, and Wendy Mayer and Pauline Allen, *John Chrysostom*, The Early Church Fathers (New York: Routledge, 2000). We shall return to this homily again on several occasions because of its theological and spiritual profundity. I shall interact with these two translations on crucial points of commentary.

20 *On Blessed Philogonius*, PG 48:756.

21 *On Blessed Philogonius*, PG 48:756.

Church Fathers, it would be *philanthropia*, the love of humanity. This word is scattered not only throughout the writings of John the Golden Mouth but throughout the work of most of the Greek Christian writers of the first eight centuries of the Church. They see the Triune God as the Lover of Humanity and that love as the foundation of all creation.

John's perception of the love of God for humanity best explains the frequent plaintive tone of his homilies. Rather than commanding his people on the basis of a moral obligation, John often appeals to the beneficence and goodness of God to motivate his congregants to appreciate the majesty of the Eucharist. The liturgy is certainly a gift of divine providence. So, in section 6 of Chrysostom's work on *The Providence of God*, he begins his demonstration of God's goodness with an affirmation of love:

> For those who are well disposed the declaration of God by itself is sufficient even before the demonstration from his works, showing not only his providence but also his extreme love toward us. For he does not simply watch over us; he rather loves with an exceedingly irresistible love. This is a love without [the fluctuations of] passion, the most ardent, most vigorous and genuine, unbreakable and incapable of being snubbed out. Since the Sacred Scriptures want to present this love, it sets before men images, it presents many examples of love, of providence, and of care. They wish not only to establish us with these [examples], but also to surpass reason with examples. And not being satisfied in showing these things as a love-charm, the things known to those listening also show this.[22]

God could see ahead of time—providence in Greek is *pronoia*, meaning "seeing ahead"—that humanity would need both verbal affirmation and visible signs of his love. In this beautiful appeal John piles adjective upon adjective to express what cannot be expressed in human language. The love of God seen through his providence is "an exceedingly irresistible love."[23] Unlike the fickleness of human love, God's is exempt from passing passions (ἀπαθῆ), but his love is warm and intense, genuine, indissoluble, and unparalleled. This twofold reality, God's incomprehensible being and our inability to understand it, demonstrates the loving intention of the Creator in giving the liturgy of the heaven to humanity. The liturgy and the Eucharist it contains is not a human invention; it is a gift from the very heart of God. This

22 *The Providence of God*, 6.1, SC 79, 94, no numbered lines.

23 "Irresistible" translates ἀμήχανον, which could also mean "extravagant" in this context.

explains why John can speak of the liturgy as the earthly Church joining the choir of heaven. They are only two parts of one and the same choir. Liturgy, centered on the eucharistic sacrifice, is God's way of wrapping his arms of love around his people, the Church.

As John matured through life, he came to a deeper appreciation of that love over time. Nowhere is this more vividly taught than in a *Homily on the Betrayal of Judas*. When Scripture has Jesus expressing his troubled heart at the prospect of betrayal by one of his own, John astutely asks, "Why was he troubled?" His answer may surprise us. Jesus was troubled not over himself being betrayed but over Judas's act of unspeakable evil: "When the Master saw the insanity of the disciple, his merciful heart was troubled and wept."[24] In other words, Jesus's heart was full of compassion over Judas's failure to repent and change his course: "This was the reason that the Master who loves humanity was troubled and wept when he saw the audacity of the disciple. He showed his sympathy for the disciple and the greatness of this love for humanity because until the betrayal itself he did not cease to keep in view the possible correction of the disciple."[25]

John twice invokes his favorite designation for the Lord in as many sentences. He is "the Master who loves humanity" (ὁ φιλάνθρωπος Δεσπότης) who, amidst his own pain, "showed . . . the greatness of this love for humanity" (τῆς φιλανθρωπίας τὸ μέγεθος). Chrysostom goes on to say that we should weep more for those who commit evil than for those who suffer evil. The latter can count themselves blessed, as Jesus said, "Blessed are those who are persecuted for the sake of righteousness, for theirs is the kingdom of heaven" (Mt 5:10), but those who commit evil stand upon the precipice of destruction. So he urges his hearers to follow Jesus's example and to pray for evildoers more than for those who suffer evil. And what could be more an example of selflessness than praying for those who have betrayed the Lord? No wonder John can hardly contain himself:

> Oh how great the compassion, what goodness the Master shows!
> The One betrayed grieves for the betrayer!
> How great is his patience and his love for humanity!
> Oh how he spares the foolish one![26]

24 *Homily 2 on the Betrayal of Judas*, PG 49:383.

25 *Homily 2 on the Betrayal of Judas*, PG 49:383.

26 *Homily 2 on the Betrayal of Judas*, PG 49:383.

The themes of compassion toward great sinners, of forgiveness of wrongdoing, and of love modeled on Jesus's tender love even for those who turn away are so important that we must return to them in later chapters, for they constitute the greatest fruit of eucharistic communion in Chrysostom's theology. Like Jesus himself, the Christian must learn to grieve for the betrayers among humanity. The only way to achieve this is to have the same love for humanity that Christ himself had. That love comes through the Eucharist, but without Christ coming into the world as a man, there would be no Eucharist.

CONDESCENSION (*ΣΥΓΚΑΤΑΒΑΣΙΣ*) IN CHRYSOSTOM'S THOUGHT

Earlier we noted how condescension played an important role in John's theology. While many of Chrysostom's interpreters have indicated how central the concept of condescension is in his thought, Bertrand de Margerie especially pointed out the pervasive presence of this condescension in Chrysostom's corpus.[27] For Chrysostom, the condescension of God can be seen in the gradual revelation of his plan of salvation (οἰκονομία). This gradual unfolding of God's plan of salvation in the old covenant prepared the world for the ultimate manifestation of himself in Christ. This assumption makes sense of John's use of typology in his expositions of Scripture. As Bradley Nassif points out, John Chrysostom's method of contrasting the old and new is predicated on a prior continuity between the revelation to Israel and the culmination of that revelation in the Incarnation.[28] Margerie takes this arrangement a step further by connecting history, Scripture, and liturgy: "We will catch a glimpse that Scripture is for Chrysostom a prolonging of the Incarnation. Scripture paved the way for it and also manifests it in the liturgy which is the place of the Divine Word being received and effective par excellence."[29]

27 Bertrand de Margerie, *Introduction à l'histoire de l'exégèse les pères grecque et orientaux* (Paris: Editions du Cerf, 1980), 214.

28 Bradley Nassif, "Theoria in St. John Chrysostom's Exegesis: A Study in Biblical Hermeneutics and the Spiritual Life" (PhD diss., Fordham University, 1991), 230–48, where Nassif explains typology and the unity of the Testaments. Of course, John is by no means unique in this regard. The extensive use of typology reaches back as far as the second century to figures like Melito of Sardis in his Paschal homilies.

29 Margerie, *Introduction*, 216.

The infinite distance between God and humanity forms the necessary background for understanding the love that motivated the Incarnation and the necessary condescension entailed by it. As John claimed in his criticisms of the Anomoeans, it is God's initiative "to appear and show himself, not as he is in himself, but such as he can be seen by those who are capable of such a vision as he proportioned his presentation of himself to the weakness of those who look for him."[30] In his goodness God has not remained aloof, and so his condescension to humanity should evoke an appropriate response: "Let us glorify the God who was made flesh [τὸν σαρκωθέντα Θεὸν] for such great condescension. According to our ability, let us render him worthy honor and recompense. Now there can be no repayment to God from us other than the salvation of our souls and our care for [living a life of] virtue."[31] Jean Daniélou argues that in John's theology this condescension was not limited to the Incarnation but must also be seen in the liturgy of the Church as well.[32]

The condescension of Christ displays God's method in the plan of salvation or *oikonomia*. God was not only motivated to send his Son out of his love for humanity; he also structured that plan out of the same love. One of John's clearest statements occurs in his *Homilies on Colossians*, where he explains that in the divine *oikonomia*, "God does not do everything all at the same time but has employed condescension because of his great love of humanity."[33] John borrows Paul's phrase about "the fullness of time" (Gal. 4:4) to explain why God waited until the right moment, the *kairos*, to reveal the fullness of life in Christ. All this was part and parcel of his condescending love to prepare for the reception of his Son. Because love is not often recognized without proper preparation, God planned to reveal his love for humanity only at the right moment, the right *kairos*, so that it could be understood and embraced.

Chrysostom loved to use the prophet Jonah as an example of God's love for the nations. In Jon 4:11 God asks Jonah why he should not have

30 *On the Incomprehensibility of God*, Homily 3, quoted in Margerie, *Introduction*, 217.

31 *On the Birth of Christ*, PG 49:360.

32 See Daniélou's introduction to *Sur l'incomprehensibilté de Dieu*, SC 28 (1970), 15–63.

33 *Homily 4 on Colossians*, PG 62:328. The Greek text reads, Ὁ γὰρ Θεὸς οὐκ ἀθρόως πάντα ποιεῖ, ἀλλὰ κέχρηται συγκαταβάσει διὰ τὴν πολλὴν αὐτοῦ φιλανθρωπίαν. Margerie quotes only the second half of this statement (after ἀλλά) but the temporal reference is crucial. Margerie translates the second clause, "Dieu use de condescendance en vertu de sa grande philanthropie" (*Introduction*, 216).

compassion on the Ninevites if Jonah had such great concern for the plant that had withered. John comments, "Defending himself to Jonah because of the plant [that withered], God says, 'You felt pity for the plant for which you did nothing; shall I not spare [them] for the sake of the great city of Nineveh in which live more than one hundred and twenty thousand people?' He mentioned the number for a reason, that you might learn that prayer with unanimity has great power."[34] While in the immediate context Chrysostom is arguing for the superiority of corporate prayer (e.g., in liturgy), he notes the extent of God's love as seen in his concern for noncovenantal people. John expands on the incident of Jonah at the end of his life in his treatise *On the Providence of God*. In chapter 6, which treats the love of God, John again invokes Jonah. The story of Jonah tells of his complaint to God that he did not bring to pass the threat of destruction upon Nineveh which he had foretold. Jonah, however, had missed the divine intention; it was ultimately not to punish but to show mercy if Nineveh repented. So, in John's preaching God rebukes Jonah with the example of a gardener who loves his plant and adds that "he [God] wanted to show in this example his love for men in the form of a love charm."[35] This divine love, Chrysostom says, is seen not only in God's provision, but also in the kind of love God has. "God loves with an exceedingly irresistible love, love without human passions, a love that is very warm, very vigorous, very genuine, indestructible, and cannot be snubbed out."[36]

Since the Incarnation with its condescension to the human race is so central to Chrysostom's preaching, it makes perfect sense that he would emphasize the earthly life of Jesus as a source of inspiration and grace. For John, the believer of his time is able to experience Jesus Christ in his humanity in the same way that Christ was present on earth. When his people would express a desire to see Jesus, to know his appearance, and to experience him as those did who were on earth at the time of the earthly sojourn, John reminded them that "you do see him, you touch him, you eat him. . . . He gives you himself not only to be seen but to be touched, eaten, and taken

34 *Homily 3 on the Incomprehensibility of God*, SC 28 (bis), 220, lines 419–26.

35 *The Providence of God*, 6.19, SC 79, 104, no numbered lines. See also Monk Moses, *On the Providence of God* (Platina, CA: St. Herman of Alaska Brotherhood, 2015). See page 58, from which my translation diverges slightly.

36 *The Providence of God*, 6.1.

within."[37] It is at the table of the Eucharist that the fifth-century Christian could find Jesus no less than one of the first century. The eucharistic altar then was an implicit call to set on their journey to the kingdom: "They [the Israelites] were about to enter Palestine and so they walked with a roadmap; but we are about to go on a journey to heaven."[38]

The exercise of faith not only allows one's eyes to behold Christ, but the Eucharist even affords an opportunity not given to those who walked on earth with Jesus. They could see, hear, and touch him, but at the mystical table of the Church the faithful can consume Christ, something infinitely better. This superiority is underscored in two ways by John. Not only does he contrast the Hebrews ready to leave Egypt with Christians ready for their journey to heaven, but he highlights the difference between those who knew Christ on earth and those who take him within (λαβεῖν ἔνδον). If believing hearts of Jesus's time could be moved by his presence, later generations can and should "be enflamed, all full of zeal, all fully awake."[39] All confidence depends upon taking the Son of God at his word when he said, "This is my body." To do so, of course, requires "spiritual eyes" to see metaphysical realities. Our modern contrast between the physical and the spiritual parses into a threefold division in John's vocabulary. The real world is not physical and spiritual but physical (φυσικός), metaphysical (νοητός), and spiritual (πνευματικός). Because "Christ has delivered to us nothing that can be seen with the senses but metaphysical realities in observable things,"[40] then the acts of seeing, hearing, touching, and even consuming Christ entail a metaphysical reality that is in no way inferior to his earthly existence. Accordingly, one is not surprised that John Chrysostom ties the eucharistic experience of the Church to specific events in the life of Jesus.

In the liturgy, the Eternal Word (*Logos*) descends from heaven. In God's *oikonomia*, the presence of the mystical sacrifice of the cross is real. Through the calling down (the Epiclesis) of the Holy Spirit, the liturgy becomes a kind of second incarnation as the Word-Become-Flesh comes again to earth. It is easy for those inside the Church and out to think of Christianity as a copious system of laws, rules, and demands, but apart from Christ and his saving mysteries nothing in the laws and rules makes sense. It is Christ's presence

37 *Homily 82 on Matthew*, PG 58:743.

38 *Homily 82 on Matthew*, PG 58:743.

39 *Homily 82 on Matthew*, PG 58:743.

40 *Homily 82 on Matthew*, PG 58:743.

which gives meaning to the liturgy. John was also well aware of *how* Christ became present in the worship of the Church and so in his admonitions to other priests, he reminds them of the contrast between the old and the new. The story of Elijah on Mount Carmel dueling with the prophets of Baal presents a dramatic manifestation of divine power. The power of Elijah's prayer in 1 Kg 18:36–37 seems unparalleled in the new covenant, but that is only the appearance. In reality, the power of a priest's prayer in the Epiclesis is much greater. Elijah's prayer and the subsequent answer from heaven served to demonstrate that Israel's God, not Baal, was the true deity. If the hearts of the people were changed at all, it was from the outside by way of a dramatic event. The priest of the new covenant calls down grace that can lift up souls by an awe-inspiring rite. None of the events of the old covenant could accomplish that.[41] John often highlights the drama of the Old Testament stories, but his purpose is to contrast the inferior (e.g., Elijah) to the superior, the Christian priest, who calls down the Holy Spirit. This Epiclesis is a clear case of how the presence of Christ comes in and through the Spirit. As we will see in later chapters, the priest is an essential but still only the human agent in the Epiclesis; it is what he calls down that transforms the gifts into sacred realities. That is nothing less than God himself.

Chrysostom underscores the same truth again and again in different contexts. In his homily *On the Resurrection of the Dead* he once more emphasizes the supernatural presence of the Holy Spirit that makes the contemporary experience of worship in John's time the same as when the apostles were on earth. Just as signs and wonders accompanied the apostles, so none of the supernatural gifts of the mysteries would be possible without the Spirit's presence: "You are not devoid of the grace of the Holy Spirit. Still now, there are many signs of that gift among those things that are even greater and more awesome. . . . If there were no down payment of the Spirit now [then we would] enjoy no mysteries. There can never be any mystical body and blood without the grace of the Spirit.[42] In due course, John will remind his hearers that the Church was formed out of the side of Christ, from which flowed blood and water. Here and elsewhere, however, Chrysostom brings out the central role of the Holy Spirit in bringing about that union of heaven and earth that *is* the liturgy and its sacraments. In calling the Eucharist "the

41 *On the Priesthood*, 3,4.

42 *Homily on the Resurrection of the Dead*, PG 50:431.

mystical body and blood" John wished to emphasize that it can only be so by the agency of the Holy Spirit.[43]

APPROACHING THE EUCHARIST: FEAR OR PEACE?

For John there is nothing like the liturgy of the Church and the Eucharist that is its center. These should have an unparalleled effect on those who are present and who partake of the sacrament. Peace, tranquility, and lack of animosity are some of the results of receiving the Holy Eucharist, and we will explore these more fully in part 3. In contrast, the communing believer must reject confusion, clamor, and strife. By embracing reverence and devotion, the communicant is transported to a higher level of existence, to the celestial realms to sing with the Seraphim and, like them, to burn with God's love and grace. Yet there is another angle from which to view the sacrament, one that might engender fear.

John would frequently speak of the liturgy and the Eucharist as full of "awesome mysteries" (φρικτὰ μυστήρια). He employs a family of words of which the adjective *phriktos* could be translated "fearful, dreadful, awesome, awe-inspiring" (φρικτός, φρικώδης). Sometimes John uses the term in reference to God's judgment, in which case "fear or dread" is appropriate, but other times he joins this word with the mysteries (sacraments).[44] In those cases, *phriktos* shades over into the meaning of awe, wonder, and amazement.[45] Of these new covenant mysteries, John says, "awesome and fearful are the mysteries that have so much depth. If the types were so fearful, how

43 The use of the expression "mystical body" has a fascinating history as explained in Henri de Lubac, *Corpus Mysticum l'Eucharistie et l'Eglise un Moyen Age Etude historique* (Paris: Editions du Cerf, 2009), originally published in 1944. For the most part, the expression "mystical body" was used of the sacrament for many centuries, after which it began to be applied to the Church.

44 Leyerle devotes a long chapter to "fear" in Chrysostom but she does not consider *phriktos* or its cognates because her focus is on the emotions. See Blake Leyerle, *The Narrative Shape of Emotion in the Preaching of John Chrysostom*, Christianity in Late Antiquity 10 (Berkeley: University of California Press, 2020), 112–49.

45 Some form of the word *phriktos* occurs 177 times in his corpus. Cardo cites other Eastern Fathers (Theophilus of Alexandria and Theodore of Mopsuestia) who frequently use a vocabulary of awe and fear to describe the Eucharist. See Daniel Cardo, *The Cross and the Eucharist in Early Christianity: A Theological and Liturgical Investigation* (Cambridge: Cambridge University Press, 2019), 50–51.

much more the truth."[46] The table of the new covenant, then, can be called *phriktos* by metaphorical extension as he asks, "Do you turn away from this awe-inspiring table?"[47] and this table (altar) is exactly what leads into the mysteries of heaven: "Being about to come to this awesome and divine table and sacred mystagogy, you do so with fear and trembling."[48] Communicants can and should stand in amazement, left as it were in a state of stupor for the wonder they feel in the presence of heaven come to earth. Thus, the silence, tranquility, and depth of thought implicit in the eucharistic celebration invite the participant into something much greater than himself.

The connotations of *phriktos* become clearer when we see it conjoined with "ineffable" in describing the mysteries (τὰ ἀπόρρητα καὶ φρικτὰ μυστήρια). Sometimes he simply affirms this close relation, "You see the ineffable and awesome mysteries" (ὁρᾷς τὰ ἀπόῤῥητα καὶ φρικτὰ μυστήρια); other times he constructs his sentences to highlight the nature of the sacrament, "For this is a view of the awesome and ineffable [nature] of the mystery."[49] John, however, stresses that while the mysteries are inherently ineffable, they nevertheless can be experienced by those who are attentive. "It is not the case that hearing is not pure enough to see the height of the things said, as they should be seen, nor to know, as should be the case, the awesome and ineffable [nature] of these mysteries, nor of any other virtue in divine revelation."[50] Stated less cumbersomely, John is affirming a kind of knowledge attained not by rational investigation but by mystical participation.

John was ever concerned with the moral implications of the Eucharist and so he uses this same linkage of terms to focus on the disparity between participation in the sacred mysteries and immoral living afterwards:

> Consider that you guide [the Eucharist] not only to your hand but also to your mouth. Guard then your tongue from shameful and arrogant speech, blasphemies, lies, and other such things. It is destructive that the tongue that is served with the most awesome mysteries and that is reddened

46 *Homily 23 on Ephesians*, PG 62:165.

47 *On the Baptism of Christ*, PG 49:370.

48 *Homily 1 on the Betrayal of Judas*, PG 49:380.

49 *Homily 11 on the Gospel of John*, PG 59:80. θέα μοι τὸ φρικτὸν καὶ ἀπόῤῥητον τοῦ μυστηρίου. Here John is speaking of baptism. When he uses the word *mystery* in the singular, he usually means a particular sacrament or its underlying reality, while the plural tends to refer to the Eucharist.

50 *Homily 1 on the Gospel of John*, PG 59:27.

> with such blood becomes a golden sword to start reviling, boasting, and ribald jesting. Have respect for the honor that God has bestowed on it [the tongue]. And do not bring it down to a level of cheapness. Ponder again that the heart receives that awesome mystery and then don't contrive malice against your neighbor. But maintain your mind pure of evil. So too you will be able to keep your eyes and ears safe. How can it not be inappropriate that after that mystical sound is brought down from heaven, I mean that of the Cherubim, you defile your hearing with fornicating songs and weakened members? How is this not worthy of the last punishment for the eyes with which you see the ineffable and awesome mysteries to view harlots and to engage in adultery in your mind?[51]

The manner in which John uses awesome (*phriktos*) with ineffable (ἀπόῤῥητος) in close connection suggests he is thinking of the inner reality contained in the sacrament. That invisible reality comes from heaven above. The same ears that hear the mystical sounds of the Cherubim above cannot be exposed to ribald songs of the brothel and remain without guilt. The Eucharist is a call not only to heaven but also away from the worldliness that corrupts the soul. The mysteries of the Church are truly awesome and ineffable.

Why should John think of the mysteries of the altar in such moving terms? Why describe them as ineffable or beyond all words? Is he only stating the negative? Is he here only apophatic? I think not. Perhaps the best answer lies in what we observed about his view of God. God is also ineffable, beyond human understanding, and incapable of being defined in words. And divine providence is also incapable of rational explanation. What appears chaotic and capricious to the human mind is really meaningful to God and his guidance, but that providence can never be articulated, at least not fully. So, if the sacraments (mysteries) are gifts of God and thus carry the presence of God, as they surely do for John, then they also reflect their origins in God. They contain something of the divine, something beyond what human beings can put into words. Those same awesome mysteries make the communicant awesome as well.

The experience of heaven in the liturgy of the Church is unmatched, incomparable, and unsurpassed. The iconic character of liturgy makes it more than bare analogy between different and separate worlds. The realities of heaven are actualized, that is, made present, for all on earth who dare to

51 *Catechetical Lectures*, PG 49:233–34.

come to the mysteries. There is a union of upward movement in which the minds and hearts of the faithful are united with Christ as their high priest. This experience of transcendence while remaining on earth allows one to see what can only be perceived by faith:

> When you see the Lord sacrificed and lying there and the priest standing with the sacrifice praying along with all who have become red with that precious blood, then do you still think you are among men and standing on earth? Rather, aren't you immediately transported into heaven? Once you cast aside every carnal thought of your soul, don't you see the things in heaven with a bare soul and a pure mind? O what a wonder! O the love of God for humanity! He who sits above with the Father holds all things in his hands at that hour and gives to those who want it to enfold and embrace him. Now all this is accomplished through the eyes of faith.[52]

What is so powerful as to allow people on earth to grasp "the One who sits above with the Father" and to engage the same worship as those reddened with "the precious blood"? The Master's love of humanity forms the ultimate motive in John's understanding of why the Church can enjoy the dignity of heaven. Yet, as we will see in chapters 2 and 3, this *philanthropia* is not a bare emotion in the godhead but the deepest ground of the divinely established economy of salvation. God's *oikonomia* tells the story of salvation from beginning to end, but its apex is most assuredly in the Paschal Mystery (death and resurrection). That high point also becomes the font from which flows all the grace needed for the Church. The rationale for the Eucharist is located in the cross and its aftereffects, but the whole life of Christ on earth is encompassed in the divine *oikonomia*. In one of his most captivating adages, John Chrysostom insists that "this table fulfills the order of the manger."[53] What could this remarkable statement possibly mean? I believe that John sees in the Eucharist more than a sacramental addition to an already completed story of salvation. The manger (birth) of the Savior is an essential part of that process of *oikonomia* because it is a crucial step in the order (τάξιν) of God's saving acts. If that is the case, then it is also true that the Eucharist is an irreplaceable part of that same order. The order represented by the manger finds its fulfillment in the table of the Eucharist.

52 *On the Priesthood*, 3,4.

53 *On Blessed Philogonius*: ἡ γὰρ τράπεζα αὕτη τάξιν τῆς φάτνης πληροῖ; PG 48:756.

This explains why Chrysostom's preaching was often invitatory, because it was the liturgy, not only his preaching, that permitted the faithful to experience heaven on earth. The desire of John's heart was so forcefully put in a homily on 1 Corinthians:

> This mystery here makes earth heaven for you. Fling open the gates of heaven and look in. Or rather not those of heaven but of the heaven of heavens. That which is the most precious of all is lying on earth. As the most venerable thing in the royal palace is not its walls or its roof but the royal body sitting on the throne, so also the body of the king is in the heavens. But you are permitted to see this on earth. I will show you not angels nor archangels nor heaven nor even the heaven of heavens but the One who is the Master of all these. Do you know how you see what is more precious than all on earth? And you not only see it, you can touch it. And not only touch but eat it. Wash your soul clean. Prepare your mind for the reception of these mysteries.[54]

The liturgy is the real, albeit imperfect, experience of heaven, of eternity, of eschatological glory. Yet, it can only be so because in the Eucharist human sinners can not only touch heaven but taste it too. With the Eucharist they can "taste and see that the Lord is good" (Ps 34:8). John will return to this theme many times in his homilies because one of his greatest fears was that his flock would despise these heavenly gifts in favor of earthly attachments. He worried that the Christians to whom he preached would neglect to grasp the sublimity and majesty of the Eucharist. So, when he exhorted them to prepare their minds for the reception of the mysteries, he quickly likened this act to being charged with the responsibility of caring for a royal child.[55] Chrysostom saw the distractions of a busy and noisy megalopolis and observed the temptation of Christians to allow worldly distractions to obscure their appreciation of heavenly goods.

Being distracted by earthly delights or being prone to despise the wonders of heaven in the liturgy requires countervailing measures to resist their lure. As we will see in later chapters, John proposes remedies for such weaknesses and temptations, but none is more arresting than his suggestion of a kind of holy inebriation. Speaking of being filled with the Holy Spirit, John

54 *Homily 24 on 1 Corinthians*, PG 61:205.

55 "And if you were entrusted to carry a royal child with jewelry, a purple robe, and a crown, would you just toss all this to the ground? But now it is not the royal child of a human being but the only-begotten child of God that you are receiving" (*Homily 24 on 1 Corinthians*, PG 61:199).

exhorts his flock, "Let us get drunk with this [kind of] drunkenness. Let us abstain from that other kind [of drunkenness] that we may not disgrace the present feast. For the present feast is not only of the earth but of heaven as well."[56] His exhortation stands against the background detectable in a number of homilies preached at Antioch, where Christians had abused their festivals by excess drinking and carousing. We will observe this again in that powerful homily *The Cemetery and the Cross*, preached in a cemetery outside Antioch on Good Friday. John urges a different kind of dissipation, to be drunk with a holy love of heaven that can be acquired by participation in the liturgy of the Church, because the liturgy is an inexhaustible source of joy for the willing participant. As elsewhere, John here cannot contain his exuberance: "Today there is joy on earth; there is joy in heaven. If there is joy in heaven when one sinner turns back, how much more is there joy in heaven when the whole world was snatched from the hands of the Devil."[57]

From here to eternity. That is the path the liturgy affords. In the same way that the creation is a harmonious and exquisitely lavish product of God's providential goodness, so the liturgy of the Church and the Eucharist within it are God's finely tuned gift to lift Christians out of the humdrum of everyday existence and to transport them into the eternal kingdom, from which vantage point we are able to look down upon our daily lives and see, at least in part, the eternal significance of what we do every day. The liturgy is not a retreat from the world but an entry into the kingdom in such a manner that it provides a perspective on the world of everyday life. If the liturgy is a true union of heaven and earth, then the Eucharist affords an opportunity to participate in the life, sufferings, death, and resurrection of Jesus Christ. The same Jesus who taught the crowds, healed the sick, and suffered a shameful death is present in the Eucharist and is present for the people of God today. The past and the future meet in the liturgy, as Robert Taft has put it so beautifully:

> The reality that it [the liturgy] initiates and signifies, however, is neither past or contingent but ever present in God, and through faith to us, at every moment of our lives. And if the past event is both permanent cause and contingent historical sign of salvation, the ritual memorial is the present

56 *Homily against Those Who Are Drunk and on the Resurrection of Christ*, PG 50:436.

57 *Homily against Those Who Are Drunk and on the Resurrection of Christ*, PG 50:436.

> efficacious sign of the same eternal reality. The ritual moment, then, is a synthesis of past, present, and future, as is always true in God's time.[58]

Given John Chrysostom's view, it is no wonder that he would frequently speak of the liturgy and the Eucharist as full of awesome mysteries, as awe-inspiring. He tried to capture what could not be explained or even described. The very nature of mystery defies explanation. The bread, the wine, the altar, and even the entire ritual itself are not strictly speaking the mysteries even though the language of both East and West seems to suggest this at times. The mysteries are in truth what is hidden or concealed inside these visible and tangible realities. The mysteries are the intangible, metaphysical realities that inspirit the physical symbols so that the symbols themselves become life-giving (ζωοποιέω). The true location of the mysteries is in God himself, but these mysteries are actualized in liturgy, all of which is a gift.

58 Robert F. Taft, "Toward a Theology of the Christian Feast," in *Beyond East and West: Problems in Liturgical Understanding*, 2nd ed. (Rome: Edizioni Orientalia Christiana, 2001), 17.

2

The Eucharist Anticipated in the Old Testament

For John Chrysostom, as for so many of the Church Fathers before him, the revelation of the Old Testament foreshadowed the realities fulfilled in Christ and in the Church. The pattern was already established in the pages of the New Testament but was developed further in the earliest writings of the sub-apostolic age. The author of the Letter to the Hebrews, in seeking to prove the superiority of Jesus Christ and the new covenant, contrasts the worship of the old covenant with that of the new:

> You have not approached a mountain that can be touched with hands and burning with fire, of darkness, gloom, and storm, to the sound of trumpet blast or words spoken such that those who heard them begged that no further word be added. For they could not bear what was commanded, "Even if an animal touches the mountain, it shall be stoned." This sight was so fearful that Moses said, "I am scared and trembling." No, you have come to Mount Zion and to the city of the Living God, the heavenly Jerusalem, to myriads of angels in festal assembly. You have come to the church of the firstborn enrolled in heaven and to God, the Judge of all, and to the spirits of the righteous made perfect. You have come to Jesus, the Mediator of the New Covenant, and to the sprinkled blood that speaks better than that of Abel. (Heb 12:18–24)

This biblical contrast of the two covenants reverberates in Chrysostom's insistence on the union of heaven and earth in the divine liturgy. John certainly believes in the continuity of the old and the new but, like the author of Hebrews, John can equally stress the discontinuity. In a homily on 2 Corinthians, he employs language reminiscent of Hebrews 12:

> Behold a new soul (for it was purified) and a new body and new worship and new promises. Here is a new covenant, life, a table, and a garment. In essence all is new. Instead of the Jerusalem below we have received the one mother city above. Instead of a visible temple we see a spiritual one. Instead of stone tablets, we have a fleshly one. Instead of circumcision, baptism. Instead of manna, we have the Master's own body. Instead of water from the rock, we have blood from his side. Instead of Moses's or Aaron's rod, we have the cross. Instead of the promised land we have the kingdom of heaven. Instead of thousands of priests we have one High Priest. Instead of an irrational lamb we have a spiritual Lamb. As Paul thinks about all such things, he said, "All things are new." All these things are from God through Christ and his gift.[1]

In speaking of the new covenant one can hear in Chrysostom's overtones the Johannine contrast where truth is the antitype of the types in the old covenant. Here the meaning of "true" or "truth" is opposed not to "false" but to the imperfect and incomplete. Israel was named the vine that God planted (e.g., Is 5:7; Ps 80:8–18), but the true vine is the Messiah, the true son of Israel (Jn 15:1ff). In this same vein, Chrysostom draws out contrasts never mentioned in the Bible: "Instead of manna, we have the Master's own body. Instead of water from the rock, we have blood from his side. Instead of Moses's or Aaron's rod, we have the cross."

This dynamic of continuity and discontinuity impelled Chrysostom to comb the entire Old Testament to find clear types and figures of Jesus and the Eucharist. One major line of continuity and contrast has already been noted, the liturgy itself. In his exhortation to priests, he not only reminds them of their dignity as agents of God, he also points to the contrast between the accoutrements of worship in the two dispensations:

> For the things before grace are fearful and most dreadful such as the bells, the Urim and Thumim, the stones on the chest, the shoulders, the girdle, the lyre, the sash, the golden leaf, the holy of holies, the calm of things

1 *Homily 11 on 2 Corinthians*, PG 61:476.

> within. But if anyone scrutinizes the things of grace, he will find those fearful and dreadful things to be small. He will find it true what was said concerning the law, "that which has glory is not glorious in comparison to the surpassing glory."[2]

John's quotation of 2 Cor 3:10 seems directed against the perennial Christian temptation to look back to the concreteness of the old covenant with a nostalgic glance as if the present Christian worship experience lacked some of the tangible manifestations of God's glory. This theme, already detectable in the Hebrews passage quoted above, functions in Chrysostom's mind to signal the higher and deeper awe that should be evoked from the Christian worshiper.

Even though, at one level, John was simply following the pattern set in the New Testament, he may have had a heightened reason for making strong contrasts between old and new covenants. Chrysostom has been long known for his acerbic preaching against the Jews. Yet new light has been thrown on John's anti-Judaism by placing his comments in a new context. Robert Wilken recontextualizes John's preaching against the Jews by arguing that in fact he was preaching against Judaizing Christians in his own flock. We know that there was a sizable Jewish community in fourth-century Antioch with Jews in every strata of society, including the wealthy landowners. Relying on solid previous scholarship, Wilken is not overstating the case when he says that "the Jews continued to be a significant factor [in Roman society] through the third and fourth centuries."[3] The continuing practice of the Jewish religion sometimes lured baptized Christians into Jewish celebrations. John was very jealous for his flock as he tried to call Christians away from such Jewish rituals, which he regarded as inherently inferior. The recognition of Judaizing Christians in Antioch not only suggests a slightly different audience than previously thought but also makes better sense of John's interpretations of the Old Testament.[4]

Bradley Nassif has elucidated this dynamic by stressing the role of *theoria* in the homilies of John Chrysostom. He attempts to refine the received contrast between Alexandrian allegorism and Antiochene literalism by showing

2 *On the Priesthood*, 3,4.

3 Robert Wilken, *John Chrysostom and the Jews: Rhetoric and Reality in the Late 4th Century* (Eugene, OR: Wipf and Stock, 1983), 46.

4 Wilken's whole book is an illuminating read but I especially recommend *John Chrysostom and the Jews*, 46–48, 158–64.

that John's literal interpretation also contained a mystical dimension that, among other things, searches out the deeper unity between the testaments.[5] That unity was literal in the sense of real historical events (e.g., Passover, tabernacle) bearing a typological significance. This typology grew out of and depended on the "christological content and soteriological purpose within the framework of salvation history" so that one should be able to see a "deeper spiritual meaning connected to the historical sense."[6] This implies that while there was indeed a great difference between such allegorism as one finds in Origen and John's approach to the Old Testament Scriptures, the Antiochene Father was not bereft of deeper spiritual meanings. They were rooted in salvation history and elucidated by *theoria*. In Nassif's judgment, salvation history was John Chrysostom's metanarrative. *Theoria* was not, however, a purely exegetical tool. René Bornert traces the interaction of biblical and liturgical exegesis in the Byzantine tradition by showing that they reach back into the catechetical instructions to the newly baptized. This led to what Bornert calls "the mystical commentary," whose purpose was to explain the *mysterion* behind the visible signs and rites of the liturgy.[7] The connection and continuities between the liturgy and exegesis are not hard to see. Both the rites of the Church and the sacred page of the Church reveal deeper mysteries behind the visibly historical and factual instances.

In this chapter I will explore John's interpretations of the persons and events of the Old Testament that pointed forward to the new covenant realities. While three of the most prominent figures (Moses, Elijah, Melchizedek) play singular roles in his thinking, he also comments on classic texts with eucharistic connections, preeminent of which is Mal 1:11–14. His commentary of persons, events, and texts displays his conviction of both continuity and discontinuity between the old and new dispensations, and his interpretations also show similarities and dissimilarities with those of New Testament authors who comment on the same material. It is here that I introduce two

5 Nassif's work began in "Theoria in St. John Chrysostom's Exegesis: A Study in Biblical Hermeneutics and the Spiritual Life" (PhD diss., Fordham University, 1991) and continued in other publications noted below.

6 Bradley Nassif, "Antiochene θεωρία in John's Chrysostom's Exegesis," in *Exegesis and Hermeneutics in the Churches of the East*, ed. Vahan S. Hovhanessian (New York: Peter Lang, 2009), 51, 53.

7 I am indebted to Nassif for his summary of Bornert's treatment of the liturgical commentarytradition in "Theoria in St. John Chrysostom's Exegesis," 248–64. See also René. Bornert, *Les Commentaires byzantines de la divine liturgie de VIIe au XVe siècle*. Archives de l'Orient chrétien 9. Paris: Institut francais d'Etudes byzantines, 1966.

central concepts of this book that seek to unify and make sense of these diverse phenomena: anticipation and participation. The latter concept is more than one point of theology among many. In later chapters we shall often return to participation as a central idea in his view of the Eucharist.

TWO AXES OF HISTORY

Drawing on these studies of Antiochene hermeneutics, I would like to sketch a general framework that underlies John Chrysostom's reading of the old covenant and how it relates to the Eucharist. In this regard, John is by no means unique or unusual, for many other Church Fathers employed the same framework evident in Paul's epistles and the Letter to the Hebrews.[8] These New Testament authors all divided history into the overarching dispensations of the old and the new covenant. The quotations above show clearly that John saw these two dispensations in liturgical as well as in historical terms. In order to capture this picture, which functions as an archetype for John, I would like to introduce two axes that relate the old covenant to the new and simultaneously relate both to the central event of salvation, the Paschal Mystery. To speak of the Paschal Mystery (the death and resurrection of Christ) as the central event of salvation is to bring to light an unchanging tradition from the New Testament to contemporary theology. In commenting on Paul's use of *anakephalaiosis* (ἀνακεφαλαίωσις) in Eph 1:10, Lawrence Feingold summarizes this long tradition: "Christ recapitulates all things in himself by being the Antitype of all salvation history. Everything before the Incarnation was a preparation for and prefigurement of Christ, and everything after him is to be conformed to his image in the Church, which shall finally be brought into the splendor of his glory."[9] These two axes represent a unifying line of direction that explains how the events of the old covenant relate to Christ's salvific work and how that work is communicated to the Church in the new. An axis is an imaginary line around which something revolves, such as the earth spinning on its axis, producing the difference

8 Even though modern scholars tend to ascribe the Letter to the Hebrews to someone other than Paul, John firmly believed that he was the author of the document. I suspend judgment on this issue since it affects nothing in our treatment.

9 Lawrence Feingold, *Touched by Christ: The Sacramental Economy* (Steubenville, OH: Emmaus Press, 2021), 29n60.

between night and day. From the perspective of the new covenant, the life and worship of ancient Israel in the Old Testament all revolved around an *Axis of Anticipation*. Israel's elaborate temple liturgy (or cult), its governing monarchy, whether united or divided, and its annual calendar all make sense from the standpoint of the new covenant as anticipating the coming of the fullness of time (see Gal 4:4) and the arrival of the Messiah. The prophets have multiple ways of speaking of the Messiah and the messianic age to come. The truths they predicted, intimated, and hinted at increased the sense of anticipation in the Jews of Jesus's day. Both explicit (e.g., Is 53) and oblique (e.g., Is 2; Mi 4) references to the Messiah in the prophets deepened the longing of the ancient people of God. The Psalms too, as Israel's prayer book, contained multiple ways of foreseeing the consummation of Israel's hope (Psalms 2, 22, 110). As Paul makes clear in speaking of the experiences of Israel: "All these things happened to them as examples and were written for our instruction on whom the end of the ages has come" (1 Cor 10:11). This awareness of the two dispensations, old and new, surfaces again in Heb 1:1–2: "God, having spoken in many partial and manifold ways of old to the fathers in his prophets, has spoken to us in these last days in a Son." The arrival of the end of the ages is reflected in Paul's declaration that "Christ is the end (*telos*) of the law" (Rom 10:4). So the Axis of Anticipation is a line running through Israel's history around which events revolve and to which texts refer:

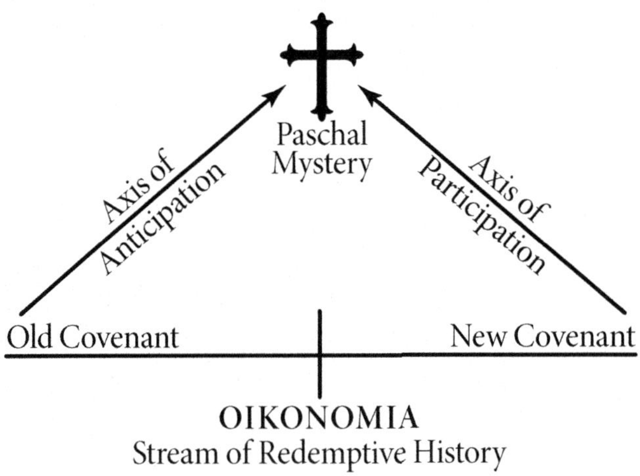

As we will observe presently, the major events of the old covenant (e.g., Passover) and the major personages involved (e.g., Moses, Elijah,

Melchizedek) were all understood by Chrysostom as harbingers or indexes pointing to future realities. The Axis of Anticipation, however, is only one side of picture because for those in the new covenant there is also an *Axis of Participation*. I contend that for John, the Christian in the new covenant participates in the Paschal Mystery of Christ in virtually everything in life. This means that the orientation of the Church (and the individual Christian) is always directed back to those saving events. Although the Christian looks forward to the consummation of all things in the second advent of Christ, his daily experience largely revolves around an axis that looks back to the cross and resurrection (Paschal Mystery) of Christ. Participation or *koinonia* is the proper term to capture Chrysostom's preaching because he sees the liturgical celebration of the Church as the primary means by which all that was anticipated in the old covenant is experienced in the new. None of this is surprising to one immersed in the idea of memory or remembrance present in the stories and texts of the Old Testament. Over fifty years ago Brevard S. Childs explicated this phenomenon in his widely acclaimed 1962 work, *Memory and Tradition in Israel*. Childs drew upon a confluence of studies that pointed out that memory or remembrance for the Israelites was more than mental recollection of past events.[10] It was participatory, and it has profound implications for our understanding of Chrysostom's eucharistic theology.

This Axis of Participation is then far greater, far more powerful, far more sanctifying than anything known before the coming of Christ. These two axes, taken together, capture John Chrysostom's approach to the Eucharist based on the unity of the two testaments.[11] In the liturgy the Axis of Anticipation and the Axis of Participation converge once again as they once did in the Paschal Mystery of Christ. The Eucharist is at once a participation in Calvary as a past event and an anticipation of Calvary's consummation as a future event. The actualization happening in the liturgy of the Church brings both the past and the future into the present. In a way similar to the centrality of the Axis of Anticipation in the old covenant, the Axis of Participation is the invisible line around which the liturgy, sacraments, and preaching revolve. Both axes stand out more clearly in John's treatment of old covenant events.

10 Brevard S. Childs, *Memory and Tradition in Israel* (London: SCM Press, 1962).

11 "Liturgical images of the Exodus, the sacrifice of Melchizedek, the paschal lamb and others . . . presuppose a typological *theoria* which is grounded in the unity of the Testaments and implicit in the mystery of the sacraments" (Nassif, "Theoria in St. John Chrysostom's Exegesis," 253).

THE PASSOVER AND THE EUCHARIST

In the Old Testament, the Exodus from Egypt is the central event of redemption for the people of Israel. The later authors of the Hebrew Bible repeatedly return to this complex of events as the sign and assurance that the Lord has chosen Israel as his own.[12] The book of Deuteronomy, for example, is set in the Transjordanian desert where Moses delivers his last speeches to the children of Israel before they enter to conquer the promised land. These sermons are replete with references back to God's saving work in Egypt and the forty years of wandering in the desert. Here Israel is commanded never to forget what the Lord has done (see Dt 8:1–2). In fact, when Moses reiterates the Ten Commandments as the summary of the moral, liturgical, and civil laws of Israel, he prefaces that summary with a reminder of the character of the God who commands them, "I am the Lord your God who brought you out of the land of Egypt, out of the house of slavery" (Dt. 5:6), just as the original promulgation had done (see Ex 20:2). Already in the old covenant, obedience flows out of an awareness of God's saving acts.

The New Testament authors provide the model for John's preaching, of course, by viewing the event of the Passover as a type and foreshadowing of the redemption brought by Christ. Both John the Evangelist and Paul see Christ as the Lamb of God sacrificed for sins (Jn 1:29; 1 Cor 5:7). The emphasis on the lamb being unblemished in Exodus 12:5 is developed by Peter: "You were not redeemed with corruptible things such as silver and gold . . . but with the precious blood of Christ like one unblemished and spotless" (1 Pt 1:18–19). Even Peter's specific language of "precious blood" (τιμίῳ αἵματι) found its way into the Greek Christian vocabulary of the Eucharist.[13] This blood from the unblemished lamb of every Hebrew household had to be applied to the doorposts (Ex 12:7), which the Letter to the Hebrews appropriates by saying that "without the shedding of blood there is no forgiveness" (Heb 9:22).

John Chrysostom views the Passover and the Exodus in this biblical light. He often contrasts the Passover celebrated by the Jews of Antioch with the Christian celebration that he considers the true fulfillment of the Old

12 Among many other texts, see Psalm 136 and Hos 11:1.

13 The phrase is used widely in the Greek Fathers. In the Chrysostom corpus it occurs sixteen times as a clear reference to Christ's blood. Among these, several have clear eucharistic referents, as in "to come and commune in the sacred table and to partake of the precious blood" (ἐλθεῖν καὶ κοινωνῆσαι τῆς ἱερᾶς τραπέζης, καὶ τοῦ αἵματος μετασχεῖν τοῦ τιμίου; *Against the Jews*, PG 48:861).

Testament memorial; the latter is predicated on the divine institution of the original Passover. The ancient feast was only a preparation for the real Passover in which the only thing that could save humanity was Christ, the Sun of Righteousness:

> "When your son asks you, what is this?" you say that they poured the blood of the sheep on the doorposts and they caused death to flee which the Destroyer brought on all those in Egypt. Because of this blood the Destroyer was not able to force his way in and bring in the plague. [The sheep] of the old Passover did this unwillingly but in this case Christ is willingly sacrificed. Why? Because that one back then is a figure [τύπος] of the spiritual one. And so you may learn, look at what kind of relation there is. Lamb and lamb but one is nonrational and the other is rational. Sheep and sheep, shadow and truth. But the Sun of Righteousness appeared and the shadow ceased. The shadow was hidden by the sun's presence. Therefore, there is a lamb and a mystical table for us to be sanctified by his blood. Let the lamp no longer shine once the sun comes. For they are figures [τύποι] of the events of the future.[14]

None of the particulars of the Passover escape John Chrysostom's notice as they become important in his exhortations to the Christians of his day. In his catechetical sermons, John desires his hearers to learn from the Old Testament Passover: "Do you want to learn the power of this blood? Let us have recourse to its type, to the ancient stories in Egypt" and "Learn the power of this type so that you learn the power of the truth."[15] The truth is the fulfillment of the type in Christ. Like Paul in the New Testament, Chrysostom draws on the Old Testament narratives to bring understanding of the liturgy and Eucharist.[16] For the preacher of Antioch, the blood of the lamb in the Passover is a type of the real blood that redeems. As the author of the fourth Gospel contrasts the Mosaic dispensation of law with "grace and truth through Jesus Christ" (Jn 1:17), so his fourth-century namesake contrasts shadow with reality:

> What did Moses [say]? "Sacrifice the spotless lamb and put its blood on the doors." What is that you say? Does he think that the blood of irrational animals saves rational men? Yes, he says, since it is not blood but a type

14 *Homily 2 on the Betrayal of Judas*, PG 49:388.

15 *Baptismal Catecheses*, 3,13.

16 *Baptismal Catecheses*, 3,13.

> of the blood of the Lord. Just as royal statues that are without souls and sensation save men who flee to them, men that have sensation and possess souls, not because of the bronze but because they are images of the king, so the blood [of those animals] without sensation and souls saved men who have souls, not because it was blood but because it was the type of the blood [of Christ].[17]

John assumes the early patristic reasoning found in Athanasius's *On the Incarnation* that only like can redeem like. How can an irrational animal redeem rational beings like human beings? Only because the redemption was accomplished not in the Passover from Egypt nor in the blood shed there, but in the blood shed in the death of Christ. This implies the objective superiority of the new covenant realities to which the old economy of salvation pointed forward. That is why the Christian can have high confidence in the victory that Christ has won and communicates to him in the eucharistic blood. For Chrysostom, the superior reality of the new covenant Passover is why Paul can say, "Christ our Pascha is sacrificed for us" (1 Cor 5:7):

> In this way, the story is a type but the reality is this. We ourselves eat the Pascha who is Christ for "Christ our Pascha has been sacrificed." And so we eat the Pascha that is much better than that of the [Jewish] law. So too we should eat shod and girded. Why? That we may be ready for our exodus, our departure from here [i.e., this world]. Let none who eats look back to Egypt but to heaven, to the Jerusalem that is above. For this reason, you should eat girded and shod that you may learn that as you begin eating, you should depart on your journey.[18]

The exhortation to be prepared to depart is as relevant for the Christian of the new covenant as it was for the Jew of the old, but the destination is different. For the Christian, it is the New Jerusalem, the heavenly promised land. In that same homily on Ephesians Chrysostom reminds his baptized hearers of Paul's words "Our citizenship is in heaven" (Phil 3:20), and therefore Christians must be more prepared than the Israelites of old since they partake of a much greater meal. Gird about and feet shod, John's hearers must be ready:

17 *Baptismal Catecheses*, 3,14.

18 *Homily 23 on Ephesians*, PG 62:166.

> The mysteries are awesome, inspiring, and have so much depth. If there are such awesome things in the types, how much more are there in the reality [*aletheia*]? They come out of Egypt; they eat the Pascha. Pay attention to the scheme of those who are making their way out. They have sandals, staffs in their hands, and they eat standing up.[19]
>
> So let us gird ourselves around, and we will be able to go on our journey, even amid hardships. Whenever we pass through open country, the Devil stands ready, cunningly devising things so that he may seize those who are saved from Egypt, those who pass through the Red Sea, those who are delivered from demons and a thousand plagues.[20]

As arduous as the journey may be, as daunting as the malevolent enemy seems, John sees the reinforcements of grace at the Christian's side: "If we stay vigilant, we have a pillar of fire, the grace of the Holy Spirit. The same One enlightens and shades us. We have manna but we have more than manna. We have a spiritual drink but not water flowing from a rock."[21] The spiritual food and drink of the Eucharist can sustain the heart of the believer on the journey through the desert of this world. Manna, yes, but more than manna feeds the spiritual hunger of the traveler as he sets his sights on the promised land of his true citizenship.

This homily in Ephesians stresses the difference between the manna and the Eucharist, but John could nevertheless emphasize the continuity between the two on occasions. *In Homily 23 on 1 Corinthians*, John lays the emphasis on how Christ was operating through the figure of the manna, even suggesting that it was something beyond the natural realm:

> As you eat the Lord's body, so they ate the manna. As you drink his blood, they drank water from a rock. Even though the things that happened were visible, yet they are shown to be spiritual not by nature, but by the gift of grace. With the body they nourished the soul by leading it to faith. For this reason he said nothing about food for it had already been changed not only in the manner but in the nature as well. For it was manna.[22]

And when he speaks of the water brought from a rock, he reminds his hearers that it was Christ who was the true rock slaking their thirst. This

19 *Homily 23 on Ephesians*, PG 62:165.

20 *Homily 23 on Ephesians*, PG 62:166.

21 *Homily 23 on Ephesians*, PG 62:165.

22 *Homily 23 on 1 Corinthians*, PG 61:191.

strong continuity between the experiences of the old and the new explains in John's mind how Paul can say that the ancient Israelites were "baptized into Moses" (1 Cor 10:2). John explains, "As we believed in Christ and in his resurrection, we were baptized, so they partook of the same mysteries."[23] I doubt John is thinking of the fullest sense of participating in the same mysteries that the Christian in the new covenant would, but he sees Paul's stress on the continuity when he says, "He [Paul] wishes to introduce a type close to the truth; he does not say it this way. Rather he used the names of the truth in the type. Now this was a sign of redemption, but what came after these things was the holy table."[24]

Whenever John reflects on the interplay of the old order and the new, he reintroduces the continuity between them to emphasize the discontinuity and the greater experiences of believers in the new covenant. In his commentary on Matthew, John focuses his attention on the timing of Christ's institution of the Eucharist and finds something significant in it:

> "While they were eating, he took bread." Why did he choose to accomplish this mystery at the season of the Passover? For you to learn that in every instance he is the lawgiver of the old covenant and so things were written in cryptic form. Because the type is there, he brings forth the reality. The evening of the fullness of times was a proof and the affairs of that time had come to an end. He gives thanks, by teaching us that we should celebrate this mystery, by showing us that he was not approaching his passion involuntarily, and by instructing us that whatever we suffer, we should gladly bear and keep up useful hopes. If this type of slavery could become deliverance, how much more will the truth set free the whole world and be given for the benefit of our nature. For this very reason, the mystery was not passed on before this, [but was delayed] until the things of the law finally ceased. And their chief feast is abolished and they are transferred to a thoroughly awe-inspiring table. And so Christ says, "Take, eat. This is my body, which is broken for you."[25]

Christ, the lawgiver of the new covenant, now substitutes new signs in place of the old, which implies that the older order will be done away with to make room for the new. As "the things of the law finally ceased," so now

23 *Homily 23 on 1 Corinthians*, PG 61:193.

24 *Homily 23 on 1 Corinthians*, PG 61:191.

25 *Homily 82 on Matthew*, PG 58:737–38.

is the time "to celebrate this mystery" (Eucharist). The superiority of the new covenant Passover is also seen in the wider scope of salvation enjoyed. The old Passover showed that "this type of slavery [Egypt] could become deliverance." The new Passover contains the "truth [that] sets free the whole world" by being "given for the benefit of our nature."

Thus, the "thoroughly awe-inspiring table" (τράπεζαν φρικωδεστάτην) will make it possible for Christians to be far more than a liberated nation. By their participation in the sacred table they are elevated to the status of sons. These privileges demand an even greater obedience than could ever have been expected of the ancient Israelite. That is undoubtedly why Chrysostom encourages them to follow the example of voluntary suffering seen in Christ, who showed by his life that "whatever we [Christians] suffer, we should gladly bear and keep up useful hopes."[26] So for John the old Passover serves several functions. It is the necessary background for the Eucharist in a manner consistent with Jesus's institution. It is an index pointing to God's goodness, demonstrating that the divine intention was always to bestow untold blessings on his children, blessings that came to fulfillment in the new Passover. And most importantly, the new Passover provides an even greater incentive to pursue a life of virtue and holiness.

The Exodus from Egypt was without a doubt the supreme act of divine redemption for the children of Israel, and the Passover is the meal celebrating that deliverance. These events, as glorious as they must have seemed to the ancient people of God, pale into insignificance compared to the sufferings of Christ and the meal he instituted to commemorate those sufferings. The enduring reality has superseded the temporary type. The Old Testament pictured the future redemption of a reunited Israel in terms of a second Exodus (Hos 11:1 and Mt 2:15). For John, as for so many other Church Fathers, that anticipated redemption is now a reality. It is no longer anticipated; it is realized, fulfilled. It only remains now to participate in it.

26 *Homily 82 on Matthew*, PG 58:737–38.

ELIJAH AND THE CONTEST ON MOUNT CARMEL

The Eastern Churches have always placed great importance on the Transfiguration, and so it is not unusual that Elijah should also be an important figure since Moses symbolizes the Torah (Law) and Elijah the Prophets in that biblical story. For John, Elijah does indeed represent the greatest of the Old Testament prophets, but even that honor contrasts with the greater glory of Christ the Master. In one of his sermons on the ascension of Christ we hear John making a strong contrast: Elijah the servant was taken up to something like heaven whereas Christ the Master ascended into heaven itself. The modes of their transport were also different, Elijah in a chariot, Jesus on a cloud representing the throne of heaven. Most importantly, Elijah and Jesus differ with regard to what they left behind:

> When the servant had to be called home, a chariot was sent. But in the case of the Son, it was when the Royal Throne and not simply a royal throne, but the Father's throne itself, called. Listen to what Isaiah said about the Father, "Behold the Lord sits on the fluffy cloud."[27] So he sent a cloud for his Son. Elijah who went up left a mantle for Elisha. When Jesus ascended into heaven, however, he left gifts for his disciples. He did not make one prophet but thousands of Elishas. These are much greater and more illustrious than him.[28]

These contrasts clearly indicate not only the superiority of Christ's ascension but also their incommensurability. Any similarity is only superficial because Christ's gifts are infinitely greater. The greater majesty of Christ's ascension consists of the gifts he gave to the Church when he made all prophets or "thousands of Elishas" (μυρίους Ελισσαίους). This text from the homily on the ascension represents a wider phenomenon in Chrysostom's preaching emphasizing the greater superiority of new covenant realities. Such a contrastive mindset plays strongly into his view of the Eucharist.

Chrysostom does not specify what gifts Christ gave to his Church, though his wording may be drawn from Eph 4:7–8, but the contrast between Elijah's unusual departure from this world and that of Jesus is not limited

27 John appears to refer to Is 14:13–14, although his version does not correspond to any of the known versions. He may in fact be combining several texts into one.

28 *Sermon 2 on the Ascension*, PG 52:796.

to homilies on the ascension. In his more famous homilies on the statues in Antioch John connects Elijah with the gift of the Eucharist:

> Elijah left his mantle for his disciple. When the Son of God ascended on high, he left us his own flesh. But there is this difference. Elijah shed his cloak but Christ left us his flesh and took it up at the same time. So, let us not fall away or lament our fate, or fear the discontent of our times. He did not refuse to shed his blood for all and share his flesh and blood with us again. What will he refuse to do for the sake of our salvation? So, bolstered by these hopes, let us entreat him continuously and devote ourselves to prayers and supplications, let us take care of the remaining virtues with every careful attention that we may escape the danger pressing on us and obtain the good things to come.[29]

John here becomes very specific about the gift left to the Church. It is the gift of Christ himself. And not a gift of self in a general sense but a gift of the same flesh and blood that was sacrificed on the cross. This then becomes the basis of his exhortation to greater prayer and holiness. When John notes a difference between Christ and Elijah, it is ultimately a difference between what a human being can give and what only God himself can give. That "Christ left us his flesh and took it up at the same time" is something only the Son of God could do. Elijah is again invoked to emphasize the inferiority of the old covenant in comparison with the new.

Elijah contrasts not only with Christ himself but even with a human priest. John introduces Elijah in his treatise *On the Priesthood*, where he compares the sacrificial service of the Christian priest with the sacrifice offered by Elijah. One can hear behind the text a temptation to denigrate the meager trappings of Christian worship in the light of such dramatic events of the old covenant as Elijah's calling down divine fire to consume the sacrifice on the altar at Mt. Carmel. In 1 Kings 18, Elijah stands alone against the prophets of Baal. Taunting them with ridicule, Elijah calls down fire and "suddenly a flame descends from heaven upon the sacrificial animal." This fire is a vivid demonstration of the Lord's power over evil forces while the people of Israel stand in silence. Silent too is the "sacrifice lying on the stones." Thinking of the fire falling on Elijah's makeshift altar, John can declare that,

29 *Homily 2 to the People of Antioch*, PG 63:645.

"These amazing spectacles are full of dread" and he readily acknowledges that all this is "awesome to see, but it surpasses all amazement."[30]

Yet the burning flame manifested in Elijah's confrontation is cold compared to what takes place in the liturgical sacrifice offered by the priest of the new covenant. He invokes not fire but the Holy Spirit. The result is not destruction but the open river of grace flowing down so that "the grace coming on the sacrifice may through it lift up the souls of all, and shine forth more brightly than silver refined by fire." This is not the fire that consumes material sacrifices but the grace that enlivens and enlightens believers. In fact, the presence of God in the eucharistic sacrifice is so intense that "a human soul was not even able to bear the fire of that sacrifice but . . . all would be utterly destroyed if there were not a lot of help from the grace of God."[31] The momentous physicality and visibility of Elijah's experience remains in John's mind inferior to every Christian priest at the altar. It is precisely because this table is full of spiritual fire that the Eucharist far exceeds even the most dramatic events of the old order. The priest invokes not physical fire but the fire of the Holy Spirit. This fire brings grace, not destruction, and lifts souls up to God. How could anyone who understood the power of the Christian sacrifice be contemptuous? John employs the visible and earthly types to heighten the invisible and heavenly realities. The imagery of fire we observed in his description of the liturgy is more than flowery rhetoric. The true fire of God comes from heaven to the altar of the Church.[32]

MELCHIZEDEK: HARBINGER OF CHRIST'S OFFERING

It is only natural that John Chrysostom would treat the enigmatic figure of Melchizedek who surfaced on the pages of Genesis chapter 14 and became a harbinger of the Messiah even before the arrival of the new covenant and the

30 All the quotations in this paragraph come from *On the Priesthood*, 3,4.

31 *On the Priesthood*, 3,4. This passage will be discussed again in chapter 6.

32 The imagery of fire for eucharistic communion will persist in Eastern writers for centuries to come. See John Damascene, *On the Orthodox Faith*, 4,13: "Let us approach him with burning desire and forming our palms in the shape of a cross let us receive the body of the one Crucified. Touching our eyes, our lips, and forehead let us receive the divine coal that is the fire of the desire within us, and once received, the burning from the coal may consume our sins and enlighten our hearts and we burn by partaking of the divine fire and be deified."

Letter to the Hebrews. John's lectures on Hebrews, his commentary on Psalm 110, and his treatment of Genesis would all be apt occasions for treating this "priest of the Most High God" who was, in the language of the author of Hebrews, "made like unto the Son of God" (Heb 7:3). While this is not the occasion to address the biblical treatments of Melchizedek, it is clear that John follows the biblical texts closely while at the same time expanding their meaning in directions that go beyond the texts themselves. In his short, self-contained homily on Melchizedek, Chrysostom enlarges the statements of Heb 7:3 that Melchizedek was "without father, without mother, without a genealogy." This becomes an occasion for him to compare the "birth above" and the "birth below." In the case of Jesus the "birth above" was without a mother while the "birth below" was without a father. John repeatedly quotes Heb 5:11, which says that the matter of Melchizedek is "a subject great and hard to interpret," and applies this to the eternal generation of the Son by the Father and to the virgin birth by Mary. John is fully aware of the paradoxes entailed by the use of these categories as he asks, "If he is without a father, how is he a son; if without a mother, how is he the Only Begotten?" He openly confesses the limits of his—and everyone's—knowledge of how all these things could be true but he is not afraid to affirm them.[33]

The author of Hebrews does not even mention the bread and wine in Gn 14:18 inasmuch as his purpose is to contrast the priesthood of Melchizedek with that of Aaron and the Levites. John, however, does not pass up the opportunity to speak of "the apostolic table" (ἀποστολικὴν τράπεζαν) while also contrasting the Aaronic priesthood with that of Melchizedek, or rather with the fulfillment of the image of the enigmatic figure:

> This Melchizedek was a righteous man and truly bore the image of Christ, since he was moved by the prophetic spirit. It was the future offering on behalf of the nations that he brought, thinking to honor God with bread and wine as he imitated the future Christ. Now since the synagogue of the Jews offered a sacrifice to God in the order of Aaron, not bread and wine, but bulls and lambs, he [Aaron] glorified God with sacrifices by blood. But speaking of the Christ to come, Jesus, born of the virgin Mary, God cries out, "You are a priest forever in the order of Melchizedek," not in the order of Aaron who served with bulls and lambs. Rather, "You are a priest forever

33 All the quotations in this paragraph come from *Homily on Melchizedek*, PG 56:257–62. See also *Homilies on Genesis*, PG 53:328.

> in the order of Melchizedek," by bringing forth perpetually with bread and wine the offering of the gifts.[34]

John sees in Melchizedek a foreshadowing of Christ as priest not only in general, as the author of Hebrews does, but also in the kind of offering he brought. The bread and wine were anticipations or types of the gifts offered in the Eucharist. John makes this explicit again in his comments on Psalm 110: "What was the reason for his saying 'in the order of Melchizedek'? He says it with the Eucharist in mind, because he too offered bread and wine, to Abraham, and because of the independence of this priesthood of the Law and its being without end and without beginning, as Paul too says."[35]

It may be helpful to reminder ourselves how important Psalm 110 was in the New Testament. In addition to being quoted and commented on in the Letter to the Hebrews, it also forms the background of Mt 22:41–46, where Jesus poses the conundrum of how the Messiah could be simultaneously David's son and David's Lord. John seems to offer a solution to this conundrum that reveals truly who the Messiah is. In his commentary of Psalm 110, John makes much of the words, "The Lord said to my Lord" and asks how there can be more than one Lord when Scripture says to worship the One True Lord (Dt 6:4–5). John takes this as sufficient evidence to counter errant Christologies, insisting that this text shows the divinity of Christ. Yet John is no less attentive to indicators of the humanity of Christ and sees in the Psalm and the Gospels emphasis on both: "Do you see how once again he [the Psalmist] brings his speech down to a more concrete level, discoursing in one place of his divinity and in another of his humanity?"[36] John then contrasts Melchizedek and Jesus by explaining the words of Heb 7:3, "without father, without mother, without a genealogy." The controlling contrast between shadow and reality plays a significant role here as John explains the difference between the lack of a genealogy in the case of Melchizedek and that of Jesus. In the case of the priest of Salem there simply was no mention of a genealogy, not that he did not have one, for he was after all only a man. But in the case of Jesus Christ, he truly had no genealogy since he was the Son of God. This all bears on the Eucharist because Christ as God commanded the

34 *In Illud: Ascendit Dominus in templo*, PG 61:742.

35 Robert C. Hill, *Commentary on the Psalms* (Brookline, MA: Holy Cross Orthodox Press, 1998), 2, 27–28; translation modified.

36 *On Melchizedek*, PG 56:257–62.

sacred meal, while as a human priest he brings the gifts of bread and wine. John again makes a eucharistic reference in his homilies on Genesis when he comments on Melchizedek. Since the enigmatic King-priest of Salem was a type of Christ, his actions pointed to "a kind of a mystery."[37] In *Homily 36* he explicitly connects the mystery to the gifts: "In another way he was a type of the things happening in Christ. And he indicates a kind of mystery by the offerings."[38] While there is nothing unexpected in his commentary on Melchizedek, Chrysostom does connect the shadowy figure with the Eucharist in a way that the author of Hebrews does not. For John, the bread and wine offered by the King of Salem foreshadowed that which Christ would offer as well.

OLD TESTAMENT TEXTS ANTICIPATING THE EUCHARIST

John Chrysostom is not limited to the personages and events of the Old Testament; he often draws on familiar texts and weaves them into his speeches. He prepared for this during his time in the caves outside Antioch where he spent days, weeks, and months memorizing long passages of Scripture. Among these texts, Mal 1:11 stands out as perhaps the most important text for the Eucharist among the early Church Fathers. It was quoted from the earliest times to demonstrate that the Eucharist was a true sacrifice pleasing to God and that it truly pleased God more than the sacrifices of the temple in Jerusalem.

John was by no means the first Church Father to quote or refer to Mal 1:11. Among the earliest occurrences, *The Didache* quotes Malachi in chapter 14:

> On the Lord's day, once you have gathered, break the bread of the Lord, and hold Eucharist, confess your transgressions that your sacrifice may be pure. Let not anyone who has a quarrel with his friend join you until they reconcile that your sacrifice not be defiled. This is what was spoken by the Lord, "In every place and time offer to me a pure sacrifice because I am a great king, says the Lord, and my name is marvelous among the Gentiles."

37 *Homily 35 on Genesis*, PG 53:328.

38 *Homily 36 on Genesis*, PG 53:337.

When the Didachist quotes Malachi, he does not follow the Septuagint precisely and he combines verse 11 with verse 14 of Malachi's text.[39] Nevertheless, he is clearly putting the Old Testament text in a eucharistic context so that the offering made to God by the Gentiles is thought better than the sacrifices of the old covenant.

Justin Martyr too quotes Malachi as he describes Christian worship in the mid-second century. Justin is justly famous for the description of the liturgy in chapters 65 and 66 of his *First Apology*, but it is in his *Dialogue with Trypho the Jew* that he argues most persuasively for understanding the Eucharist as a fulfillment of Old Testament types and images. In chapter 41, one can hear Justin's interlocutor contending for the superiority of the Jewish faith based on having sacrifices to offer to the true God whom Justin claims Christians worship. In this context Justin cites Mal 1:11–14, in which the words of the text itself suffice for Justin to conclude, "Now he speaks beforehand about the sacrifices offered by us Gentiles in every place—that is, the bread of the Eucharist and similarly the cup of the Eucharist—when he says that we 'glorify his name, but you defile it.'"[40] Later in the same century, Irenaeus of Lyons cites the same text to argue that the Jewish form of sacrifice is no longer valid. "This shows very clearly that the first people [of Israel] ceased to offer a sacrifice to God, but that in every place a sacrifice is offered to him [God], one that is pure, and that his name is glorified among the nations."[41] After quoting the text of Malachi, Irenaeus condemns both the Jews who have no sacrifice and the heretics (Gnostics) who distort the sacrifice by their false teachings. The universal and apostolic Church alone has a pure sacrifice: "For it is necessary that we make to God an offering and be found grateful to God the Creator in all things: in pure opinion and faith without hypocrisy, in firm hope, in fervent love, offering the first fruits of his creation. And the church alone offers this pure offering to the Creator, offering it to him with gratitude out of His creation."[42]

39 For a further discussion of this problem see Kenneth J. Howell, *Clement of Rome and the Didache: A New Translation and Theological Commentary* (Zanesville, OH: CHN Resources, 2012), 75–77, and Willy Rordorf, *La Doctrine des Douze Apotres*, SC 248 (bis) (Paris: Editions du Cerf, 1998), 193.

40 Justin Martyr, *Dialogue with Trypho the Jew*, 41,1–3, PG 6:563.

41 Irenaeus, *Against Heresies*, 4,17,5.

42 Irenaeus, *Against Heresies*, 4,18,4.

These earlier figures are only a part of the interpretative tradition that preceded Chrysostom, but they will suffice to show the background common to many, if not all, who commented on the eucharistic sacrifice.[43] In the light of this tradition, it is not surprising that we discover John Chrysostom quoting or alluding to Mal 1:11 a number of times.

It turns out that Chrysostom does more than earlier writers in that his use of Malachi differs considerably from theirs. In *Homily 5 against the Jews* John invokes the prophet Malachi in greater detail to show that only the sacrifice of Christians can be a legitimate fulfillment of the prophet's words. If the sacrifices of the old covenant, whether then or now, were sufficient, then they would have to be in one place, the place chosen by God as fitting for sacrifice. John is alluding to Dt 12:11 and similar texts that indicated that the God of Israel was to determine the locale for sacrifices. That place, of course, became the temple in Jerusalem, which no longer stood in John's day. Chrysostom very astutely observes that Malachi's words "in every place" and "among the Gentiles" are in contradiction to the law if he were speaking about the standard sacrifices of the old covenant. No, he insists, the prophet is speaking about a different sacrifice:

> when the prophet says that "in every place incense and a pure offering will be offered," it opposes and contradicts Moses. But there is no contradiction or rivalry. The prophet was speaking about something different and he later prophesied something different. What makes this clear? From the words and more signs. First, from the place. Not in one city as the Jews did. But "from the rising of the sun to its setting" he said this service was to be completed. Then also from the manner of the sacrifice. He called it a pure sacrifice. By this he showed what he was talking about. And from the character [lit. "faces"] of those bringing it. He did not say, "in Israel" but "among the gentiles."[44]

John then proceeds to paraphrase Malachi's words to show that only the Christian sacrifice that is "in every place" and "among the Gentiles" can truly be a fulfillment of the prophecy. Although Chrysostom is clearly using this Old Testament text in a polemical context, he nevertheless emphasizes that it is grace that is now conveyed through the sacrifice of the Church for

43 For a fuller treatment of the use of Malachi's prophecy in early Christianity, see Mike Aquilina, *The Eucharist Foretold: The Lost Prophecy of Malachi* (Steubenville, OH: Emmaus Road Press, 2019).

44 *Homily 5 against the Jews*, PG 48:902.

"it brings the grace of the Spirit." The "surpassing glory" of the new dispensation over the old means that "the saving grace of God has appeared to all people teaching us to deny ungodliness and worldly passions" (Ti 2:11–12). Invoking Jesus's words to the Samaritan woman in the fourth Gospel (chap. 4), John stresses the universality of the gospel and the Church. All this shows that "Christianity is unalloyed and legitimate" (εἰλικρινῆ καὶ γνήσιον τὸν Χριστιανισμὸν ἐπιδείξωνται). While John then does not quote the Malachi prophecy extensively, his usage is in keeping with his typical exegesis that is "with great care" (μετὰ ἀκριβείας).[45]

John also makes eucharistic references and employs eucharistic language in his commentaries on various Psalms. Here too are the contrasts between the old and the new dispensations, between the heavenly and the earthly realities. Psalm 78:24–25 is a natural place for such commentary: "He rained down manna for them to eat and he gave them bread of heaven. Man ate the bread of angels and he sent them provision to the full."[46] A number of patristic figures before Chrysostom including Athanasius and Ambrose had commented on this text, and many after John continued the tradition. Ambrose, for example, cites this text in explaining the mysteries as a fuller manifestation of grace in the new covenant than in the old. His contrast is between the temporary and the permanent, the latter being that bread which gives "the substance of eternal life" (*vitae aeternae substantiam*).[47] That same contrast shows up in John's *Homily on Holy Pentecost*. While quoting Ps 78:25 and not denying the good things of the old covenant, those of the new dispensation are far greater, "things truly worthy of God's love for humanity."[48] The superiority of the new over the old shows up in one of his homilies *Against the Jews* where John contrasts the heavenly gift of bread given to the Old Testament people of God and their misuse of the divine gifts.[49] In a quite different tone is John's homily on *Rachel and the Infants* (i.e., the slaughter of the Holy Innocents, Mt 2:16–18). In a passage too beautiful to omit, John seeks to comfort the mourning mother:

45 All quotations in this paragraph other than the statement from Titus are from *Homily 5 against the Jews*, PG 48:902.

46 Translated from the LXX: καὶ ἔβρεξεν αὐτοῖς μαννα φαγεῖν καὶ ἄρτον οὐρανοῦ ἔδωκεν αὐτοῖς· ἄρτον ἀγγέλων ἔφαγεν ἄνθρωπος, ἐπισιτισμὸν ἀπέστειλεν αὐτοῖς εἰς πλησμονήν.

47 Ambrose, *On the Mysteries*, 8,47.

48 *Homily on Holy Pentecost*, PG 50:455.

49 *Homily 5 against the Jews*, PG 48:906.

> But come now and stop your crying. Cease from your sorrow, Rachel. Herod murdered your infants on earth, but God is feeding them in heaven. Herod robbed them of temporal light, but these are the ones God fills with his own light in heaven. You can't observe them growing up on earth but at that time you will see and rejoice when you see them skipping like lambs in Paradise. Now you sorrow because you don't see them extending their hands at table but at that time you will see and rejoice when you see them eating heavenly bread sumptuously with the angels.[50]

This last reference to eating in heaven is certainly an allusion to Ps 78:25. Athanasius had spoken of the bread of angels as contemplation in *Easter Letter 7* and Augustine would introduce the same idea in his preaching. The contrast then in John's mind is twofold: old versus new covenant and heavenly versus earthly. We saw in chapter 1 how the second contrast pervades John's conception of the liturgy. The contrast of the old and new covenants, however, comes out even more powerfully at the end of his third lecture to the catechumens. In pursuing multiple contrasts between the old and the new Moses, John highlights the difference between the kinds of bread bestowed:

> What was the real characteristic of that Moses? Moses was "the meekest of all men on the earth." Someone who said this about this Moses [Jesus] would not have erred. In fact, the meekest Spirit was present with him as having the same nature and of the same kind. Moses once extended his hands into heaven and brought down manna as the bread of angels. This Moses extended his hands into the heaven and carries eternal nourishment. That one struck the rock and out came a flood of waters. This one touched the table and strikes the heavenly table and makes founts of the Spirit gush forth. This is why the table is set like a spring in the middle that on every side the flock may satisfy themselves at the fount that they may enjoy the saving streams.[51]

Though Moses was considered the meekest man on earth (Nm 12:3), John sees this as more appropriately applied to Jesus. Alluding to Ps 78:25 John cites Moses as the bread giver but Jesus as providing "eternal nourishment" (τὴν αἰώνιον τροφήν). Antoine Wenger saw the use of "this Moses"

50 *On Rachel and the Infants*, PG 61:699. Even though the Migne editors classified this homily as spurious, it reflects well the kind of thinking characteristic of Chrysostom.

51 *Catechetical Lecture*, 3,26.

as referring to John's Bishop Flavian with the understanding that Jesus is working through the bishop.[52] While the language of touching the table toward the end of the paragraph could possibly be so read, I prefer to see "this Moses" as mainly intending Christ himself. It is clear that the contrast between old and new is not about a Christian pastor but about the Good Pastor and the table he sets.

This repeated contrast between the old and the new, between the earthly and the heavenly, raises a thorny question. In what sense is the old covenant with all its earthly marvels inferior to the new with much less outward fanfare? Did not Ps 78:24 say that God rained down manna? The whole point of the narrative of the manna in Exodus 16 seems to be that it was a supernatural provision. And if Ps 78:25 calls it "the bread of angels," it may be because angels were then mediating messengers. Would that not qualify such a gift as heavenly? And why did Jesus seem to reinforce the same equation of the food of the old covenant as earthly? Did he not deny that the manna Moses gave came from heaven in Jn 6:32? And the passage from Hebrews 12 that opened this chapter could certainly be read as implying that behind the author's concern for his recipients lies a meager form of worship in the new covenant that contrasted with the glorious synesthesia of the temple worship in the old. So in what sense could the old covenant with its manna be thought of as earthly? The answer, I aver, lies in two extremely important values for John. Later we will again see how he values the heavenly and the spiritual over the earthly and mundane. Though John could be very down-to-earth, he always sought to warn his people against indifference to higher values. The second reason for seeing the old covenant as earthly and the new as spiritual is implied in the *Catechetical Lecture* quoted above. The symbols of the new covenant are truly sacramental in that they contain the realities they signify. Nothing in the old covenant, no matter how glorious in appearance, could match that truth.

Psalm 145 is another natural place for John to introduce the Eucharist into his commentary although its reference to food is less direct than in the previous psalm: "The eyes of all look to you and you give them food in due season" (Ps 145:15). Although this psalm is largely one of praise to God, the simple mention of the provision of food evokes for John a deeper spiritual meaning. As the psalm opens, it invites the reader to join in the praise of

52 Antoine Wenger, *Huit catéchèses baptismales inédites*, SC 50 (Paris: Editions du Cerf, 1957), 161.

God, a praise that also suggests a father-child relation between God and the people of Israel:

> It is right to pay attention to this psalm with great care. This one has the words that the initiated sing assiduously by saying, "The eyes of all hope in you and you give them food in the right time." The one who became a son and enjoys the spiritual table would be righteous to glorify the Father. For he says, "A son glorifies his father and the slave will fear his master" (Mal 1:6).[53]

There are indicators that he may have preached this homily at Easter Vigil or another occasion when the newly baptized were present ("the words that the initiated sing"). They adopted verse 15 as their own. The mention of food at the right time evoked the Eucharist for John as he goes on to speak of "the spiritual table." And this is reinforced by his emphasis on the sonship of the initiated, who now are privileged to enjoy the table of the Master. In the Ancient Near East—and apparently in Chrysostom's own place and time—to be invited to join the Master's table was a sign of filial privilege. We see that reflected in the story of David and Mephibosheth in 2 Samuel 9. The dignity that is due God as Lord and Master is reciprocated by God to those he has made his sons and daughters:

> You have become a son and you enjoy the spiritual table by eating the flesh and the blood that gives you new life. Make your repayment for such a benefit and glorify the One who has had such things. When reading these words, measure your opinion by the things said. Say, "I will exalt you, my God, my King." Show how much you appropriate this that God may say about you, as he did about Abraham, Isaac, and Jacob, "I am the God of Abraham, the God of Isaac, and the God of Jacob." When you say, "my God, my King" and not only say this but demonstrate such a great love, he will say the same things about you, "my servant and my helper," as was said of Moses.[54]

What are these great benefits that invite the newborn child to extol God himself? The food on this table is "the flesh and the blood that gives you new life." John's choice of "gives new life" translates τὸ ἀναγεννῆσάν σε and suggests the regenerative power of baptism since this verb (ἀναγεννάω) was

53 *Homily on Psalm 145 (LXX 144)*, PG 55:464.

54 *Homily on Psalm 145 (LXX 144)*, PG 55:464.

regularly associated with baptism. If this is the setting of the homily, then John is leading his initiates from the waters of baptism to the eucharistic table to be fed with the bread of life. What could anyone do to repay God for all such benefits? It only requires living a life that demonstrates appropriation of God's grace. Such appropriation will truly make sons and daughters of the newly initiated, so much so that the words spoken to the patriarchs may also be theirs. The Eucharist then is connected with adoption into God's family and compels the new Christian to say the words of the Lord's Prayer with a new depth of meaning. That prayer, given as a gift to the people of the new covenant, is the basis of present praise for the Creator and future blessing for the creature: "I will bless your name forever and ever. You saw how he showed the prelude of eternal life. Here he speaks a blessing, not with words but with actions. Surely then God is exalted and surely blessed. We are commanded to pray, 'Hallowed be your name,' that is, 'let it be glorified.' I will bless you every day and praise your name forever."[55]

Psalm 134 presents a different case from Psalms 78 and 145 because there is no mention of food at all, but this does not prevent John from introducing a contrast between the old and new covenants that involves the Eucharist. John exhorts his faithful to embrace holiness and purity, which will beautify the mind. This exhortation is based on the greater gifts received in the new covenant. Since the psalm speaks of standing in the house of the Lord, John reminds his hearers that in the old covenant this approach to God's temple was accorded only to those who entered with ritual purity. As he likens the house of the Lord to heaven, John helps them recall their privilege, saying, "You became a temple yourself" (αὐτὸς ἐγένου ναὸς):

> Consider how great is the holiness you should have for having received greater symbols. Of these the holy of holies was received at that time. You don't have Cherubim but you have the Master of the Cherubim dwelling within you. Nor do you have an earthen jar or manna, or stone tablets and the rod of Aaron. But you have the Master's body and blood, the Spirit instead of the letter and grace transcending human reason and an indescribable gift. The greater the symbols and the awe-inspiring mysteries you have been made worthy of, the greater you are accountable for holiness and the more punishment if you transgress his commandments.[56]

55 *Homily on Psalm 145 (144 LXX)*, PG 55:464.

56 *Homily on Psalm 134 (133 LXX)*, PG 55:386.

The differences John sketches between the types (e.g., rod of Aaron, manna) and the reality of the new order climax in the contrast between the Cherubim and the Master of the Cherubim. Having the Master's body and blood (σῶμα καὶ αἷμα δεσποτικὸν) confers an indescribable dignity on God's children. While this dignity is meant for rational creatures, the gift itself transcends human reason (χάριν ὑπερβαίνουσαν λογισμὸν ἀνθρώπινον). Such a gift also bestows a heightened duty to pursue holiness, one that attempts to expel "evil thoughts, remembrance of evil, and avarice" (διαλογισμῶν πονηρῶν εὔχεσθαι δεῖ, χωρὶς μνησικακίας, χωρὶς πλεονεξίας). These last two vices are ones to which we will return because the remembrance of evil (μνησικακία) and greed (πλεονεξία) are deadly poisons of the mind that John abhors.[57]

In this context, however, John's emphasis lands on the blessing and liberties that Christians can enjoy because they are members of the Church in the new covenant. John sees hints of the future era already latent in the psalm when it contrasts implicitly the temple of Jerusalem with the universality implied in the description of God as "the one who made heaven and earth" (Ps 134:3). Prayer is no longer limited to a place like the temple but may be exercised "in every place, in every locale, in a house and marketplace, in a desert, in a boat, in an inn, or wherever."[58] This means that in the new covenant the true nature of God is seen in the catholicity of the Church in a manner superior to that in the old. The Lord God wishes to stand alongside (παραστήσεται) and be joined to (συνεφάψεται) his people so that everything becomes easy for them. God himself will make them worthy of the good things to come. Such dignity comes to God's children most realistically in the awe-inspiring mysteries of grace, which are a clarion call to holiness. Without any mention of food, this psalm still suggests to John's mind the greater realities of the Eucharist.

Psalm 23 evokes the eucharistic cup in John's mind. If the simple mention of food as in Ps 145:15 can stimulate Chrysostom's mind, the cup overflowing in Ps 23:5 positively inebriates his thinking. In his *Homily against Those Who Are Drunk and on the Resurrection of Christ* he contrasts ordinary drunkenness with a kind of spiritual inebriation that comes from the cup of salvation:

57 The brief quotations in this paragraph all come from *Homily on Psalm 134 (133 LXX)*, PG 55:387.

58 *Homily on Psalm 134 (133 LXX)*, PG 55:387.

> There is a good cup of drunkenness, a cup that leads to prudence and not dissolution. What sort is this? It is a spiritual cup, an immaculate cup of the Lord's own blood. That cup does not produce drunkenness; it does not give dissolution. It does not dissolve power but strengthens it. It does not dissolve ties but reinforces them. It makes for sobriety, veneration for the angels, fear of the demons, honor for men, love for the Master. Do you see what David says about this spiritual cup sitting on the table? "You have prepared a table before me among those who afflict me. You anoint my head with oil and your cup makes me strong." So that you won't be immediately afraid when he uses the word *drunkenness* and think of the drink as weakness, he adds that it is powerful and strong. This is a new manner of drunkenness, one that puts strength in, making one powerful and strong. It flowed from the spiritual rock. There is no alteration of thoughts but an addition of spiritual thoughts.[59]

As John quotes Psalm 23 he clearly takes his cues from the Septuagint version as it differs from the Masoretic Text. He sees spiritual inebriation suggested in verse 5 because the Greek translators chose μεθύσκω, "to intoxicate" (Ps 22:5 LXX), for the Hebrew verb, which can be used of saturation or intoxication. Those translators also chose "your cup" instead of "my cup," which John takes to refer to God's chalice. He leaves us in no doubt about what cup the Psalmist is referring to. It is the cup of the Eucharist: "It is a spiritual cup, an immaculate cup of the Lord's own blood." To call this chalice "an immaculate cup" underscores its purity as a source of power in his mind. Absent from the Hebrew is any mention of strength, of which John makes a central point, but the Septuagint clearly has ὡσεὶ κράτιστον, "as strong as possible" or "like the strongest." So John urges his hearers to take spiritual fortitude from the cup of the Lord's own blood. John clearly reads this psalm in the light of his eucharistic theology.

THE DIVINE *OIKONOMIA* OF CONDESCENSION

The descent of the Son of God into the world was the crucial turning point for humanity, and that is not only what distinguishes Christianity from the

59 *Homily against Those Who Are Drunk and on the Resurrection of Christ*, PG 50:436.

pagan religions of the ancient world but also what distinguishes the experience of believers in the old covenant from that of believers in the new. In a remarkable passage from *Homily 58 on Genesis*, Chrysostom reflects on Jacob's encounter at the River Jabbok with the shadowy divine/human figure in Gn 32:22–32. Paraphrasing this pericope with an emphasis on human weakness, seen so clearly in Jacob the patriarch, John brings together three angles implicit in his view of the Incarnation: condescension (*sugkatabasis*), the redemptive order (*oikonomia*), and God's love for humanity (*philanthropia*):

> Do you see how the Master condescended to human weakness and acted and accomplished everything so that he might demonstrate his very own love for humanity? Beloved, don't be astonished at the greatness of this condescension but consider the case of the patriarch [Abraham] when he was seated by the oak tree. [The Master] came to this righteous man in the form of a man with angels, indicating above and from the beginning that he was going to take human form and so liberate the entire human nature from the tyranny of the Devil and lead it to salvation.[60]

The entire history of the old covenant patriarchs is colored by God's adaptation to human limitations. If in an abstract and unrealistic manner, one asks why God did not erase human limitations and weakness, and simply raise humanity to divine heights, John readily knows the answer. God attempted to meet human weakness on its own level because the patriarchs could not—nor could any—embrace the truly transcendent nature of God. So, adopting Paul's language from Phil 2:7 ("the form of a servant"), John vividly portrays Christ's humanity:

> When he counted it right to take on the form of a servant and to make known our first fruit, [it was] not in a dream nor did he only seem to plunge into flesh. Rather [it was] in truth. For this reason, he chose to come by way of all our [experiences], to be born of a woman, and become an infant, to be wrapped in swaddling clothes, to be nourished on milk, and to engage everything about us to confirm the truth of the *oikonomia* and to shut up the mouths of heretics.

For John the earthly experiences of Jesus were more than mere appearances. They included all the infant experiences of a normal baby. This was essential

60 *Homily 58 on Genesis*, PG 54:510.

because the Redeemer truly had to become "the first fruit" of what his followers would also experience. For this reason, the adult life of Jesus was no less thoroughly human:

> He too slept in a boat, walked along the way, and felt tired, and also endured all other human things that he might be able to fulfill everything through actions. For this reason also he stood in the court and was crucified. He stood in the court of death, was crucified and endured a shameful death, was buried in a tomb, that the things of the *oikonomia* might become manifest. If he did not take on our flesh in truth, or was not crucified, or did not die or was not buried or did not rise again, and if he was not raised again, then the entire rationale of the *oikonomia* is overturned. Do you see how those who do not want to follow the canon of the divine scriptures fall into error by insisting on their own reasonings?[61]

This is not the last time we shall see John speaking in concrete terms about the life of Jesus. He certainly felt the horror of the heretics who denied the true humanity of Christ. Here in this text, however, I would like to note his emphasis on the *oikonomia* of God because without that divine arrangement, there would be no salvation. As he summarizes it, the entire rationale (*logos*) of that arrangement rests on God's accommodation of himself in the person of Christ.[62]

All the persons, events, and texts of the Old Testament anticipated this intimate union of God and his people. In and of themselves, they were but shadows and types that only vaguely foreshadowed the truth (ἀλήθεια) later revealed. Yet placed within the matrix of Israel's corporate life and history, they all pointed forward not only to the person of the Anointed One (Χριστός) but even to the sacramental *oikonomia* present in liturgy. None of the types, figures, or texts of the old covenant makes any sense without the centrality of Christ, the condescending Son of God. Taking Paul as his cue for placing Christ in the forefront, John views Jesus as the consummation of all that the ancient people of God looked forward to and all that the Christian can now experience. This explains why John Chrysostom can at times construct litanies of praise to Christ as the complete fulfillment of all God's salvific purposes:

61 Both quotations come from *Homily 58 on Genesis*, PG 54:510.

62 Jacky Marsaux translated the passage from *Homily 58 on Genesis* into French in *Jean Chrysostome, lecteur de l'Ecriture*, Cahiers Evangile Supplement 188 (Paris: Editions du Cerf, 2019), 69–70. I am indebted to Marsaux for bringing this passage to my attention.

Christ is himself our fullness.
He is the way, the husband, the bridegroom.
He is the root, the drink, the food, and the life.
He is the apostle, the high priest, the teacher, and the father.
He is the brother, the co-heir, the sharer in the tomb and the cross.
He is also [our] Suppliant.
He is an advocate with the Father.
He is the house and the residence [ἔνοικος].
He is a friend.
He is the foundation and the cornerstone.[63]

All these appellations drawn from the repertoire of New Testament images signal the incomparable place Jesus Christ holds in John's view of reality. Yet even in this context John cannot overlook how all the realities about Christ imply something wonderful about the members of his Church. The Church is Christ's body, his field, his building, his fellow workers. The intimate connection between the members and the Head flow from Christ's unbounded love of the Church, for "He is one who loves greatly" (ὅπερ τοῦ σφόδρα φιλοῦντός ἐστι). And it is the union of Head and members that will provide the background for understanding communion. John perceives Jesus's motives in the strongest possible terms, in the intimacy of union and communion: "What does he [Christ] not want to be for us when he joins and unites himself to us in every way?"[64] Christ takes up his residence in us that he may be "everything for us on the inside and out."[65]

63 *Homily 24 on Romans*, PG 60:624. I have omitted John's parenthetical scriptural quotations associated with each line above to highlight the multiplicity and variety of praises to Christ. The full text is as follows: Καὶ γὰρ πλήρωμα ἡμῶν αὐτός (καὶ γὰρ Πλήρωμα τοῦ τὰ πάντα ἐν πᾶσι πληρουμένου)· καὶ ὁδὸς καὶ ἀνὴρ καὶ νυμφίος (Ἡρμοσάμην γὰρ ὑμᾶς ἑνὶ ἀνδρὶ παρθένον ἁγνήν)· καὶ ῥίζα καὶ ποτὸν καὶ τροφὴ καὶ ζωή (Ζῶ γὰρ, φησὶν, οὐκέτι ἐγὼ, ζῇ δὲ ἐν ἐμοὶ Χριστός)· καὶ ἀπόστολος καὶ ἀρχιερεὺς καὶ διδάσκαλος καὶ πατὴρ καὶ ἀδελφὸς καὶ συγκληρονόμος, καὶ τάφου κοινωνὸς καὶ σταυροῦ (Συνετάφημεν γὰρ αὐτῷ, φησὶ, καὶ σύμφυτοι γεγόναμεν τῷ ὁμοιώματι τοῦ θανάτου αὐτοῦ)· καὶ ἱκέτης (Ὑπὲρ γὰρ Χριστοῦ πρεσβεύομεν)· καὶ πρὸς τὸν Πατέρα συνήγορος (καὶ γὰρ Ἐντυγχάνει, φησὶν, ὑπὲρ ἡμῶν) καὶ οἶκος καὶ ἔνοικος (Ὁ γὰρ ἐν ἐμοὶ μένων, κἀγὼ ἐν αὐτῷ), καὶ φίλος (Ὑμεῖς γὰρ φίλοι μού ἐστε)· καὶ θεμέλιος καὶ λίθος ἀκρογωνιαῖος·

64 *Homily 24 on Romans*, PG 60:624.

65 *Homily 24 on Romans*, PG 60:624.

✠ ✠ ✠

John's treatment of Old Testament texts and events as anticipations of the Eucharist presupposes the two axes of history mentioned earlier. He clearly follows the lead of the New Testament writers in his attempts to show the superiority of the new covenant over the old. Whereas in the first century, that contrast focused on the historical and ecclesiological differences between ancient Israel and the Church, Chrysostom extends this fundamental contrast into the liturgical and sacramental realms. The importance of condescension (συγκατάβασις) in John's theology cannot be overestimated, for it is so prominent that scholars have long claimed it as essential to understanding his view of God's action in history. Yet condescension also stands at the center of his view of the Eucharist and its home in the liturgy of the Church. This ongoing sacramental condescension is what allows the Christians of his day to encounter Jesus Christ in the same way as those who knew Jesus on earth, albeit in an entirely different and mystical mode of experience.

The Axes of Anticipation and Participation are complementary ways of looking at the life of Christ. The first was directed toward his advent and was populated by events, persons, and proclamations that obliquely indicated his arrival. The second only makes sense in the fulfillment of Christ's life on earth, culminating in the Paschal Mystery. It is directed back to that Mystery by the liturgy and rituals of the Church, at the center of which is the Eucharist. If Christ in his mysteries is so important, then it naturally follows that knowing him in personal experience is of paramount importance. What does it mean to know Christ in his present state of existence? Seeking the answer leads Chrysostom to consider the earthly life of Jesus and its connection to the Eucharist.

3

The Eucharist and the Earthly Life of Jesus Christ

Christians have always longed, so it seems, for real contact with Jesus Christ. They have long dreamed of being there when Jesus was on earth. That sentiment resided in the hearts of Antiochene Christians in the late fourth century as much as it has in any era. And if it was lacking in some hearts, John Chrysostom wanted it to be in there. Perhaps that explains why he connected the Eucharist with Jesus's earthly life as he did in *Homily 82 on Matthew*:

> So many say, "I would like to see his form, his distinctive appearance, his clothes, his sandals." Look, you do see him, you touch him, you eat him. Yes, you desire to see his garments, but he gives you himself not only to be seen but to be touched, eaten, and taken within. Let no one approach this staggering nor dissolute. All should be enflamed, all full of zeal, all fully awake. If the Jews stood ready with their sandals and staff in hand, and ate with haste, how much more should we be sober and disciplined? They were about to enter Palestine and so they walked with a roadmap; but we are about to go on a journey into heaven.[1]

Because Christ is truly present in the Eucharist, it is in fact an extension of his earthly life. Just as Jesus Christ on earth was a

1 *Homily 82 on Matthew*, PG 58:743.

fulfillment and extension of the economy of salvation in the old covenant, so the life of Christ finds its fulfillment and extension in the eucharistic celebration of the Church. The Eucharist is not simply a recalling or remembrance of past events, even of those saving events of Christ's life. Rather, those saving events had an end or purpose (*telos*) beyond their own time. They are projected forward, as it were, into the future celebrations of the Church so that the saving efficacy of events like the cross and resurrection is the same in the Church today as it was in the past when they were accomplished. All this flows from what we discovered about the liturgy of the Church as an embodiment of heavenly realities. Those heavenly realities in turn contain the saving mysteries of Christ's life on earth.

In this chapter we will see how closely John Chrysostom ties his teaching on the Eucharist to the events in the life of Jesus.[2] While some Church Fathers, both East and West, mention the Eucharist in preaching on the life of Christ, John seems to surpass them all in specificity of analysis and depth of spiritual theology. Whether he is treating the birth or the baptism, the healings or the resurrection, all seems to circle back to the cross as the apex and triumph of Christ over the forces of evil. This focus on the earthly life of Christ provides the foundation for his view of the presence of Christ in the Eucharist, to be explored more fully in chapter 4.[3]

In the historical development of the Byzantine liturgy the events of the life of Jesus Christ played an increasingly important role. In the early stages the anagogical function of the liturgy was prominent, which is what we see in the homilies of John Chrysostom. The liturgy was thought to be a guide (anagogy) back into the life of Christ and the Eucharist was a participation in that same life. Later in time, the liturgical culture of Byzantium began to tie specific moments of the liturgy to specific events in the earthly life of Christ, a development evident in *Commentary on the Divine Liturgy* by Germanos of Constantinople in the first half of the eighth century. At this later stage, the liturgy becomes even more symbolic than it had been before. This illustrates

2 Some of the material in this chapter appeared previously in Kenneth J. Howell, "The Eucharist and the Life of Christ in the Preaching of John Chrysostom," *Nova et Vetera* 19, no. 3 (2021): 791–824.

3 Brian Dunkle shows that Thomas Aquinas also relied on Chrysostom's emphasis in his own exposition of the *acta et passa* of Christ's life in his *Summa Theologiae* III qq. 27–59. This suggests that for Aquinas, as for John, each mystery of Jesus's life held significance. See Brian Dunkle, "Thomas Aquinas's Use of John Chrysostom in the *Catena Aurea* and the *Tertia Pars*," in *Thomas Aquinas and the Greek Fathers*, edited by Michael Dauphinais and Andrew Hofer (Ave Maria, FL: Sapientia Press, 2019), 163.

what Paul Meyendorff calls the movement from *theoria* to *historia*. In *theoria* the Greek Fathers seek the meaning of the liturgy as a revelation of Jesus Christ; in *historia*, later Greek writers seek the meaning of each event of Christ's life represented in the liturgy. Although some modern scholars have viewed this tradition in a negative light,[4] an increasing focus on the life of Christ connected to the liturgy shows both how central the liturgy was in the East and how important was the redemptive sense of the life of Jesus for the Byzantines.[5] The development from a general representation of Christ's life in the time of John Chrysostom to more specific links between Christ's *oikonomia* and the liturgy in Germanos's day is a very natural one. And this becomes especially clear when we study how John himself made the links between the Eucharist and history. He repeatedly drew significant moral and spiritual lessons out of the events of Jesus's earthly sojourn, which he often connected to the Eucharist.

When John turned his gaze to the life of Christ, he probably realized that his preaching would strike a cord with his hearers. The linkage between Christ's earthly life and the Eucharist revolves around the second axis in our diagram. In the last chapter we posited that many events in the old covenant revolve around an *Axis of Anticipation* that runs like an arrow through the diverse and multifaceted events of the economy of redemption. When John read the Scriptures of the old covenant, he saw how they anticipated the coming of the Messiah and the eucharistic economy he instituted. Standing on the other side of that fulfillment, John views the liturgy of the Church along an *Axis of Participation*. The liturgy runs like an arrow pointing back to the Paschal Mystery, and all the aspects of the eucharistic celebration revolve around that invisible line. This line is best understood as participation because *koinonia* is at the heart of everything which happens in the liturgy.[6] No participation would be possible without the Eucharist because it is the earthly dimension of *theosis*. *Theosis*, or deification, requires the communication of divine life to the faithful. The process of deification therefore requires participation, which is the invisible line, or axis, along which every

4 For example, Alexander Schmemann, *Introduction to Liturgical Theology* (London: Faith Press, 1966), 99–115.

5 See Paul Meyendorff's excellent discussion in short compass *On the Divine Liturgy: Germanus of Constantinople* (Crestwood, NY: St. Vladimir's Press, 1999), 9–54.

6 John uses several words for participation (μέθεξις, μετοχή, κοινωνία) on different occasions, but he sees *koinonia* as the strongest synonym. We explore this more fully in chapter 7.

part of the life of the faithful proceeds. Without participation there could be no salvation because the Paschal Mystery is the *source* of all *theosis*.[7] And without the eucharistic liturgy there could be no communication in the Paschal Mystery. So the Axis of Participation is a way of understanding how all the various aspects of the liturgy and the consequent life of the believer are unified around the Paschal Mystery and its embodiment in the Eucharist. It is this that makes all the events in Jesus's life relevant.

THE NATIVITY OF JESUS CHRIST

Many of John Chrysostom's topical homilies seem to treat quite disparate subjects, and sometimes they end with a section discussing the eucharistic mystery, although his sequential homilies on books of the Bible generally stay close to the biblical text. John's attention to detail may account for his reputation as a literal exegete of the Antiochene school although, as I have noted, more recent studies demonstrate that the classic categories of literal (Antiochene) versus allegorical (Alexandrian) interpretation must yield to more subtle descriptions. His topical sermon *Homily on the Birth of Christ*[8] displays the same detailed reading of the biblical texts, but he does weave his homily around a common theme, or at least makes connections between various themes in a manner easily missed.

As a man who loved detail in his exegesis and presentation, John's meticulous nature comes out in this homily when he argues for the celebration of Christmas Day. One can almost hear the objection that the nativity of Christ should not be celebrated because that practice cannot boast of great antiquity. We learn here that the celebration of Christmas had arrived in Antioch (or Constantinople) only recently from the West. John, however, argues that the celebration of the Savior's birth is proper because it has been accepted by both East and West. His second argument for its appropriateness comes from the details of Scripture about the birth of Christ. It was God's own plan being worked out that is celebrated. Surely, John argues, celebrating

7 *Theosis* has become a prominent topic in Catholic and Orthodox theology of late. *The Oxford Handbook of Deification*, soon to appear, promises to be the most comprehensive treatment of the subject to date. See also the discussion of deification in Andrew Hofer, *The Power of Patristic Preaching: The Word in Our Flesh* (Washington, DC: The Catholic University of America Press, 2023), 17–23.

8 *Homily on the Birth of Christ*, PG 49:347–62.

the birth of the Savior is important and valuable if God revealed so many details about his birth.

The Incarnation is his last and most important reason for celebrating Christmas, and it is here that he argues against the cultural derision hurled at God-becoming-man. John turns this criticism on its head by asking, "If it is shameful for God to dwell in a human body, how much more so is it that he would dwell in stone and wood? And all the more so since stone and wood are less honorable than a human being, unless of course our race seems to them to be cheaper than this senseless matter."[9] John gives a kind of argumentation similar to the medieval West—the argument from fittingness (*convenientia*). God born as a man in fact shows the superior dignity of the human race and at the same time dignifies that nature even more. What was the ultimate purpose of the Incarnation? John says it was for God to prepare a temple so that he might bring heaven to earth residing in the human soul: "God, once he prepared a holy temple for himself, introduced into our daily life the citizenship of heaven by that means."[10] The Incarnation, then, is the lynchpin that connects the event of Christ's birth to the celebration of that event in the liturgy of the Church. That connection naturally leads him to the Eucharist, but only after he again stresses the condescending love of God: "Let us glorify the God who was made flesh for such great condescension [συγκατάβασις]. Now there can be no repayment to God from us other than the salvation of our souls and our care for [living a life of] virtue."[11] How then does one glorify the God-Made-Flesh? By properly approaching the Eucharist: "Inasmuch as you are about to approach this awesome and divine table and sacred entrance into the mystery, do so with fear and trembling, with a clean conscience, with fasting and prayer, not causing a commotion, nor in rebellion, nor fighting your neighbor."[12]

Chrysostom proceeds to contrast our lowly condition with the utmost dignity of the sacrament: "Even though you are dust and ashes, you partake of the blood and body of Christ."[13] But why is the Eucharist so worthy of these accolades? Perhaps the very union of heaven and earth in the

9 *Homily on the Birth of Christ*, PG 49:359. John may have drawn his language from the taunts against false gods in Is 44:9–20.

10 *Homily on the Birth of Christ*, PG 49:359.

11 *Homily on the Birth of Christ*, PG 49:360.

12 *Homily on the Birth of Christ*, PG 49:360.

13 *Homily on the Birth of Christ*, PG 49:361.

Incarnation and its extension in the Eucharist is simultaneously enough to evoke admiration and purity of approach. Yet John does not leave the matter there; rather he stresses the saving power of the sacrament: "What lies before you is the saving medicine for our wounds. His wealth is unfailing; he is the patron of the kingdom of heaven."[14] John adopts the medical metaphor in use since Ignatius of Antioch but makes it more explicit.[15] The "saving medicine" (φάρμακόν σωτήριον) is emphasized in John's syntax as he underscores both its medicinal effect ("for the wounds sustained by sin") and its character as a gift from God himself ("patron of the kingdom of heaven"). What could be more inviting and powerful than the gift of the sacrament? "Let us enfold [it] with our eyes, let our minds be warmed [with it] that we might not come to judgment or condemnation but to a sobriety of the soul, to love, to virtue, and to reconciliation with God, to confident hope, to the practice of a thousand goods. This is also for us to sanctify ourselves and to edify our neighbor."[16]

The dignity of the sacrament derives from the liturgy as a union of heaven and earth: "When God calls you to his table, and sets before you his own Son, when the angelic powers attend with fear and trembling as the Cherubim hide their faces and the Seraphim cry out, you too cry out, 'Holy, Holy, Holy Lord.'"[17] Chrysostom never tires of repeating the union of heaven and earth made possible by the Eucharist. In his *Homilies on Isaiah* (chapter 6) he seeks to lift the mind of his congregants by reminding them, "That altar [in the church] is a type and icon of this altar [heavenly], that fire a type and icon of spiritual fire." The means by which a believer can see that celestial fire on the earthly altar resides in the love of God for humanity (φιλανθρωπία): "When you fix upon your Master's love for humanity, [then you realize that] the grace of the gifts was not reluctant to descend to our lowliness."[18]

The only appropriate preparation to this awesome mystery is silence and calm. "Will you then attend this spiritual banquet in a confused state? Don't you know that your soul must be filled with calmness [γαλήνη] at that very moment? There is a need for much peace and silence, not confusion, anger,

14 *Homily on the Birth of Christ*, PG 49:361.

15 Ignatius of Antioch, *Letter to the Ephesians*, 20,2.

16 *Homily on the Birth of Christ*, PG 49:362.

17 *Homily on the Birth of Christ*, PG 49:361.

18 Both quotations come from *I Saw the Lord: Homily 6,3* on Isaiah.

and disturbance. These things make your soul unclean as it approaches."[19] Confusion, anger, and wrath will only condemn the communicant because these vices lead to an arrogance unfit for the King.[20] Still, the silence and calm urged are not empty or vapid. They consist of a living humility and self-abnegation that should characterize every approach to the Eucharist: "Let us then tremble as we approach, let us give thanks, let us fall down, confessing our faults, let us weep as we mourn our own evil. Let us offer fervent prayers to God. We will thereby purify ourselves quietly and with a fitting good order. So let us come as approaching the King of Heaven. After receiving [the sacrament], let us kiss the blameless and holy sacrifice."[21] With such exhortations one can readily understand why John would see a deep connection between the birth of Jesus and the celebration of the Eucharist.

This connection becomes even more evident in a rather unexpected place. In his homily *On Blessed Philogonius*, an earlier bishop of Antioch, Chrysostom takes the occasion to highlight the power and value of the sacrament.[22] This homily, preached five days before the nativity of Christ, contains a variety of themes, but one toward the end that stands out is how the celebration transports the Christian back to the very circumstances in which Christ was born:

> Because of this I greet and love this day [of Christ's birth] and I put love front and center that I may make you sharers of this love-charm. For this reason, I beg and entreat you all to be here with all diligence and readiness, for each should empty his own house that we may see our Master lying in a manger, wrapped in swaddling clothes, that awesome and incredible spectacle. What defense can we have, what excuse, when he has come down from heaven for our sake, but we don't come out of our house to him? When the Magi, those barbarians and foreigners, ran from Persia to see

19 *Homily on the Birth of Christ*, PG 49:361.

20 *Homily on the Birth of Christ*, PG 49:362. "Confusion and wrath become arrogance [ὕβρις] in the presence of the sacrifice lying before us. It is the last [and greatest] contempt for a defiled man to present himself to God."

21 *Homily on the Birth of Christ*, PG 49:361.

22 Two fine translations of this homily exist: Paul W. Harkins, *Homilies on the Incomprehensible Nature of God by St. John Chrysostom*, FC 72 (Washington, DC: The Catholic University of America Press, 1984), 164–83, as well as Wendy Mayer and Pauline Allen, *John Chrysostom*, The Early Church Fathers (New York: Routledge, 2000), 184–95. The latter date the homily 20 December 386 (in Antioch). There are divergences in the manuscript tradition. This homily is only tangentially about the incomprehensibility of God but is titled Homily 6 in that series; see Harkins, 164. My translation will differ at times from both of these otherwise excellent options.

> him lying in a crib, but you, O Christian, do not remain a little while so as to enjoy this blessed sight. For when we approach with faith we too will certainly see him lying in the manger, for this table fulfills the order [*taxis*] of the manger.[23]

Recall that the love-charm (φιλτρον)[24] of which John speaks could be a potion or any object by which the recipient is rendered unable to resist the advances of a lover. The comparison with the Magi is an argument from the greater to the lesser (*a majore ad minorem*) because the effort of the Magi was so much greater than what is required of the Christian in John's day. The end result, however, is the same, that is, worshiping the infant Christ.[25] To come to the Eucharist is to place oneself at the manger and to adore Christ in his humble condition. What is striking is John's practical equivalence of the manger with the table of the Church. The purpose of the birth is to allow the Christian to partake of Christ himself. John's choice of vocabulary astounds. This table "fulfills [πληροῖ] the purpose [or order] of that manger."[26] The choice of "order" (τάξις) suggests another favorite term of John's—*oikonomia*, God's plan or design. In short, the Eucharist is more than an arbitrary divine choice. The sacrament is the purpose or order of God's saving acts because it incorporates the communicant into God's plan. Participation in the table is the fulfillment of the Incarnation.

The grandeur of the Eucharist then also explains why John insists on a right approach to the sacrament. The presence of the same man who walked the earth implies that the Christian is in no inferior position to those who lived at the time of Christ's earthly sojourn:

> For the Master's body shall lie here too, not wrapped in swaddling clothes as then, but wrapped on every side with the Holy Spirit. Those initiated into the mysteries know the things said. Now the Magi only worshiped, but you, if you approach with a pure conscience and receive, we will be united to

23 *On Blessed Philogonius*, PG 48:753–56.

24 Mayer and Allen, *John Chrysostom*, 191, translate, "I put my love on show to make you share in my affection for it." It is not obvious that John is speaking about his own love at this point. It may be referring to God's love. Further, I would rather retain the noun "love-charm" than flatten it out as they have done.

25 Some earlier scholars have seen the remarkable connection between the manger and the altar. See August Naegle, *Die Eucharistielehre des Heiligen Johannes Chrysostomus* (Freiburg, Germany, 1900), 66.

26 Mayer and Allen, *John Chrysostom*, 192, translate, "this table fulfills the role of the manger." In my opinion, "role" is too weak for τάξις.

> you and you can depart for home. Come then and bring your gifts, not like those of the Magi but rather more solemn. They brought gold. But you, you bring discretion and virtue. They offered frankincense but you, you bring pure prayers, spiritual sacrifices. They offered myrrh, but you, you should offer humility, a humble heart and alms. If you approach with these gifts, you will enjoy this holy table with much confidence. For this reason, I want to motivate you now with these words since I know that certainly many will approach on that day and will stumble over the spiritual sacrifice.[27]

Among the rich ideas expressed in this passage John attempts to place his audience back in front of the manger where Jesus was born. He does so not by some rhetorical skill or trick but by pointing to the realities hidden within the narrative of the Gospel account in Mt 2:1–12. John's wording again suggests the contrast, not between the old and new covenants, but between those who lived in the time of Jesus's earthly life and those who lived later. The Magi *only* (μόνον) worshiped, as if to suggest acts of outward homage rather than inward prostration. "But you" (σὺ δὲ), you Christian, are in a superior position for by your interior dispositions of discretion and virtue, of humility and alms, you may arrive at the true purpose of Jesus's birth. He came not to have foreigners adore him but to transform the peoples of the world into children of God. This then is the purpose of the eucharistic table and why the Church's liturgy extends Christ's life into the future.[28]

THE BAPTISM OF JESUS

Baptism and Eucharist were universally considered to be the two most prominent sacraments in the ancient Church, so it is not surprising that Chrysostom would preach on the baptism of Jesus, but his method in doing so shows some distinctive characteristics. John was always aware of the background of salvation history when treating mysteries of the new covenant, always ready to invoke texts and images of the Old Testament: "This is the reason for baptism. All that was said beforehand was to fulfill the whole law.

27 *On Blessed Philogonius*, PG 48:753.

28 The idea of the Church and the Eucharist as a kind of ongoing incarnation, rather than simply juridical entities, became a prominent theme in nineteenth-century German Catholic theology, e.g., Johann Adam Mohler, *Symbolism* (New York: Crossroads, 1997), and Matthias Scheeben, *The Mysteries of Christianity* (St. Louis: B. Herder, 1951).

So the Spirit came down in the form of a dove, for where there is reconciliation with God, there is a dove. On Noah's ark the dove was also carrying an olive branch, a symbol of God's love for humanity and of relief from winter."[29] The presence of the dove in both the Noachic narrative and in the baptism of Jesus evoked the theme of purity in John's mind, but the purity of the dove in the story of Noah was only a pointer, an index of a greater purity that lay in the Son of God, who "is now at the right hand of the Father in a pure and undefiled body."[30] As John compares the two stories, he sees the truer ark in the Church; "that ark [of Noah] stayed on the earth even though the harshness of winter was unleashed, so this ark [the church] snatches one up to heaven."[31] The liturgy of the Church, uniting heaven and earth, means that "Christ is present, the angels [are] standing in attendance, the awesome table prepared."[32] This reality induces John to warn his hearers against a casual indifference to the glories contained in the mysteries:

> As your brothers [i.e., catechumens] are still being led into the mysteries, will you leave this and turn away? When you have been invited to a supper, even if you are satiated, you would not dare to leave the other guests in front of friends. Here Christ is enacting awe-inspiring mysteries, the sacred liturgy is still being performed, are you going to leave and depart in the middle? What sort of defense can you give? May I tell you whose work it is that those who leave before the conclusion are doing? They are not bringing the eucharistic hymns to the purpose [*telos*] of the table.[33]

John is warning his congregants against the temptation to receive communion because it is a high feast day rather than because of the state of their hearts. As he reminds them of the presence of Christ's body, he warns against perfunctory communion: "I know that many among us are running toward this holy table because of the custom of the feast." What then is necessary for the believing Christian? "Not to observe the feasts but to cleanse the conscience and then to touch the sacred sacrifice."[34] Even worse would be to leave the liturgy before the consummating end of communion, an act

29 *On the Baptism of Christ*, PG 49:369.

30 *On the Baptism of Christ*, PG 49:369.

31 *On the Baptism of Christ*, PG 49:369.

32 *On the Baptism of Christ*, PG 49:369.

33 *On the Baptism of Christ*, PG 49:370.

34 Both quotations are from *On the Baptism of Christ*, PG 49:370.

which John likens to Judas leaving the Passover supper of Christ: "Judas shared in the last supper on that very last night while all the others were sitting at table but he alone jumped up to leave. These here who leave before the last thanksgiving [εὐχαριστίας] are imitating him."[35] So to be worldly minded like Judas is to despise the glorious reality resident in the Eucharist, that "spiritual food which surpasses the whole creation, visible and invisible, [and] being a man and of the same vile nature [as Judas], won't you remain in thanksgiving in words and deeds?"[36] In the end, treating baptism or Eucharist with contempt or even indifference results from a profound lack of understanding of the effects that they can produce: "Where there are mysteries, there is tranquility. So let us touch this sacred sacrifice and cleanse our soul with much tranquility, much good order, and with fitting piety that we may be drawn to God into greater kindness and obtain eternal goods."[37]

Baptism naturally leads to the Eucharist, and the latter forms a kind of completion (*telos*) of the former, but both flow from the redemptive work of Christ. Nothing in the previous history of salvation can compare to what Christ accomplished and what he transmits to the Christian in the mysteries. This becomes evident in Chrysostom's baptismal catecheses, where he contrasts the blood on the doorposts in Egypt with the blood of Christ. The former was a type (τύπος) of the latter and only the latter is effective in protecting the Christian from the Destroyer.[38] The superiority of Christ's blood induces John to introduce what he terms "a different mystical word."[39] The blood and water that flowed from Jesus's side (Jn 19:34) are "symbols," but not in the modern sense of bare signification. They are signs that carry the reality of what they signify:

> The first was a symbol [σύμβολον] of baptism; the second of the mysteries. For this reason it did not say, "blood and water flowed out," but first came water and then blood since baptism comes first and then the mysteries. So the soldier pierced his side, he dug through the wall of the holy temple and I found the treasure and received wealth. Thus, it was the lamb too.

35 *On the Baptism of Christ*, PG 49:371.

36 *On the Baptism of Christ*, PG 49:372.

37 *On the Baptism of Christ*, PG 49:372.

38 See *Catechesis*, 3, in *Huit catéchèses baptismales inédites*, translation and notes by Antoine Wenger, SC 50 (Paris: Editions du Cerf, 1957), 158–62.

39 *Catechesis*, 3,17.

> The Jews sacrificed the sheep and I have found the fruit of salvation from the sacrifice.[40]

John is commenting on the passage in Jn 19:31–36, which recounts the Roman soldier piercing Jesus's side, from which flowed "blood and water" (Jn 19:34). Strangely, John insists on the reverse order of "water and blood" to align with the temporal administration of the two sacraments. Scholars have puzzled over this because this is not the only place where John argues this way.[41] Scholars have suggested different solutions to this conundrum, but the general thrust of John's point is sufficient for our purposes.[42] The flesh of Christ is a "holy temple" that housed the sacred waters of baptism and the precious blood of the Eucharist. The change from the third to the first person in the middle of the sentence of the last quotation is also significant. The soldier's action had the effect that "*I* [*ego*] found the treasure and received wealth." The Jews' sacrificing the lamb also made it possible that "*I* [*ego*] have found the fruit of salvation from the sacrifice." The members of the new covenant Church are the beneficiaries of all salvation history, both before and during the earthly life of Christ:

> "Water and blood came from [his] side." Beloved, do not pass by the mystery. I have a different mystical word. I said that this blood and water were a symbol of baptism and of the mysteries. It was out of these two that the Church was born "through the washing of regeneration and renewal of the Holy Spirit," through baptism and through the mysteries. The symbols of baptism and the mysteries flow from [his] side. So it was from his side then that Christ created the Church as it was from Adam's side that he formed Eve.[43]

When John exhorts his hearers not to let the mystery escape them, the choice of the singular "mystery" is significant. He normally uses the plural to designate the Eucharist, as he does above toward the end of this quotation. Speaking of "mystery" in the singular probably refers to the broader idea of

40 *Catechesis*, 3,16. See notes by Wenger, *Huit catéchèses baptismales inédites*, 160, 161.

41 In *Homily 85 on the Gospel of John*, Chrysostom makes the same point. See PG 59:463B. As Wenger notes, John does give the correct order on other occasions. See *Huit catéchèses baptismales inédites*, 60n.

42 See Wenger's discussion of suggested solutions in *Huit catéchèses baptismales inédites*, 160n1.

43 *Catechesis*, 3,17.

the birth of the Church from the side of Christ. This means that the Church was born not only as a result of Christ's will but from his very inner being. As Eve was taken from Adam ontologically, so the Church as Christ's bride derives ontologically from Christ himself.[44]

John's teaching on baptism, both that of Jesus and of the Christian, means that there exists a deep linkage and inner unity between all the mysteries in Jesus's earthly life. His nativity, baptism, and death are all connected. What John's eucharistic language suggests is that those mysteries of Christ's earthly life are active and efficacious in the consummating sacrament of the Church.

THE HEALING MINISTRY OF CHRIST

John preached on many of Christ's miracles, as one would expect when preaching on the Gospels.[45] One of his more striking expositions treats the story of the woman with a hemorrhage, as it appears in Matthew's Gospel.[46] This story is embedded in the account of the synagogue official who came to plead with Jesus for his dying daughter, and so it has the flavor of an inadvertent miracle within a greater miracle story. Unlike many other such stories, the hemorrhaging woman is not healed because of some deliberate action on Jesus's part. It is she who initiates the healing by touching Jesus's garment. In this John finds something very relevant to his audience:

> The woman with a hemorrhage taught us how to find wisdom. But the Evangelist showed that Jesus went up into those parts for a long time: "The men knew the place and they sent them into the surrounding region and they brought the sick to him." But the extended time not only did not destroy her faith but rather made it stronger by preserving her who was at the prime of life.[47]

44 John proceeds to draw on and develop marital imagery in the following sections of *Catechesis*, 3,18–19.

45 Chrysostom never preached a series of expository homilies on Mark or Luke as he did on Matthew and John. He may have thought it unnecessary since he had dealt with the major themes of Christ's life in treating Matthew. Here I select only one healing story for brevity's sake.

46 Mt 9:20–22. The fullest account of this miracle is in the shorter gospel of Mk 5:25–34.

47 *Homily 50 on Matthew*, PG 58:507.

This poor woman's faith becomes the centerpiece of John's reflections. Her wisdom lay in her perception that even a mere touch of Jesus's clothes would bring her the relief she had been seeking for twelve years. Of all the accounts in the Gospels, only Matthew uses the term "hem" or "edge" (κράσπεδον) of Jesus's garment. John finds this significant for his own audience as well. Where could a Christian in the late fourth or early fifth century find the hem of Jesus's garment to touch? John does not hesitate to introduce the Eucharist as the answer:

> Dare to touch the hem of his clothes. Or rather, if we wish, we can have all of him. For Christ's body lies before us now. Not only his garment but his very body. Not only to touch but to eat and enjoy. So, let us approach with faith, each of us who is weak. For if those who touch the hem of his garment can draw out such great power, how much more can those who have him whole? And they can approach with faith not only to receive what lies here but to touch with a pure heart, to be disposed in this way as approaching Christ himself. What then? Only when you hear his voice? But you see him lying here.[48]

John's appeal moves from the lesser to the greater (*a minori ad majorem*). The Christians of his day may have been tempted to think that such a great miracle could not be repeated in their own day, that the historical Jesus was not present with them as he was to the hemorrhaging woman. John, however, sees the miracle recorded in the Gospel not as the greater but as the lesser of two realities: the historical and the eucharistic. The eucharistic presence of Christ allows for more than touching the hem of Jesus's clothes. It provides not only a visual reality ("Christ's body lies before us now") but the mystery of consuming his very body ("not only to touch but to eat and enjoy"). In this way, the Christian consuming the Eucharist is in a superior position to the suffering woman. Yet, like the bleeding woman, every person too is weakened by sin ("each of us who is weak"). The only remedy is the same as the woman manifested: faith. Approaching with faith allows one to eat the same body of Christ that healed the woman. The touch which Christians can have is more than the woman's. It is an inner, spiritual touch ("to touch with a pure heart") that reaches not the hem of Jesus's garment but into his very heart.

This practical equation between the body of Christ on earth and that same body in the celebrations of the Church is a doctrine held by many,

48 *Homily 50 on Matthew*, PG 58:507.

if not all, the Church Fathers. Later in history, the Western Church would struggle to define this relation more carefully, but even then the Church would hearken back to ideas such as John expresses here. Like every act of communion, in this woman and in believers of later generations objective and subjective factors come into play. The body of Jesus is objectively present and holds within itself the power of healing, but the faith of the recipient acts as the subjective catalyst to bring that healing power out of the body of Christ. The Christian now as then only has to believe that the supper makes a difference.

THE PASSION AND DEATH OF JESUS

From time to time we have noticed how important the love of God for humanity (*philanthropia*) was for John Chrysostom. That such love had to be manifested by divine action was necessary because of the infinite distance between God and the human race.

The condescension (*sugkatabasis*) of the Eternal Son, therefore, is in the service of demonstrating the *philanthropia* of God, since human efforts could never reach God nor even begin to comprehend him. When John contemplates the passion and death of Jesus, that same focus on God's love for humanity comes back into play. In his two homilies on the thief on the cross, John sees Christ's love for the repentant thief in stark terms: "Now it is not only from the cross but from the words of the cross that his ineffable love for humanity could be seen. While being nailed, ridiculed, derided, and spit on, he kept saying, 'Father, forgive them their sin for they don't know what they are doing.' As he was being crucified, he prayed for those crucifying him."[49] As John emphasizes the contrast between the treatment Jesus received ("nailed, ridiculed, derided, and spit on") and his response of forgiveness, he also believes that same love is operative in Jesus's interactions with the dying thief.

> Do you promise admittance there to the thief? Yes, he says. I am the Master of the Cherubim. I have authority over flame, and Gehenna, and life and death. So, he says, "Today you will be with me in Paradise." When those powers see the Master, they immediately move aside and make way. . . . The

49 *Homily 1 on the Cross and the Thief*, PG 49:405.

> Master who loves humanity did this very thing. It is into the holy homeland that he enters and brings the thief with him, not to dishonor Paradise with the feet of the thief—may it never be—but to honor it.[50]

John views the good thief much the same as the prostitutes and tax collectors who were admitted to Paradise. As he seems to put himself in their place, he exclaims, "What a great honor! Abundant is the grandeur of God's love of humanity! Ineffable is the excellency of his goodness! For it is a greater honor to be with the Master than to enter into Paradise."[51] The transition from a life of sin to the reward of Paradise hangs on confession and repentance, which is what John sees in the thief on the cross. The one who is mercy itself could not resist the pleas of one who knew and acknowledged his own sin.[52]

This magnanimous love is even more on display in the case of Judas, because if anyone deserved to be rejected by Jesus, surely it was Judas.[53] Yet, in John's thinking, the love that Jesus had for Judas was no less than he possessed for the thief on the cross and the other disciples:

> O Christ's love for humanity! O the madness of Judas! O the lunacy! Judas sold him for thirty pieces of silver; Christ after this did not refuse his blood to be sold to give the forgiveness of sins for him who sold him. . . . Yes, Judas was present and he shared in the holy table. As Christ washed his feet along with the other disciples, so he partook of the holy table that Judas might have no excuse if he continued in evil.[54]

It is hard to imagine a greater contrast between the sanity of love and the lunacy of hate with respect to what motivated Jesus and what motivated Judas. Such a contrast hearkens back to the opening paragraphs of this first

50 *Homily 2 on the Cross and the Thief*, PG 49:410.

51 *Homily 2 on the Cross and the Thief*, PG 49:410.

52 *Homily 2 on the Cross and the Thief*, PG 49:413: "You see how great his confession was even on the cross. When you hear these things, do not despair about yourself any longer, but minding the unspeakable love of God for humanity, press on to correct your sins. If Christ counted the thief on the cross as worthy of such honor, how much more will he count us worthy of his own love if we are willing to make a confession of our faults. So that we might enjoy that great love from him, we should not be ashamed to confess our own sins, for great was the power of that confession and so is the power of this one. Look, he confessed and found Paradise opened. He confessed and he who was a thief received confidence to ask a King."

53 John preached two homilies on Judas, PG 49:373–92.

54 *Homily 1 on the Betrayal of Judas*, PG 49:380.

homily when Chrysostom painted the difference between the betrayer and the betrayed in vivid terms:

> He who was betrayed saved the inhabited world.
> He who betrayed him lost his own soul.
> He who was betrayed sits on the Father's right hand in the heavens.
> He who betrayed him is now in hell awaiting inevitable punishment.[55]

The one betrayed loves the one betraying. Judas could and did receive all the benefits that the other disciples enjoyed, but his response to such grace was horribly deficient. Judas's partaking of the first Eucharist was an opportunity for repentance or for making his betrayal more egregious if he did not repent. His madness, his lunacy, lay in his obstinate refusal to turn back from his crime. Still, this only highlights the love of Christ more fully:

> O how great is the Master's kind heart! The One betrayed suffers pain for the betrayer. When he saw him, he was troubled and said, "one of you will betray me." For whom was he despondent? At once showing his own love, he taught us that it is right to sing a dirge not for the one who suffers evil but for the one who does evil. What is worse than this? Suffering evil is not evil but doing evil is. Suffering evil procures the kingdom of heaven whereas doing evil becomes the cause of Gehenna and punishment. "Blessed are those who are persecuted for the sake of righteousness for theirs is the kingdom of heaven" [Mt 5:10].[56]

And here we arrive at Chrysostom's deepest reason for seeing Jesus's love. Love is willing to suffer evil for another but never willing to do evil to another. One should more readily weep and mourn for Judas than for Jesus. Consequently, John exhorts his hearers to lament not the Master's fate but Judas's: "Weep and groan for him; grieve for him since the Master shed tears for him."[57] Since Chrysostom sees Jesus's attitudes toward Judas as based on his love of humanity, John exhorts his congregants to proper preparation for receiving from the holy table. Judas provides the example of one who was poisoned with evil intent; his actions are to be avoided at all costs: "Let them not carry one thing in their mouth and another in their heart."[58]

55 *Homily 1 on the Betrayal of Judas*, PG 49:373.

56 *Homily 1 on the Betrayal of Judas*, PG 49:373.

57 *Homily 1 on the Betrayal of Judas*, PG 49:373.

58 *Homily 1 on the Betrayal of Judas*, PG 49:380.

> So then let no one be deceitful, let no one be full of evil with any poison in his mind so that his reception may not lead to condemnation. And then, after receiving the offering, the Devil rushed into Judas without any thought of the Lord's body that was there. He looked only at the shamelessness of Judas. This happened to teach you that to those who partake of the divine mysteries in an unworthy manner, it is these that the Devil rushes into and enters continuously as was the case with Judas at that time.[59]

On the basis of Jesus's example Chrysostom urges his people to show mercy, kindness, and forgiveness to their enemies. If Jesus could love Judas even amidst "the unspeakable madness," how much more should his followers forgive lesser sins? Such divine love overcomes the treachery of others. These thoughts lead John to the shedding of Christ's blood, which in turn leads him to the Eucharist. What could be a greater exemplar of forgiving love than Christ's willingness to forgive even Judas? As we shall later see, love toward one's enemies is one of John's most cherished themes in applying the Eucharist to his hearers. Communing in the holy mysteries demands such imitation of Christ. Yet John realizes that such a call is not easy to fulfill. The wounds caused by an enemy are "not easily healed by prayer. It is not healed by prayer. It has been healed by the forgiveness of sins against one's neighbor." Such forgiveness is so far beyond human power that only the grace of the Eucharist can accomplish it.

When partaking of the holy table of Christ, one must remember not only the treachery of Judas but also the love of Christ for humanity. Judas was lost, not because he betrayed Christ—Peter did the same—but because he failed to confess his sin and repent. In John's estimation, the contrast between the repentant thief and Judas stands as a powerful index pointing to the love of Christ, a love that bore the impossible ignominy of a merciless crucifixion.

The death of Christ left so great a mark on John's soul that he could never leave it to the side for long. Nor could John disassociate Christ's crucifixion from the Eucharist. One was intimately bound up with the other. When Paul uses the phrase "one body" (Eph 4:4), it evokes eucharistic connections for John:

> But since the subject is the Lord's body, let us also recall him who was crucified, nailed, sacrificed. If you are the body of Christ, bear the cross for he himself bore it too. Bear the spitting, bear the slaps, bear the nails. Such

59 *Homily 1 on the Betrayal of Judas*, PG 49:380.

> was his body. That body was without sin, for it says, "He did not commit sin nor was guile found in his mouth" [Is 53:9]. His hands were only for benefitting others. They would do anything for those who asked. Nothing inappropriate came out of his mouth. "You have a demon," he heard, and he answered nothing back. Now since the subject has to do with the body for us, as many of us as share the body, and taste this blood, you should ponder that in communion we share in him who makes himself no different nor divides himself because we taste of him as he sits above, is worshiped by angels, as we are close to the power of the Undefiled One.[60]

How easily John can move between the Church as the body of Christ and the physical body of Christ is demonstrated in the vivid descriptions of the crucifixion: the mocking, the nails, the flogging. Paul's doctrine of the Church as the body of Christ might be thought of as a mere analogy in the minds of some, but the quotation above points to more in Chrysostom's mind. The physical body of Christ that underwent the ignominy of death is mystically present in the Church and so can be present in the bread and wine on the sacred table.

The intimate connection between the death of Christ's physical body and the birth of the Church as his mystical body was probably seared into John's memory by a common tradition of interpreting the story of the soldier who thrust the lance into Jesus's side. As we observed above in treating baptism, John took the blood and water that flowed from Jesus's side on the cross as meaning not only that Jesus commanded the sacraments but also that he provided their reality and power. He spoke of them as symbols while transposing the order in Jn 19:34 from "blood and water" to "water and blood" to match the order of sacramental administration ("The first was a symbol of baptism; the second of the mysteries"). Although I have translated *sumbolon* as "symbol," Chrysostom's meaning cannot be read through modern eyes, meanings that pare down the richer content shared by almost all the Greek Fathers. *Sumbolon* can certainly be translated "sign" but not with any connotation of arbitrariness.[61] The signs of blood and water were not arbitrary, because they are natural signs of life (blood) and cleansing (water). Yet they were true signs in the economy of redemption because they pointed forward to the future sacraments, which would cleanse, nourish, and perfect

60 *Homily 3 on Ephesians*, PG 62:27.

61 For an enlightening explanation see Alexander Schmemann, *The Eucharist: Sacrament of the Kingdom* (Crestwood, NY: St. Vladimir's Press, 1987).

the Church in generations to come. Those sacraments (mysteries) were not arbitrary signs in the modern sense; they carried what they signified. So in Chrysostom as in other Fathers, the *sumbolon* was a sign that contained the very reality it showed outwardly. For John this piercing at the end of Jesus's earthly life became the source of everything that the Church was to become.

THE TRIUMPH OF THE CROSS

The death of Jesus must be viewed from many different angles to be understood and appreciated. John's reflections on his death are like a kaleidoscope that, if turned in a certain direction, yields a multichromatic vision. While the West increasingly focused on Christ's Passion as a source of sorrowful meditation, the East retained an emphasis on the cross as a triumph over the forces of evil. In many ways the death of Jesus takes the most prominent position in John's preaching. Like other Eastern Fathers, he sees the cross as a triumph over death and the Devil. For him, as for them, death destroyed death. Christ turned the instruments of deception against the Deceiver and overcame him who had overcome the weakness of the first human pair.

John is supremely happy to focus on the cross. Nowhere is this more evident than in his *Homily on the Cemetery and the Cross.*[62] Although it is difficult to know when and where many of Chrysostom's homilies were preached, J. N. D. Kelly places this one in the cemetery outside Antioch on a Good Friday.[63] As John explains, it was the custom of their Antiochene predecessors to journey out to the cemetery north of the city on that occasion, but John is ever after a deeper explanation, which he happily finds in Heb 13:12–13, "Therefore Jesus, that he might sanctify the people through his own blood, suffered outside the gate. So then, let us go outside the camp to him bearing his reproach." But then there were many memorials of martyrs (μαρτύριον) within the city. Why come to this particular place of martyrdom? John reminds them of what their own language readily provided, namely, that the word *cemetery* (κοιμητήριον) meant a place to sleep. From this he draws the all-important lesson that Christ changed death to sleep

62 *The Cemetery and the Cross*, PG 49:393–98.

63 J. N. D. Kelly, *Golden Mouth: The Story of John Chrysostom; Ascetic, Preacher, Bishop* (London: Duckworth, 1995), 88.

for all who belong to him. Christ's victory over death then becomes the occasion of exultant joy.

Although *The Cemetery and the Cross* is somewhat shorter than most of John's homilies, it is full of powerful, gripping language.[64] Thinking of Paul's words in 1 Cor 15:54 (quoting Isaiah) about death being swallowed up in victory, Chrysostom hails the cross as a war memorial:

> The cross is
> the war memorial against the demons,
> the sword against sin,
> the blade that Christ used to prick the serpent.
> The cross is
> the will of the Father,
> the glory of the Only Begotten Son,
> the Spirit's transport of joy,
> the world of angels,
> the safety of your church,
> the boast of Paul,
> the wall of the Saints,
> the light of the whole earth.[65]

The term "war memorial" (τρόπαιον) is not used in the New Testament, but the word was all too familiar from John's military culture and hallowed by previous Christian writers.[66] Although Chrysostom's favorite saint Paul did not use the word, the latter's words in Col 2:14–15 certainly justify the term for John. The war memorial captured John's imagination as a means of exulting in the triumph of the cross.

64 The Greek text has 2,356 words. Most of John's homilies ranged from about 4,000 to 5,000 words.

65 *The Cemetery and the Cross*, PG 49:396–97. σταυρὸς τὸ κατὰ τῶν δαιμόνων τρόπαιον, ἡ κατὰ τῆς ἁμαρτίας μάχαιρα, τὸ ξίφος, ᾧ τὸν ὄφιν ἐκέντησεν ὁ Χριστός· σταυρὸς τὸ τοῦ Πατρὸς θέλημα, ἡ τοῦ Μονογενοῦς δόξα, τὸ τοῦ Πνεύματος ἀγαλλίαμα, ὁ τῶν ἀγγέλων κόσμος, σῆς Ἐκκλησίας ἡ ἀσφάλεια, τὸ καύχημα Παύλου, τὸ τῶν ἁγίων τεῖχος, τὸ φῶς τῆς οἰκουμένης ἁπάσης. I have arranged this section in a semi-poetic form justified on the basis of its contents. No printed version has it thus. Although neither of the two homilies Chrysostom preached treating the thief on the cross who found forgiveness from Christ (Lk 23:39–43) has any definite references to the Eucharist, both contain similar encomia of the cross.

66 For earlier Christian writers, see G. W. Lampe, *Patristic Greek Lexicon* (Oxford: Oxford University Press, 1961), under τρόπαιον, 1411.

> Mind what is poured out. It is the blood that wiped away the written condemnation of our sins. This is the blood that cleansed your soul, that washed away the stain, that triumphed over the evil rulers and authorities. "For he stripped the rulers and authorities and displayed them openly by triumphantly parading them on the cross" [Col 2:15]. The war memorial has many symbols of victory, he says. The spoils of war hang on high on the cross above. A noble king, once he wins the most difficult battle, places the armor, the shield, and the weapons of the tyrant and of the defeated soldiers up high on the memorial. So also Christ, once he won the war against the devil, hung high upon the cross all his weapons: death and the curse, as if it were a war memorial that all may see the memorial, the powers above in heaven, and men below on earth, as well as the evil demons that had been destroyed.[67]

The mention of the blood poured out is a reference not only to the historic crucifixion but to the eucharistic celebration presently taking place. When John says "mind" or "take note" (ἐννόησον) it is the second in a pair, the first of which refers to Christ's body on the altar:

> **Body:**
> Mind the offering and from what cause it came. He was slain for your sake and you are abandoning him who was sacrificed when you see him. He said, "Where the carcass is, there the eagles gather" [Mt 24:28]. We approach not as eagles, but as dogs. How great is our shamelessness![68]
>
> **Blood:**
> Mind what is poured out. It is the blood that wiped away the written condemnation of our sins. This is the blood that cleansed your soul, that washed away the stain, that triumphed over the evil rulers and authorities.[69]

The eucharistic connection is strengthened when we hear John saying that the altar of the cemetery is as if one were with Jesus: "We are about to stand, not next to an empty tomb, but next to the table itself that has the lamb."[70] One can easily imagine John standing before a tomb used as an altar while he preaches this encomium of the cross. He seems keenly aware of being both an instrument of God and simultaneously only a human one whose role is

67 *The Cemetery and the Cross*, PG 49:398.

68 *The Cemetery and the Cross*, PG 49:398.

69 *The Cemetery and the Cross*, PG 49:398.

70 *The Cemetery and the Cross*, PG 49:397.

to invoke the presence of the Spirit, who will actually bring the Christ of the cross to the altar in the cemetery:

> When the priest stands in front of the table stretching out his hands to heaven, calling on the Holy Spirit to come down and touch the offerings, there should be much silence, much quietness whenever the Spirit gives the grace, whenever he comes down and touches the offerings. When you see the lamb slaughtered and prepared, will you also introduce disturbance and confusion, then rivalry and ridicule? How can you enjoy this sacrifice while approaching this table with so much confusion?[71]

John's call to sobriety and silence seems to arise from his realization of all that the cross of Christ accomplished. The Eucharist itself is a kind of war memorial in a manner of speaking, for it too brings the reality of death's defeat to the present. As Christ is present on the table, so too are the hosts of heaven, for "where Christ is, there too is heaven."[72] Nothing could more succinctly capture the triumph of the cross than the fact that Christ himself came to set those in prison free:

> A virgin, and wood—these are the symbols of our defeat. Eve was a virgin for she had not yet known a man. The wood was a tree. And death was Adam's price. But look! Again, there is a virgin, wood, and death. These symbols of our defeat are now the symbols of victory. Instead of Eve there is Mary. Instead of the wood of the knowledge of good and evil, there is the wood of the cross; Instead of Adam's death, the death of Christ. You see, by the very things by which he [the Devil] conquered, he was defeated.[73]

So the defeat of the Devil, evil, and death results from the presence of Christ. Christ took heaven even down to Hades to destroy the last enemy. Now through the Eucharist that same victory belongs to the Christian. No wonder John never tires of exhorting his congregation to silence, sobriety, calmness, and tranquility.

71 *The Cemetery and the Cross*, PG 49:398.

72 *The Cemetery and the Cross*, PG 49:395.

73 *The Cemetery and the Cross*, PG 49:396.

THE RESURRECTION OF JESUS CHRIST

For Christians of most ages the resurrection of Christ has been an occasion of great joy and it was certainly considered the high point of the liturgical year in the late fourth and early fifth centuries. This was so not only because of the inherent reality of new life in Christ but also perhaps because the season of Pascha followed upon the long and arduous fasting of Lent. So an occasion of spiritual joy could easily degenerate into a distorted form of celebration. In fact, John was so concerned about the sinful behavior of his fellow Christians that he devoted an entire homily on the resurrection to correcting the drunken behavior of some.[74] The celebration of Easter and the resurrected Christ apparently occasioned inebriation and riotous behavior among some Christians. Perhaps after the rigors of Lenten fasting, the Christians of Antioch and/or Constantinople entered the Pascha season with an immoderate attitude. Chrysostom picks up on Paul's warning against drunkenness in Eph 5:18 ("Do not be drunk with wine in which is excess") and explains two salient points. First, he contrasts inebriation by means of ordinary wine with a spiritual inebriation that leads not to dissolution but to sobriety and joy:

> Let us get drunk with this [kind of] drunkenness. Let us abstain from that other kind that we may not disgrace the present feast. For the present feast is not only of the earth but of heaven as well. Today there is joy on earth; there is joy in heaven. If there is joy in heaven when one sinner turns back, how much more is there joy in heaven when the whole world was snatched from the hands of the Devil. Now the angels are skipping, now the archangels rejoice, now the Cherubim and the Seraphim celebrate the present feast. They are not ashamed of their fellow servants but rejoice with our good things. Even if our grace comes from the Master, yet our happiness [ἡδονή] is common to all. And what do I say of these fellow servants? Their Master and ours is himself not ashamed to feast with us.[75]

It is this spiritual drunkenness that Chrysostom wants for his people, that is, to be filled with a higher joy that makes all other joys superfluous. In his allusion to the parable of the Prodigal Son in Luke 15 ("If there is joy in

74 *Homily against Those Who Are Drunk and on the Resurrection of Christ*, PG 50:433–42.

75 *Homily against Those Who Are Drunk and on the Resurrection of Christ*, PG 50:436.

heaven when one sinner turns back"; Lk 15:7) John raises a second point that brings him back to a favorite theme, the neglect of those in need. John makes a link between drunkenness and the misuse of resources such that the poor are deprived. In explaining what drunkenness leads to, he says, "We call the young dissolute who receive their father's inheritance and taking everything together, they don't think about who might need it and then give. Rather, taking clothes, gold, and silver, they divide their paternal inheritance among prostitutes and lechers. Such is drunkenness."[76]

Drunkenness turns the sinner in on himself and causes him to forget the very purpose of having worldly goods. But the mystical table is a reminder of the inherent solidarity which in fact all people have and which should impel the Christian to charity. By recognizing that only "one and the same table is set for the King . . . and for the poor man who sits begging for alms" the Christian who has a sober mind sees clearly that "grace is divine" and the mystical realities of the sacred table "are the Lord's gifts." This means that discriminatory attitudes according to common social norms are completely out of place for those at the table of Christ.[77] The resurrection of Christ stands as a beacon to call all Christians to the sobriety of new life but that new life is never lived in isolation. It is a call away from self-indulgence to service of others. In the Pascha celebration John is begging his people to turn away from the cultural customs of the season to a deeper faith. He hopes that the superior joy of being inebriated with Christ through communion will instill the same attitudes and actions that Jesus himself demonstrated. Love for the salvation of others and their temporal welfare are natural extensions of the resurrection life in Christ. The Eucharist is a call to live that life of Christ in service to others.

PEDAGOGY AND MYSTAGOGY

The power of John's preaching lies as much in what it is about as in his rhetorical skill. Readers of patristic sermons have long noted how the Fathers' preaching moved back and forth between pedagogy and mystagogy.[78] They

76 *Homily against Those Who Are Drunk and on the Resurrection of Christ*, PG 50:434.

77 *Homily against Those Who Are Drunk and on the Resurrection of Christ*, PG 50:437.

78 Augustine being the most famous, but other examples exist. Peter Chrysologus was influenced by Augustine in this regard. See Caroline Tolton, "From Memory to Topology: The Architecture

did intend to instruct but they also aimed at something more. John Henry Newman was one prominent Victorian who caught the mystagogical flavor of patristic preaching. As Newman put it, the Fathers "deal with things [*res*], not words [*verba*]" in their preaching and writing. Consequently, they allow modern readers "to get through and beyond the letter into the spirit."[79] Such a characterization certainly captures Chrysostom. John's preaching is historical, contextual, and philological, at least as much as any other Church Father, East or West, but it is preeminently mystagogical in that John wants his hearers to enter into the mysteries of salvation, not just to understand them from a distance. Those mysteries are most of all the life of Jesus himself on earth. All his life, but especially his suffering and death, are the mysteries that contain salvation.[80] It is those same saving events that are embodied in the Eucharist.

For John Chrysostom the Eucharist must always be viewed in the context of the larger liturgy. One cannot exist without the other. Now we can more fully appreciate why this is the case. It is because the Eucharist and its attendant liturgy embody the realities of Christ's earthly life. The Christian of his day—and for that matter ours—suffers no disadvantage compared to those who were alive in Jesus's day. The liturgy relives salvation history, not just recounts it, and therefore the sacred table really contains the human Jesus.

With this overview of the life of Christ in John's preaching it becomes evident that the Eucharist was in his mind the means to be connected with the earthly experience of Jesus. Christ's terrestrial sojourn was more than an amorphous thought that each believer can access through mental recall while reading the pages of the Gospels. The Eucharist was in fact the embodiment of each of the mysteries contained in Christ's earthly life. All that John Chrysostom preached had its center and focus in Jesus Christ, and he reveled in the details of Christ's earthly life. In this regard, John was not unique, for it seems to have been the common inheritance of the Church both East and West. That the ancient Church reflected much on Christ's earthly life shows

---

of Persuasion in the Sermons of Peter Chrysologus" (PhD diss., University of Chicago Divinity School, 2005). For one of the greatest influences on Augustine, see Craig Alan Satterlee, *Ambrose of Milan's Method of Mystagogical Preaching* (Collegeville, MN: Liturgical Press, 2002).

79 See Thomas J. Norris, *Cardinal Newman for Today* (New York: New City Press, 2010), 55–56.

80 "From the swaddling clothes of his birth to the vinegar of his Passion and the shroud of his resurrection, everything in Jesus' life was a sign of his mystery" (CCC §515).

up in the lesser-known witness of Greek Christian poetry, which seems to have been overlooked by many scholars:

> Today we have beheld our Lord Jesus Christ on the altar.
> Today we have grasped the coal of fire of which the Cherubim sang in a shadow.
> Today we have heard that great and sweetest voice crying out.
> This is the body that burned off the thorns of sins and enlightens human souls.
> This is the body the woman with a hemorrhage touched and was delivered from her suffering.
> This is the body which the daughter of the Canaanite woman saw and was healed.
> This is the body that the prostitute, by approaching with her whole soul, wiped away the filth of her sins.
> This is the body that Thomas when touching cried out "My Lord and My God."
> This is the body that brought us so great and wondrous a salvation.[81]

Although the author of this encomium is completely unknown, it has been dated from about the fourth century. John would certainly have agreed with its content and underlying sentiments inasmuch as the eucharistic references are unmistakable; its repetition of the body points to a demonstrative referent before its hearers and readers. And the content suggests more than a purely human body. John Chrysostom would have welcomed such language as fitting for the Eucharist and edifying for those who desire to encounter Christ.

THE WONDER OF CHRIST'S CONDESCENSION

Earlier, we made note of the place of divine incomprehensibility in the thought of John Chrysostom. Since God is infinitely above every human thought and rational exercise, God himself had to descend to earth in order

81 This text was originally published in the early twentieth century in F. Cabrol and H. LeClercq, *Reliquiae liturgicae vetustissimae*, Monumenta Ecclesiae liturgica 1 (Paris, 1913), and reproduced in Jesus Solano, *Textos Eucaristicos Primitivos* (Madrid: Biblioteca de Autores Cristianos, 1952), 1:1062.

to meet human need. John was well aware that the Incarnation was also difficult to grasp and even harder to embrace. Yet he was also convinced that nothing in the Church or the Christian life contained any reality more important than the mysteries of the life of Jesus Christ, and so without the Incarnation no grace could ever be imparted to the human race:

> The message of the Incarnation is very difficult to receive because the superabundance of his love of humanity and the greatness of his condescension were filled with stupefying awe. There had to be a great preparation so it could be received. Mind then how great a thing it was to hear and to learn that God is ineffable, incorruptible, incomprehensible, invisible, beyond understanding, "in whose hand is the ends of the earth, the one who looks down on the earth and makes it tremble, who touches the mountains and they smoke." Not even the Cherubim could bear the moment of his condescension. Rather, they hid their sight with the protection of their wings. God is the one who surpasses every thought, surmounts all reason, transcends the archangels and all the intellectual [νοερὰς] powers above. Christ consented to become a man to take on flesh from the earth and clay, and to come into the virgin womb and for Mary to be pregnant for nine months, to be fed with milk, and to suffer everything that is human. Since what was about to happen was paradoxical as if it was not to be believed by many, he first sent prophets to declare it.[82]

Jean Daniélou expressed John's sentiment well when he said that the mystery of Christ died and resurrected was the one truth that made sense of all the other aspects of Christianity, but Chrysostom's way of drawing out the meaning of that truth shows how much the details of Jesus's earthly life meant to him, none of which would be known without the Incarnation. The stupefying impact of that historical event resulted from those same three truths which we observed in the Chrysostom corpus in chapter 1: the incomprehensible transcendence of God, the divine love of humanity, and the condescension of Christ. These three, properly triangulated, leave the observer filled with "stupefying awe" (φρίκη).

82 *Father, If Possible, Let This Cup Pass*, PG 51:36–37.

✠ ✠ ✠

God's utter otherness, when finally grasped, leaves the human mind in a state of stupor. Richard Feynman, the Nobel-prize physicist, once famously quipped, "Nobody understands quantum mechanics," because it seemed to go beyond and against human reason. If observations and theories of nature could render the human voice speechless and leave the human mind baffled, how much more would human powers fail before divine transcendence. However, Chrysostom expresses the same perplexity in the face of the Incarnation. The only way to make the descent of Christ to this world palatable is to recall the excellence (ὑπερβολὴ) of God's love for the human race (φιλανθρωπία). That love did not make God's nature comprehensible to human beings, but it did make his condescension easier to embrace. Or perhaps one should say that Christ's condescension made accepting God's love easier. A person may embrace the paradox of God's hiddenness and Jesus's humanity but in doing so has to say, "Nobody understands the condescension." There is something puzzling about the invisible God becoming a visible and real human being, and that without any loss of divinity or humanity. But the bewilderment lies not only in the *fact* of this condescension but also in the *motive* behind it, because such a divine love for the human race is beyond anything that anyone might have hoped for. If that is true of the Incarnation, it is equally true of the Eucharist. No one understands how the real flesh and blood of the historical Jesus could be present in bread and wine. Nor how each event of his earthly life could be present to all subsequent generations of Christians.

Part II

✣ ✣ ✣

Presence

4

The Presence of Christ's Sacrifice in the Eucharist

The study of the Eucharist in any Church Father naturally raises the question of the real presence and the sacrificial nature of the sacrament. The term *real presence* is a relatively modern one. It cannot be found in any Father of the Church and there are only vague approximations in the medieval West, even after the extensive debates issuing from the Berengar controversy in the eleventh century. The term makes sense in a post-Reformation context because it became a shorthand designation for the belief that Christ's body and blood are truly and really present in the sacred species after transubstantiation. In Western histories of the Eucharist since the sixteenth century, the questions of real presence and sacrifice loom large. Catholic historians generally sought to show a uniformity of belief in the real presence and true sacrifice in the Church Fathers, thus bolstering the claim of the Church that its doctrine was in continuity with the witness of the early Church. Protestant historians sought to argue for more nuanced readings of the Church Fathers, arguing varying kinds of presence are evident in their writings. Most Protestant theologies denied that the Eucharist was a propitiatory sacrifice while allowing other definitions of the sacrifice.

In this chapter, I will argue that John Chrysostom does indeed teach what was later called the real presence but also that he has a multidimensional view of Christ's presence. He transcends any putative division or tension between the words of consecration and the Epiclesis of the Spirit, considering them both necessary for the Eucharist. His view of divine omnipotence operative in the Eucharist agrees with that of Ambrose. The putative oppositions between East and West, sometimes placed front and center, can hardly be justified on the basis of John Chrysostom's texts. John's insistence on the true presence of the earthly Jesus in the Eucharist carries with it a plenary view of Christ's sacrifice and power.

Earlier we saw that John Chrysostom made connections between the Eucharist and the events of the life of Jesus while on earth. For him, the Eucharist embodies and extends the earthly life of Christ into the Church and the world today. If someone were to ask what significance the life of Jesus has for today—or for any time after his earthly sojourn—John would answer that because of the Eucharist we can experience Jesus as directly as did those who knew him in his own lifetime. But how is this possible? In what sense is Christ as present in the Eucharist as he was on earth in the first century? This claim may seem absurd on the face of it, but its odd appearance can be a spur to dig more deeply into the mystery of the Eucharist. Whatever the outcome, we would like to know if John Chrysostom believed in anything like what was later called the real presence and the sacrificial nature of that presence. In this chapter, I will produce evidence that John was fully convinced of the Eucharist as a true and proper sacrifice to God the Father because all that Christ was on earth, including his death and resurrection, are present now in the privileged moment (*kairos*) of the Church's worship.

THE PRESENCE OF CHRIST IN THE EUCHARIST

If John Chrysostom never addressed this problem like later writers, what, if anything, does he have to say about the question of Christ's presence? The best place to begin is with John's clear affirmations or his assumptions while addressing other matters. Since John largely invokes eucharistic references while speaking about moral and spiritual growth, the belief in the real presence is usually assumed by default. But at times he does employ stark language, as when he speaks of the "body of God" (τὸ σῶμα τοῦ Θεοῦ). If John is an ardent defender of the incomprehensibility of God because he knows that God's nature is immaterial, how can he speak of "the body of God"? He uses this phrase to underscore how careful the recipient of the Eucharist must be in approaching the sacred table:

> What if someone would not receive the king simply? What do I mean by king? No one would touch a royal garment with unclean hands, even if he were in a desert, or alone, even if no one were present, although there was no other garment or the web of a worm. If you are amazed at dye, this is only the blood of a dead fish. But at the same time, no one would choose to approach him boldly with filthy hands. But if someone would not dare to touch a mere human garment in this way, how would he dare to touch the body of the God who is over all, the blameless and pure one, to be in union with the divine nature that is the cause of our being and life, by which the gates of death were destroyed and taken up into the vault of heaven? How can we receive this with such great arrogance?[1]

Here John invokes a rhetorical strategy seen in many of his homilies, arguing from the lesser to the greater (*a minori ad majorem*). If one would not think of approaching an earthly king with unclean hands, how could one be so bold as to dare to touch God himself? It is the exalted status of the thing to be handled that must guide the one approaching. In the end, there can be no comparison between a human king with his royal vestments and that which carries the very God of all. John reminds his hearers of the absolute uniqueness of God ("over all," ἐπὶ πάντων). Although nothing human is commensurable with the divine nature, it is precisely this nature that is in the bread and wine. When he speaks of the blameless and pure, he is not speaking of God in general but of the body of God.[2] It is this body, united to the divine nature, that gives human beings their existence and life. John chooses a term for union, ὁμιλῆσαν, that he elsewhere uses to describe marriage. The kind of intimacy enjoyed by husband and wife reflects the deepest union between the divine and human in Christ. The communing Christian enjoys an even greater intimacy with the body of God.

A little later in this discourse he speaks of what the Christian may hope for: "This is why I hope for heaven and hope to receive the good things in it: life without death, a share with the angels, communion with Christ."[3]

1 *Homily 24 on 1 Corinthians*, PG 61:203.

2 As indicated by the neuter gender of the adjectives (τὸ σῶμα . . . τὸ ἄμωμον . . . τὸ καθαρὸν).

3 *Homily 24 on 1 Corinthians*, PG 61:203.

This yields some insights into what he means by the phrase τὸ τῇ θείᾳ ἐκείνῃ φύσει ὁμιλῆσαν, which I translated provisionally as "to be in union with the divine nature." For a person to be in ὁμιλίαν with another suggests an intimate union and exchange to the greatest extent possible. So the "ομιλιαν of Christ" that awaits the believer in the future life is not only a state of being but an active participation in which the believer experiences an exchange with Christ. It may even imply a kind of eternal deification. When John speaks of Christ's body as possessing τὸ τῇ θείᾳ ἐκείνῃ φύσει ὁμιλῆσαν, he probably means a union of the material body with the divine nature in which there is a perpetual exchange taking place. John may also be thinking of the Incarnation as a definitive moment that brought this exchange about.[4] Thus, a looser paraphrase seems justified, "the body that is in perpetual union with and participation in the divine nature." The blamelessness and purity of this body then derives from that union with the divine.

Such is the nature of the body received in the Eucharist. It can be called the body of God because of the intimate union that that body enjoys with the divine nature. No wonder then that this body of God "is the cause of our being and life by which the gates of death were destroyed and taken up into the vault of heaven."[5] Chrysostom is no doubt thinking of the climactic destruction of evil that Christ procured by his passion and death, but from this complex of saving acts flows the very life of heaven and the entry into that celestial world. There seems little doubt that John believed what we call in modern theological parlance "the real presence." What could such a phrase mean if not precisely what Chrysostom meant by a body of God that destroys all the barriers to life and heaven? The real presence was for him the intimate union and exchange of the divine and human in Christ conveyed through the sacramental elements.

Surely, though, the presence of Christ's body in the bread and wine is not the same body that walked the roads of Galilee, taught the poor, healed the sick, and suffered under Pontius Pilate! The medievals, beginning in about the tenth century, posed the question and answered it by focusing either on the signs (Berengar) or on the underlying spiritual reality (Paschasius Radbertus). The latter answer became the accepted view in the West and led to the distinction between substance and accidents. None of that discussion, however, was known to John Chrysostom. Even though there had been many

4 Which would accord with his choice of the aorist infinitive (ὁμιλῆσαν) over the present (ὁμιλεῖν).

5 *Homily 24 on 1 Corinthians*, PG 61:203.

affirmative answers before and after Chrysostom, the answer seems so unbelievable and even irrational. John Chrysostom was aware of the problem of appearance and reality, perhaps from his own musings, but certainly from the yearnings of his flock. John not only gives an affirmative answer to the question of Christ's presence; he also elaborates on it in a manner designed to astound. Recall that in *Homily 82 on Matthew*, Chrysostom employed vivid language to show that the Christian in his day can share in Jesus's life just as much as those who lived contemporaneously with him.[6] He insisted that the experience of the Christian in the eucharistic liturgy is not in any way inferior to that of those who saw Jesus in his earthly life. We saw how important this truth was for John in chapter 3, but here we should allow the accent to fall on a slightly different point. If the faithful living after Christ can really touch him and "take him within," then it is hard to deny that John sees Christ's presence in the Eucharist as not only real but even transformative. That is why the proper dispositions (not "staggering nor dissolute") are so important. This is the same Lord who walked the earth who is now present to the Church in the liturgy.

John Chrysostom, however, was not an irrational man although he firmly believed God was far above and beyond human understanding. That latter fact becomes important in John's distinction between appearance and reality when discussing the eucharistic presence of Jesus in this same homily:

> But let his word be stronger than our machinations and sight. And we do so in regard to the mysteries, not only focusing on the things we see before us, but holding to his words. His word cannot deceive but our senses can be easily deceived. God has never failed but our senses have been overturned many times. So since he says, "This is my body," let us be persuaded and believe and let us look on with spiritual eyes. For Christ has delivered nothing to us that can be seen with the senses but metaphysical realities in observable things. Everything is metaphysical. So also in baptism the gift comes through the sensible element of water, but what is produced is metaphysical, that is, birth and regeneration. If you did not have a body, he would have given you the gifts in bare reality without physical form. But since the soul is bound up with the body, he gives you metaphysical realities in physical things.[7]

6 *Homily 82 on Matthew*, PG 58:743.

7 *Homily 82 on Matthew*, PG 58:743. At times I have alternated between "spiritual" and "metaphysical" in my translation of νοητός.

We hear in this section of *Homily 82 on Matthew* echoes of Cyril of Jerusalem (d. 386), who emphasized the same difference between the appearance of the elements and the reality underneath them. Cyril was keenly aware of the ever-present temptation to downplay the reality of Christ's physical life and death.[8] The reality of that death, however, was essential because it was that death into which the neophyte was baptized. That same issue of appearance and reality surfaced again for Cyril when he stressed the reality of Christ's body and blood in the bread and wine:

> Do not think of the bread and wine as mere bread and wine, for they constitute the body and blood of Christ by the Lord's own declaration. For even if your sense experience suggests this to you, let your faith rather confirm it for you. Do not judge the matter from taste. Rather, from your faith become fully persuaded without a doubt because you have been made worthy of the body and blood of Christ.[9]

Cyril proceeds to use a salient designation to express this difference when he asks the meaning of Ps 23:5, "'You have prepared a table before me.' What does it mean other than a mystical and metaphysical table?" Within a half century John would speak in this same tradition of νοητά, that is, metaphysical realities embodied in physical things. Many Latin Fathers chose the term *intelligibilis* to express this difference between appearance and reality. The term "intelligible," which has long been used in English translations, is singularly uninformative since it typically designates something mental and cognitive. And the choice of "spiritual" misses the mark because in the modern mind it connotes the supernatural or even the unreal. Recall that the modern physical/spiritual divide parses into a threefold difference in an ancient Christian mode: physical/metaphysical/spiritual.

John follows the tradition attested in Cyril in the quotation above from *Homily 82*. Four times Chrysostom invokes the noetic (νοητά) nature of the mysteries and applies it in slightly varying ways. Like Cyril before him, John stresses that the divine realities cannot be understood from human sight, which is why the believer must use "spiritual eyes" (νοητοῖς ὀφθαλμοῖς), perhaps better translated "eyes of the mind." Like numbers or other intangibles,

8 Cyril of Jerusalem, *Baptismal Rite, Lecture 2*. See *St. Cyril of Jerusalem's Lectures on the Sacraments*, ed. F. L. Cross (Crestwood, NY: St. Vladimir's Press, 1986), 2.

9 Translated from Gerardo di Nola, *La Dottrina Eucharistica dei Secoli I-IV* (Vatican City: Libreria Editrice Vaticana, 2000), 130.

the realities hidden in the visible bread and wine are perceived only with the mind because they are "metaphysical realities in observable things" (ἀλλ' ἐν αἰσθητοῖς μὲν πράγμασι, Πάντα δὲ νοητά).[10] What are those intangible realities? Stressing again the disjunction between the sensible and the noetic he speaks of "metaphysical realities in perceptible things" (ἐν αἰσθητοῖς τὰ νοητά σοι παραδίδωσι) precisely because human beings are body and soul. To underscore the realities in the Eucharist, John reminds his audience of baptism, in which the tangible element of water is the instrument by which the metaphysical is accomplished. By "accomplished" or "completed" (νοητὸν δὲ τὸ ἀποτελούμενον) John doubtless means the act of baptism with its attendant words, but in this lies an astounding reality. What is accomplished is "birth and renewal" (ἡ γέννησις καὶ ἡ ἀνακαίνωσις), evoking the language of Ti 3:5. More than a mere verbal parallel, Chrysostom sees this implantation of the metaphysical as at the heart of the gospel, for that same action was done in the Incarnation of Christ. The noetic is therefore not an epistemological category; it is ontological. Baptism and the mysteries convey the metaphysical through the physical. That is why John can boldly proclaim that Christ in his condescending love "gives you himself not only to be seen but to be touched, eaten, and taken within." It is hard to imagine how Christ's presence in the Eucharist could be more real.

Chrysostom still has other ways of affirming Christ's presence. Like a great storyteller, John uses varying images and analogies to make his point. His third *Baptismal Catechesis* offers an extended example.[11] As we observed in chapter 2, John always wishes to contrast the superiority of the revelation in Christ with the inferior prefigurements in the history of Israel. Here John compares the blood of Christ with the blood of the lambs slaughtered by the Hebrews in Egypt. Moving from the type (*tupos*) to the reality (*aletheia*), John argues that the true blood of Christ is much more powerful than anything the Jews knew, so powerful in fact that the Devil will flee from a Christian when he sees the precious blood of Christ reddening his lips.[12] The table then that holds this blood acts as a weapon stronger than any other. Yet John is careful to note that the type in the Old Testament derives its power from the reality manifested later. John's use of the abstract word "truth" rather than

10 The construction μέν . . . δέ suggests a strong contrast in John's mind.

11 I use here the text in Antoine Wenger, *Huit catéchèses baptismales inédites*, SC 50 (Paris: Editions du Cerf, 1957), 158–60.

12 *Baptismal Catecheses*, 3,12–13.

some concrete adjective such as "true blood" may indicate that he is thinking of the body and blood of Christ as part and parcel of the revelation of truth through the appearance of Christ as Messiah in a wider sense. The final manifestation of truth is the revelation of Christ. The truth of the Eucharist can only be understood in that context.

The superiority of the new covenant derives mainly from Christ himself, whom John here designates a temple when he says, "the blood of truth smeared on the believers' mouth, like doors of the temple holding Christ."[13] Wenger notes that in Antiochene Christology Christ was the temple of God and cites Chrysostom's homilies on Matthew for support.[14] And, of course, John was fully aware of his inspired namesake's passage about Jesus calling his own body a temple in Jn 2:12–22. If Christ is the new temple of God, then his body and blood, united to the divine presence, can save those who receive it. Baptism and the Eucharist are intimately tied together in Chrysostom's mind since both are saving ordinances.[15] The presence of God in both sacraments is certainly real because Christ's body held the saving waters of baptism and the nourishing blood of the Eucharist. As the slain lamb was Israel's means of redemption, so the Lamb of God is for the world. This latter Lamb is what allows John to say, "I found a treasure and received wealth" and "I have found the fruit of salvation as the fruit of the sacrifice."[16] The flesh of Christ is a holy temple that housed the sacred waters of baptism and the precious blood of the Eucharist.

One final comparison between the old covenant and the new reinforces John's underlying belief in the sacred presence of Christ in the eucharistic meal. In section 18 of his *Baptismal Catechesis 3* he aligns the birth of the Church with the creation of Eve from the side of Adam:

> Moses, commenting on the first man, speaks this way, "bone of my bone, and flesh of my flesh," intimating the side of the Lord. For as God then took [from] the side and formed the woman, so he gave us blood and water from his side and formed the church. As he took the side while Adam was sleeping in an ecstasy, so now he gave blood and water after [Christ's] death, in

13 *Baptismal Catecheses*, 3,15.

14 *Homilies on Matthew*, 4 (PG 57:43) and 8 (57:86). See Wenger, *Huit catéchèses baptismales inédites*, 161.

15 See further exploration of the relation of baptism and Eucharist see Rudolf Brändle "Eucharistie und christliches Leben" 1193-1194.

16 *Baptismal Catecheses*, 3,16.

> the first place, water and then blood. But then it was an ecstasy, now a death has occurred that you may learn that this death was only a form of sleep.[17]

By invoking the original creation of Eve from Adam, John is forthrightly implying that there is a communication from one human being to another. As Eve derived her own humanity from her husband, so the Church as the bride of Christ derives her own life from the humanity of her husband too. While in the preceding section (17) John employed the language of birth to show how the Church was born from Christ's side, this section makes the union even more complete by implying the reality of conjugal union. No greater act of human intimacy can be imagined. As life is communicated through marital union, so the divine life of Christ is communicated through the mysteries.

Although there seems little room for doubt about John's faith in Christ's bodily presence in the Eucharist, he never attempts to explain that presence by any philosophical or theological reasoning. There is, however, one passage that borders on an explanation. John uses his usual acuity of observation and language to speak of something he knows is beyond explanation. He speaks of two important conditions that make Christ present in his body and blood at the liturgy of the Church: words and the Holy Spirit. In his *Homily on the Betrayal of Judas* he gives one of his most explicit statements of the verbal component:

> Christ is present and now he who once arranged that [historical] table also arranges this [present] one. For it is not a man who makes the gifts become the body and blood of Christ. Rather, it is Christ who was crucified on our behalf. The priest stands fulfilling the form [σχῆμα] by uttering those words, but the power and the grace are from God. He says, "This is my body." This utterance transforms the gifts.[18]

Here John echoes the view common among the Church Fathers that Christ the priest is the principal actor in the liturgy. Wanting to show the

17 *Baptismal Catecheses*, 3,18.

18 *Homily 1 on the Betrayal of Judas*, PG 49:380. Jesus Solano, *Textos Eucaristicos Primitivos* (Madrid: Biblioteca de Autores Cristianos, 1952), 1:705. Πάρεστιν ὁ Χριστὸς, καὶ νῦν ἐκεῖνος ὁ τὴν τράπεζαν διακοσμήσας ἐκείνην, οὗτος καὶ ταύτην διακοσμεῖ νῦν. Οὐδὲ γὰρ ἄνθρωπός ἐστιν ὁ ποιῶν τὰ προκείμενα γενέσθαι σῶμα καὶ αἷμα Χριστοῦ, ἀλλ' αὐτὸς ὁ σταυρωθεὶς ὑπὲρ ἡμῶν Χριστός. Σχῆμα πληρῶν ἕστηκεν ὁ ἱερεὺς, τὰ ῥήματα φθεγγόμενος ἐκεῖνα· ἡ δὲ δύναμις καὶ ἡ χάρις τοῦ Θεοῦ ἐστι. Τοῦτό μου ἐστὶ τὸ σῶμα, φησί. Τοῦτο τὸ ῥῆμα μεταῤῥυθμίζει τὰ προκείμενα.

supernatural origin of the sacred meal, Chrysostom stresses that the human priest is a necessary but secondary actor in the consecration of the eucharistic elements. In his choice of vocabulary, John stands almost alone, for no one else seems to have chosen the words he chose, τοῦτο τὸ ῥῆμα μεταῤῥυθμίζει τὰ προκείμενα ("this utterance transforms the gifts") in speaking of the consecratory formula.[19]

Understanding Chrysostom's words is aided by another version of this passage because this homily has come down to us in two forms. It is quite possible that John preached largely the same homily on two different occasions, because the passage in question has slightly different wording: "Christ is present arranging the table, for it is not a man who makes the gifts the body and blood of Christ. The priest only stands fulfilling the form [σχῆμα] and offering petitions. But it is the grace and power of God that is working it all. 'This is my body,' he says. This utterance transforms the gifts."[20]

Slight variations in the wording of these two homilies do not seem to be significant, but his addition of "only" (μόνον) and the priest's petitions (δέησιν προσφέρει) in the second version would seem to underscore the limitation of the priest in contrast with the divine power of Christ speaking through him. In a later chapter, we shall see John's high and lofty view of the priest, but even that view does not rise to the level of the power necessary for the eucharistic transformation.

If the words of Christ transform what lies on the table, what does *transform* mean in this context? What does μεταῤῥυθμίζειν mean in this context? While "transform" may be an adequate first approximation, are there any indications as to what is transformed or how? The root ῥυθμίζειν is also used by Chrysostom in a variety of contexts.[21] John uses the verb in parallel

19 I am not aware of any published English translation of this homily. Batiffol translates the sentence in question "Cette parole transforme les oblats" and comments, "Chrysostome de plus précise un point, savoir, que la convérsion ou sanctification des oblats est produite par la parole même du Christ prononcée par l'évêque" (Pierre Batiffol, *L'Eucharistie: La Presence Réele et la Transubstantiation* [Paris: Libraire Victor Lecoffre, 1930], 415). Rudolf Brandle has a slightly more literal translation, „Durch dieses Wort wird das, was vor uns liegt, verwandelt." See „Eucharistie und christliches Leben" 1200.

20 *Homily 2 on the Betrayal of Judas*, PG 49:389: Πάρεστι καὶ νῦν ὁ Χριστὸς τὴν τράπεζαν κοσμῶν· οὐ γὰρ ἄνθρωπός ἐστιν ὁ ποιῶν τὰ προκείμενα γενέσθαι σῶμα καὶ αἷμα τοῦ Χριστοῦ. Σχῆμα πληρῶν μόνον ἕστηκεν ὁ ἱερεὺς, καὶ δέησιν προσφέρει· ἡ δὲ χάρις καὶ ἡ δύναμίς ἐστιν ἡ τοῦ Θεοῦ ἡ πάντα ἐργαζομένη. Τοῦτό μου ἐστὶ τὸ σῶμα, φησί. Τοῦτο τὸ ῥῆμα τὰ προκείμενα μεταῤῥυθμίζει.

21 Some form of the verb occurs 151 times in the Chrysostom corpus.

with διαπλάττειν in his homilies on the Gospel of John: "Nothing, nothing is stronger than a godly and wise woman to form [ῥυθμίζειν] a man and to shape [διαπλάττειν] his soul in whatever way she pleases."[22] He uses it also in his homily on the widow: "I commanded to shape [διαπλαττειν] and form [ῥυθμίζειν] the one who is tender."[23] So, if ῥυθμίζειν means "to shape or to form," what does μεταῤῥυθμίζειν mean? Here too we find the parallel verb μεταπλάττειν to assist us. In a homily on Hebrews John uses these verbs to stress God's sovereign independence over nature. Speaking in God's voice, John emphasizes that God is not bound by nature and adds, "I am able to alter [μεταπλάττειν] and transform [μεταῤῥυθμίζειν] them, that is, the things of nature."[24] A similar point is made in his commentary on the episode of Noah in Genesis, "Because he is the Creator [demiurge] of nature, he transforms and alters according to his will."[25] These texts witness to the sovereign independence of God over the creation. In John's mind, God is free to create and to change nature according to his will.

This emphasis fits well with Chrysostom's words in the *Homily on the Betrayal of Judas*, for immediately after the consecratory words we have been considering, he invokes the creative power of God. He cites Gn 1:28 ("Be fruitful and multiply") to show how God, who spoke once, can establish a lasting effect in the creation. "It was said once, but through all time it works to enable our nature to bring forth children. In the same way, [Christ's] word once spoken effects the perfected sacrifice on each table in the churches from that time until now, even until his coming."[26] While John makes no attempt to offer a philosophical or theological explanation for the transforming event in terms of substance or being, he is sure of its reality. It might even be accurate to say that Chrysostom would endorse the statement that after the consecration, what looks like bread is not bread but the body of Christ, what appears as wine is not wine but the blood of Christ. Chrysostom desires above all for his hearers to know the transformative power of Christ

22 *Homily 61 on the Gospel of John*, PG 59:340: Οὐδὲν γὰρ, οὐδὲν ἰσχυρότερον γυναικὸς εὐλαβοῦς καὶ συνετῆς, πρὸς τὸ ῥυθμίζειν ἄνδρα, καὶ διαπλάττειν αὐτοῦ τὴν ψυχὴν ἐν οἷς ἂν θέλῃ.

23 *On the Words: Let the Widow Be Chosen*, PG 51:327: Ἀπαλὸν ὄντα διαπλάττειν ἐκέλευσα, καὶ ῥυθμίζειν. He uses a similar construction in *Against the Opponents of Monastic Life*, PG 47:381.

24 *Homily 25 on Hebrews*, PG 63:175: διὸ καὶ μεταπλάττειν καὶ μεταῤῥυθμίζειν αὐτὰ δύναμαι.

25 *Homily 25 on Genesis*, PG 53:224: Δημιουργὸς γὰρ ὢν τῆς φύσεως κατὰ τὸ αὐτῷ δοκοῦν ἅπαντα μεταῤῥυθμίζει καὶ μεταπλάττει.

26 *Homily 1 on the Betrayal of Judas*, PG 49:380.

himself. In the context of the homily on Judas's betrayal, he draws attention to Christ's words so that he may exhort his hearers to prepare their hearts for holy communion and to avoid the deception of Judas. The strength of those exhortations rests on a firm conviction that the Eucharist contains the presence of Christ as real as if he were on earth. The presence is made real in the Church's liturgy because Christ speaks his own words to give his body and blood.

John's invoking of Christ's eucharistic words as an agent of transformation certainly has echoes in the Western Church. Ambrose speaks of the transforming power of Christ's consecratory words:

> But if a human blessing could accomplish something so great, what can we say of the divine consecration itself where the very words of the Lord and Savior are at work? For that sacrament which you receive is made [*conficitur*] by the word of Christ. If Elijah's word accomplished so much, won't Christ's word be powerful enough to change the nature [*species*] of the elements? You read about the entirety of the works in the universe, "Because he said it and it happened; he commanded and they were created." So, the word of Christ, which was able to make from nothing [*ex nihilo*] what did not exist, can it not change what does exist into something else? For it is not anything less to bring about new things than it is to change their natures.[27]

While there are numerous witnesses from the Western Fathers expressing similar ideas, Ambrose (d. 397) is particularly apposite because he was an older contemporary of John Chrysostom. This concurrence suggests that in the fourth century the transformative power of the consecratory words of Christ was embraced by both East and West. If a greater emphasis on those words as a transformative instrument resided in the West, the same was not absent from the East. As we will see, these varying emphases became a wide rift between the East and West, so much so that Nicholas Cabasilas in the fourteenth century was compelled to answer the objections of the Latins against the Eastern order of liturgy.[28]

John Chrysostom believed in what would later be called the real presence, but he never named it as such. He was sure that Christ's presence in the

27 Ambrose, *On the Mysteries*, 9.52. The Latin text with Italian translation can be found in Gerardo di Nola, ed., *Cristo, Eucaristia, la Vergine Madre del Signore* (Vatican: Libreria Edictrice Vaticana, 1997), 134–37.

28 Nicholas Cabasilas, *A Commentary on the Divine Liturgy*, trans. J. M. Hussey and P. A. McNulty (Crestwood, NY: St. Vladimir's Seminary Press, 2002); see sections 27–30.

Eucharist could not be a result of human ingenuity or effort. It had to be a divine work. The ordained priest had a necessary role to play, but his human powers were unequal to the holy and supernatural event that takes place in the liturgy. If words were important to John in general, the words of Christ were infinitely more so. Those words were essential for making the bread and wine into the body and blood of Christ. Of themselves, however, those words were not the only supernatural power needed to make the sacrament of Christ's humanity present on the sacred table (altar). The presence of the Holy Spirit was needed. When the Spirit and the Word combined, then every Christian could be certain that "the body here is the fullness of Christ."[29]

EPICLESIS: THE ROLE OF THE HOLY SPIRIT

The liturgy was certainly a meeting of heaven and earth in Chrysostom's mind. What was the active principle in bringing about that union? What role did God play and what role did the earthly Church play? The Eastern churches have from ancient times insisted on the importance of the Epiclesis, the calling down of the Holy Spirit to make the sacramental signs into the true body and blood of Christ. *Epiclesis* became a technical term in Christian Greek to designate the portion of the liturgy in which the Holy Spirit is invoked to come down on the gifts of bread and wine. Such a usage must have been a development later than Chrysostom's time because he never uses the noun *Epiclesis* to speak of a portion of the liturgy in this way.[30] John does, however, use a number of verbs that point to the same reality and that remind his hearers that there is nothing good in the liturgy or in the Christian life without the work of the Holy Spirit. Toward the end of a

29 *Homily 82 on Matthew*, PG 58:745.

30 By the early eighth century John Damascene is clearly using the word as a technical term: "God said, 'This is my body' and 'This is my blood' and 'Do this in remembrance of me.' And it comes about by his all-powerful ordinance 'until he comes.' So he said, 'until he comes' and the rain takes place in this new vineyard through the Epiclesis, that is, the power of the Holy Spirit overshadowing it." And Damascene continues, "Now you ask how the bread can become the body of Christ and the wine and water the blood of Christ? I tell you, the Holy Spirit visits with his presence and makes these things something beyond reason and understanding" (*On the Orthodox Faith*, 4,13).

homily on the resurrection John gives a clear and ringing affirmation of the essential role of the Spirit in the life of the Church:

> If there were no down payment of the Spirit now, there would be no baptism, no forgiveness of sins, no righteousness and holiness. We would have no adoption and enjoy no mysteries. There can never be any mystical body and blood without the grace of the Spirit. We would have no priests. And all these things could never be established apart from that visitation. And there are many other symbols of the grace of the Spirit so that because you have the down payment of the Spirit, the death of the soul can be taken away, the hardening of thought and an impure life can be eradicated. So let us not be vexed at future things, because we receive such things as pledges.[31]

Here Chrysostom attempts to reassure his congregation of the certainty of the future resurrection of believers. The "down payment of the Holy Spirit" is one among many signs that God will bring about what he promised. Here too John asserts that "there can never be any mystical body and blood without the grace of the Spirit." While the ordained priest must perform the form (σχῆμα) of the divine liturgy, words are not enough because an active agent is needed to bring about the transformation of bread and wine into Christ's body and blood. The Holy Spirit is that agent who is present behind and within the Church's sacramental ministry. When John speaks of the Eucharist as spiritual food, it is not because it is immaterial but because the food from heaven is made life-giving by the presence of the Holy Spirit. It is spiritual because it comes from and by the Spirit.

That the Holy Spirit is actively at work in the Church, manifested most fully in its liturgy, John has no doubt. It is the visitation of the Spirit that marks the Church's distinctiveness among the human institutions of this world. No other organization has "the down payment of the Spirit" that is able to lift Christians from the mundane affairs of this world to the glories of the world to come: "And there are many other symbols of the grace of the Spirit . . . because you have the down payment of the Spirit." Chrysostom picks up on Paul's use of ἀρραβών in 2 Cor 1:22; 5:5 and Eph 1:14. In the Corinthian passages "the down payment of the Spirit" is a gift from God and in Ephesians the phraseology slightly varies. "The down payment of our inheritance" is a result of the believer being "sealed with the Holy Spirit of promise." John

31 *Homily on the Resurrection of the Dead*, PG 50:432.

reads the Corinthian passages epexegetically so that "the down payment of the Spirit" means that the down payment is "the Spirit in our hearts."[32] He makes explicit what is implicit in Eph 1:14. This text might be read as saying that the Spirit's presence produces the down payment, but John sees the Spirit itself as the down payment.[33] The present reality of the Spirit ensures the future reality in much the same way as the present Eucharist is a kind of down payment on the future reality of the kingdom.

References to the work of the Holy Spirit in the divine liturgy and in the lives of Christians are scattered through a wide range of Chrysostom's works. We observed earlier in the treatise on the priesthood how John viewed the episode of Elijah on Mt. Carmel as an anticipation of the superiority of the new covenant and the Eucharist. He saw Elijah's calling down fire from heaven (1 Kgs 18:36–40) as prophetic of a greater fire falling, the fire of the Holy Spirit:

> So now, move from there to the sacrifice being now completed. Not only is it awesome to see, but it surpasses all amazement. For the priest stands there, not bringing down fire, but the Holy Spirit. And the priest himself makes much supplication, not so that a kind of torch may consume the gifts lying there. Rather, it is so that the grace coming on the sacrifice through [that prayer] may lift up the souls of all, and shine forth more brightly than silver refined by fire.[34]

The fire that fell on Elijah's sacrifice consumed what was upon the altar; the Spirit's fall on the sacred table brings grace capable of lifting up the recipient to something greater than natural fire. And yet for all the differences between the old sacrifice on the stone altar and new sacrifice of the Eucharist, both have the same goal of having the people recognize the true and living God (1 Kgs 18:39). Chrysostom does not let the opportunity pass to emphasize that God's grace is also a consuming fire: "Or don't you know that a human soul was not even able to bear the fire of that sacrifice but that

32 In the phrase of 2 Cor 1:22, τὸν ἀρραβῶνα τοῦ πνεύματος ἐν ταῖς καρδίαις ἡμῶν, the genitive τοῦ πνεύματος is in all probability epexegetical. The Spirit is another way of saying, "the down payment": see F. Blass and A. Debrunner, *A Grammar of the Greek New Testament and Other Early Christian Literature* (Chicago: University of Chicago Press, 1961), 92.

33 The textual variants of Eph 1:14 show the ambiguity perceived by the copyists. Some MSS have *ho*, which is read by the Nestle text 28th ed. and the UBS5. Nestle 22nd has the masculine ὅς.

34 *On the Priesthood*, 3,4.

all would be utterly destroyed if there were not a lot of help from the grace of God?"[35]

It is significant, I aver, that John included this analogy between Elijah and the Epiclesis in his treatise on the priesthood. Thereby he perhaps hoped to accomplish two goals at once, that is, to remind priests and people of the inherent dignity of the priesthood and at the same time to remind every priest that the privilege and power of the Eucharist come not from himself but from God, who transforms the gifts so as to nourish souls to heaven. A little later in that same treatise John teaches both: "When he [the priest] calls on the Holy Spirit and completes that awesome sacrifice, he touches the one who is the common Master of all. In what order shall we place him [the priest]?"[36]

The descent of the Holy Spirit on that same sacrifice on the sacred table creates a unique and unrepeatable reality in the liturgy. In the cemetery outside Antioch John exhorted his pilgrim church to stand in awe of the Spirit's work: "When the priest stands in front of the table stretching out his hands to heaven, calling on the Holy Spirit to come down and touch the offerings, there should be much silence, much quietness whenever the Spirit gives the grace, whenever He comes down and touches the offerings."[37] What results from the Spirit's touching the sacrifice of the priest and the Church? As we saw in chapter 3, it is to make Christ as really present in the Church as he was on earth in the Incarnation, "for the Master's body shall lie here too, not wrapped in swaddling clothes as then, but wrapped on every side with the Holy Spirit."[38] Just as the true divinity of the Son of God lay wrapped and hidden in swaddling clothes, so the true humanity and divinity of the same in the Eucharist lies wrapped in the embrace of the Holy Spirit. And that means that the table of Christ becomes an instrument for giving the Spirit: "That table [of Christ's last supper] was not at that time made of silver nor the cup of gold in which Christ gave his blood to his disciples, but everything there was nevertheless precious and awe-inspiring because he filled them with his Spirit."[39] It was the Holy Spirit who made the table of the Lord that

35 *On the Priesthood*, 3,4. In chapter 6 we return to the importance and function of the priesthood.

36 *On the Priesthood*, 3,4.

37 *The Cemetery and the Cross*, PG 49:398.

38 *On Blessed Philogonius*, PG 48:755.

39 *Homily 82 on Matthew*, PG 58:740.

the martyr Luciano recalled when tempted to eat defiled food: "Seeing that defiled and cursed table, he remembered a different table that was awe-inspiring and full of the Holy Spirit. And so he was burning with fire when choosing to endure and suffer rather than taste of those defiled meats."[40]

All these texts, diverse though they are, stress the importance of the Holy Spirit in sanctifying both the gifts of the altar and the people of the Church. One passage in the fourth *Homily on Holy Pentecost*, however, stands out in its emphasis on the role of the Spirit in the Church. Some of its language is reminiscent of that in the *Homily on the Resurrection* when it says, "If there were no Holy Spirit, there would be no shepherds and teachers in the Church. These come through the Spirit, as Paul says, 'Among whom the Holy Spirit has set you as shepherds and bishops' [Acts 20:28]. Don't you see that this is through the Spirit?"[41] As the shepherds of the Church have been given through the Spirit's work, so too their ministry at the altar would be impossible without the presence of the Holy Spirit:

> But whenever he stands at this sacred table, when he is about to offer that awesome sacrifice—those initiated know what is being said—he does not first touch the gifts until he invokes grace from the Lord. And you say to him, "and with your Spirit," reminding them with this response that he who is present does nothing nor are the gifts from human nature. The grace of the Spirit being present and hovering over all, prepares the mystical sacrifice.[42]

Perhaps worried that the people needed to be reminded again, John thus stresses that "the one present is a man, but it is God who is working through him"[43] who effects the required transformation and nothing of this work is a result of human ingenuity or achievement. It is the grace brought by the Spirit "hovering over" the gifts that produces "the mystical sacrifice." This all resonates with Cyril of Jerusalem's insistence that it is not the visible and the tangible that makes the Eucharist great. "Don't pay attention to the nature of what is seen but attend to the invisible grace. There is nothing human in what happens in this sacred seat [βῆμα]. If the Spirit were not present, the church would not be constituted here. But since the church is constituted, it is

40 *Homily on Saint Luciano Martyr*, PG 50:524.

41 *Homily 4 on Holy Pentecost*, PG 50:458.

42 *Homily 4 on Holy Pentecost*, PG 50:458–59.

43 *Homily 4 on Holy Pentecost*, PG 50:459.

evident that the Spirit is present."[44] Like his predecessors, John Chrysostom wanted to lift the eyes of his flock up to heaven, to a celestial table where the sacrificial lamb truly resided. What he knew was that there could no participation in the heavenly realm without the Holy Spirit's presence and work. In fact, John even goes so far as to say that the Church's very existence depends on the presence of the Spirit. The glory and majesty of the liturgy consists of its bringing that heaven down to earth. The mystical sacrifice on the sacred table made the union possible, a union only made real by the descent of the Holy Spirit on the Church and the altar.[45]

THE EPICLESIS IN EAST AND WEST: A SHORT INTERLUDE

While our focus is not on the history of liturgy, it may be well to pause and reflect on the Epiclesis for a brief moment since it became so important in the Eastern traditions of which John Chrysostom was a participant and exponent. At the heart of the Eastern conception of Christian faith is the belief that in the divine liturgy one encounters the kingdom of God in a profound way.[46] As Alexander Schmemann explained, the ancient Christian idea of "symbol" is a far cry from the modern idea of a bare, arbitrary signification without any interior meaning or presence.[47] Entrance into the liturgy of the Church is entrance into the kingdom of God, where *sumbolon* is a manifestation of something real, in this case the Holy Spirit, that makes present a spiritual reality from the world beyond.

The role of the Holy Spirit in transforming the gifts of bread and wine, however, is not the exclusive possession of the Christian East. The current eucharistic prayers of the Roman West contain the Epiclesis as well, which

44 *Homily 4 on Holy Pentecost*, PG 50:459.

45 Two recent prominent Orthodox theologians have emphasized how the Eucharist makes the Church: John Zizioulas, *Eucharist, Bishop, Church: The Unity of the Church in the Divine Eucharist and the Bishop during the First Three Centuries* (Brookline, MA: Holy Cross Orthodox Press, 2001), and Alexander Schmemann, *The Eucharist: Sacrament of the Kingdom* (Crestwood, NY: St. Vladimir's Press, 1987), 166.

46 This theme is explored in Vassilios Papavassiliou, *Journey to the Kingdom: An Insider's Look at the Liturgy and Beliefs of the Eastern Orthodox Church* (Brewster, MA: Paraclete Press, 2012).

47 Alexander Schmemann, *For the Life of the World* (Crestwood, NY: St. Vladimir's Press, 1973), 27–31.

usually comes in two forms. One is the descent of the Spirit on the gifts and the other is the fullness of the Spirit invoked on the people of God. In Western liturgies, the Epiclesis for the gifts *precedes* the words of consecration. In the third canon of the current Western Mass, for example, the priest invokes the Holy Spirit with these words as he approaches the institution narrative:

> And so, Father, we bring you these gifts.
> We ask you to make them holy by the power of your Spirit,
> that they may become the body and blood of your Son, our Lord,
> Jesus Christ.

The second eucharistic prayer, adapted from the Canon of Hippolytus, contains similar language:

> Lord, you are holy indeed,
> The fountain of all holiness.
> Let your Spirit come upon these gifts to make them holy
> So that they may become for us
> The body and blood of our Lord, Jesus Christ.

Even the Roman canon (first eucharistic prayer), though less direct in its language, expresses similar teachings in a more general manner:[48]

> Which oblation may you, O God, consider it right
> to make blessed, approved, ratified, reasonable, and acceptable
> that it may become for us the Body and Blood
> of Your most Beloved Son
> Our Lord Jesus Christ.[49]

48 See a discussion of the problem of the lack of an Epiclesis in the Roman Canon in Daniel Cardo, *The Cross and the Eucharist in Early Christianity: A Theological and Liturgical Investigation* (Cambridge: Cambridge University Press, 2019), 142–49. Cardo argues that although there is not an explicit "pneumatological epiclesis" in the Roman Canon, "the ancient gesture of signing with the Cross confers this benedictory sanctification, fulfilled through the recitation of the Institution Narrative and the whole anaphora" (149).

49 The usual translation is "Bless and approve our offering / make it acceptable to you / an offering in spirit and truth / let it become for us / the body and blood of Jesus Christ / your only Son, our Lord." I have chosen to update an older translation of this prayer rather than employ the one currently in use. I find the current translation too loose and inaccurate.

In the second canon, after the consecration and memorial acclamation (*anamnesis*), the priest again prays for the invocation of the Holy Spirit, this time to come on the people for great unity in the Church:

> May all of us who share in the body and blood of Christ
> Be brought together in unity by the Holy Spirit.

The third eucharistic prayer is even more explicit:

> Grant that we, who are nourished by his body and blood,
> be filled with his Holy Spirit,
> And become one body, one spirit in Christ.[50]

John Chrysostom may not have known any of this language in the liturgies of Antioch or Constantinople, but the underlying theological meaning was familiar enough. The Liturgy of St. John Chrysostom, although likely originating after John's time in its present form, honors his name with the same invocation of the Holy Spirit as we see in the current Western canons. Unlike the Western order, in this liturgy the Epiclesis comes *after* the words of consecration:

> Again we offer to You this reasonable worship without shedding blood
> And we appeal to You, we ask, and beg,
> Send down your Holy Spirit on us and on these gifts presented here.
> Make this bread the precious body of your Christ
> And in this cup [make the wine] the precious blood of your Christ.
> Changing them by your Holy Spirit, Amen, Amen, Amen.[51]

While these words may not have been the exact ones John Chrysostom used in his liturgies, the reference to the Spirit and his transformative work would have no doubt been deeply embedded in the worship of his time. And what we saw scattered throughout his homilies shows the same teaching

50 The various canons (anaphora) currently used in the Western Church were instituted under the liturgical reforms of Paul VI and are based with modifications on the Antiochene structure. See Enrico Mazza, *The Celebration of the Eucharist: The Origin of the Rite and the Development of Its Interpretation* (Collegeville, MN: Liturgical Press, 1999), 49–61.

51 Translated from the Greek text in *The Divine Liturgy of Saint John Chrysostom* (Brookline, MA: Holy Cross Orthodox Press, 1985), 22. My translation differs slightly from the English in current use. I have chosen "reasonable" for *logikos* rather than "spiritual" to make the reference to Rom 12:1 clear.

reflected in this Epiclesis. With the Spirit's descent, the body and blood of Christ is a true sacrifice that draws the people of God into reasonable worship without shedding blood.

There has long been a perception that the East and the West differ over the relation of the Epiclesis to the words of consecration inasmuch as the West has emphasized the consecratory words of Christ as the moment of the transformation while the East has placed greater emphasis on the Epiclesis without any further specification as to the moment of transformation. This seemed to be crystallized in the medieval dogmatic definition at the Council of Florence (1431–49). That council defined the words of the Savior as the "form of the sacrament," but the later *Catechism of the Catholic Church* (1994) distinguished between the words as a formal cause and the Holy Spirit as a kind of efficient cause without using the exact term.[52] I suggest that there is an underlying unity in the differences between the East and West in the theology of the Epiclesis. It seems to me unnecessarily narrow to insist on either the words of institution or the Epiclesis as the sole or even primary means of transformation. My appreciation for the work of Alexander Schmemann is enormous, but he seems to have downplayed the role of the words of consecration when stating that "the Orthodox Church has always insisted that the transformation (*metabole*) of the eucharistic elements is performed by the epiclesis—the invocation of the Holy Spirit—and not by the words of institution."[53] In the West, Frans van der Pavard seems to have adopted the same attitude about the East. even to the point of denying any consecratory value in the words of institution.[54]

Yet it seems that the transformation of the bread and wine was understood by John Chrysostom as a symbiotic relation between the work of the Spirit and the role of the human priest speaking Christ's words. That same symbiosis of the divine and the human surfaced ten centuries later when this difference between the East and the West became acute. In his *Commentary on the Divine Liturgy*, Nicholas Cabasilas (1322–92) states in vivid language the definitive power of the consecratory words:

52 CCC §1353. For a discussion of this matter see Lawrence Feingold, *The Eucharist: Mystery of Presence, Sacrifice, and Communion* (Steubenville, OH: Emmaus Academic Press, 2018), 205–12.

53 Schmemann, *For the Life of the World*, 43–44.

54 Frans van de Paverd, *Zur Geschichte der Meßliturgie in Antiocheia und Konstantinopel gegen Ende des vierten Jahrhunderts - Analyse der Quellen bei Johannes Chrysostomos* (= Orientalia Christiana Analecta 187) Rome, 1970. See the discussion by Brändle in "Eucharistie und christliches Leben" 1200-1207.

> Once these words [of consecration] are spoken, the entirety of the divine liturgy is done and complete and the gifts sanctified. The sacrifice is complete and the great, divine sacrificial victim, slain for the world, is seen lying on the holy table. The bread of the Lord's body is no longer a type nor a simple gift as if bearing an image of the true gift nor bearing in itself an inscription of the saving sufferings like on a tablet. Rather, now it is the true gift, the all-holy body of the Master.[55]

These words, isolated from their context, may give credence to the idea that the words of consecration are as determinative for the East as they are for the West. And as we have seen, there is no doubt that Christ's words are transformative for Eastern believers, but Cabasilas proceeds to answer objections of the "Latins" that they leveled against the East. While Cabasilas's answers to these objections are worthy of close attention, I would like to emphasize how he avoids unnecessary polemics and argues in the end for a similarity in underlying theology between the East and West. Nicholas cites passages from the Roman liturgy to show that "it is not the whole Latin church which condemns the prayer for the offering after the words of consecration, but only a few innovators who are causing her harm in other ways."[56] Cabasilas appears to me to be a guide for understanding differing emphases of the East and the West. And John Chrysostom is a source of faith (*lex credendi*) for both East and West.

The relation of Christ's words of consecration to the Epiclesis of the Spirit is more than a theological conundrum or a passing fancy of theologians. It is another expression of the *oikonomia* in which there is a delicate cooperation of the divine and the human, a symbiosis that runs like an arrow through all redemptive history. Its climax of course is in the Word-Become-Flesh. The Incarnation itself in which the power of the Holy Spirit brings about the impregnation of the Theotokos requires Mary's consent. Both were vital to the miracle (Lk 1:35–38). So if at the most important juncture of history—the moment that made salvation possible—divine power is manifested in union with human cooperation, should we expect anything less in the liturgy of the Church that celebrates that salvation? Although there are differing emphases between the Byzantine and the Latin liturgical traditions, both acknowledge

55 Cabasilas, *A Commentary on the Divine Liturgy*, section 27.

56 Cabasilas, *A Commentary on the Divine Liturgy*, 79.

that the two aspects of the word of Christ and the power of the Holy Spirit are vital to the eucharistic transformation.

WHAT KIND OF SACRIFICE?

John Chrysostom never hesitated to speak of the Eucharist as a sacrifice. Whatever specific meaning he attributed to the word with reference to the sacrament, he was happy to celebrate not only the presence of Christ's body and blood but its presence as a sacrifice. The sense of wonder we detected in his words about the liturgy could be equally applied to the sacrifice of the Eucharist in particular:

> The sacrifice is in the hands [of the priest] and everything is ready. The angels and the archangels are present. The Son of God is present. All are standing with that awesome sacrifice. Those stand by shouting while the rest are silent. Do you think these things simply happen? Are the other things simply [there]: the things [prayers] done for the Church, and the gifts offered for the priests and the things [offered] for the fullness of the congregation? May it never be! But all this happens with faith.[57]

What then was the nature of that sacrifice in the hands of the priests? Perhaps the answer lies in how John views the cross. In his *Homily on the Cross and the Thief*, John insisted that the crucifixion of Christ was a sacrifice and that the cross was the altar on which he offered that sacrifice:

> It was on the cross that Christ was sacrificed. Where there is a sacrifice, there is the forgiveness of sins, there reconciliation with the Master, there a feast and joy. "For Christ, our Passover, has been sacrificed for us." Where was he sacrificed? Up on a high scaffold, a new altar for this sacrifice since it is both new and startling. The same man was both sacrifice and priest, a sacrifice according to the flesh, a priest according to the Spirit.[58]

The sacrifice of the cross, then, is an occasion of great joy and festivity precisely because of its place both in history and in liturgy: "You see how there was a sacrifice and a priest, and the cross was his altar."[59] So John

57 *Homily 21 on the Acts of the Apostles*, PG 60:170.

58 *The Cross and the Thief*, PG 49:399.

59 *The Cross and the Thief*, PG 49:399.

attempts to draw out several implications from the details of the crucifixion. He asks why Christ was crucified high on a scaffold and not under the roof of the temple or within the city walls. John has more than a practical answer; there are two theological reasons. One is that he wanted to "cleanse the nature of air"; the other to show that Christ's sacrifice was universal (καθολική), not limited to one nation. Christ's "offering was for the whole earth . . . common to all" and thereby he "cleansed the whole world [and] every place became a place of prayer." The fact that the eucharistic sacrifice opens up the doors of heaven to join the celestial world to the mundane world surely points to a profound belief in the sacrificial nature of the Eucharist.

With these guiding thoughts, we may well ask what the connection is between the sacrifice of the cross and that of the sacred table. Is the Christian sacrifice Christ's real body and blood? And what sense of sacrifice does John mean? Is it the sacrifice of praise? The sacrifice of thanksgiving? Is the sacrifice on the church's altar the same as that of Calvary? The texts quoted earlier from *On the Priesthood* certainly point to the fullest sense of sacrifice one can imagine: "When you see the Lord sacrificed and lying there and the priest standing with the sacrifice praying along with all who have become red with that precious blood," etc.[60] The Lord sacrificed on the altar? Was Christ crucified once again? Was "the precious blood" on the lips of believers a mere symbol of the blood shed? Or was this the blood of the cross? What is the connection between the sacrifice on the altar of the church and the altar of the cross? If both are true sacrifices, then how are they related to each other?

To my knowledge, John Chrysostom never addresses these questions directly, but he does provide indirect evidence in his homilies, of which two of the most important have to do with multiplication of liturgies and celebrants. Does the timing of the liturgy make a difference? Does it matter which liturgical season is being celebrated? If so, what difference does it make? For John, no one divine service is more efficacious than another:

> The mystery in the Pascha contains nothing more than what is now being done. It is one and the same, this grace of the Spirit. It is always Pascha. You who are initiated know this. On Friday, Saturday, and from Sunday to Sunday as well as the martyrs' days this sacrifice is accomplished [ἐπιτελεῖται]. . . . Paul did not circumscribe the sacrifice with a specific limitation of time. How was it then called the Pascha? Because it was at that

60 *On the Priesthood*, 3,4.

> time that Christ suffered for us.[61] Pascha [Easter] is for proclaiming [his] death. The offering that happens today and the one yesterday and every day is like the one that takes place on the Sabbath day and that is not more solemn than this nor is this one more paltry than that one. Both are one and the same; both are awesome and full of salvation.[62]

One can hear beneath his words the natural tendency of his congregation to think of Pascha (Easter) as more important, more celebratory, and more life-giving than other liturgies. While the uniqueness of Pascha days lies in being the time when the Lord died and rose again from the dead, the essence of every liturgy is the same. John then holds to a principle of liturgical unity in which the sameness of every divine service can best be explained by what is there in the liturgy. In every celebration the same reality is present:

> There is one power, one value, one grace, one body and the same body, not one holier than the other nor one less than the other. And you know this too when you see nothing newer than these worldly veils and an illustrious multitude. Now those days of Pascha have something more because our day of salvation took its beginning from them since Christ was sacrificed on that day. In sum, by the mysteries [those days] have no superior claim.[63]

The unity implicit in and between every liturgy resides in the same realities being present there. If the realities of salvation are present in every liturgy, then they can only be so because of an identity between the body that lies on the altar of the Church and the body that hung on the altar of the cross. This comes out even more clearly in John's *Homily 17 on Hebrews*. John is commenting on Heb 10:3, where the author says that the reason that God commanded the Jews to have an annual celebration was to remind them of their sins. John contrasts the repeated sacrifices of the Jews with the one final sacrifice of Christ in the Eucharist. He has either heard or anticipates the natural objection:

> But do we not bring an offering every day? We do indeed bring an offering, but it is a remembrance of his death. There is only one, not many. How is there only one and not many? It is because he [Christ] was offered up once for all like that [sacrifice] was brought into the holy of holies. This thing

61 *Homily 5 on 1 Timothy*, PG 62:530.

62 *Homily 3 against the Jews*, PG 48:867.

63 *Homily 5 on 1 Timothy*, PG 62:530.

> [*touto*] is a sign of that sacrifice and this sacrifice is also a sign of that one. It is always the same One we offer, not one sheep today and another tomorrow. It is always the same so there is only one sacrifice. By the same token are there many Christs since he is offered in many places? Absolutely not! The one Christ is offered everywhere, being fully present here and there, one body. As he who is offered in many places is one body and there are not many bodies, thus also there is only one sacrifice.[64]

The overriding message here is the oneness of every Eucharist. John's stress on the unity of every liturgical sacrifice leaves little doubt that he saw a deep connection and identity between the sacrifice on the altar of the cross and those in the liturgy of the Church. This belief explains the unity of all liturgies—different times and different places, but they all possess the same offering, the same sacrifice, because each one is in fact the sacrifice of Christ on the cross.

If there is a real presence of Christ's sacrifice in every divine service, then what does John mean in this homily by "the remembrance of his death"? Quoting Jesus's words, "Do this in remembrance of me," John gives this gloss, "We are bringing about the remembrance of the sacrifice." Perhaps John simply means that a memorial is taking place, a ceremony in memory of the one original sacrifice of Calvary. Yet I would contend that by *remembrance* John means something much more than the bare meaning of *anamnesis* (ἀνάμνησις) as "memory" or "remembrance." Earlier, I argued that *sumbolon* cannot be understood in the modern signification of "symbol" but must be understood in the manner of a sacrament as a sign that carries what it signifies. In a similar way *anamnesis* points to an extra-mental reality. In its classical (pre-Christian) usage, the word did sometimes simply mean "recollection" or "remembrance," but in Plato *anamnesis* took on a heightened meaning as the process whereby the realities in the world of forms are instantiated in the material world. This added meaning underlay Christian usage to signify that the mental recall provoked by the Church's celebration was triggered as it were by the presence of the reality. Thus, the recall of the death of Christ was possible because that sacrificial death was present in the liturgy. *Homily 17 on Hebrews* certainly suggests this with its emphasis on the unity and identity of all eucharistic celebrations. This hearkens back to the idea of actualization, which is hardly an invention of the ancient Church,

64 *Homily 17 on Hebrews*, PG 63:131.

much less only those in the East like John.[65] As noted earlier, the roots of this important idea stretch back into ancient Israel. Israel's corporate worship aimed at a cultic retrieval of past redemptive history. Actualization made the events of salvation such as the Exodus present in the experience of worship, or as Childs puts it, "Israel in every generation remembers and so shares in the same redemptive time."[66] Their collective memory was rather a liturgical, cultic experience in which personal memories were stimulated and engaged by the cult of the ancient tabernacle/temple.

When John referred to the sacrifice of Christ on the sacred table of the Church, he did so for more reasons than simply to affirm an identity between the two. As in so many of his homilies, his overriding concern was to exhort his hearers to a better Christian life. Nothing could be better than love, the kind of love Christ himself showed in his sacrifice. As the Paschal Mystery of Jesus was for the salvation of the world, so the Christian must live for the salvation of his neighbor. And there could be no more effective way than to recognize the saving power of eucharistic mystery: "The offerings are not given in vain for the dead nor are prayers or alms in vain."[67] His emphasis that these offerings are not "in vain" reveals both that he shared the universal faith in the efficacy of the Eucharist for the deceased and that he was deeply concerned that his flock not minimize the power of God's spiritual order.

We will observe in chapter 7 how John was anxious to wake his people from the complacency of indifference, something quite akin to acedia. Indifference to higher realities sometimes plagued ancient Christians as much as it does modern ones. The practical equation John makes in his *Homilies on the Acts of the Apostles* between the offerings on the altar, prayers, and alms reflects the Lenten advice of many ancient writers in which spiritual benefit and progress is made because of the underlying unity of all these pious exercises. What could be more like Christ and bring his forgiveness more than to live in charity with the living and the dead? To live for the salvation of others is the preeminent way to Christ: "You have become the cause of salvation for someone while he is the cause of alms for you. Do not doubt that something beneficial has borne fruit."[68] The Christian then enters into

65 For references to *anamnesis* in other Fathers of the Church, see Cardo, *The Cross and the Eucharist*, 49–50, 148.

66 Brevard S. Childs, *Memory and Tradition in Israel* (London: SCM Press, 1962), 54.

67 *Homily 21 on the Acts of the Apostles*, PG 60:170.

68 *Homily 21 on the Acts of the Apostles*, PG 60:170.

the salvific plan of God and thereby becomes a conduit of divine grace, not only in giving alms to others but in receiving alms as well. Both giver and receiver reap spiritual benefits for each other because they come to embody the sacrificial life of Christ.

It is therefore inconceivable for a Christian to be indifferent to the need to live in peace with his fellow believers in particular and his fellow human beings in general. Perhaps the highest expression of Christ's sacrifice is to live in peace:

> Christ lies here slaughtered. For what reason and why? It is to make peace between things in heaven and things on earth, to make you a friend of angels, to reconcile you to the God of all, you who are an enemy and adversary. He did it to make you his friend. He gave his life [ψυχήν] for those who hate [him]. But do you remain at enmity with your fellow servant? How can you approach the table of peace?[69]

John's vivid language ("Christ lies here slaughtered") highlights his strong exhortation to reconciliation based on understanding the purpose for which Christ was sacrificed, "Yes, he says, this sacrifice is here for the sake of peace with your brother."[70] If it is true that "the Son of God came down to reconcile our nature to the Master," then the Christian has the highest moral obligation to seek reconciliation and peace. Yet the flip side is also true. The sacrifice of the slain Lamb lying on the altar is the very strength opening up the possibility of peace.

John Chrysostom—and a host of later theologians East and West—spoke of Christ's presence in the Eucharist in spite of the inherent limitations involved in the enterprise. Many have affirmed it and all have assumed it but none has explained it. John affirms not how the Eucharist is a real sacrifice but who the real agent of bringing it about is:

> It is not the priest's life or virtue that accomplishes so great a thing, is it? Aren't such things given by God as accomplished by priestly virtue? The entire matter comes from grace. The priest only opens his mouth and God accomplishes the entire affair. The priest only acts as a symbol. . . . No man can be so much greater than John the Baptist was with respect to Jesus. But

69 *Homily 1 on the Betrayal of Judas*, PG 49:381.

70 *Homily 1 on the Betrayal of Judas*, PG 49:382.

> the Spirit came down on him that you might know that the whole thing is accomplished by God because it is God who does the whole thing.[71]

John's insistence on the priest as a human conduit through whom the Divine Author works aids in a better understanding not only of the origin of the power involved but also the nature of the eucharistic sacrifice itself. He continues to expound this truth by emphasizing that not only is Christ himself the principal actor but that fact makes each and every celebration of the Eucharist the same:

> This offering is the same whether it is Paul or Peter doing it. It is the same in fact that Christ did and that he gave to the disciples; the same as the priests now do. This is nothing less than that [offering] because it is not men who make this holy but the One who sanctifies it himself. As the words that God uttered are the same that the priest now speaks, so also the offering is the same like the way he gave baptism. Everything comes from the Faith. . . . Whoever considers this to be less than that body does not know that Christ is now present and at work.[72]

So while John never sought to explain the presence of Christ in the Eucharist, he did make clear the essential truth that Christ's presence is the same as when Jesus was on earth. More importantly, he identified the one sacrifice of Christ's death with each and every sacrifice (offerings) on the Church's altars. The same priest, Jesus Christ, was acting behind and through every priest on earth in offering himself as sacrifice.

In *Homily 82 on Matthew* we noticed the vivid language John uses when he speaks of Christ being present to the believer living well after his time on earth: "Look, you do see him, you touch him, you eat him. Yes, you desire to see his garments, but he gives you himself not only to be seen but to be touched, eaten, and taken within." That such graphic phrases could be used of Christ in the Eucharist surfaces again in his *Homily 46 on the Gospel of John*, where we hear, "Christ did this to lead us to a greater love of friendship, showing us his desire, that he not only gives to those who desire to see him, but even to touch him, to eat, and to bite their teeth into his flesh,

71 *Homily 2 on 2 Timothy*, PG 62:612.

72 *Homily 2 on 2 Timothy*, PG 62:612.

to be interwoven [with him], and to be filled with all desire."[73] It is hard to imagine how Christ could be more real for the Christian people who approach his table.

✠ ✠ ✠

Earlier we wondered out loud how the historical Jesus could be present to subsequent generations of Christians who had never known him in his earthly sojourn. Although John Chrysostom clearly affirmed the real presence of Christ in the eucharistic liturgy through the ministry of the Holy Spirit and his descent on the gifts (offerings), we can still ask if this really answers our question of the how (i.e., the means or mechanisms) of such a presence. If such a question were put to John today, I am convinced that he would reject the formulation of the question, not by being overly dismissive but by pointing out that the question does not fit the nature of mysteries. For a question to be meaningful it must fit the category of the thing questioned.

The Eucharist does indeed call for reflection on the nature of an explanation, but such thought must be engaged with the recognition of the limitations in human understanding. This is an important point because the underlying problem has led to repeated misunderstandings between Christians in the East and in the West. There are two extremes to be avoided. One occurs frequently when Eastern theologians criticize the West for attempting to explain the Eucharist, objecting that a mystery cannot be explained by concepts like substance and accidents, or focusing on sacramental causality. The other extreme occurs in the West by not recognizing the limitations inherent in the process of explaining the Eucharist. If there is any answer, it lies in avoiding the extremes.

One cannot understand a Christian mystery as having mechanisms like valves on the heart or gears on a machine. Nor can it be understood as a particular instance of a general law like gravity. The nature of the mystery of Christ is of a different order, but not in the way that the modern secular mind may easily dismiss as unreal. The fact that it is a mystery does not mean that it is not capable of being understood, at least to some degree. No Church Father, no theologian, no Church council, no episcopal decree has ever been able to explain this truth in ways accessible to our normal patterns of human

73 *Homily 46 on the Gospel of John*, PG 59:260.

reason. Nor have many theologians been under the delusion that they could explain this mystery, a point often lost on Eastern writers who think Western theologians too rationalistic.

Western theologians have not always recognized something the East has emphasized, namely, that mysteries are not waiting to be explained but waiting to be entered into. The explanations offered for the eucharistic mystery are like putting a fence around a piece of land. The fence protects what is within by fending off what does not belong there and by preserving what is good, but in and of itself, the fence cannot explain what is inside it. John Chrysostom's words are much like that fence. He wanted to protect the truths of the Eucharist while inviting his people into the realities that those truths pointed to. Many major Christian doctrines act like fences. The Nicene formulation of the Trinity does not explain the three-personed God nor does the Chalcedonian formula the two natures of Christ. These creeds fence off heretical notions and preserve the truths inside the fence.

The mystery of Christ died and risen is the content of the Eucharist. It is the same content as what is lived mystically in souls. In the end, whether in souls or under the appearances of bread and wine, it is Christ as presence and sacrifice that is embraced. Theological formulation is an exercise in explication of what cannot be explicated—not what could be explicated if only there were sufficient intellectual finesse. In fact, even if it could be so explained, our comprehension would still fall short of the mark because Christ's presence in the Eucharist as well as in all its other manifestations transcends linguistic expression. John Chrysostom's insistence on the incomprehensibility of God applies not only to the divine essence and to divine providence but even to his real presence in the sacrament of his body and blood.

5

Chrysostom on the Bread of Life Discourse (John 6)

It is inevitable that Chrysostom would comment on the Gospel of John chapter 6 while he preached on the fourth Gospel among the Antiochenes. The Eucharist, however, is not the special focus of John's six homilies on John 6 (homilies 42–47), as it might be in a modern polemical context, but neither could he avoid dealing with such an important topic inasmuch as it forms the core and the climax of John 6. John the Expositor always tried to stay close to the biblical text of John the Evangelist without being caught up in flights of fancy. He was always concerned with accuracy (μετὰ ἀκριβείας) of understanding but in this case that entailed the limitations of human understanding of divine mysteries. Chrysostom is very aware of the mysterious character of his subject when he turns to the Gospel of John chapter 6.

The eighty-eight homilies on the Gospel on John were preached in Antioch around the year 390, just a few years after the famous revolt against the Eastern Emperor Theodosius I, who imposed a special tax (380).[1] The people of Antioch destroyed statues of

1 See the introduction to Sr. Thomas Aquinas Goggin, SCH, *Homilies on Saint John the Apostle and Evangelist: Homilies 1-47*, FC 33 (Washington, DC: The Catholic University of America Press, 1957) and *Homilies on Saint John the Apostle and Evangelist: Homilies 48-88*, FC 41 (Washington, DC: The Catholic University of America Press, 1959). Homilies 46 and 47 are in volume 33. I shall make liberal use of Goggin's translation with some minor corrections and occasional major departures.

the imperial family and one of Theodosius himself, and during this period John attempted to calm his flock with homilies that called for repentance. It was within or near this Sitz-im-Leben that John gave his homilies on the Gospel bearing his own name.[2] He structured his eighty-eight homilies on a sequential exposition of verses in the Gospel.

Although the focus of this book is on John Chrysostom, I will depart from that plan slightly in this chapter to examine and compare Chrysostom's treatment of John chapter 6 with that of his Latin contemporary St. Augustine (354–430).[3] Since John and Augustine were close in time, and yet had no contact that we know of, the comparison of their expositions may reveal interesting beliefs about the Church in the East and in the West during their lifetimes. Their most foundational commonality was their belief in the Eucharist as the true body and blood of Christ. Beyond this, we will observe three important points of shared faith. They both saw the Incarnation and the Eucharist as intimately tied to one another, the former providing the necessary ground for the latter. They similarly believed the Eucharist and the Church to be two aspects of one great reality since both are the body of Christ. And finally, both Fathers held to the Eucharist as a sign and instrument of God's love for humanity, which naturally overflows into the Christian's love for other human beings. These commonalities, however, do not exhaust their expositions. Chrysostom's treatment of John 6 contains an extraordinary encomium on the blood of Christ not unlike other litanies of praise on the cross or the body of Christ.

When we read John's homilies on the sixth chapter of the fourth Gospel, we would do well to understand the broader context evident from his earlier sermons on the Evangelist's craft. The two homilies on the Eucharist in John 6 (46 and 47) presuppose themes found in earlier homilies. In the very first homily on this Gospel, Chrysostom exhorts his hearers to prepare their ears to listen carefully to the wisdom of the Evangelist.[4] Drawing a cultural

2 There are 21 homilies titled *To the People of Antioch*, PG 49:15–222.

3 John 6 is quoted and alluded to incalculable times in patristic writings but extant complete commentaries on the whole Gospel are not that numerous. Three of the more prominent ones, in chronological order, are Chrysostom's (ca. 390), Augustine's (early 400s), and Cyril of Alexandria's (412).

4 In *Homily 2* Chrysostom treats the life of the Evangelist and the superiority of his philosophy to that of acclaimed Greek philosophers, especially Plato.

analogy with athletic games or musical entertainment, Chrysostom urges them to prepare themselves to hear a messenger from heaven. Why should John's audience pay special attention to the Evangelist? Because he teaches "the naked truth" and draws on "deep spiritual resources" in order to lay bare "the awesome mysteries" that are beyond human comprehension.[5]

This Evangelist is a harp of the Holy Spirit; the Paraclete speaks through him.[6] Unlike the sights and sounds of the theater, the voice of the Evangelist does not disturb any of the faithful and it actually "frees from terror and confusion."[7] Another analogy affords John a handy illustration. If anyone wanted to know the goings-on in the royal palace, he would search out a friend of the king; the Evangelist is also a friend of Christ the king inasmuch as he called his disciples his friends (Jn 15:14–15). Since Jesus had heard what the Father had spoken (Jn 15:15), he also passed it on to his disciples, his friends. So to listen to the Evangelist is the same as entering heaven, in contrast to the inane stage plays or athletic theaters, which offer nothing lasting or valuable. The stage for this Evangelist is the world and even the angels are his audience.

The stage is set and the Evangelist has "a beautiful soul." He is clothed with Christ. The only thing that remains to be done is for the Christian to prepare his soul to hear and to be attentive to the divine words spoken by the Evangelist. And yet herein lies the quandary. No human power is sufficient to prepare the soul. Grace is needed. True listening takes preparation, and the person who has no heart to listen attentively will not profit from the teachings of the Evangelist. And this is especially true when he recounts the "hard saying" (Jn 6:60) about eating the flesh and drinking the blood of the Son of Man. This call to listening with spiritual ears provides the background for all that John will expound from the pages of the Evangelist whose name he bears.

The sixth chapter of John contains an extended contrast between the manna of the old covenant and the bread of life in the new covenant, a contrast that broadens throughout the Gospel of John to encompass almost every discourse. The contrast between old and new lies underneath the dialogue between the Samaritan woman and Jesus (John 4); it undergirds the contrast between darkness and light in the dialogue that follows the healing

5 *Homily 1*; Goggin, 5, 6.

6 *Homily 1*; Goggin, 6.

7 *Homily 1*; Goggin, 7.

of the blind man in chapter nine. However, the contrast in chapter six is especially noteworthy because the Jews with whom Jesus was arguing took great pride in the fact that God had provided sustenance for his people in the barren desert. The manna carried a symbolic value of God's loving goodness to Israel. Jesus seemed to deny this, something that would have shocked the sensibilities of his contemporaries. But, as with many other contrasts in the Gospel, it is a contrast not of true versus false but of shadow and reality, promise and fulfillment. All this was prepared for within the controlling perspective of the Prologue itself: "From his fullness we have all received grace upon grace because the law was given through Moses but grace and truth came through Jesus Christ" (Jn 1:16–17). Chrysostom dedicated an entire homily (14) to these words.

We saw in chapter 2 that John's preaching filled the air with the often-repeated differences between the temporary dispensation of the figures and types in the old covenant and the fullness of spiritual realities in the new covenant. In *Homily 14* Chrysostom enlarges this pattern with his characteristic concern of exactitude (ἀκρίβεια). He asks what the Evangelist meant by "from his fullness we have all received" and the even more puzzling "grace upon grace" (χάριν ἀντὶ χάριτος).[8] John explains the meaning of these phrases on the pattern of continuity and discontinuity that we observed earlier. The former phrase provides the underlying structure on which the latter is built: "There was holiness before and there is holiness now. There was a baptism before and a baptism now. There was a sacrifice before and a sacrifice now. There was a temple before and a temple now. There was a circumcision before and a circumcision now. So also, there was grace before and grace now."[9]

In so many ways the old covenant economy laid the groundwork for the new, but the differences are even more important: "The first-named as types and the others as reality have kept the same name but not the same meaning."[10] John inches his way to a definitive statement of the differences: "In so far as a thing was a type, it was not completely divorced from truth. But, in so

8 Goggin translates "grace for grace."

9 *Homily 14*; Goggin, 132–33. While Goggin's translation here is not as literal as possible, it captures the meaning very well. καὶ ἁγιασμὸς, καὶ ἁγιασμός· καὶ βάπτισμα, καὶ βάπτισμα· καὶ θυσία, καὶ θυσία· καὶ ναὸς, καὶ ναός· καὶ περιτομὴ, καὶ περιτομή· οὕτω καὶ χάρις, καὶ χάρις (PG 59:92).

10 *Homily 14*; Goggin, 133.

far as it continued to be shadow, it was less than the truth."[11] The language of shadow and reality is especially significant, as he illustrates using the idea of adoption or sonship. The people of Israel were honored with this title of sons, but believers in the new covenant have "the cleansing of regeneration and the renovation of the Holy Spirit."[12] What then is the difference between the grace given in the old covenant and that of the new? As John insists that "the working of grace in us is not the same as in them," he explains that grace for believers today is not only the forgiveness of sins as in the old, but the granting of "justice, and holiness, and adoption of sons, and the grace of the Spirit, much more splendid gifts and richer by far."[13] So grace was given to them, but the reality of grace was so much greater than what Israel could experience. The grace given in the new covenant is an interior reality that the shadow only reflected. This greater grace becomes important in the contrast between the manna and the bread of life in chapter 6 of the Gospel.

Another schema of continuity and discontinuity that John reiterates is the incomprehensibility of God paired with condescension (συγκατάβασις) in *Homily 15*, a correlation that we insisted was important for the whole of Chrysostom's theology. And it seems pertinent to the bread of life discourse in two respects: the bread of life comes down from heaven and the truth of consuming the flesh of the Son of Man brings incomprehensibility down from the ethereal to daily existence. In this homily Chrysostom is explaining Jn 1:18, "No one has ever seen God. The only begotten Son who is in the bosom of the Father, he has revealed him."[14] How could the Evangelist say that no one has ever seen God when there are so many references in Scripture to people seeing God? Did not the prophet Isaiah himself, so loved by John Chrysostom, say he had seen the Lord high and lifted up (Is 6:1)? John explains that there are times when reading the Scriptures too literally leads to trouble. In fact, John insists that not only has no human ever seen God, no angel has either. He cites the different appearances of God to human beings in Scripture and shows that the Lord must have appeared by an act of condescension: "I condescended to them; I did not appear as I was."[15] John's theological accuracy is hard to dispute; "Could created nature see the

11 *Homily 14*; Goggin, 133.

12 *Homily 14*; Goggin, 133. John is quoting Ti 3:5.

13 *Homily 14*; Goggin, 135.

14 *Homily 15*; Goggin, 141.

15 *Homily 15*; Goggin, 143.

Uncreated?"[16] In other words, what these human beings saw was not God in his essence or his substance but God in some condescending visible form that allowed them to comprehend the Incomprehensible One.

Yet the force of Jn 1:18 is that since the Son was in the bosom of the Father, he was able to reveal the inner heart of God. As John sees it, "to be in God's bosom is a much greater thing than to see him."[17] The Father and the Son "have full conformity and agreement of substance. . . . Their knowledge is identical. . . . Their power is equal."[18] And the greatest declaration of all is the undeniable answer to a question, "Do you see the mercy and providence of God?" God's goodness is manifested through the gift of his Son as a teacher of truth, and here again we see the contrast: "He condescends to such an extent that he no longer wills to speak to us through servants but through himself. . . . To be sure, they had Moses as instructor, we have the Lord of Moses."[19] Jesus Christ did what no servant of God could ever do. He became the mouthpiece of the Father because he came from the bosom of the Father. His teaching therefore is definitive, final, unquestionably true. All this becomes important for John as he approaches the bread of life discourse in John 6 with its startling pronouncements.

THE HEART OF *HOMILY 46*

Homily 46 is where John gives his fullest expositions and reflects on the eucharistic bread and wine. Among other things, Chrysostom answers three crucial questions when he asks, "Therefore, we must learn the wondrousness of the mystery: what it is, why it was given, and what is the benefit to be derived from it?"[20] In sum, John is posing the following questions:

1. What is the essence or reality of the eucharistic bread and wine?
2. What motivated Christ to promise and to give the Eucharist?
3. What benefits accrue to those who receive the Eucharist?

16 *Homily 15*; Goggin, 143.

17 *Homily 15*; Goggin, 145.

18 *Homily 15*; Goggin, 146.

19 *Homily 15*; Goggin, 148.

20 *Homily 46*; Goggin, 468.

As he proceeds to answer these questions, his language strikes a balance between being overly obfuscating and being hopelessly simplistic. On the one hand, the mystery of the sacrament is beyond human explanation; on the other, an overly simple explanation runs the risk of turning something exalted into something common, which might alienate his hearers rather than draw them into the mystery. John is highly sensitive to the flow of the text and the appropriateness of certain words at certain junctures. John the Evangelist portrayed Jesus's words as increasingly enigmatic as the chapter proceeded, and John the Expositor is ever aware of that progression and sense of climax. So when Jesus said, "I have come down from heaven" (Jn 6:38), Chrysostom anticipates an objection: "If anyone would inquire why he tossed in an explanation of the mysteries, we would respond to him that the timing was especially opportune because the obscurity of his words always provokes the hearer and makes him more attentive."[21]

While those who listened to Jesus should have inquired more fully into the depths of his meaning, John says that their perversity lay not in the doubtful meaning of the Master's words but in their inability to transcend the physical realm of meaning. Chrysostom sees in this instance another example of the obtuseness evident in other cases. Nicodemus in John 3 had similar objections precisely because he could not imagine a higher spiritual meaning to Jesus's words "You must be born again" (Jn 3:3–5). So when Jesus says that his flesh must be eaten, they ask, "How can this man give us his flesh to eat?" (Jn 6:52). If they found it so impossible to believe this statement, they should have likewise found the multiplication of the loaves impossible. If they were able to believe the latter, they should have believed the former.

Still, John is not unaware of the difficulties with Jesus's eucharistic claims. Like Jesus in John's Gospel, however, John the Expositor reaffirms the poignant reality of the eucharistic bread being his flesh:

> Christ did this too to lead us to a greater friendship and to show the great longing he had for us, not only to provide for those who desired to see him but also to touch, eat, and sink their teeth into his flesh, to be entwined with him and to be filled with all desire. Like lions breathing fire, so let us depart

21 *Homily 46*, PG 59:259. Εἰ δὲ ἐξετάζοι τις, τί δήποτε καὶ τὸν περὶ μυστηρίων ἐνέβαλε λόγον; ἐκεῖνο ἂν εἴποιμεν πρὸς αὐτὸν, ὅτι καὶ τούτων σφόδρα τῶν λόγων ὁ καιρὸς ἦν. Τὸ γὰρ ἀσαφὲς τῶν εἰρημένων ἀεὶ τὸν ἀκροατὴν διανίστησι καὶ προσεκτικώτερον ἐργάζεται. My translation has one significant disagreement with Goggin's (466). She takes περὶ μυστηρίων as mystery in general ("Why did he shroud the explanation in mystery"), whereas I take the phrase as referring to the sacraments.

> from that table, being a threat to the Devil, while you contemplate the head [i.e., Christ] and the love he has demonstrated toward us.[22]

Here John partially answers the first two of the questions posed. He affirms what would later be called the real presence as well as the motivation for the gift of the Eucharist. Christ's love prompted him not only to offer a special food but to offer himself as that food.[23]

Chrysostom's words make it clear that in his mind there is a sacramental equivalence between the earthly body of Jesus and the eucharistic body. The reality of Christ in the mysteries is reinforced by John's contrast of the Old Testament types and the New Testament antitypes. We observed above the pattern of such contrasts as seen in his commentary on the Evangelist's statement that grace and truth came through Jesus Christ. Here John again draws on this same interpretation:

> Now, if its type had so much power, both in the temple of the Hebrews and in the midst of the Egyptians, when sprinkled on the doorposts, how much more power does the reality have. In its types this blood sanctified the golden altar; without it the High Priest did not dare to enter the sanctuary. This blood has ordained priests; in its types it has washed away sins. And if it had such great power in its types, if death shuddered so much at the figure, how would it not be in terror of the reality itself?[24]

As we saw in the case of other Old Testament institutions in chapter 2, so too the blood of Christ in the Eucharist is seen as the final reality of which the blood of bulls and goats was the shadow (cf. Heb 9:13–14). True redemption could only come through the blood of the true Lamb who takes away the sin of the world, which is why John eulogizes Christ's blood: "This Blood is the salvation of souls; by it the soul is cleansed; by it beautified; by it inflamed."[25] John emphasizes the identity of the sacramental blood with the real blood of Christ by underscoring its power. We again hear John reiterating the union of

22 *Homily 46*, PG 59:260.

23 Despotis rightfully sees Chrysostom's interpretation of John 6 as based on the recognition of love. "The mystery of the Eucharist is a mystery of love, revealing God's love for human beings and satisfying the love of those seeking God. From this perfect love relationship results the healing of human souls and bodies" (Athanasios Despotis, "The Philosophical-Religious Hybridity in John 6 and Its Reception in the Commentaries of Origen and Chrysostom," in *Drawing and Transcending Boundaries in the New Testament and Early Christianity*, ed. Jacobus Kok, Martin Webber, and Jermo van Nes (Münster: LIT Verlag, 2020), 61.

24 *Homily 46*, PG 59:261. The above is Goggin's translation, 469–70.

25 Goggin, 470.

heaven and earth that we observed in chapter 1 when he praises the objective effects of communion in the blood of Christ: "Those who share in this Blood have taken their stand with angels, and archangels, and the Powers from on high, clad in the royal stole of Christ and possessing spiritual weapons. But I have not yet mentioned anything really great, for it is the King Himself with whom they are clothed."[26]

There are two kinds of effects of the Eucharist that John draws on: objective and subjective. The former are effects *ex opere operato* that need no consent from the communicant to be the case while the latter are *ex opere operantis* and can only have their desired effect with the consent of the communicant. Yet the line between these two types of effects sometimes grows very thin in John's eucharistic teaching. When John speaks of communion as bringing about union with the mystical body of the Church, this is true apart from the awareness or consent of the communicant. We hear echoes of Paul's notion of union with Christ in baptism (Rom 6:1–11) and membership in the Church (1 Cor 12:13). John also sees a subjective side to this mystical reality, for he quickly adds, "This, in truth, is characteristic of those who have great longing [πόθος]."[27] The longing of the Christian corresponds to Christ's longing for union with the Christian. Just how deeply John muses on this point can be seen in his appropriation of Jb 31:31, the wording of which is close to Jn 6:52, "How can this man give us his flesh to eat?" Chrysostom no doubt referred to the text in Job because it contained the words "Who will give us his flesh that we may be filled," and he was intent upon emphasizing not only the reality of Christ's flesh in the Eucharist but even more the plenitude of grace and virtue that derived from that flesh in communion. Those who long for Christ better dispose themselves for being united more deeply and more intimately with the Church in its mystical dimension. Later in *Homily 46* John again dwells on the benefits that accrue to the believing Christian when he likens the mysteries of the Church to a fountain watering the land to bear fruit and to cool the fiery temptations assaulting him. John has no doubt that "the gifts lying before us [on the altar] affect the soul far more" than even something turning to gold when immersed in molten gold. The river of grace that flows from the sacred altar (fountain) does not consume but cleanses.[28]

26 *Homily 46*, PG 59:262. I have modified Goggin's translation somewhat. For hers see 471.

27 *Homily 46*; Goggin, 468.

28 *Homily 46*, PG 59:262.

INCARNATION AND EUCHARIST: CHRYSOSTOM AND AUGUSTINE

The Incarnation stands in the background of Chrysostom's eucharistic discussion in *Homily 46*. When John contrasts the manna of the old covenant with the food Christ provides, as Jesus does in Jn 6:30–35, his emphasis falls on the utterly unique character of Christ's provision. Taking on the voice of Christ himself, John uses language reminiscent of the Letter to the Hebrews:[29]

> I don't give food in the way others do. Rather, I feed you with my own fleshes; I furnish myself to you and want all of you to be noble as I extend you kind hopes for the future. For here the one who gives himself to you now will do so much more in the future. I wanted to become your brother; I shared in flesh and blood for your sake. I distribute again the same flesh and blood by which I become your kinsman.[30]

Here John alludes to the common lot of humanity which Christ assumed; otherwise he could not have become their "kinsman" (συγγενὴς). The emphasis falls on the desire of Christ to "become your brother" (ἀδελφός ἠθέλησα ὑμέτερος γενέσθαι). By sharing in the flesh and blood of all human beings, Christ has not remained a God aloof from the struggles and pain of humanity. Yet Christ's voice, as conceived by John, proclaims an even greater good than the bare fact of Incarnation. It is his own flesh that Christ gives for food, and this functions as a sure promise of future blessing. The promise of resurrection that Jesus gives in chapter 6 is not only intimately tied in John's mind to faith, as Jn 6:40 suggests, but is even related to consuming his flesh and blood, as Jn 6:50 and Jn 6:54 suggest. The nature and reality of that flesh to be consumed is in no doubt: "I distribute again the same flesh and blood by which I become your kinsman."[31]

Augustine too sees a close link between the Incarnation of Christ and the Eucharist. In section 10 of tract 26 on John's Gospel, he uses eternal life as a substitute for the name of Christ himself, "Eternal Life assumed death;

29 Heb 2:14: "Since therefore the children share in flesh and blood, he himself likewise partook of the same things, that through death he might destroy the one who has the power of death, that is, the devil" (ESV).

30 *Homily 46*, PG 59:261.

31 The text of John 6 uses δίδωμι ("give" exclusively, but Chrysostom seems to strengthen this idea by glossing it with παρατίθημι ("furnish," "provide") and ἐκδίδωμι ("give out," "distribute").

eternal life wanted to die but only for you, not for himself. He received from you something in which he might die for you."[32] He emphasizes this to show how humans may have him, as Jesus says in John 6. To have Jesus is to have eternal life, but that is only possible because of the self-humiliation of the Word-Made-Flesh. For Augustine Christ is God and has eternal life within himself, but that reality had to be communicated to humanity somehow. In taking on human flesh Christ communicated divinity to the humanity he assumed: "Eternal life himself gave eternal life to the flesh he assumed."[33] The statement may either mean that the divinity of the Word (*Verbum*) communicated itself to Jesus's own personal flesh or that he communicated it to humanity as a whole. I understand him to be saying the latter. If this interpretation is correct, then participation in the Eucharist has a close parallel to what took place in the incarnate Christ himself.

This becomes clearer in section 19, where Augustine treats the words of Jn 6:57, "The living Father sent me, and I live because of the Father, and he who eats me will live because of me." Supposing that this might be misunderstood, Augustine clarifies that it is not as if the Son ate the Father while the way to receive Jesus is to eat him. Eating functions here as a metaphor for participation: "He did not say 'as I eat the Father, I also live because of the Father, and he who eats me will live because of me.' The Son did not become better by participation in the Father. He was equal by nature. In our case, we are made better by participation in the Son through unity with his body and blood. This is what eating and drinking signify."[34]

When Augustine says, "through unity with his body and blood" (*per unitatem corporis eius et sanguinis*), does he mean unity of Christ's humanity with his divinity or the communicant's unity with Christ's body and blood? I am inclined to think he means the latter while the former is not out of the question. Augustine seems to be saying both that Christ's bodily life participated in his divine nature (eternal life) and likewise that believers participate in eternal life through sharing in his flesh. This undoubtedly explains why

32 Augustine, *Commentary on John* 26,10: *Vita aeterna mortem assumpsit, vita aeterna mori voluit; sed de tuo, non de suo: accepit a te, ubi moreretur pro te.*

33 Augustine, *Commentary on John* 26,10: *Ipse vita aeterna, dedit et carni susceptae vitam aeternam.* That Christ communicated his divinity to his human nature is also a prominent theme in Cyril of Alexandria. See Daniel A. Keating The Appropriation of Divine Life in Cyril of Alexandria Oxford: Oxford University Press, 2003).

34 Augustine, *Commentary on John* 26,19.

he emphasizes Christ's death. That death won eternal life, which then must be communicated to believers.

Yet how does such communication take place? Section 19 contains a sentence that is both unclear and pregnant with meaning, "My emptying of myself has made that condition in which he sent me. But so that anyone may live on account of me, participation makes the condition possible by which he eats me."[35] The unclarity of the Latin is not only for the translator, but it would have probably puzzled native speakers as well. The Latin itself is not very well-formed and so may be open to different readings, but the theological meaning still seems accessible. Consistent with other statements in tract 26, Augustine is saying that the Incarnation was ordained by the Father as a form of humiliation for the Son. He had to participate in human flesh to redeem humanity and so lower himself. Similarly, human sinners must participate in the Son to have eternal life. And Augustine equates participation with the eating of flesh in Jesus's discourse (*participatio facit qua manducat me*). So in Augustine's exposition of John 6, the Eucharist depends on the reality of the Incarnation with its plenitude of divinity and humanity united. At the same time, the Eucharist is a kind of extension of the Incarnation because both share a common term of participation.

JOHN AND AUGUSTINE ON THE CHURCH AND THE EUCHARIST

The sixth chapter of John's Gospel says nothing explicitly about the Church, but John Chrysostom sees allusions to the Church in the ebb and flow of the discourse recorded there. I would propose three reasons why he does so. John was deeply immersed in the Pauline epistles and he calls Paul his dearest and favorite saint. Margaret Mitchell rendered an invaluable service to Chrysostom studies by her elucidation of the obvious affection John had for Paul.[36] We noticed in an earlier chapter how John viewed events in the life of Christ through a Pauline lens and so it is not surprising that he would look at John 6 with eyes colored by Paul's view of the Church. From that theology

35 Augustine, *Commentary on John* 26,19. Exinanitio mea fecit, in qua me misit; ut autem quisque vivat propter me, participatio facit qua manducat me.

36 Margaret Mitchell, *The Heavenly Trumpet: John Chrysostom and the Art of Pauline Interpretation* (London: Westminster John Knox Press, 2002).

there emerges an image of the Church as a mystical, organic reality. While the Church has a juridical, legal aspect to its existence, the weight of Paul's ecclesiology falls on the reality of Christ's members being living members of his body. And the term *body* suggests the Eucharist, because this is the middle term between Christ himself and the Church. Christ's own life is communicated to the Church through the sacrament of the altar.

The three questions mentioned earlier that John posed and answered occurred in the context of John explaining why Jesus's audience could not believe his words. John explains that Jesus first worked the miracle of feeding the five thousand to point to a higher miracle, the gift of the mystery of the Eucharist. In John's mind the third question about the benefits to be received from the Eucharist leads him to consider the union of Christ with the Church. The passage in context reads: "At that time, they [the Israelites] had no fruit from what was told them but we have enjoyed the benefits through the very things themselves. So we need to learn the marvel of the mysteries: what it is, why it was given, and what benefit there is in the matter. It is one body that we become and members, he says, of his flesh and bones."[37] John immediately paraphrases Gn 2:23 and combines it with Paul's motif of "one body and many members" into one sentence with breathless ease. The word order in the original and the use of the indicative (γινόμεθα) justify the reading that John sees one great benefit of the sacrament consisting of incorporation into the one body of Christ, the Church. This reading is strengthened when we attend to what immediately follows:

> So, let us become this [body] not only in accord with love but also in the very fact itself. Let us be mingled with that flesh. For this is what came through that nourishment which he bestowed, wanting to show the longing that he had for us. For this reason, he fused himself with us and mixed his body with us that we may exist as one thing like a body joined to the head.[38]

In standard Pauline fashion, John builds his hortatory subjunctive on the indicative. Because the Church is in fact one body in many members, John exhorts his hearers to live in accord with that fact ("let us become one body by love"). That this is dependent on the Eucharist is evident from John's choice of three verbs—mingle (ἀνακερασθῶμεν), mix (ἀνέμιξεν), and join (ἀνέφυρε)—while a few lines later he becomes even more graphic in his

37 *Homily 46*, PG 59:260.

38 *Homily 46*, PG 59:260.

vocabulary choices: "Who may give of his fleshes, they say, so as to be filled up? Christ did this to lead us to a greater friendship. And showing the great longing he had for us, he not only provided for those who desire to see him but even to touch, eat, and sink their teeth into his flesh, to be intertwined and to fulfill their whole desire."[39]

The language mounts up to the only possible conclusion that John sees the Church as an organic extension of Christ in the world. The reason the Church is Christ's body is because it takes his body from the sacrament and is formed into a body of his members, bone of his bone and flesh of his flesh. This realistic view also explains his exultant language in which he cannot help himself from exclaiming, "O how truly awesome are the mysteries of the church, how truly awesome this altar![40]

This same connection between the Church and the Eucharist can be found in Augustine's commentary on John 6. Reading Augustine's works over time, one cannot help being struck by how he sees every revealed truth in Scripture as intimately related to some other truths, often in a complex but illuminating correspondence. In section 13 of tract 26 Augustine argues that to be imbued with the Spirit of God, one must be in the body of Christ. He appeals to a belief shared by him and his readers, namely, that the human body lives because of the human spirit, not the reverse. Nor can one person's body live because of another's spirit: "My body lives from my spirit; your body from yours."[41] Augustine then argues from this commonsense belief to the nature of the Church: "the body of Christ cannot be alive unless from the Spirit of Christ."[42] Now if living from the Spirit of Christ had nothing to do with the Eucharist, then Augustine's next quotation would not be understandable. As the Bishop of Hippo cites 1 Cor 10:17 ("one bread," "we the many are one body"), he cannot hold in his joy:

O sacrament of devotion!	*O sacramentum pietatis!*
O sign of unity!	*O signum unitatis!*
O bond of charity!	*O vinculum caritatis!*

39 *Homily 46*, PG 59:260.

40 *Homily 46*, PG 59:261.

41 Augustine, *Commentary on John* 26,13.

42 Augustine, *Commentary on John* 26,13.

Why would Augustine be so jubilant, so overjoyed, so beside himself with confidence? Because the answer to true piety, genuine unity, and faithful charity lies in one Church. One wonders if behind expressions like the above there is always in Augustine's heart anxiety over the Donatist schism. And if not the formal schism, at least the spirit of division and rivalry. He never tires of calling Christians back to the unity of the Church: "He who wants to live has a place where he may live, he has that from which he may draw his life."[43] The Church is the place where the Spirit of God lives. And so for Augustine a call back to the Church is a call back to the Spirit and the Eucharist: "Let him not abhor the bond of members, let him not be a rotting member that ought to be cut off. May he not be a distorted member about which he may be embarrassed. May he be a beautiful, fitting, healthy member. Let him cling to the body; may he live for God from God; let him now labor on earth that he may reign afterwards in heaven."[44]

Augustine then insists that partaking of the body and blood of Christ is to partake of the "one loaf" which is found on the one altar of the one Church. It would seem that both John and Augustine believed the body of Christ, of which all must partake to have eternal life, is inseparably tied to loving the Church and to being a member of that Church.

Section 15 of the same tract emphasizes the contrast between normal food and the food that leads to eternal life. It is as if Augustine is worried that his people might take the Eucharist as less than the divine gift it is, or might even disassociate it from the visible Church. Here Augustine clearly shows the divine intention of drawing all into the Church. God intends the reality (*res*) of the sign (*sacramentum*) for the salvation of all: "The sacrament of this reality, that of the unity of the body and blood of Christ . . . is prepared on the Lord's table and is received from the Lord's table, by some for life, by others for destruction. But the reality itself, of which it is a sacrament, is for everyone who partakes of it for life, none for destruction."[45] The objective reality of the sacrament is designed for all but not all who partake of it will have life. It is in this same context that Augustine now makes clear his conviction that to partake of the body of Christ means that one must consider himself a member of the bond (*societas*) that unites the members of the Church together: "By this food and drink [Jesus] wants the bond of the body and

43 Augustine, *Commentary on John* 26,13.

44 Augustine, *Commentary on John* 26,13.

45 Augustine, *Commentary on John* 26,15.

of his members to be understood, which is in fact the holy church in those predestined, called, justified, glorified."[46] Since the reality of the sign binds the recipient to Christ and Christ is bound to his body the Church, it follows that anyone who is bound with Christ must be bound to the Church as well. For both John and Augustine, the middle term, the link, between Christ and the Church is the Eucharist. As Christ himself makes the Eucharist, so the Eucharist makes Church.

Praise for the Blood of Christ

While John and Augustine share many points of contact in their reading of John 6, there are distinctives of each not shared by the other. Nowhere in Augustine's commentary do we find anything comparable to Chrysostom's encomium on the blood of Christ. We observed in chapter 3 how John rhapsodized the cross as the instrument of victory whereby death destroyed death. Perhaps it is not surprising, then, in the context of the Eucharist, that John would wax eloquent about the blood of Christ. Though never printed in the form of a poem, one section of *Homily 46* takes on poetic qualities by the reiteration of the pronoun *this* (*touto*).[47] John heaps word upon word, phrase upon phrase, to underscore the exalted nature and power of the eucharistic blood. In his characteristic manner, Chrysostom hopes to entice his hearers into a deeper apprehension of what the Eucharist effects in the lives of the faithful:

This blood
stamps the royal image brightly on us.
This blood
gives birth to an irresistible beauty.
This blood
does not allow the nobility of soul to be tarnished, feeding and watering
it constantly.

46 Augustine, *Commentary on John* 26,15.

47 The neuter form of the pronoun "this" specifically refers back to *haima* (blood). Though *haima* is not always repeated in this section with *touto*, the pronoun clearly references the noun and thus I have added it in my translation to bring out what is implied in the Greek text. Other scholars have created poetic renditions of classical texts, such as Carolyn Hammond in translating Augustine's *Confessions* 10,27,38 in the famous passage *Sero te amavi*. Like Augustine, Chrysostom's artful use of rhetoric begs for poetic expression.

This blood

came to us from the grains.

This does not happen immediately but in another way.

This blood

does not work this way but immediately moistens the soul and produces great power.

This blood

received worthily drives demons far away from us and calls angels to our side. Yes, even the Lord of angels. Demons flee when they see the Lord's blood but angels run to us.

This blood

Poured out has washed the world.

Blessed Paul spoke many times wisely about this blood in the Letter to the Hebrews.

This blood

Has purified the sanctuary and the holy of holies.

If the type had such great power in the Hebrews' temple and in the midst of Egypt when poured on the doorposts, how much more does the truth have?

This blood

Sanctified the golden altar.

This blood

Was what the high priest did not dare to leave behind when entering the sanctuary.

This blood

Was used to ordain priests.

This blood

Washed sins away in the types.

If it had such great power in the types, if this shadow made death shudder

Tell me, how can the reality [truth] not inspire reverence?

This blood

is the salvation of our souls.

This blood

Washed souls.

This blood

> Makes them beautiful,
> enflames them
> makes our mind brighter than fire.
> This blood
> Makes the soul brighter than gold.
> This blood
> Poured out makes heaven accessible.[48]

John is referring at times to the use of blood in the old covenant, at others to the blood of Christ shed on the cross and given in the Eucharist; he again works against the background of continuity and discontinuity in the transition from old to new. His contrast between the type and the reality (sometimes called simply "the truth") leaves no doubt about the superior nature of the blood of the new covenant. In its old covenant types, this blood "purified the sanctuary and the holy of holies, sanctified the golden altar, was what the high priest did not dare to leave behind when entering the sanctuary, was used to ordain priests, washed sins away in the types." Such high praise for the blood shed in the case of Israel still does not attain to the greater reality of the true blood of Christ shed in the new covenant. That blood attained the forgiveness of sins. That blood "poured out has washed the world" and therefore "is the salvation of our souls."

John's praise of the blood of Christ can be seen from two perspectives: rhetorical and iconographical. It is not surprising to find him engaging in such flights of laudatory acclamation when his training as an orator prepared him so well for it, but that is only the background. In the foreground stands his own Christian frame of reference. In delivering these words, John intended to bring to the hearer the reality of what the words represented. Like a visual icon, the words are meant to be windows into heaven. So when John says that the blood of Christ "stamps the royal image brightly on us," he is expressing literally what this whole section of the discourse aims at, namely, to have the words become conveyors of the ontological effects of Christ's blood. This is not unrelated to John's way of reading the Gospel narratives, because he sees in each story the higher reality represented. The story goes beyond being a narrative about an event in the past; it becomes a reality present to those who read or hear it. Like a visual icon, whose details

48 *Homily 46*, PG 59:261. My translation differs from Goggin's at significant points.

can depict a multifaceted truth, his poetic portrayal accomplishes the same for those who know how to listen.

In *Homily 46* Chrysostom goes further and deeper than preaching *about* the blood of the chalice; he hopes to captivate his audience when he speaks of the beautifying effects of the Eucharist. In addition to stamping "the royal image brightly on us," this blood "gives birth to an irresistible beauty." It "does not allow the nobility of soul to be tarnished, feeding and watering it constantly." This blood "moistens the soul and produces great power." By this blood the soul is made beautiful. It "enflames" the soul, "makes our mind brighter than fire" and "makes the soul brighter than gold." And as if this were not enough, the eucharistic presence of Christ "received worthily drives demons far away from us and calls angels to our side. Yes, even the Lord of angels. Demons flee when they see the Lord's blood but angels run to us." And most of all the Eucharist "poured out makes heaven accessible." All this hearkens back to the union of heaven and earth in the liturgy, but it also focuses on the necessity and power of the eucharistic presence.

A moment's reflection indicates the difference between the language John chose and that which a modern Christian might be inclined to choose. He combined terms of beauty with the imagery of fire. Fire does not normally suggest beauty in our minds. What did John have in mind? Toward the end of this poem-like section he has four noteworthy statements:

> By this [blood] the soul is beautified [τούτῳ καλλωπίζεται].
> By this [blood] it is enflamed [τούτῳ πυροῦται].
> This [blood] makes our mind brighter than fire [τοῦτο πυρὸς λαμπρότερον ἐργάζεται τὸν νοῦν τὸν ἡμέτερον].
> This [blood] makes the soul more shining than gold [τοῦτο χρυσίου φαιδροτέραν τὴν ψυχὴν ποιεῖ].

Fire, or what John occasionally specifies as spiritual fire, has a purifying effect on the soul. It burns away the dross of sin and lethargy, and this is what permits the believer to see heavenly realities with greater clarity and deeper love. When John says that the soul is enflamed (πυροῦται) by the eucharistic blood, he may be referring not only to greater clarity of heart and mind but also to a fiery passion to pursue the will of God. In this way, the soul is truly beautified (καλλωπίζεται) and is enabled to respond to the descent of the angels at its side and to embrace the Christ present in the sacraments.[49] The four lines above pick up on those from the beginning of this poem which employ the language of image (εἰκων), beauty (κάλλος), and nobility (εὐγένεια):

> This [blood] stamps the royal image brightly on us [Τοῦτο τὸ αἷμα τὴν εἰκόνα ἡμῖν ἀνθηρὰν ἐργάζεται τὴν βασιλικὴν].
>
> This blood gives birth to an irresistible beauty [τοῦτο κάλλος ἀμήχανον τίκτει].
>
> This blood does not allow the nobility of soul to be tarnished, feeding and watering it constantly [τοῦτο ἀπομαρανθῆναι τῆς ψυχῆς τὴν εὐγένειαν οὐκ ἀφίησιν, ἄρδον αὐτὴν συνεχῶς καὶ τρέφον].

These lines afford greater insight into John's desire for his hearers on the basis of the power of the Eucharist to shape and form the soul into a greater conformity with God. Only God's own life and presence can give the soul an "irresistible beauty" (κάλλος ἀμήχανον), and John's choice of "give birth" (τίκτει) may suggest that this beauty comes through baptism. The adjective ἀμήχανον, which I have translated "irresistible," is sometimes translated "impossible,"[50] but whatever may be the precise translation, it is clear that John is emphasizing that such beauty is beyond human ability and even beyond what anyone could possibly hope for. The nobility of soul mentioned in the third statement above may refer to the pristine state of the human being prior to the ancestral sin, or to the future state that results from grace communicated through the sacrament. In either case, we may be certain that for John the Eucharist is a powerful instrument to lift the communicant out of a tarnished state of sin and to make the soul beautiful by Christ's saving presence. This entire panegyric on the blood of Christ stands almost unique among the Fathers as an example of effusive praise for Christ's redemptive death. That it should occur in the context of Chrysostom's exposition of John 6 means that he was fully convinced of Christ's sacramental intention in this chapter of the Gospel and was fully aware of the benefits enjoyed by believers who would "eat the flesh and drink the blood of the Son of Man" (Jn 6:53).

49 Some form of the verb καλλωπίζειν (to beautify) occurs over 250 times in Chrysostom's corpus. A more careful study of its use thus seems justified.

50 Goggin chose "inconceivable."

The Sacrament of Love: John and Augustine

Throughout our study of John's eucharistic doctrine we have observed how his view always has in the background a sense God's love for humanity. Although his treatment of John 6 does not contain an abundance of references to love, the context of what he does say highlights that the Eucharist is a preeminent expression of God's love. The vocabulary of mingling and mixing that we saw earlier comes from the realms of love. And the fact that the Church is more than a juridical entity but is formed from the body and blood of Christ himself means that love is the glue that holds the body of the Church together. And John sees the eucharistic table as an expression of Christ's desire for friendship with us, leading us "to a greater friendship" and showing us "the great longing he had for us." It was this love that compelled Christ to give his flesh for the life of the world (Jn 6:51). It is this love communicated through the Eucharist that empowers the believer to resist the wiles of the Evil One. The reception of the Eucharist enables the believer to be simultaneously threatening and loving, a menace to the Master of Evil and a humble servant to the Master of Love. Most of all, it is this love, once perceived in sacramental communion, that leads the believer to "contemplate the head and the love he has demonstrated toward us."[51] The sense of love in the believer will no doubt grow when he considers the friendship that Christ wishes to have with him. The famous proclamation of Francis of Assisi, "Love is not loved," is overcome in the Eucharist because love is precisely the mingling, mixing, and union of one Lover with the other. That mutual indwelling of Christ and the believer yields both love for Christ and love for the Church as the body of Christ. The Eucharist conveys that love of Christ and engenders it as well in the heart of the believer. This love impels the believer to be part of the body of Christ's Church because he has received the body of Christ. The language John chooses here sounds the note of intimacy, and that is what the Eucharist provides, intimacy with Christ.[52]

Augustine too sees the Eucharist as a sign of love when he treats the words of Jesus, "No man has greater love than that he lay down his life for his friends" (Jn 15:13).[53] Prima facie, one may not imagine that this text has much to do with the Eucharist, but Augustine ties them together by quoting and

51 *Homily 46*, PG 59:260–61.

52 *Homily 46*, PG 59:260.

53 Augustine, *Commentary on John* 84,1.

expounding Prv 23:1, "If you sit down to dine at the table of a powerful man, with careful thought consider what is placed in front of you and so stretch out your hand knowing that you ought to be prepared for such things."[54] The mention of eating at the table of a powerful man evokes the Eucharist for Augustine:

> For what is "the table of a powerful man" except the place where the body and blood of him who gave his life for us is received? And what does it mean "to sit at that table" except to approach it in humility? What is it to "consider and know that which is placed in front of you" except to think worthily of so great a grace? What is it "to stretch out your hand" that you may know how to prepare for such things except what I already said that as Christ laid down his life for us, we ought to lay down our lives for our brothers?[55]

I aver that John would have been very pleased with Augustine's attempt to show that receiving the sacrament of love should issue forth in loving one's brothers and sisters, for John will lay considerable emphasis not only on loving one's fellow believers but even on loving one's enemies. Being "prepared for such things" means preparing for a sacrificial death, which is why Augustine invokes the example of the martyrs. Their actions arose out of ardent love (*ardenti dilectione*) that was enflamed by the banquet where they themselves were satiated (*in convivio quo et ipsi saturati sunt*).

✠ ✠ ✠

Because of its richness, John Chrysostom is anxious to apply this teaching to his people. He speaks of the necessity of receiving the Eucharist even if those seemingly impossible words of Jesus in John 6 run counter to normal human understanding. Anticipating the attempt to soften the exacting demands of Jesus's words, Chrysostom reiterates the absolute necessity of eucharistic reception because it was the only way that the soul could be beautified and so made ready for eternal glory. The gift of self that is the Eucharist demonstrates God's love of humanity (*philanthropia*). With Augustine and many other Church Fathers, we may even say that it is the highest expression of that love known to the human race. The only other truth about Jesus

54 Augustine's Old Latin translation follows the LXX fairly closely.

55 Augustine, *Commentary on John* 84,1.

Christ which matches that love is the power of his sacrifice, the shedding of his blood. This second truth is what captured John's imagination because in the end Christ's love and sacrifice are one and the same.

6

The Priesthood and the Eucharist

Few human institutions in this age are as admired and despised as much as the priesthood. As men who are both greatly loved and deeply hated, priests occupy a unique position in this world. Their whole ministry has no parallel in any other profession, though different aspects of their service to humanity bear superficial resemblance to others. They speak publicly, counsel privately, and listen endlessly. They visit the sick, feed the hungry, and comfort the dying. They must articulate moral norms while knowing that they have often failed to live up to them. They must be students of languages, history, philosophy, and theology while having little time to delve into any one of them in much depth. They must be men of concerted prayer while being distracted by a myriad of other duties. But most of all, priests must perform a service that is utterly unique to their vocation; it is their duty to celebrate the Eucharist. That is also their highest privilege. John Chrysostom seems to have understood this unique position of the priest. Early in his own ministry, he penned a long and diverse treatise, *On the Priesthood* (*De Sacerdotio*) that reflected his own high estimation of the priest's unique position.[1] I have previously claimed that for John the central

1 *Six Books on the Priesthood*, trans. and intro. Graham Neville (Crestwood, NY: St. Vladimir's Press, 2002). I shall interact with Neville's translation at selected points. I

purpose of the liturgy and the Eucharist is to unite heaven and earth into a chorus of praise and adoration, to bring the glories of heaven down to earth and to lift up the common experiences of humanity into the eternal realities of heaven. None of this would be possible without priests. In what follows, I will interpret *On the Priesthood* with an intratextual approach and seek to explicate its contents from within John's theology.[2]

This chapter explores Chrysostom's understanding of the priesthood in relation to the Eucharist by examining his view from a distinction between objective and subjective aspects. The former deals with the inherent nature and structure of the priesthood while the latter takes into account the human priest as a person and agent of something larger than himself. What stands out is that the priest of the new covenant enjoys an unparalleled dignity of which he is manifestly unworthy. John seems keenly aware of this fact as he seeks to understand the majesty of offering the sacrifice of the altar. It is this sacrifice that gives greater specificity to that union of heaven and earth that I argued was the essence of Christian worship. It is not a vague ethereal union of spirits, but a real metaphysical communion made possible by the sacrifice that the priest offers. The priest is an essential player in the *oikonomia* of redemption because it is ultimately Christ the high priest who acts behind, on behalf of, and through the human priest. For all this dignity and glory, the priest is still a mere man, and so John considers the subjective side of the priesthood as well by looking at the temptations and moral dangers that attend the life of a priest.

It is perhaps significant that John titled his treatise *On the Priesthood* (περί ἱερωσύνης) rather than *On the Priest* (περί ἱερέως) in his desire to speak more broadly than dealing with the life of the priest per se. Although he uses the terms *priest* and *presbyter* more than *priesthood* in this treatise, John shows clearly that he sees the priest as serving something greater than himself. He repeatedly speaks of the majesty and honor of the priesthood, reminding himself and others that this is a privilege that no one deserves.[3]

---

shall also make use of Anne-Marie Malingrey, *Jean Chrysostome: Sur le sacerdoce*, SC 272 (Paris: Editions du Cerf, 1980), for points of comparison. Two dates have been proffered for *De Sacerdotio*. The traditional date has it in the first year of his diaconate. More modern editors opt for a slightly later date (ca. 388–90). For our purposes it is a matter of indifference.

2 This approach contrasts with an external approach that seeks to read the document in a socio-political context. See Chris L. De Wet, "The Priestly Body: Power-Discourse and Identity in John Chrysostom's *De Sacerdotio*," *Religion and Theology* 18 (2011): 1–29.

3 Dom Chrysostomus Baur, the greatest Chrysostom scholar of the first half of the twentieth century, called *On the Priesthood* "one of his most beautiful compositions." After years of reading

That idea seems to underlie the opening two chapters of this treatise, where he constructs a dialogue between himself and his friend Basil about John's integrity and honesty in light of his refusing priestly ordination while his friend accepted it. John is charged with deceit for tricking Basil into accepting ordination while he cleverly avoided it himself. Basil echoes what he says is a common charge that John was interested in vainglory (κενοδοξία) and pride. It would have been very natural for people in John's Church community to think that he was interested only in worldly honors because of his advanced education in the school of Libanius. His rhetorical education, provided for at his mother's considerable sacrifice, set him up for an illustrious career. In the treatise, Basil gives voice to these objections and John retorts with more than expected. He not only defends his own integrity, he does so on the basis of a high view of the priesthood.

Before examining *On the Priesthood* in some depth, it would be valuable to note that this treatise is not the only text in which John expresses his views on the priesthood.[4] As will be evident shortly, Chrysostom is remarkably consistent over time in diverse expressions of the priesthood while recognizing the varying challenges facing a priest. In one homily John discusses Paul's exhortation to examine oneself before partaking of the body and blood of Christ (1 Cor 11:27–28) and warns his hearers about becoming guilty of the Lord's body. He likens it to the guilt of those who crucified Jesus. The severity of such an equation does not escape John so he proceeds to soften the blow in what is certainly one of his tenderest expressions of solidarity between laity and priest:

> The love of God for humanity has come so that the speaker and the hearers are subject to the same laws that are shared in nature itself. . . . This is the reason that God did not send angels down from heaven; he appointed teachers with the same human nature. This was so that they might not make the censures against us more unsparing by their superiority of nature or from an ignorance of human weakness. On the contrary, he gave mortal men as teachers and priests, men set about with weakness, that this whole matter may be the same responsibility for all speakers and the hearers, that

Chrysostom daily Baur concluded that this treatise "gave the author an occasion of writing the most beautiful things concerning the dignities and burdens of the priesthood that had ever come from a Christian pen" (*John Chrysostom and His Time*, trans. Sr. M. Gonzaga, RSM [Westminster, MD: Newman Press, 1959] 1:181).

4 Baur treats a number of texts dealing with Chrysostom's view of the priesthood that time and space do not allow me to handle. See *John Chrysostom and His Time*, 1:180–89.

> the tongue of the speaker may have a bit so that there would be no place for accusations beyond measure.[5]

Chrysostom quotes briefly from Heb 5:1–2 (men set about with weakness) to emphasize that priest and people are all subject to the same spiritual laws of grace. A priest's own weakness as a man can be very beneficial in that he will learn compassion for his fellow sinners: "You see that weakness is the ground of sympathy and the affinity of nature does not permit the one rebuking into excess even if he is very contentious."[6] This awareness of the subjective reality of priests and priesthood is an important theme to which we will return, but we must recognize above all the objective realities inherent in the priestly ministry, for it is those that make the Eucharist what it is.

ON THE PRIESTHOOD: OBJECTIVE CONTENT AND ASPECTS

For our purposes chapter 3 (section 4) is one of the most important passages in *On the Priesthood* because it contains a rich discussion of the material content of the priesthood. Its opening paragraph sets the stage for John's adoring description of the dignity of the priestly ministry in the new covenant. For the backdrop of his praise, he trots out the priestly attire of the old covenant:

> The priesthood exercises itself on earth but possesses an array of heavenly orders. This is very fitting. It is not a man, not an angel, not an archangel, not any other creature, but the Advocate [Paraclete] himself who has commanded this arrangement. He impelled those who remain in the flesh to make the ministry of angels visible. Therefore, it is necessary for the priest to be pure as he stands in the heavens among those powers. For the things before grace are fearful and dreadful, such as the bells, the pomegranates, the stones on the breastplate, the ephod, the miter, the lyre, the sash, the golden crown, the holy of holies, the calm of things within. But if anyone scrutinizes the things of grace, he will find those insignificant things to be fearful and dreadful. He will find it true what was said concerning the

5 *Non esse ad gratiam concionandum*, PG 50:654.

6 *Non esse ad gratiam concionandum*, PG 50:654.

law, "that which has glory is not glorious in comparison to the surpassing glory" [2 Cor 3:10].[7]

There is an aspect of a priest's ministry in this passage that would be easy to overlook. Throughout this treatise, Chrysostom speaks of the priest in kinetic terms. In other words, the priest is an actor and agent of movement in at least two directions: movement from the past to the present and movement from earth to heaven. And these movements roughly correspond to what we earlier dubbed the Axis of Anticipation and the Axis of Participation. As we saw in chapter 2, John often appeals to examples from the ancient Scriptures to compare and contrast the Jewish worship of the temple and tabernacle with the superior rites of the Church. Such a contrast involves a mental movement from shadows to reality, from promise to fulfillment. A second and ultimately more important movement stretches from earth to heaven. This vertical movement is the purpose of the liturgy.

The opening sentence of the passage above strongly reaffirms the liturgy as a union of heaven and earth ("The priesthood exercises itself on earth but possesses an array of heavenly orders"). When it speaks of the priesthood as having an array of heavenly things (τάξιν δὲ ἐπουρανίων ἔχει πραγμάτων), it leaves open the question as to what John is thinking of by the use of πρᾶγμα since the word allows a wide range of translations (thing, matter, reality, business).[8] Yet the context later aids us by stating that the priest makes "the ministry of angels visible" and that the servant of the altar "stands in the heavens among those powers." John's invitation to scrutinize "the things of grace" and to discover their true character as incomparably greater than the order of the old covenant suggests that the heavenly πράγματα are the preternatural company that the earthly Church imitates and joins. John does not explicitly name a hierarchy of angels here, as Pseudo-Dionysius will later do, but he does intimate such a structure by his insistence that "it is not a man, not an angel, not an archangel, not any other creature" that has made this arrangement. He insists rather that the liturgical order derives its authority from God since it is "the Advocate himself who has commanded this arrangement." Chrysostom adopts the use of Paraclete (Παράκλητος) from 1 Jn 2:1, where his model (the Apostle John) used the same term to refer

7 *On the Priesthood*, 3,4; Malingrey, *Sur le sacerdoce*, 142.

8 Neville chose "ordinances" (70), while Malingrey translated it as "things" (*les choses*, 143).

to Jesus Christ.[9] The term "Advocate" with its legal connotations seems the appropriate choice here because of John's emphasis on the authorization of the eucharistic liturgy. John rarely leaves such a description without some call for a human response. His invitation to scrutinize the heavenly realities means that people's minds must view "the things in heaven with a bare soul and a pure mind," as he will go on to say in just a few lines. If Christians approach the sacred table with proper dispositions, they will be able to live in the environs of the angels and see how glorious this new arrangement of grace is in comparison to the old.

As an agent of movement, the priest has at his disposal the stories of the Old Testament as well as the descriptions of Israel's cult. As John later comments on the story of Elijah on Mt. Carmel, he emphasizes the astounding spectacle of fire falling from heaven.[10] Yet this is as nothing compared to the rites of the new covenant. His exhortation to move on from Elijah to a greater reality underscores his belief that nothing is more awesome than the eucharistic table:

> Picture Elijah with your eyes, and a boundless crowd standing around with the sacrifice lying on the stones, and all the rest of the people in quiet and silence with only the prophet praying. Then suddenly a flame descends from heaven upon the sacrificial animal. These amazing spectacles are full of dread. So now, move from there to the sacrifice being now completed. Not only is it awesome to see, but it surpasses all amazement. For the priest stands there bringing down not fire but the Holy Spirit. And the priest himself makes much supplication, not so that a kind of torch may consume the gifts lying there by descending from above, but that the grace coming on the sacrifice through it may lift up the souls of everyone and shine forth more brightly than silver refined by fire. So will anyone be able to think of this awe-inspiring rite with contempt except through madness or lunacy? Or don't you know that a human soul was not even able to bear the fire of that sacrifice but that all would be utterly destroyed if there were not a lot of help from the grace of God?[11]

One suspects that John is thinking of how Christians may downplay their own experience of worship in comparison with the dramatic stories

9 Of its five occurrences in the Johannine writings, only 1 Jn 2:1 refers the term to Jesus Christ. The other four refer to the Holy Spirit.

10 This event is narrated in 1 Kings 18.

11 *On the Priesthood*, 3,4.

like Elijah and the prophets of Baal. When the victim on the altar is not an animal but the Lamb of God, John calls for his people to stand in amazement of this greater reality. The superiority of the new covenant sacrifice over the old is much like a contrast between reality and a picture of reality, between substance and the outward appearance of substance. John contrasts the descent of fire with the descent of God himself. His love of meditating on God's condescension comes out again in his emphasis on the Epiclesis, the calling down of the Holy Spirit. He seems very cognizant of the priest as a human agent, not the source or the power of the eucharistic sacrifice. It is the Holy Spirit, not the priest, who brings the grace of God to the people of God. It is pertinent to ask why John would make this contrast. Nothing in the Old Testament suggests that Elijah's sacrifice was anything like those offered in the temple or tabernacle. His sacrifice is purely for demonstrating the power of the true God. A more fitting contrast would have been between Christ's sacrifice and those prescribed in the Torah. Yet John wanted to use the Elijah example because of the common themes of descent and fire. For Chrysostom, the Eucharist is a spiritual fire that enlivens the souls of Christian people because the Holy Spirit, also depicted as fire in the New Testament, brings a grace so potent that "it may lift up the souls of everyone, and shine forth more brightly than silver refined by fire."

In these substantial passages the priest is both all-important and insignificant at the same time. He holds an office unparalleled among human institutions but infinitely inferior and subordinate to the true priest, Christ himself. This is the reason I speak of the priest in kinetic terms; he is an agent of movement, primarily vertical. He is the divine choice to embody movement from heaven to earth and earth to heaven. He is also free, however, to move from the older shadows and signs of God's grace in the Old Testament to the realities revealed in the new covenant. The old serves the new just as the earthly serves the heavenly.

However dignified the priesthood may be, a priest is still a man subject to the same weakness as other men. And to many in the world his work does not seem important or effective. There are often no tangible results or benefits. He cannot command people, only persuade them. He cannot rule over people, only guide them. Why then would John Chrysostom be so intent on speaking in such lofty terms about the priesthood? John was well aware of the struggles and temptations facing priests, but he spoke thus because of the supernatural origin and significance of the priestly ministry. And while he was more than familiar with priestly failings, he nevertheless reminded himself and his audiences of the high calling of the priest:

> Away with madness! For madness clearly overlooks such a great foundation [ἀρχή], without which we neither have salvation nor obtain the good things proclaimed to us. For if no one can enter the kingdom of heaven except he is born again through water and the Spirit, and unless he eats the flesh of the Lord and drinks his blood, then he is cast out of eternal life. Then all these things are done through no other means but only through those holy hands, those of the priests I mean. Then how can anyone without these escape the fire of hell, or obtain the crowns stored up? These men are those who have been entrusted with spiritual birth pangs and who have been entrusted with giving birth through baptism. Through these we are clothed with Christ and buried with the Son of God. We become members of that blessed head! So then they [the priests] are more to be feared than rulers and kings. And not only this; they are honored more than parents. They [parents] give birth from blood and the will of the flesh, but they [priests] are the source of our birth from God, of that blessed regeneration, of that true freedom and adoption by grace.[12]

To understand the priesthood, it is necessary to distinguish its objective aspects from its subjective appropriation by a particular man. Here John concentrates on the objective features of the institution when he speaks of the necessity of the priesthood for salvation. Quoting from Jn 3:5 (on the necessity of baptism) and Jn 6:53 (on the necessity of communing in the Eucharist), Chrysostom insists that "all these things are done through no other means but only through those holy hands, those of the priests I mean." A key word in this context is "entrusted" (πιστευθέντες), because John certainly embraces Paul's self-description as "stewards of the mysteries of God" (1 Cor 4:1) even if he doesn't quote it at this point. And picking up on Paul's words, the priest's baptismal ministrations make a person "buried with the Son of God" (Rom 6:4) and clothe that person with Christ (Gal 3:27). The priest can command even greater respect than parents because God has entrusted him with "spiritual birth pangs" (τὰς πνευματικὰς ὠδῖνας) and with nourishing the faith of the children of God through the Eucharist. The honor due to the priest is as high above natural parents as the world of heaven is to this world.

12 *On the Priesthood*, 3,5–6.

SACRIFICE OF CHRIST: THE INDISPENSABLE MINISTRY OF PRIESTS

In chapter 4 we claimed that the presence of Christ's humanity in the Eucharist entailed the notion of sacrifice. We pointed to texts that taught that there is an identity between the sacrifice of Jesus on the altar of the cross and the body of Christ lying on the altar of the church. I even partially quoted from *On the Priesthood* 3,4 to show that it was consonant with other expressions of the sacrificial nature of the Eucharist. Now let us return to that text to examine the connection between priest and sacrifice:

> When you see the Lord sacrificed and lying there and the priest standing with the sacrifice praying along with all who have become red with that precious blood, then do you still think you are among men and standing on earth? Rather, aren't you immediately transported into heaven? Once you cast aside every carnal thought of your soul, don't you see the things in heaven with a bare soul and a pure mind? O what a wonder! O the love of God for humanity! He who sits above with the Father is held in the hands of all at that hour and gives to those who want to enfold him and to embrace him. All do this through the eyes [of faith]. Are these things only worth being despised by you or can such things be lifted up with them?[13]

A contextual analysis of *On the Priesthood* 3,4 shows that in following upon 3,2 there seems to be an abrupt change of topic. In the preceding section John is still defending himself to Basil regarding the charge of ambition as a reason not to accept ordination. This accusation, leveled by some in Antioch, falls flat because John would certainly have accepted ordination if he had been motivated by vainglory. Then the text seems to switch in a completely different direction. Commentators have read it so. Yet I think there is a deeper connection in the sequence of the text. By beginning 3,4 in the way he does, John is offering a notion of the priesthood in accord with his view of the liturgy. The priesthood participates in a higher reality, one where human aspirations are empty (κενοδοξία) and meaningless. When he exclaims, "O what a wonder! O the love of God for humanity!" John is implicitly answering his own questions, "Rather, aren't you immediately transported into heaven? Once you cast aside every carnal thought of your soul, don't you see the things in heaven with a bare soul and a pure mind?"

13 *On the Priesthood*, 3,4.

There simply is no common measurement between what humans can conceive and what the priest is privileged to celebrate. Why should this be so? The passage gives an answer through a striking progression.

The progression moves from the earthy altar (table) that is the focus of prayer for both priest and people to the corollary worship of heaven; it then climaxes in the One who is both Gift and Giver. Behind this progression lies the centrality of Christ crucified. He is the One who lies sacrificed on the table (τὸν κύριον τεθυμένον καὶ κείμενον) but, as the passage later makes clear, this same sacrifice is the One who sits above with the Father (Ὁ μετὰ τοῦ πατρὸς ἄνω καθήμενος). The presence of Christ as the sacrifice is the indispensable foundation of earthly worship, and that same presence is what makes for the transport into heaven. It is that same sacrifice that allows the worshipers to see the celestial realities present in the earthly. This union of heaven and earth, which we made our focus so much in chapter 1, is here understood to be possible only through the sacrificed Jesus. And there is a tantalizing unclarity in the reference to all those "who have become red with that precious blood" (καὶ πάντας ἐκείνῳ τῷ τιμίῳ φοινισσομένους αἵματι). Are these the people in liturgy who have united themselves with the priest in his sacrificial offering? Are these ordinary people who have communed in the blood of Christ? Or could this refer to the denizens of heaven who have been washed in that same blood for their entrance into celestial glory? Chrysostom may be alluding to those who "washed their robes and made them white in the blood of the Lamb" (Rv 7:14). I am inclined to think that Chrysostom is referring to the glorified saints in heaven since the next phrase refers to a transposition from earth to heaven.

In any case, this experience of transcendent glory is only possible through the sacrifice of Christ. That sacrifice, though accomplished once at Calvary, is still effective for communicants, and one is tempted to add "for the forgiveness of sins" (Mt 26:28). Yet John's choice of language emphasizes the humility of Christ and his intimacy with his participants: "He who sits above with the Father is held in the hands of all at that hour and gives to those who want to enfold him and to embrace him. All do this through the eyes [of faith]."[14] That the Incarnate Son would allow himself to be held in the hands of humans (ταῖς ἁπάντων κατέχεται χερσὶ), sinners at that, shocks the sensibilities of all who know that God is beyond our comprehension. But John embellishes that fact with two highly descriptive verbs, *enfold* and

14 *On the Priesthood*, 3,4.

embrace (περιπτύξασθαι καὶ περιλαβεῖν) so as to show that the Christ who was sacrificed desires intimate union with those same sinners. In this way, the paragraph moves from earthly worship through heavenly worship to the Center of all true worship, Jesus Christ himself. I suggest that John, realizing how fearful and exacting the ministry of priests is, naturally shunned it, perhaps because he did not think himself worthy. We may never know what was in John's mind but he certainly maintained a view of the priesthood that was so exalted as to be beyond description.

Later in *On the Priesthood* 6,4, John returns to the ministry of priests to discuss specifically the work of prayer. It would not be an overstatement to say that prayer, in its widest sense, is the most important work of a priest. Kings may be charged with a portion of the human race, to rule over and govern them, but a priest is charged with the souls of everyone and he becomes a "father of all" by virtue of his ordination. His prayers, both liturgical and private, are the healing balm of salvation for his people.

> For I think that the boldness of Moses and of Elijah are not ever sufficient for such a great supplication. As he was entrusted with the whole world, and himself the father of all, so he [the priest] is attached to God to beg for the cessation of wars everywhere, for the tumults to cease, for peace, for prosperity, and asking too for the speedy change of all the evils that have privately and publicly afflicted each person. And he should pray for all who lack that they endure many things inasmuch as he is the leader of those being led.[15]

The language of this section is echoed in the later Byzantine liturgy named in honor of Chrysostom, but it may be that such a litany of prayers (for the cessation of wars, for the tumults to cease, for peace, for prosperity, etc.) was already in use in John's day and this portion of the treatise is an allusion to those prayers. In any case, John sees the priest's prayers for all people as an exercise of leadership that includes even kings and rulers. The priest therefore is to be honored above all. How ironic then that John should seem to mitigate the priest's honor at times. How does he do that?

Immediately following on the words above John gives a clue as to why and on what basis the priest is worthy of such honor. It is not because of him as a person, or his personal character, but because of the sacrifice he

15 *On the Priesthood*, 6,4.

offers. John's language combines objective and subjective aspects of priestly ministry into a seamless garment:

> But when he calls on the Holy Spirit and completes that awesome sacrifice, he lays hold of the one who is the common Master of all. In what order shall we place him? Tell me. How much purity and piety shall we demand of him? Ponder what kind of hands a priest should have to serve at such things and what sort of tongue pours forth that kind of words. And who should not be purer and holier than the soul that received such a Spirit? Then too the angels serve the priest, and the entire order of heavenly powers cries out loud. The place around the altar is brimming with these for the honor of him who lies there. And this is sufficient to be persuaded of those things then being accomplished.[16]

Chrysostom combines three historic doctrines in short compass that still animate the Churches of East and West today: the Epiclesis, the real presence, and the unique place of the priest in offering the sacrifice of Calvary. John's faith in the reality of Christ's presence in the Eucharist comes precisely from the descent of the Spirit to bring the reality of Jesus's humanity to earth. John's vivid use of "lay hold of" or "bind on" (ἐφάπτηται) suggests not only the priest's action of holding the consecrated bread in his hand but also the invisible reality behind the bread. He holds "the common Master of all" (τοῦ κοινοῦ πάντων συνεχῶς ἐφάπτηται δεσπότου).[17]

There can be little doubt that the priest holds a unique and honored position in Chrysostom's sacramental theology, but that place in the salvific economy is always at the service of Christ. In texts outside of *On the Priesthood* John returns to the theme of the priestly uniqueness when he asks, "Don't you see that it is only the priest who can lawfully present the cup of the blood?"[18] Yet the dignity and honor due to the priest only obtains because Christ himself is the one who in the priest is ministering to the people of God at the altar. In *Homily 50 on Matthew* John argues that the same Christ who acted at the Last Supper is acting in the supper at the table of the Church:

16 *On the Priesthood*, 6,4.

17 The choice of ἐφάπτω (used in the middle voice) over simply ἅπτω may indicate a strong sense of grasping or binding.

18 *Homily 45 on Matthew*, PG 58:474. A few lines later John also speaks of the priesthood of the lay faithful: "Mind what you drink and tremble! Mind that you become a priest of Christ when with your own hand you give not flesh but bread, not blood but a cup of cold water."

> Believe that that supper is also present here. In this he [Christ] is reclining because it differed in no way from this one. For it is not a man who is doing this but Christ who does that one too. He does both this and that one. When you see a priest delivering it [the Eucharist] to you, think not about the priest who is doing this but that it is Christ's hand that is stretched out. It is much like when the priest is baptizing; it is not he who baptizes you but God who holds your head with an invisible power. It is neither angel nor archangel nor any other who dares to approach and touch. The same is true now. Whenever God gives birth, the gift comes from him alone. Do you see those here being made children? How can anyone refer the matter to slaves? They are present at the court. So too God did not entrust the gift to the angels but he himself is present with this command, "Don't call anyone on earth your father."[19]

John's high view of angelic beings here yields to a greater truth. God did not commit the ministry of the sacraments to angels. How then could God be so foolish as to commit this ministry to men, who are so much less than angels? Wouldn't human agents in charge of the sacraments always put their efficacy at risk? Here are echoes of what was at stake in the Donatist controversy in the church of North Africa. I am not aware of any presence of Donatism in Antioch in the 380s, but the doctrine expressed by John is similar to how Augustine responded to the Donatists in the early 400s. The Latin Father insisted that the efficacy of the sacraments does not depend on the degree of holiness of the priest. A priest may be a sinner, even a notorious sinner, but his sacramental ministry is not null and void because of his sin. Augustine rightly argued that if that were true, no sacraments would be valid because all priests were sinners. Like John here, Augustine maintained that it is Christ who is the main and principal actor behind the human priest. The efficacy of the sacraments, whether baptism or Eucharist, depends not on the human priest but on the theandric priest, Christ himself. So John reminds the faithful that it is Christ who is stretching out his hand with his own body and blood in the Eucharist.[20]

Christ not only commanded the Eucharist. He is the one whose power makes it possible, but it is a power exerted through the agency of

19 *Homily 50 on Matthew*, PG 58:507.

20 In a similar vein Naegle pointed to Chrysostom's *Homily 86 on the Gospel of John* (PG 54:472), where he says the priest lends his tongue to Christ and offers his hand to this work. See August Naegle, *Die Eucharistielehre des Heiligen Johannes Chrysostomus* (Freiburg, Germany, 1900), 130.

the Holy Spirit. Set like a diamond among other gems there is a passage in Chrysostom's *Homily on Holy Pentecost* that spells out the role of the Holy Spirit in establishing the Church and its sacraments. What is striking is how John telescopes two different perspectives into one picture; the historical and the liturgical unite to teach John's people the necessity of the ministry of the Holy Spirit:

> If there were no Holy Spirit, there would be no pastors and teachers in the church, for these come from the Spirit, as Paul himself says: "The Holy Spirit set you as pastors and bishops." Do you see that this comes through the Spirit? If the Holy Spirit were not in concert with the Father and the Teacher, then there would not be any of the other things such as when he mounted the sacred *Bema* a little before this and gave you all peace and you all uttered together, "And with your spirit." So you didn't utter this saying only to the one who mounts or to him who dialogues with you or to him who prays for you. Rather, when he stands at the sacred table, when he is about to offer the awesome sacrifice—those initiated know this—he does not touch the gifts before he prays down grace from the Lord. And you may utter "And with your spirit," reminding them with this response that the one present does nothing himself nor are the offered gifts effective from human nature. On the contrary, it is the grace of the Spirit present and hovering over that prepares the mystical sacrifice. For even if a man is present, it is God who works through him. So do not fixate on what is visible but consider the invisible grace. There is nothing human of what is happening on this sacred *Bema*. If the Spirit were not present, the church would not be constituted, if the church is constituted, it is abundantly clear that the Spirit is present.[21]

John opens a window on the power and dignity of the priesthood by showing its purpose is always to shepherd the people of God. His quotations from Eph 4:11 (pastors and teachers) and his rewording of Acts 20:28 both stress how it is only by the work of the Holy Spirit that the pastoral work of the Church can be accomplished. That John may be collapsing two perspectives here hinges on the word *Bema* (βῆμα), which is used in Paul of Christ's judgment seat (Rom 14:10; 2 Cor 5:10). We know, however, that it is used in some patristic writings to indicate the raised platform of the sanctuary of the Church, or the bishop's cathedra.[22] If he is in fact drawing on Paul's use,

21 *Homily on Holy Pentecost*, PG 50:459.

22 See G. W. Lampe, *Patristic Greek Lexicon* (Oxford: Oxford University Press, 1961), 296.

he may be referring to Christ's ascension, which of course took place just prior to Pentecost, and John may simply be referring to that event. After all, he does refer to Christ as Teacher—and to the Trinitarian persons—in the protasis of the conditional sentence. So, he may be referencing the historical event. Yet he is clearly referring to the liturgy when he quotes the people's response, "and with your spirit." Then comes a curious statement, "You didn't utter this saying only to the one who mounts or to him who dialogues with you or to him who prays for you."

These three clauses seem to refer to the priest, but John is denying that only the human priest is involved. Does he mean that Christ is the recipient of the people's response? Who is he referring to when he says that "he stands at the sacred table, when he is about to offer the awesome sacrifice"? He seems to refer to the human priest because he proceeds to say, "He does not touch the gifts before he prays down grace from the Lord," but there also seems to be something more, or rather *someone* more. In any case, John goes on to say that there is no awesome, mystical sacrifice without the presence and work of the Lord. Whether he is referring to Christ as Lord or to the Spirit, the implication for the priesthood is the same. There can be no priestly ministry at the sacred table without the Spirit's work. The human priest is only a conduit for that presence. It is grace that "prepares the mystical sacrifice" (τὴν μυστικὴν ἐκείνην κατασκευάζει θυσίαν). John reinforces this reality when he contends, "For even if a man is present, it is God who works through him." What John says of the Church being constituted by the Spirit's presence can perhaps be said also of the priesthood. It is the Spirit's presence that constitutes a priest. And as the Church is in fact constituted, so the presence of priests in the Church makes it "abundantly clear" (εὔδηλον) that the Holy Spirit is present too.

This all implies the divine origin of the priesthood—and therefore the sacrament of the Eucharist—as well as the objective reality of priestly operations. The same emphasis surfaces again in *Homily 2 on 2 Timothy*, where John exhorts Christians to be obedient to their priests in accord with Heb 13:17. Chrysostom then cites several New Testament texts teaching that to hear God's messengers is to hear God (Mt 10:40). To support his exhortation, he restates something we saw in the *Homily on Holy Pentecost* about the necessity of the priesthood for salvation. While insisting that despising a priest is tantamount to despising the God who ordained him, John answers an objection in the strongest possible terms: "What shows that God has ordained him? Unless you have this assumption [of his ordination], then your hope is empty. If God does nothing through the priest, you have no washing in baptism, you partake of no mysteries, you enjoy no [priestly] blessings. In effect, you would be no Christian at all."[23] This counterfactual argument (if he were not ordained, there would be no salvation) hearkens back to Athanasius's method of defending the Incarnation, for the Alexandrian Father argued that if God had not become a man, there would be no salvation. And Paul said that if there were no resurrection, the Christian would have no hope (1 Cor 15:14). Yet, if it is true that God's divine effort to save the human race acts through priests, then is it not all the more important that the priest be a holy man? We will address this problem presently but first it is crucial to note how John believes in the objective efficacy of priestly work. Later in the same homily John says: "It is not the priest's life or [his] virtue that accomplishes so great a thing, is it? The things that God gives are not results of priestly virtue. The entire matter comes from grace. The priest only opens his mouth and God accomplishes the entire affair. The priest only fulfills the role of a symbol."[24]

There can be no doubt that John's use of "symbol" (σύμβολον) here is key to understanding his teaching; both the syntax (emphatic order) and the semantics (original meaning) indicate his larger point. Calling a priest a "symbol" both limits his importance in the divine *oikonomia* and enlarges the scope of divine work through him. Being a symbol, the priest is a sign, an index pointing to a greater reality. He is not the source of the work, as John emphatically insists, "the entire matter comes from grace." But the term "symbol" for John, as for most other Greek Fathers, means much more than our modern cognate allows. As we explained earlier, σύμβολον meant that a visible sign carried the reality that it signified. For them, the symbol was in accord with the signifying reality of the world as a whole. As Schmemann put it, "To be symbolical belongs to ontology."[25] So, to paraphrase the language of the liturgy named after John, the priest is one who "mystically represents" the work of God but even more than the laity because of his ordination. In an earlier chapter we observed how the earthly liturgy actualizes the already existent liturgy of heaven. So too the priest actualizes the grace of God by

23 *Homily 2 on 2 Timothy*, PG 62:610.

24 *Homily 2 on 2 Timothy*, PG 62:612. ἀρετῆς ἀνύεσθαι· τὸ πᾶν τῆς χάριτός ἐστι· τούτου ἐστὶν ἀνοῖξαι μόνον τὸ στόμα, τὸ δὲ πᾶν ὁ Θεὸς ἐργάζεται· σύμβολον οὗτος πληροῖ μόνον.

25 Alexander Schmemann, *For the Life of the World* (Crestwood, NY: St. Vladimir's Press, 1973), 139–40.

becoming an instrument of that grace. Heaven can visit earth because the priest is a true embodiment of God's action; he is a σύμβολον.[26]

Earlier we observed John in *Homily 2* assuring himself and others of the objective value and power of the eucharistic sacrifice flowing from the nature of the priesthood. Noting again that "it is God who does the whole thing" (ὅτι τὸ πᾶν ὁ Θεὸς ποιεῖ), Chrysostom emphasizes that the eucharistic offering (προσφορὰ) does not depend on which priest acts in Christ's place:

> I want to tell you a paradox, but don't be perplexed or disturbed. So why is this? This offering is the same whether it is Paul or Peter doing it. It is the same in fact that Christ did and that he gave to the disciples; the same as the priests now do. This is nothing less than that [offering] because it is not men who make this holy but the One who sanctifies it himself. As the words that God uttered are the same that the priest now speaks, so also the offering is the same and the baptism he gave. The whole matter is of the faith.[27]

If it does not matter which of the two apostolic pillars of the Church celebrates, then the offering certainly does not depend on the person or character of the priest. John explicitly grounds the eucharistic offering in two realities: one historical, the other supernatural. Christ gave the Eucharist to his apostles and he is also the one who sanctifies the gifts (αὐτὸς ὁ καὶ ἐκείνην ἁγιάσας) at every liturgy. And that explains the objective reality of the Eucharist. As other Church Fathers say, the priest lends his voice to God to sanctify the gifts. John reassures his hearers by affirming that "the whole matter is of the faith" (οὕτω τὸ πᾶν τῆς πίστεώς ἐστιν). I rather think that John here means "the faith" in its objective sense (*fides quae creditur*) rather than faith as a subjective reality (*fides qua creditur*). In sum, what John has expressed about the divine origin, authorization, and action of the liturgy through the ministry of a priest is part and parcel of the faith delivered to the holy Church (Jude 3).

26 My translation differs from that of Schaff, who translates σύμβολον οὗτος πληροῖ μόνον as "the Priest only performs a symbol." To choose "perform" for πληροῖ suggests that the act of consecration is a symbolic act, which makes it subject to the possible misunderstanding of many moderns who see the act as a bare symbol devoid of any deeper reality. The verb πληροῖ means "to fulfill, to make full" and can be distinguished from τελέω, which is the normal word in Chrysostom for "perform" or "act" in regard to the liturgy.

27 *Homily 2 on 2 Timothy*, PG 62:612.

THE PRIESTHOOD: THE SUBJECTIVE SIDE

For all his emphasis on the objective nature of the priestly ministry, John also speaks of the person of the priest and the weight of responsibility that falls on him. John repeatedly expresses his reticence, even fear, of all that the priesthood requires of a man, of all the burdens laid on his shoulders. Our earlier quotation from *On the Priesthood* 6.4 spoke of how much greater the priest's pastoral responsibility is than was that of Moses and Elijah. This greater work is based on the contrast of "the things before grace" and those coming in Christ and the fullness of redemption. John seems to think the enormous weight on a priest would be enough to scare normal men away, but he is also drawn to the elevated and sublime work of priestly ministry. The great dignity of the priestly office derives from the exalted service he performs in consecrating the Eucharist: "When he calls on the Holy Spirit and completes that awesome sacrifice, he lays hold of the one who is the common Master of all. In what order shall we place him?"[28] That order belongs to another world: "Then too the angels serve the priest, and the entire order of heavenly powers cries out loud. The place around the altar is brimming with these for the honor of him who lies there."[29] Immediately, however, John realizes that this celestial reality on earth demands of the priests something beyond what a man is capable of: "How much purity and piety shall we demand of him? Ponder what kind of hands a priest should have to serve at such things and what sort of tongue pours forth that kind of words. And who should not be purer and holier than the soul that received such a Spirit?"[30] The celebration of the Eucharist, which stands at the very center of a priest's ministry, calls forth a life and vision from the priest that encompasses the whole world.

Transcending the intercessory ministries of Moses and Elijah, the priest in the time of grace becomes "a father of all people" (αὐτὸς ὢν ἁπάντων πατήρ) and, like the Son of God (Heb 5:7) makes supplication (ἱκετηρία) for the whole world. Chrysostom would never have doubted or denied that all baptized Christians are intercessors for one another and for the world, but in a heightened sense the priest plays that all-important role. The difference is

28 *On the Priesthood*, 6,4.

29 *On the Priesthood*, 6,4.

30 *On the Priesthood*, 6,4.

not absolute but relative. Yet the prayers of priest and people all derive their efficacy from the same source, namely, the sacrifice of Christ lying on the altar. The power of the priesthood lies not in the priest himself, neither in his personal wisdom nor in his virtue. It seems that ancient Christians fell prey to the same temptations that modern ones do. They were tempted to think that it was the personal qualities of the priest that made him effective or not. Chrysostom is clear that such a belief is wrong, and he vigorously opposed it as strongly as Augustine did the Donatists who advocated the same mistake.

Yet at the same time it is true that the priest must be a holy man. The temptations facing the priest are what seem to have scared John, because he found the life of a public priest to be far more dangerous than that of a monk. No doubt remembering his time in the caves outside Antioch, John views the monk as taking great precautions to maintain "spotless purity" (καθαρότητος εἰλικρινοῦς) and angelic virtue (ἀγγελικῆς ἀρετῆς), but even heroic measures do not always protect the priest living in the city. One clear and present danger comes from women who seek to entice him into sin. The words John chooses to describe this generic woman make it clear that he is first talking about the woman who is seeking a sexual liaison. None of this surprises John, but what does astonish him is that it is not only the sexually overt woman who might ensnare the priest; the unassuming and needy woman might also become a trap if the priest is not careful. John now describes a generic woman who is not seeking a sexual liaison at all and yet may pose a temptation to a priest just by her feminine nature. The priest's compassion for her spiritual needs may give way to something less than appropriate. Perhaps John is aware of the wiles of the Evil One in this latter case where a noble sentiment (compassion) can easily give way to self-gratification. In this case too, the fault lies not so much in feminine enticement as in masculine self-interest. In both cases, the end can be destruction.[31]

Sexual temptation, no matter the circumstances, presents a clear threat to purity and holiness, but other forms of allurement may not be so obvious. These come in the form of daily distractions that can "abate men's concerns for the things of God."[32] These include the business affairs of the city, domestic duties, and even hardships that accompany ordinary life. The duties of a priest to his people are distracting enough, but his duties to God far surpass

31 *On the Priesthood*, 6,2; see Neville, 137–38.

32 *On the Priesthood*, 6,4; Neville, 140.

any comparison. Still, these distractions cannot compare to what is perhaps the greatest danger facing a priest.

The history of the Church has borne out John's anxiety over temptations arising from involvement with the opposite sex. The clergy have been no more able to resist sexual engagement with women than any other class of people. Because of the intensely personal nature of their work in helping souls, priests are sometimes even more vulnerable than those whose daily work is not so interpersonal. However, reading *On the Priesthood* leads me to conclude that sexual temptations are not as problematic as a whole other class of allurements. John returns again and again to vainglory and worldly honors as a form of spiritual suicide for the priest as well as every Christian. Yet because a priest is such a visible public figure, these vices are likely to affect him more severely than ordinary Christians. But what exactly is vainglory? In *On the Priesthood* 6,12 John glosses vainglory (κενοδοξία)[33] with several other expressions that afford us some understanding: "What is the food that feeds these beasts? It is made up of vainglory. Whether it is honors and praise, arrogance, excessive authority and power, jealousy, approval of your neighbors, love of money, ambition of getting from donors, intemperance, luxury, or the constant company of women."[34]

Chrysostom often used wild animals as metaphors for the passions because they both have uncontrollable natures. There is little difference between savage beasts and wicked men, but the greatest threat to sanctity comes not from the outside but from the inside, from passions that wage war against the soul. John certainly believed that a priest's attraction to women could be problematic, even his downfall, but I rather think that the threat of vainglory was even more ominous in his mind. Note his vocabulary: authority and power, approval of your neighbors, ambition of getting from donors. All these share the common denominator of sycophancy, that fawning after human approval and praise that sometimes comes to priests. To be placed in a position of trust is to be tempted to abuse the powers of the trust for one's own advantage. This is especially true in currying the favor of benefactors. And after John was installed as the Patriarch of Constantinople that temptation was no doubt very present in his mind, but we know from his personal history that he did not give in to that temptation. It was his opposition to

33 Some form of κενοδοξία occurs ten times in the treatise.

34 *On the Priesthood*, 6,12.

the royal throne that in fact alienated him from the city and eventuated in his banishment.

Earlier in *On the Priesthood* 6,3 John gives us examples of seeking empty glory and its effects. Two possible faults can emerge in a man who has been honored by others. These can often conflict with one another: sycophancy, or what John calls the "servility born of flattery" (τῇ τε τῆς θωπείας δουλοπρεπείᾳ), and "insanity coming from exultant pride" (τῇ τῆς ἀλαζονείας ἀνοίᾳ). The first temptation arises from his interactions with those who stand above him in society or at least those with whom he wants to curry favor. He may end up compromising his principles or at least modifying his social behavior in unauthentic ways. The second temptation arises from his interactions with those who seem to stand below him on the social ladder, or what is worse, with those deemed less spiritual. Falling prey to the primordial sin of pride, the priest may very well be "thrust into the pit of arrogance."[35]

All these temptations can trouble the priest and make his ministry ineffective primarily because they affect his mind and his soul. The battle for purity and other virtues in the life of a priest is first and foremost an inner battle, a war that is waged in the silence of his own heart. John is realistic about success and failure. The moral trials that a priest faces can be allayed by a good will and dependence on God, but they are genuine battles nonetheless. Anger is one passion that he mentions in this context. This interior struggle is a problem shared by all human beings, and it is a menacing demon to expel. We will return to this issue again in chapter 8 under the rubric of "remembrance of evil" (*mnesikakia*), but John mentions this as a particular problem for the priest: "The memory of immoral men often arises and makes my heart swell up at the things done by them. But this is not the end."[36] No, all is not lost. John can restrain his anger by doing what he commends in other contexts, namely, to recognize that it is "futile and utterly despicable to forget our own faults and meddle with those of our neighbor."[37] All this points to the fact that the life of a priest has much in common with the lives all other human beings, but because of his heightened, even exalted responsibility, the priest can become a stumbling block in unique ways.

35 *On the Priesthood*, 6,3; Neville's translation, 139.

36 *On the Priesthood*, 6,12; Malingrey, *Sur le sacerdoce*, 360–62.

37 *On the Priesthood*, 6,2; 6,12; Neville, 152.

SCANDALOUS PRIESTS AND INJURED LAITY

Even with a solid knowledge of the dignity inherent in the priestly office, even realizing the challenges facing priests to overcome sin in their lives, even acknowledging the apparently special struggles that attend the life of a priest, there can still be great harm done to the Christian faithful when priests fail to live up to their calling. This was as much a problem in the fourth and fifth centuries as it is today. John knew the problem all too well. John distinguished between two types of complaints about priestly misbehavior. One was a legitimate feeling of hurt by faithful Christians who were sorely disappointed in their priests; the other type of complaint was more of an excuse to cover for the sins of the complainant.

We hinted earlier that Chrysostom was responding to the problem of scandal in *Homily 2 on 2 Timothy*. We previously noted how John in this homily emphasized the objective reality of Christ acting through the priest. But let's return to that homily and to these statements in their original context. In general, Chrysostom is praising Paul's pastoral sacrifice stated in 2 Timothy 2 when he asks Timothy to suffer hardship along with him because he himself suffered all things for the sake of the gospel (cf. 2 Tm 2:3). Such a holy sentiment should induce obedience from the faithful, but sometimes they are reluctant to obey their teachers. John's answer comes in the form of a rhetorical question; it is bold, even audacious: "Do you know what a priest is? He is an angel of the Lord."[38] In essence, John asks his fellow Christians to look through the person of the individual priest to the purpose and plan of God in establishing the priestly ministry. "Angel" here is certainly meant in the foundational sense of "messenger" since we know that John viewed angels and men as distinct and never to be confused. This all implies that the faithful must honor a priest for his ordained office, not so much for his person: "He who honors the priest will also honor God. He who learned to despise the priest will go on to insult God as well."[39] How the faithful think about priests will eventually transfer to God and translate into a complaint against his providence. For John, the issue is not about the priest but about the salvation of the faithful—which is why, as we saw earlier in this homily, John urges a positive disposition toward priests: "When someone is piously

38 *Homily 2 on 2 Timothy*, PG 62:610.

39 *Homily 2 on 2 Timothy*, PG 62:609.

disposed toward the priest, how much more so will he be toward God. Even if the priest is bad (φαῦλος), God sees that you are serving for the sake of honor toward him who is not worthy of such honor and God will repay you."[40] Is John here glossing over the pain and anguish Christians feel when their priests fail, whether morally or otherwise? Is he implicitly excusing priestly misconduct to shield himself and other priests? I don't think so.

Mental pain, anger, discouragement, even despair are natural human responses to priests' failures, especially when those lapses are of a moral nature. And while the faithful are generally disposed toward forgiveness of their priests, persistent and hidden evil adds insult to injury for the Christians who otherwise love their priests. In sum, John is counseling a perspective that does not injure the faith of the faithful. He asks them to remember why there are priests in the first place—it is for their own salvation. That is why it is crucial not to allow priestly misconduct to blur one's vision and deter one from the path of salvation.

The second type of complaint against priests, used as an excuse to cover one's own failures, surfaces in *Homily 21 on 1 Corinthians*. Toward the end of the homily John urges the rich to be generous toward the poor, and he especially rebukes them for making up excuses for not treating the poor with more compassion. He in fact urges the rich to be involved in the life of the poor directly and not to depend on the Church alone for almsgiving. Among the excuses often used is the failures of priests, by which he seems to refer to financial mistakes or to outright greed. But whatever the content of the objection, John offers a more generalized response. He strongly insists that pointing to priests' failures as an excuse for one's own sins will avail nothing at the judgment throne of God. John cleverly turns the objection on its head when he asks, if the teachers of the objectors were corrupt and greedy, would their wickedness justify the complainants' failure to love by the truth? Absolutely not! So too a priest's sins or failures in no way justify others in their own sins. Even if the Church provides for the poor, does this excuse the rich from being directly involved in helping the unfortunate? Absolutely not!

Yet the most important part of John's response has to do with the objective nature of the teaching of Christ. John quotes Mt 23:2–3, "The scribes and the Pharisees sit in the seat of Moses. Do and observe whatever they say but do not act in accord with their works. For they do not act in accord

40 *Homily 2 on 2 Timothy*, PG 62:609.

with their words." Thus, even if Christians have a bad teacher, they still must obey if the teaching is true and right. Clearly John is here thinking of a "bad teacher" (διδάσκαλον φαῦλον) as one who is not living the message of truth he preaches. It is not from the actions of the priest that God will judge Christians but from the teaching they received. And John is keen to remind his hearers that this is not his cleverly contrived answer; it comes from Christ himself: "The Only-Begotten Son of God, himself loving and all-wise, sees all and knows that it happens over a long time and in a far-flung world there are going to be corrupt priests."[41] John's pastoral wisdom arises from his ability to apply the objective and true teaching to the situation in such a way that he brings people back to the issue of where they stand before God. In chapter 8 we shall observe this wisdom again as he urges forgiveness of others' offenses rather than revenge. Better to be injured once by another person than twice by adding one's own self-inflicted wound on top of the first injury.

John's response in *Homily 21 on 1 Corinthians* is similar to one in *Homily 86 on the Gospel of John*, but he employs a slightly different twist in his defense of the priests. Here he is speaking not of moral lapses made by priests but of their failures to shepherd properly the souls of the faithful. There is a divine asymmetry attached to priesthood: "The priest, on the contrary, even if he orders his own life well, but does not concern himself zealously about your interests, and those of all entrusted to his care, will depart with the wicked into hell."[42] The priest will answer not only for his own life but for the lives of those under his care. This fact should evoke from the laity respect for the priestly office and make them refrain from criticism that might hamper the priest in his pastoral responsibilities. Here too John appeals to Mt 23:2–3, but now adds that priests are not in the seat of Moses but in the seat of Christ. Their authority derives not from themselves but from God; "When God is the One who appoints" it is doubly reprehensible to "despise the man chosen, insult him, keep aiming at him blows without number . . . and sharpen our tongues against our priests."[43]

The priesthood is an exalted vocation, but it is also a precarious one. It is unquestionably essential to the salvation of the world, but it can totter on

41 *Homily 21 on 1 Corinthians*, PG 61:180.

42 *Homily 86 on the Gospel of John*; Sr. Thomas Aquinas Goggin, SCH, *Homilies on Saint John the Apostle and Evangelist: Homilies 48-88*, FC 41 (Washington, DC: The Catholic University of America Press, 1959), 454.

43 *Homily 86 on the Gospel of John*; Goggin, 456.

the weak and feeble character of a man who lives the vocation every day. John seemed to recognize this doubled-sided reality, but he always placed the greater weight on the objective nature of the priesthood. I aver that he did so because of his belief in the rightness of the divinely ordained economy of salvation. The priesthood was and is an essential part of that plan inasmuch as it is an extension of the priesthood of Christ himself. Just as the Eucharist is a kind of ongoing incarnation of Christ's humanity in space and time, so the priesthood is the same because the priest and the Eucharist are bound up with each other.

The natural and understandable hurt, pain, and disappointment that the lay faithful sometimes experience because of the failings of priests cannot in any way mitigate the necessity of the priestly ministry. In yet another expression of this deeply held belief John reassures his Christian people that the Holy Spirit is no less active now than in the apostolic times:

> Still now, there are many symbols of that gift among those things that are even greater and more awesome. For there is no equality between a dead body and a resurrected body. And the soul that is dead from sins can only exchange that destructiveness through baptism. There can be no comparable healing of the diseases of the body, no removing of the burden of sin, no correction of sight, no enlightening of a darkened soul. If there were no down payment of the Spirit now, there would not be any baptism, no forgiveness of sins, no righteousness and holiness. We would have no adoption and enjoy no mysteries. There can never be any mystical body and blood without the grace of the Spirit. We would have no priests.[44]

The people have wondered why the signs and wonders attested in the New Testament are no longer seen in their time. Does it mean that the Church is impotent or that God has ceased to work in the present as he did in the past? John's answer provides two insights. One is that the same power at work in the apostolic times is still at work in his; it is only manifested in a different way. The other insight is that spiritual miracles wrought through the sacraments are even greater than the visible miracles recorded in apostolic times. The removal of sin through baptism, the enlightening of a darkened soul, and the presence of forgiveness for the sinner all point to the active power of God at work. None of this would be possible "without the grace of the Spirit." And what is undeniable proof that the Holy Spirit is still at work

44 *Homily on the Resurrection of the Dead*, PG 50:432.

in the Church? If the Spirit were not at work, "we would have no priests." The mysteries are indeed symbols, down payments on the future life, but they are real embodiments of that life to come. So too the priest points beyond himself to the greater Priest of heaven:

> And all these things could never be established apart from that visitation [of the Spirit]. And there are many other symbols of the grace of the Spirit so that because you have the down payment of the Spirit, the death of the soul can be taken away, the hardening of thought and an impure life can be eradicated. So let us not be vexed at future things because we receive such [symbols] as pledges.[45]

Here again John returns to the foundational issue of salvation. Whatever problems the priest may face, whatever the wrongs he may have committed, whatever the apparent state of the Church in the world, there is one and only one question that both priest and people need to ask: how can we be saved? The priest is an essential part of the answer because he is ordained in God's order of salvation or *oikonomia*. This is why John asks in *Homily 86 on the Gospel of John*, "Why do I mention priests?" To remind his people of who is really behind the priestly arrangement and the nature of the priestly ministry: "Not even an angel or an archangel can effect anything with regard to what is given by God, but the Father, the Son, and the Holy Spirit direct everything. The priest simply lends his tongue and furnishes his hand. This is so because it would not be right for those who have embraced the faith to suffer harm with regard to the symbols of our salvation because of the evil conduct of another."[46]

✠ ✠ ✠

The human priest must be centered on the salvation of souls and at the same time know that he is not the one who can bring about that salvation. He is a human link in a divine chain. He must love the Church and at the same time realize that the Church does not belong to him. The priest is often said to be one who acts in the person of Christ, and the imagery of marriage between priest and the people of God is often used to describe his indispensable role,

45 *Homily on the Resurrection of the Dead*, PG 50:432.

46 *Homily 86 on the Gospel of John*; Goggin, 457.

but he is in fact more like a matchmaker than bridegroom. The reason lies in the divine arrangement of the Church:

> The Church is founded both on the economy of the Son of God who became man, died, rose, and lives, and on that of the Holy Spirit who sustains his presence in those united to Christ. The sacraments are the creation of the living Christ, not simply because he established them in the past but because he is now living and acting in them and because in them man can encounter him in a personal relationship; then through Christ man encounters the Father. The Church is therefore the coming of Eternity into time, God's theophany and the manifestation of his life and love.[47]

The priest does indeed act in the place of Christ, but his role consists more of being a physician administering healing remedies. His role is that of a guide leading his people back to the Father through "the economy of the Son of God." And yet, as Joseph Raya says so sharply, "the Church is the coming of Eternity into time." The human priest is the one who unlocks the gates of eternity so that the grace of Christ can flow down into time, into the Church, and into the hearts of all the faithful.

47 Joseph Raya, *The Face of God* (Denville, NJ: Dimension Books, 1976), 93.

Part III

Participation

7

Interior Dispositions and Holy Communion

When we turn to John Chrysostom's teaching on holy communion, we enter a rich world of pastoral wisdom. John faced formidable pastoral obstacles in Antioch and especially in Constantinople. Scholars who have studied John's sermons closely have seen many social concerns lying behind his exhortations. A focus on the interior spiritual life of the individual has received less attention, but in previous chapters I have already indicated some of the richness of John's thoughts on the state of the individual in light of the Eucharist. The development of the spiritual life of a person lay at the heart of his concern, and that concern arose from two sources: his culture and his faith. Many of the philosophers and other intellectuals during this period shared the common goal of helping people grow into virtuous individuals. John's own teacher, Libanius, shows evidence of that goal. Yet, whereas Libanius thought that a return to the revered forms of ancient Rome would be the best path—a view shared by the Emperor Julian—John was convinced that the best answer lay in the Church. Faith in Christ would best shape souls into icons of goodness. How could the souls of Christians be formed in virtue? John was sure that the path forward lay in connecting his people to the life of Christ because mystical union with Jesus's humanity provided the needed medicine.

The tie between the life of Christ and the Eucharist recalls the Axis of Participation that I proffered as one side of an overarching framework to explain how the Eucharist relates to many other aspects of John's thought. So that the concept of an axis does not remain at some abstract level, we should note that participation is a carefully chosen term. While John uses several words to designate participation, such as μετοχή, μετουσία, μετάληψις, he reserves his highest praise for κοινωνία or communion, the very choice of Paul in the New Testament (cf. 1 Cor 10:16). The significance of John's choice of vocabulary lies in its ability to capture the manner in which everything in the new covenant and the life of the Christian can be related to participation or communion. All the dimensions of individual and ecclesial life are forms or expressions of participation. This implies then that communion in the Eucharist is more than just one act among many in a Christian's life. It is the zenith and the apex of all that a Christian is, and it is so because the Eucharist is the connection with and participation in the human life of Jesus.

In this chapter I explore John's wisdom for the individual Christian in the act of communing in the sacred signs. I return to several homilies cited earlier because of their richness and begin to plumb their depths in the matter of approaching the Eucharist. John does not hesitate to address the barriers to a meaningful communion, one of which hides unsuspectingly beneath the surface of life, the clandestine vice of indifference. And indifference is often manifested by a legalistic approach to communion that gauges the holy act by the liturgical season rather than by the interior state of the heart. But all the spiritual failures of a Christian are not sufficient to block profitable participation in the sacrament if he comes with an intention of receiving grace. Openness to divine working lifts the communicant up to heavenly realms, a mental ascent to the things above that simultaneously requires an ascetic denial of this world as the source of meaning and happiness. A sincere communion in the sacred species then affords abundant fruit that above all shows itself in peace and tranquility of heart. Such fruit is only possible because the Eucharist gives the same Jesus as the one who walked the earth.

Among the many texts that place the believer back into the life of Christ through the Eucharist, one of the richest can be found at the end of Chrysostom's homily *On the Birth of Christ*, which was partially treated back in chapter 3. With reminders of the objective reality of Christ's redemption embodied in the sacrament, John urges his congregation to pause and reflect on the majesty of the eucharistic sacrifice:

> Consider, O man, what kind of sacrifice you are about to touch, what sort of table you are going to approach. Think of it! Even though you are dust and ashes, you partake of the blood and body of Christ. As the King calls you to the feast, you sit down with reverence and you partake of the delights set before you with modesty and silence. When God calls you to his table, and sets before you his own Son, when the angelic powers attend with fear and trembling as the Cherubim hide their faces and the Seraphim, while trembling, cry out, Holy, Holy, Holy Lord, do you also cry out? Tell me. Will you then attend this spiritual banquet in turmoil? Don't you know that your soul needs to be filled with tranquility at that very moment? There is a need for much peace and silence, not confusion, anger, and disturbance.[48]

John's exhortation centers on the contrast between the divine preparation of the feast and the lack of human preparation, which fails to appreciate the greatness of the moment (*kairos*). Perhaps in the distant background Chrysostom is thinking of the parable of the Wedding Feast (Mt 22:1–14), where one guest fails to have the proper wedding garment for the occasion and is thrown out into the outer darkness. In this homily one can see two items of spiritual clothing that the communicant must have. One is the willingness to enter into the angelic hymn of praise, to share in the joy of heaven. The other is a silent, quiet, reverent disposition. John's fervor is evident as he piles on hortatory subjunctives ("Let us . . .") to lead his hearers to the holy table: "Let us then tremble as we approach, let us give thanks, let us fall down, confessing our faults, let us weep as we mourn our own evil. Let us offer fervent prayers to God. We will thereby purify ourselves quietly and with a fitting good order. So, let us come as approaching the King of Heaven."[49]

John sees reverential fear conjoined to a thankful spirit and diligent self-examination as all part of a proper approach to the Eucharist. One should not only confess sins but even shed tears over the evil perpetrated. He contrasts such a humble approach to "confusion and wrath [that] become arrogance [ὕβρις] in the presence of the sacrifice lying before us. This is the last [and greatest] contempt, for a defiled man to present himself to God."[50] An approach to the sacrament born of arrogance even provokes God, whereas the humble Christian desires to be reconciled through propitiation. All these exhortations suggest deep emotion within John's soul as he

48 *On the Birth of Christ*, PG 49:361.

49 *On the Birth of Christ*, PG 49:361.

50 *On the Birth of Christ*, PG 49:362.

holds in his heart a profound concern for the spiritual welfare of his flock: "Receiving [communion] let us kiss the blameless and holy sacrifice, let us enfold it with our eyes, let us warm our minds thoroughly with it."[51]

What could account for such deep emotion in Chrysostom's preaching? He gives us hints in almost passing tones as he speaks of "the king of heaven" who is at the same time "the blameless and holy sacrifice." When he speaks of "kissing the sacrifice," he may do so literally or metaphorically, but in either case he is indicating the tenderest affection for Christ present in the Eucharist. No part of the communicant, inside or out, should be left untouched as he enfolds the Eucharist with his eyes and warms his mind with it. The promise that lies waiting in such a humble and reverent approach consists of the growth in virtues that a proper reception of the Eucharist affords.

John enumerates these virtues as a result of allowing the full effect of the sacrament to penetrate deeply within the soul, "that we might come not to judgment or condemnation but to a sobriety of the soul, to love, to virtue, and to reconciliation with God, to confident hope, to the practice of a thousand goods. This is also for us to sanctify ourselves and edify our neighbor."[52] John here indirectly refers to the twofold commandment of love of God and of neighbor (cf. Mt 22:37–39). Love for God implies the desire for sanctification, which produces the other more specific virtues listed here. Reconciliation with God (καταλλαγὴν τὴν πρὸς τὸν Θεὸν) seems out of place here in that the others in the list are more internal, self-contained. Yet with a deeper look, it points to the basis for all virtues like sobriety, love, and firm hope. We must remember that John's preaching was an attempt at a Christian *paideia* to replace the pagan Greek *paideia*. He viewed himself as giving philosophical medicine to cure the soul.[53] This all implied that there could be no growth in virtue apart from the grace of God and so reconciliation with God was not one among many other virtues but the very source of all virtue.

We shall return to the subject of virtues in due course but here it is worth noting how John again mentions the idea of reconciliation at the end of the

51 *On the Birth of Christ*, PG 49:362.

52 *On the Birth of Christ*, PG 49:362. I have translated ὑπόθεσις as "practice" but it could have just as easily been glossed as "foundation."

53 See Wendy Mayer, "John Chrysostom: Moral Philosopher and Physician of the Soul," in *John Chrysostom Past, Present, Future*, ed. Doru Costache and Merio Baghos (Sydney: AIOOS Press, 2017), 193–215.

homily. He casts it as the opposite of provoking God, presumably to anger, by an improper disposition. Alienation or reconciliation; those are the options:

> So then let us not provoke God instead of [seeking] reconciliation; rather let us show attentive care and order. And with no disturbance of our soul, let us approach with prayer and a contrite heart so that with this we may propitiate our Master Jesus Christ and can obtain the good things promised to us by the grace and love for humanity [that comes from] our Lord Jesus Christ, who with the Father and the Holy Spirit is glory, power, and honor, both now and forever. Amen.[54]

Reconciliation through propitiation (ἐξιλεωσάμενοι); that is the purpose of the Eucharist, to reconcile sinners to God through the sacrifice of Christ. Once accomplished on the cross, the same oblation lies deep within the converted bread and wine. And that spiritual reality must also lie deep within the heart of every communicant. This beautiful section of *On the Birth of Christ* is but a portion of all he says about the inner dispositions of the communicant.

BARRIERS TO PROFITABLE COMMUNION

When faithful Christians are ready to approach the holy table to receive the Eucharist, are there any thoughts or conditions that they should consider before receiving? John Chrysostom certainly thought so. In fact, he discussed this question on numerous occasions and offered advice and warnings to those who were ready to commune. Before considering these barriers, however, it is important to emphasize that for John the normal expectation seems to have been to receive the Eucharist at every liturgy. This is an inference from many statements he makes, but I believe it is justified because some of the sins and vices he addresses can be reasons to come *to* communion as well as reasons to refrain *from* it. With that default expectation, we can now explore a few reasons why one might refrain from communion in the sacred elements.

In John's mind the barriers to a fruitful communion were twofold; one was theological, the other psychological. The former centered on a lack of comprehension of the significance of the act, while the latter involved a range

54 *On the Birth of Christ*, PG 49:362.

of human faults and sins that prevented benefiting from sacramental participation. The barriers to a meaningful communion for John's hearers were not only theological in the sense of a lack of appreciation for the true meaning of the act. The greater obstacles consisted of subjective conditions in the minds of the congregants. These become evident from the many exhortations John gives to put aside those things that would hinder a profitable communion for his people.

One of the most pervasive obstacles to holy communion among Christians may in fact be the most difficult to detect: indifference to holy things. Perhaps one of the greatest problems in a time such as John's was not the obvious sins of greed, anger, and sexual immorality—though John has much to say about these sins—but the more subtle sin of indifference. One can almost hear the anguish in the heart of the Golden Mouth as he laments the indifference to holy things by those who name themselves Christian: "And as Christ is about to appear on the sacred mysteries, the church is empty and deserted."[55] Deserting the Church before the celebration of the holy mysteries? This is unthinkable for John, even to the point of questioning the people's love; abandoning the mysteries of the Church is a disease (νόσημα τῆς ἐκκλησίας), the healing of which requires precisely the medicines that are being abandoned.

We saw earlier in the homily *On Blessed Philogonius* Chrysostom's desire to bring his fellow Christians back to the life of Christ because the Eucharist carries the mysteries from heaven to earth. Later in this same homily John also stresses the dignity inherent in the act of communion: "Because of this, I encourage you all to lay hold of the divine mysteries not simply on account of the necessity of the feast. Rather, since you are about to partake of this holy offering, you should purify yourselves for many days through repentance, prayer, almsgiving, and leisure about spiritual things. Make sure you don't turn back like a dog to its vomit."[56]

55 *Homily 3 on the Incomprehensibility of God*, SC 28, 216.

56 *On Blessed Philogonius*, PG 48:755. Earlier in this homily, he says, "But now many of the faithful have rushed into such great folly and neglect as if filled with a thousand evils, taking no concern even for themselves. And when they simply happen to be here during the feasts, they come to this table. They don't realize that the moment of communion is not a matter of a feast or a festive assembly but of a life that wishes to be free from accusation and possess a pure conscience. And as the one who is free of evil in his conscience ought to come daily, so too the one overpowered by sin and not repentant ought not to feel safe in coming during a feast. For having communion once a year does not set us free from guilt when we approach unworthily but in fact condemns one even more because in approaching just once we are not then approaching in purity."

This call to spiritual purification before communion highlights the greater importance of interiority over customary participation. Such interior preparation corresponds to the inherent dignity of the sacrament itself because, he says, "You are about to receive the King under your roof in communion. As the King enters your soul, you should be in much tranquility, much silence, deep peace of thoughts."[57] The language of the King coming under the roof of the communicant is an adaptation of the story of the Roman centurion whose faith rivaled that of the native people of God (Mt 8:5–13). The story was of such significance that it became incorporated into the liturgies of the East and West; for John it functions as a beacon of the power in the Eucharist. "Don't you know that this table is full of spiritual fire? As springs gush forth the nature of water, so it has a certain unspeakable flame."[58] This spiritual fire and unquenchable flame make communion the greatest act of pious devotion that a Christian can engage in.

Behind John's sermons, we can catch a glimpse of John's hearers calculating their prospects for holy communion by the liturgical season of the year. The golden-mouthed preacher constantly tried to make them understand that preparation was more a matter of the heart than of the calendar. Like Christians of every generation, these easterners were tempted to measure their spiritual progress primarily by their adherence to public worship. Without denying the unrepeatable primacy of the liturgy, John desired for his congregants to assess their preparedness by an internal examination of the heart. In his third homily on Ephesians, John confronts this problem:

> I see many simply partaking of the body of Christ, and as it happens, more by custom and law than by reason and thought. When the season of holy Lent is upon us, such a one partakes of the mysteries, as also when the day of Epiphany arrives. And indeed, this is not a season of solemn procession. For neither Epiphany nor Lent make you worthy of approaching, but sincerity and purity of soul. With this you may always come; without this never. It says, "As often as you do this, you proclaim the Lord's death," that is, you make a reminder of the salvation for you and of my kindness.[59]

Quoting 1 Cor 11:26, John interprets Paul's "as often as" (ὁσάκις) as opening up the propriety of always taking communion when the heart is in a sufficiently prepared state. The entire thrust of Paul's correcting the Corinthians

57 *On Blessed Philogonius*, PG 48:756.

58 *On Blessed Philogonius*, PG 48:756.

59 *Homily 3 on Ephesians*, PG 62:28.

assumes that holy communion is a matter of reason (λογισμός) as well as of thought or consideration (διανοία). Paul speaks of an unworthy (ἀνάξιος) communion as bringing guilt (ἔνοχος) upon the communing Christian. Such a sobering reality means that a "man must examine himself" (1 Cor 11:28) to partake worthily. Communing simply out of custom (συνήθεια) determined by the liturgical season or Church law is never enough, according to John Chrysostom. As he continues his exhortation, he reminds the congregation that the objective realities present on the altar require recognition of their nature by repentance, and penitential cleansing: "Consider this! Those who partook of the ancient sacrifice, how much care did they take? What were they practicing? What were they doing? They were constantly being purified. But you are approaching a sacrifice that angels tremble before. Will you limit this matter to a number of seasons? How will you present yourself before the judgment seat of Christ, audaciously taking the body with filthy hands and lips?"[60]

John reminds them that the heavenly liturgy where the angels assist calls the faithful to purity that emanates outward to one's behavior. If the sacrifices offered in the old covenant ("the ancient sacrifice") demanded such care, how much more the surpassing glory of the one true sacrifice of the new covenant? John again quotes 1 Cor 11:26 in *Homily 3 against the Jews*, where he stresses that Pascha is for participation in the holy table of Christ. No one, he insists, should confuse Lent with Pascha because "Pascha is not for fasting but for the offering and sacrifice that happens at each liturgy [σύναξις]." So he urges participation in communion because it is the state of one's soul that determines whether one is ready or not: "This means that as often as you approach with a pure conscience, you are fulfilling the Pascha, not when you fast, but when you partake of that sacrifice." To leave no doubt about the reality of the sacrifice of Christ in the liturgy, John underscores that all liturgies are in effect the same sacrificial reality: "The offering that happens today and the one yesterday and every day is like the one that takes place on the Sabbath day, and that is not more solemn than this nor is this one more paltry than that one. Both are one and the same; both are awesome and full of salvation."[61]

How is it that Christians become indifferent to the sacred mysteries? John was sure of one source of the problem: unprofitable and unnecessary

60 *Homily 3 on Ephesians*, PG 62:29.

61 All three quotations come from *Homily 3 against the Jews*, PG 48:866–70.

entanglements in daily life. These can be less obvious but equally pernicious enemies of the soul that can distract or disable the spiritual sensibilities of the communicant. These are not the open hostilities or shameful arrogance sometimes present in Christian communities; these are the social entanglements to such a degree that they choke out concern for one's salvation:

> Let the daily affairs begin to wail as well as business contracts. I want to save my soul. "What does it profit a man if he gains the whole world and forfeits his soul?" The Magi left Persia. But you, leave the affairs of everyday life and travel toward Jesus. . . . But now many of the faithful have rushed into such great folly and neglect as if filled with a thousand evils, taking no concern even for themselves. And when they simply happen to be here during the feasts, they come to this table. They don't realize that the moment of communion is not a matter of a feast or a festive assembly but of a life that wishes to be free from accusation and possess a pure conscience.[62]

Communion that lacks thought, compunction, and sincerity may simply be the fruit of perfunctory actions. John repeatedly shows himself to be against such superficial Christian practice. True and meaningful communion entails the same attitude as that of the Magi, who traveled far and endured much to worship the newborn King. They did not allow themselves to be distracted by the affairs of everyday life. So too the Antiochene pastor reminds his flock of Jesus's challenge to forsake all that may hinder entering into the fullness of life.

Even worse than mechanical observance of communion on certain feast days is the wrong kind of preparation so tempting to citizens of a Christian empire:

> Isn't it out of place to have such great concern for bodily care that the feast passes you by? You take the most beautiful garment out of the box, buy new sandals, and buy abundant food for your table and devise many paths on every side and brighten and beautify yourself. But doing all this you neglect your soul; it is besmirched, squalid, contaminated by famine, and you can give no account of its continuing uncleanness. You beautify the body here but leave your soul bare and full of shame. Although your fellow servant sees the outward body, and there appears to be no injury, yet the Master sees your soul and brings great punishment for such neglect.[63]

62 *On Blessed Philogonius*, PG 48:754.

63 *On Blessed Philogonius*, PG 48:755.

One can hardly imagine a more fitting warning to Christians who take delight in the outward show of religious piety but neglect the true piety of the soul. The dangers of outward forms of religion in fact may be more pertinent to most communicants precisely because of the hidden power of self-deception. As John did not hesitate to rebuke even the Empress herself, so his penetrating insight into the human condition led him to withhold nothing that might induce his hearers into more inwardly profitable communion.

Distractions through entertainments may also be a compelling reason not to receive holy communion. John received some notoriety in history for his denunciations of the theater and its portrayals of immorality. One of those condemnations surfaces in his *Homilies on Isaiah* as he shows how a mind filled with the sights and sounds of the theater can be rendered insensible to higher realities. Among his flock were some who had frequented the theater, perhaps shortly before entering the Church. Such an influence had undesirable consequences for those theater-goers:

> You should be sending up an angelic doxology with fear and trembling, and making confession to your Creator with reverence, with this praise asking for forgiveness for falling. You are led astray by actors and singers. You boldly motion with your hands in a disorderly manner, dancing with your feet and moving your whole body. . . . Don't you know that the Master himself is present invisibly and measures the movement of each one and searches the conscience? Don't you know that the angels are standing at this awesome table and are diligently caring for it in reverence? But you don't recognize these things because your mind has been darkened by the sights and sounds of the theater. And so you are mixing the things done there [in the theater] with the types of the church. So too you show outwardly a disordered soul with meaningless noise.[64]

John here castigates his people for their lack of meaningful participation in the liturgical celebration because they have been dulled in spirit by the entertainments available to them in their cities. No doubt both Antioch and Constantinople had an abundance of distractions, some of which were blatantly immoral. Such entertainments darkened the mind and heart to the point where there was an unholy mixture of the earthly and heavenly worlds. When Chrysostom uses the term *types* (τύποις), he is probably referring

64 *I Saw the Lord: Homily 1*, Jean Dumortier, *Jean Chrysostome: Homélies sur Ozias*, SC 277 (Paris: Editions du Cerf, 1981), 42.

to the mysteries since both *mystery* and *type* mean a sign that represents a deeper or higher reality. What a contrast as we recall his exhortations to leave behind the troubles of daily life, much more its immoral allurements, and enter into the world of heaven through the liturgy! John even goes so far as to name those entertainments demonic:

> Nothing so contributes to despising the words of God as the disturbances of the theater. It is for this reason that I have often exhorted [you] that no one who attends and enjoys the divine instruction and who partakes of the awesome and mystical sacrifice should go to the theater or mix the divine mysteries with demonic things. Yet some are so crazy that while putting forth an appearance of godliness, they enter old age at the same time as attending those events. They neither heed our words nor are ashamed of their own appearance. Yet, whenever we show them this, and we exhort them to have respect for their old age and for godliness, this word seems to them as meaningless [ψυχρός, lit. "cold"] and ridiculous.[65]

John here demonstrates that there is no limit to the damage done by worldly entertainments. Even the elderly, who are assumed to be mature and even wise, can fall prey to the malevolent influences of the theater. A mind filled with thoughts of the world not only has a difficult time absorbing the word of God, it even devolves to the point of "despising" (καταφρονεῖν) God's instructions through his chosen servant. Many moderns easily think John puritanical or overly ascetic, but our world today abounds in distracting entertainments much more so than his. Wise curates of souls of the twenty-first century immediately recognize the dangers John described in the fourth.

In every age the dangers of sexual allurements have afflicted Christians. In the next two chapters we shall deal with the moral implications of the Eucharist that involve more than one person, but for John the sins of the flesh begin in the heart and therefore must be addressed at that level where impurity begins. In both Antioch and Constantinople, the theaters afforded Christian men opportunities for sin that cut to the very core of their being. In the third homily on the life of David the king, Chrysostom turns his attention to men who may be in Church now but who only the day before left Church for the spectacles, which were powerful inducements to sexual immorality. John rebukes his hearers by pointing out how coming to the sacred banquet

65 *I Saw the Lord: Homily 1*, Dumortier, *Jean Chrysostome: Homélies sur Ozias*, 42.

and watching adulterous relationships on the stage are incompatible. Quoting Jesus's words, John reminds his hearers that adultery begins in the heart: "The one who looks at a woman with lust has already committed adultery with her in his heart" (Mt 5:28). Likening apathy for the condition of one's soul to neglect of the body, John asks with astonishment:

> Although there is not so great a difference between perfume and mire, between a master's clothing and that of a slave, as there is between spiritual grace and this evil activity, do you not fear, O man, to look with the same eyes on this bed onstage with its filthy rites performed and then gaze on this sacred table with its awesome mysteries enacted? Are you not afraid to hear with the same ears those shameful things about sexual matters and then the prophetic and apostolic Scriptures that lead you into the mysteries? And to receive with the same heart the deleterious drugs and the awesome and holy sacrifice?[66]

John seems to grasp what a long line of spiritual confessors have understood, expressed so well by Alphonsus Liguori, that most people fail in the pursuit of holiness in matters of sexual purity. But for Chrysostom, the issue is exposure. The more men expose themselves to sinful activity, directly or vicariously, the weaker and more unfit for the Eucharist will they be. The table where the awesome sacraments are celebrated is a constant call to purity of heart and behavior.

We again hear his warnings against sinful behavior surfacing in many of his early homilies after his arrival in Constantinople. *Against the Games and Theaters*, probably preached in July 399, warned the men of his community about the deep mark left by sexual immorality (whether mental or physical) contracted by attendance at the hippodrome. The negative effect on their marriages and family life was unmistakable, and so John warned that excommunication from the sacrament might be necessary. Short of that, Chrysostom hoped that the incongruity between the spectacles of the hippodrome and the beauty of the eucharistic liturgy would suffice to deter the men of his congregation from allowing themselves to be infected with "absurd love."

66 *Homily 3 on David and Saul*, PG 54:696. Translated in Robert C. Hill, *Old Testament Homilies*, vol. 1 (Brookline, MA: Holy Cross Orthodox Press, 2003), 41. My translation differs from Hill's somewhat.

> Tell me, isn't it in the nature of extreme vengeance to nourish such desire [i.e., sexual] and continually to be on fire, and to carry around everywhere a furnace of absurd love and the accusation of your conscience? How will you come in those holy doors? How will you touch the heavenly table? How will you hear the sermon on common sense when you're full of ulcers and so many wounds, and have a mind enslaved to passion?[67]

Secular entertainments may indeed be distracting, but when they have to do with sexual desire, the dangers become life threatening. A heart that is consumed by the fire of desire cannot be calm and recollected enough to enter into the eucharistic liturgy in a personally meaningful way. Whether John knew this struggle himself we have no way of knowing, but he certainly understood that battle in the hearts and minds of his people. His call to sexual purity was borne not so much of monastic or hermetic asceticism as it was of genuinely grasping the exalted reality of the Church's liturgical celebration of the Eucharist.

Anger is another of Chrysostom's most discussed vices. On a superficial reading he seems to rail angrily against anger but offer little advice in overcoming it. And yet a closer look unfolds a more profound understanding. While he certainly sees anger as a barrier, he also views the Eucharist as the solution to the problem. He sees all too clearly the human tendency to give in to anger, and in many homilies he mounts up terms like *wrath*, *rage*, *enmity*, and *acrimony* in order to expose the ugliness of anger. He seems rather bothered by anger, possibly because he saw this vice in himself as much as he saw it in others. In a rather explicit passage from *Homily 4 on Matthew*, John likens human anger to a roaring lion or a deadly viper:

> This one [lion] possesses hard teeth and claws. And if you do not pacify him, he destroys everything. Thus, even a lion and viper cannot tear apart [your] insides like anger, doing so constantly with iron claws. For in this case, not only is the body treated badly, it corrupts the health of the soul, devouring, ripping apart, depleting all its power and making it good for nothing. If anyone while eating gets worms in his entrails, and will not be able to breathe with everything within him spent, how can we then give

67 *Against the Games and Theaters*, trans. Wendy Mayer and Pauline Allen, *John Chrysostom*, The Early Church Fathers (New York: Routledge, 2000), 123.

> birth to something noble while we have such a big serpent devouring our insides?[68]

His preaching contains not simple denunciations of anger but attempts to bring his hearers to the awareness of the latent anger within them. He knew how frightful it could be for Christians to see raging anger within their own hearts; the verbs "devouring" (κατεσθίων), "ripping apart" (σπαράττων), and "depleting all its power" (διαξαίνων τὴν δύναμιν αὐτῆς ἅπασαν) are powerful choices of vocabulary to convey the destructive effects of anger. His preaching pointed to the only real solution for their anger problem—the real presence of the God of peace. The disabling effect of anger may lead one to despair, but John reminds his hearers that the presence of the God of peace resides in the eucharistic cup containing the blood of Christ:

> How can we, if we have a serpent [anger] devouring our insides, bring out what is noble? How will we be delivered from harm? What potion may we drink that has such power? The precious blood of Christ. If it is received with confidence, it can extinguish all disease. Add to this attentively hearing the divine Scriptures, with almsgiving added to the hearing, and by all these ways it will be able to destroy all the passions afflicting our soul.[69]

While anger may be a barrier to communion, the Eucharist can also be the healing of anger. John is thinking of anger not in its outward manifestations such as outbursts or carping criticism but as an inward disease. In the distant background John perhaps was thinking of Jesus's words, "It is not what goes into the mouth that defiles a person, but what comes out of the mouth; this defiles a person" (Mt 15:11). External expressions of anger cannot be quieted unless there is an internal change in the person. John here lists three things that help: the Eucharist, the Scriptures, and almsgiving. He seems to know that almsgiving concerns actions of the body, hearing the Scriptures addresses the cognitive side of the human person, and the Eucharist reaches into the soul at a deeper level of being. He knows that every aspect of the human being must be addressed but the deepest level is where sacramental grace must reach if it is to heal the problem of anger. When is anger an obstacle that could keep one away from communion? When the

68 *Homily 4 on Matthew*, PG 57:50. See also Gerardo di Nola, *La Dottrina Eucharistica de Giovanni Crisostomo* (Vatican City: Libreria Editrice Vaticana, 1997), 176–78.

69 *Homily 4 on Matthew*, PG 57:50.

would-be recipient fails to recognize his need. In the next chapter we will return to the theme of anger and unforgiveness as we examine John's teaching on *mnesikakia* (μνησικακία) or "the remembrance of evil," but already here we can see how even such a deadly demon as anger finds its solution in the Eucharist.

On the other end of the emotional spectrum, we find the weakness of timidity. Such fear arises in the heart because Christians underestimate the value and power of the sacrament or because they feel that they do not have sufficient preparation to partake of such an august gift. While John is never one to downplay the seriousness of sacramental communion, neither does he allow his congregation to withhold their participation on the grounds that they have insufficient time for repentance:

> Someone may say to me, I am filled with shame. I have a conscience full of sin. I bear the heaviest burden possible. The appointed time of five days is sufficient to cut off the weight of sins if you are sober, and pray, and are vigilant. Do not look at the shortness of time but rather focus on this, that the Master loves humanity. Now the Ninevites fended off such wrath in three days, and the constriction of the time hindered nothing, but the willingness of their souls, being seized by the Master's love of men, effected everything [necessary]. And the prostitute was washed clean of all disgrace when she came to Christ in a brief moment of time.[70]

Let us recall that this homily was preached just before Christmas or perhaps Epiphany. As that great feast drew near, Chrysostom urged his people not to look at their preparation in terms of earthly time, but to see the opportunity (*kairos*) that flows out of divine love (*philanthropia*). His example of the Ninevites as well as the prostitute (see Lk 7:36–50) suffice to illustrate how forgiveness is instantaneous and flowing from God's mercy. The only action that the pagans of Nineveh performed to merit forgiveness was to turn to God at the preaching of Jonah. So no Christian should be timid as if not prepared because of lack of time.

Timidity or fear can also be the prelude to discouragement, the very thing that can halt spiritual progress in its tracks. John addresses this problem under the term ἀθυμία (*athumia*). *Athumia* is an expected response to those who wish to be holy but who are crestfallen because they see

70 *On Blessed Philogonius*, PG 48:754.

themselves as so unworthy. Having concern for the health of one's own soul is a legitimate endeavor, a thought motivated not by a modern narcissism but by an ancient realization that the elimination of vice and the acquisition of virtue is a path to salvation. John discusses this problem in many places, but some of its tenderest manifestations are in his *Letters to Olympias*, his dear friend in Constantinople who had generously used her wealth to fund religious houses. Anne-Marie Malingrey provides a sensitive and insightful understanding of their correspondence on this topic that shows John at his pastoral best.[71] To understand the problem of *athumia*, one can think of its opposite θυμός (*thumos*), which refers to a soul of ardent passion and zeal. *Athumia* is its opposite, that listlessness of the soul that lacks fervency and interior motivation. John compares *athumia* to disgusting things such as maggots, rust, and tyrants. *Athumia* wounds the soul so that this malady leaves it distracted and exhausted, a state of the soul preventing good judgment and discernment: "You know how the tyranny of *athumia* darkens love and makes slaves."[72] By speaking of tyranny, John gets to the heart of the problem with *athumia*; it can become an all-controlling or all-consuming despair that blocks love and renders the mind fruitless. One can even come to find a devilish delight in this morose state of mind.

Fear, discouragement, and despair: these are obstacles that could keep one away from the Eucharist, which is the very source of healing for the troubled soul. These maladies can be just as crippling as anger or indifference. The answer is the realization that it is only God's love for the human race that can draw Christians above and beyond their own sin and limitations. God's love is the ultimate reason why no one should allow for excuses in coming to the sacrament of the altar. Attendance at liturgy while abstaining from the mystery of the Eucharist not only can be dangerous but is also an insult to God. Abstaining from the Eucharist out of a self-imposed sense of guilt and unworthiness may very well amount to a rejection of God's gracious provision. Because of the greatness of the divine table, there can be no excuse for refraining:

> The royal table is present, the angels are serving at the table. The King himself is present and you stand there indifferent? Are your garments filthy

71 Anne-Marie Malingrey, trans., *Jean Chrysostome: Lettres a Olympias*, SC 13 (Paris: Editions du Cerf, 1947), 50.

72 *Letter 3* to Olympias, Malingrey, *Lettres*, 160. John also speaks of "the tyranny of *athumia*" earlier in this letter (1.b).

> and you have no excuse? Rather, they are pure. Well, then, sit down and partake. He comes daily to see those at the supper; he converses with all. . . . If someone were invited to a feast, washed his hands and took his seat, and was ready for the feast but then did not partake, wouldn't it be insulting the one who invited him? Wouldn't it be better if such a person did not attend? But in fact, you attended. You sang the hymn. With all who are worthy you confessed to be separated from those who are not worthy. How did you remain and not partake of the table? I am unworthy, he says. Are you also unworthy of the communion in the church's prayers? It is not only through the gifts but also through the hymns that the Spirit comes down.[73]

It is an insult not to partake of the Lord's table when one has been invited and properly prepared. And here John signals an important point that is emphasized later in the Byzantine tradition. The liturgy leading up to communion is designed to help the Christian become prepared. By joining in the liturgy one's heart is readied, the soul is purified. Nicholas Cabasilas will stress this same point in the fourteenth century in his *Commentary on the Divine Liturgy*. The liturgy itself has a purifying effect on the participant: "As preparation for and contribution to this act [of holy communion] we have prayers, psalms, and readings from Holy Scripture; in short, all the sacred acts and forms that are said and done before and after the consecration of the elements." Cabasilas proceeds to explain that while God's gifts in the holy mysteries are "absolute graces" and are not a reward for anything we bring to him, God would nevertheless "not permit those who were not disposed to be thus sanctified."[74] John places reminders in bold letters that it is not only sin that can block the approach to holy communion but it can even be a misguided conscience or fear.

SEIZING THE MOMENT OF HOLY COMMUNION

The whole of the Christian profession and moral life are encapsulated in the liturgy. The unique and utterly singular position of the eucharistic liturgy

73 *Homily 3 on Ephesians*, PG 62:29.

74 Both quotations are from Nicholas Cabasilas, *A Commentary on the Divine Liturgy*, trans. J. M. Hussey and P. A. McNulty (Crestwood, NY: St. Vladimir's Seminary Press, 2002), 25–26.

means that this truth will determine the individual Christian's approach to holy communion. Preparing for holy communion means that the Christian understands the profound sanctity of the moment and begins preparation before the liturgy commences. This involves expunging the sights and sounds of the theater or, in general, a detachment from the visible world of sin, but all Chrysostom's exhortations to holiness are based on the objective realities of the Eucharist as celebrated in the liturgy. In his homilies on the incomprehensibility of God, John recalls the communicant to the true nature of the liturgy:

> Think on whose presence you stand near, with whom you are about to invoke God, with the Cherubim. Consider carefully your fellow choir members and sobriety will please you when you take to heart that though you are beset with a body and entangled with flesh, you have been counted worthy to sing the hymn to the common Lord of all along with the incorporeal powers. So, let no one whose desire has dissipated participate in those holy and mystical hymns.[75]

And casting away dissipation and a dull spirit can only be done by realizing that the communicant stands in a unique moment, God's moment (*kairos*): "At that very moment, let no one have earthbound thoughts. Rather cordon off all earthly things from your mind, having placed yourself toward the whole of heaven. As he stands near the throne of glory and flies with the Seraphim, let [everyone] offer up the all-holy hymn to the God of glory and majesty."[76] It is the objective reality of the divine liturgy as the union of heaven and earth that requires congregants to receive holy communion by appreciating the full implications of these truths. We see John connecting the objective and subjective aspects of the Eucharist in several homilies. In his homily *On the Cemetery and the Cross* John reminds his hearers of the power of the blood poured out on the cross: "Mind what is poured out. It is the blood that wiped away the written condemnation of our sins. This is the blood that cleansed your soul, that washed away the stain, that triumphed over the evil rulers and authorities. 'For he stripped the rulers and authorities and displayed them openly by triumphantly parading them on the cross.'"[77]

75 *Homily 4 on the Incomprehensibility of God*, SC 28 (bis), 260.

76 *Homily 4 on the Incomprehensibility of God*, SC 28 (bis), 260–62.

77 *On the Cemetery and the Cross*, PG 49:398.

The objective procurement of salvation, as celebrated by Paul in Col 2:15, yields a corresponding reminder that the power of Christ's redemption is communicated through the Eucharist. Being present at the table of sacrifice is like being at the cross itself on that first Good Friday.

While all the objective realities of the Eucharist are necessary for approaching the eucharistic table, they do not guarantee that the recipient is ready. All we saw above about barriers to communion requires a subjective appropriation. Thus, when John exhorts his congregants to ready themselves for the moment of communion, he does not hesitate to remind them of the wonder of the realities on the table and a vigilant approach to them. In *Homily 27 on 1 Corinthians* John challenges the mindset of his people:

> And when you take the bread of life, you make it a cause of death. And this doesn't frighten you? Don't you know how many bad things follow on the heels of luxury? Untimely laughter, inappropriate language, pleasantries filled with ruin, ignorant nonsense, and other things that cannot be mentioned. And you do these things after enjoying the table of Christ on the very day on which you are counted worthy to touch his flesh with your tongue. So, to keep this from happening, everyone should purify his right hand, his tongue, his lips, which in fact should become a front door for Christ's entry. You should place yourself next to that visible table, to that table that lifts up the mind to the Lord's supper, to that sacred watchfulness of the disciples that they had that night [in the garden]. Or rather, if we search this out more accurately, it applies to the present night. So let us keep watch with the Lord. Let us keep silence with the disciples, a moment for prayers, not drinking, always ready for the feast. And this feast is coming, not that we act shamefully, not to increase in sins, but for us to annul these present practices.[78]

At the moment of communion John urges three essential thoughts. One is to expel the practices of the secular world that Christians may bring into the liturgy ("untimely laughter, inappropriate language, pleasantries filled with ruin, ignorant nonsense"). This in turn leads to the need for self-purification ("everyone should purify his right hand, his tongue, his lips, which in fact should become a front door for Christ's entry"). It is the last consideration, however, that is delightfully ambiguous and enticing. When he urges being close to the visible table, he may be speaking of spatial proximity or of a

78 *Homily 27 on 1 Corinthians*, PG 61:231.

spiritual kind. If the churches in Chrysostom's time had iconostases, as Byzantine churches certainly did in later times, then John is probably not thinking in spatial terms. The closeness to the sacred table is spiritual and moral. This is reinforced by his reference to the historic "Last Supper" and vigilance of the disciples. Here again John assumes that participation in the eucharistic table is tantamount to participation in the original event of which it is an embodied sign (σύμβολον).

When the moment of actual communion arrives, when participation in the holy mysteries is imminent, there is no better method of preparation than meditation on the Prayer for Receiving Holy Communion used by the Byzantine Liturgy, which has long been attributed to St. John Chrysostom. Known to millions of Eastern Christians throughout the world, this prayer remains virtually unknown in the West; it never seems to be absent from the lips of individuals who claim the heritage of Constantinople. Though somewhat lengthy, its beauty and spiritual power make it worth quoting:

> Lord, I believe and confess that you are truly the Christ, the Son of the Living God.
> You came into the world to save sinners, of whom I am the first.
> I still believe that this is your undefiled body and your precious blood.
> So I ask you:
> Be merciful to me and forgive my transgressions, both voluntary and involuntary,
> Those in word, in action, in knowledge, and in ignorance.
> Make me worthy to partake of your pure mysteries without condemnation
> for the forgiveness of my sins and for eternal life.
> How can I, so unworthy, enter into the splendor of your Saints?
> If I dare to enter the bridal chamber, my clothes will rebuke me
> Since they are not a wedding garment.
> I will be seized and tossed out by the angels.
> O Lord, Lover of the human race, cleanse the filth of my soul and save me.
> Loving Master, Lord Jesus Christ, my God.
> Let not these holy mysteries be judgment for me because of my unworthiness,
> but let them be for the cleansing and holiness of soul and body.

> Let them be a pledge of the life to come and of the kingdom.
> It is good for me to be united to God and to place my hope of salvation in the Lord.
> Today accept me, O Son of God, as a partaker of your mystical supper.
> For I will certainly not tell your mystery to your enemies.
> I will not give you a kiss like Judas.
> But like the thief I confess, "Remember me, Lord, in your kingdom."[79]

In sum, the act of receiving the sacred host is the zenith and apex of liturgical participation. Nothing can compare to that moment, that *kairos*, when the king of heaven enters into the soul of the humble Christian. Such a moment is one for which every believer should long but also before which everyone should tremble; it is inviting and off-putting at the same time. It is deceptively plain and simple. A piece of bread; a sip of wine. But the world one enters into through that humble act is eternal, like God himself. While it requires careful and thoughtful self-examination, it also confers enormous benefits on the communing Christian.

AFTERGLOW: THE FRUITS OF HOLY COMMUNION

The positive benefits coming from holy communion far outweigh the dangers that may arise from improper preparation. Those benefits are to be desired by every Christian not only because they prepare the soul for heaven but also because they provide for a more peaceful and joy-filled life in this world. Recall that in *Blessed Philogonius* John exhorted, "You are about to receive the King under your roof in communion. As the King enters your soul, you should be in much tranquility [γαλήνη], much silence, deep peace of thoughts."[80] The King has entered the soul of the believer through the divine mystery of his body and blood; the recipient cannot remain unaffected. Perhaps the most common fruit of sacramental participation is peace of heart, which is experienced as silence.

79 Translated from the Greek of *The Liturgy of St. John Chrysostom* (Brookline, MA: Holy Cross Orthodox Press, 1985), 29–30.

80 *On Blessed Philogonius*, PG 48:756.

Silence is expressed by John in several standard terms (ἡσυχία, σιωπή, σιγή) that show up in many places. He uses the term as a statement of fact and as an implicit exhortation. The peace of God's presence in the soul in fact brings silence to the believer; it is the opposite of turmoil and disturbance (θόρυβος). There can be little question that John here draws his teaching from what he learned in his time in the caves outside Antioch and from his knowledge of monastic life. *Silence* is one of those terms that seems to defy description and leaves only the negative characterization that it is the absence of noise, commotion, and disturbance. John, however, occasionally gives us greater insight by the context in which he uses the term. Toward the end of *Homily 30 on the Acts of the Apostles*, we hear another of his frequent rhetorical questions, "Tell me, in the mysteries, there is no disturbance, is there? No disruption, is there? When we were baptized and did all these things, did not stillness [ἡσυχία] and silence [σιγὴ] encompass everything? This beauty in heaven was sprinkled down."[81] At times John uses *mysteries* to refer exclusively to the Eucharist, and at other times, as here, his term includes other sacraments as well. John not only valued silence; he knew its sources. The silence and peace of heaven descend through the sacraments and banish disruption and disturbance. In the homily quoted at the beginning of this chapter John spoke of receiving the body and blood of Christ "with modesty and silence" (μετὰ αἰδοῦς καὶ ἡσυχίας). The first term (αἰδώς) could easily have been translated "reverence, awe."[82] These two ideas fit together nicely. Reverence induces modesty, and that is often conjoined with silence. Before the eucharistic presence of Jesus Christ, silence is a fitting stance. Soon after in that same passage John again asks, "Don't you know that your soul needs to be filled with tranquility [γαλήνη] at that very moment? There is a need for much peace and silence, not confusion, anger, and disturbance," That very moment of the Eucharist, both in its celebration and its reception, the beauty of silence must reign supreme.

Tranquility or calm (γαλήνη) may be thought of as synonymous with silence, but the term itself originates from a different realm and evokes the image of a still sea in classical texts, a usage that can illuminate its spiritual significance; γαλήνη is used only three times in the New Testament and

81 *Homily 30 on the Acts of the Apostles*, PG 60:228.

82 *On the Birth of Christ*, PG 49:361; καὶ τῶν προκειμένων μετὰ αἰδοῦς καὶ ἡσυχίας μεταλαμβάνετε ἐδεσμάτων.

always in the natural context of the water.[83] No New Testament author applies it to the interior life. In John's case, however, with both Antioch and Constantinople in close proximity to the Mediterranean, it is easy to see why he may have used nautical metaphors to describe the state of the soul.[84] One wonders if he chose this word to imply that the holy table calms the soul so that the Christian can navigate the turbulent waters of life. As we observed earlier, the sights and sounds of the theater and hippodrome could contribute to a distracted mind and a troubled spirit, the opposite of what God's presence provides through the mysteries. What is needed in the spiritual life is that which nothing in contemporary culture could afford. The opposite of quiet and calm is "confusion, anger, and disturbance," which make the soul unclean. John is speaking of a presumptive attitude that approaches the sacrament without sufficient preparation. Elsewhere he urges Christians not to hesitate to come to the Eucharist, but in coming they must always remember that "what lies before [them] is the saving medicine for our wounds." The heavenly Physician is truly "the patron of the kingdom of heaven."[85]

Tranquility or calmness of soul denotes the stillness that results from the cessation of turbulent winds and raging storms that threaten to wear down the determination of the Christian. While John does use the term to describe the calm of the seas, his ultimate concern is with the souls of his auditors. As we might expect, John conjoins γαλήνη with close synonyms: "There is complete rest and *calm* and love and joy and peace and meekness and a thousand other goods in place of those [evil] things."[86] This concatenation of positives occurs in the context of contrasting Christian liturgy with worldly celebrations: "This is the true feast, here is the salvation of souls, here peace and unanimity."[87] A similar contrast is evident in his homily on the baptism of Christ:

> Don't you know that God has pitched the churches in cities as there are harbors in the sea that we may enjoy the greatest tranquility while fleeing from the storm of daily troubles? Of these waves there is no need to fear a triple set of waves, not an influx of thieves, not an approach of evildoers,

83 In reality, it is used only in one context, the story of the calming of the sea in all three Synoptic Gospels (Mt 8:26; Mk 4:39; Lk 8:24).

84 Γαλήνη occurs 286 times in Chrysostom, many of which refer to physically calm seas.

85 *Homily on the Birth of Christ*, PG 49:361.

86 *Homilies on Genesis*, PG 53:21.

87 *Homilies on Genesis*, PG 53:21.

> not forceful winds, not the plots of beasts, for there is a harbor in place of all these things, a spiritual harbor of souls.[88]

Outside the Church is trouble, commotion, and uncertainty; inside the Church is the safe harbor for souls seeking salvation. This fits with his usage in which he sometimes pairs γαλήνη with safety (ἀσφαλείᾳ). Why can the Church be such a place of solace and tranquility? Because it is the king who grants such peace, and on the sacred table one finds the very source of all positive virtues. It is not a modicum of tranquility that John hopes they will gain, as it were, by serendipity. He rather knows that it is "great tranquility" (πολλὴ ἡ γαλήνη) that can result from communion.[89] So, building on his knowledge of both the turbulence and calmness of the sea, John urges his hearers to come to the one place (Church) where they can find tranquility of soul. In the same way that one may experience contentment at the sight of a lake clear as crystal, so the soul that tastes of heaven through the sacrament may become as bright and beautiful as if it were gold refined by fire.

All these fruits of communion are internal to each believer, but they inevitably must show themselves in the Christian's interaction with others. The social implications of the gospel and the Eucharist are much discussed in the Church today, but there is another fruit of communion less emphasized today that John thought important: spiritual fortitude. Once a Christian has received holy communion, he is fortified and prepared for spiritual battle because holy communion gives the King of the Battle to the spiritual warrior. In case one might forget this truth, John reminds his catechumens:

> What battle? Has God only prepared weapons? No! He also prepared a table stronger than any weapon that you may not be weak when you battle, that living luxuriously you may escape from the Evil One. For when he sees you returning from the Lord's suppers as someone might see a lion emitting fire from his mouth, he will flee more vehemently than the wind. And when you show him your tongue stained with the precious blood, he will not be able to withstand you. When you show him your mouth redden with blood like a ferocious beast he will run away from you.[90]

88 *On the Baptism of Christ*, PG 49:363.

89 For example, he uses this expression (or μεγάλη γαλήνη) several times in his *Homilies on Genesis*. See PG 53:281 and 54:581.

90 *Catechesis*, 3,12, Antoine Wenger, *Jean Chrysostome: Huit catéchèses baptismales inédites*, SC 50 (Paris: Editions du Cerf, 1957) (bis), 158.

Part and parcel of the spiritual battle lying before the Christian departing from holy communion is to realize that he has an enemy who wishes to steal from him that precious gift of Christ in the Eucharist. Earlier we saw how Judas was the archetype of a man who gave in to the Devil. Chrysostom called this "the shamelessness of Judas," but the greater shame belongs to the Devil, for he it is who "rushed into Judas without any thought of the Lord's body that was there." This unworthy reception of the sacred species is to be avoided at all costs. The unworthy communicant suffers from the same danger to which Judas yielded. Judas stands as a perpetual warning: "This happened to teach you that to those who partook of the divine mysteries in an unworthy manner, it is these that the Devil rushes into and enters continuously as was the case with Judas then."[91]

John's words about a greater judgment alludes of course to Paul's warning in 1 Corinthians 11 about unworthy communion. Yet even when—and perhaps especially when—a Christian has a worthy communion, the supreme enemy of God desires to snatch away any profit that might arise from communion. Earlier John had invoked the image of a lion to represent anger, which can devour goodness within a person. Here he uses the same metaphor of a lion to speak of the Christian who has been fortified for battle against the enemy.

For a Christian to engage the enemy of Christ, he must possess certain character qualities, for the Evil One is attacking not some inanimate object but a human person. Sobriety is fundamental to this battle, which is what John stresses in his homily on drunkenness and the resurrection. John encourages a kind of spiritual inebriation in keeping with Paul's exhortation to be filled with the Spirit (see Eph 5:18), and so he glosses this verse, "Fill up the cup of the Spirit until the understanding [is full]. It is not simply about partaking of the Spirit so that the Devil cannot strike you. It is about being filled with the Spirit with psalms, hymns, spiritual songs with which you are filled today."[92] John is in no doubt about where this sobriety may be found. The Eucharist is the tangible source of being filled with the Spirit. We saw earlier in chapter 4 how important the Epiclesis was for John—and by extension for the whole Eastern Church—but another reason why the Holy Spirit's work in the Eucharist is so central has to do with the effects of communion. Recall that Chrysostom contrasted drunkenness with a holy sobriety that

91 *Homily 1 on the Betrayal of Judas*, PG 49:380.

92 *Homily against Those Who Are Drunk and on the Resurrection of Christ*, PG 50:436.

came from the Spirit. One of the greatest benefits is the strengthening of the Christian's resolve and a clearer apprehension of higher realities. The good cup of drunkenness does not dissolve one's power like normal wine "but strengthens it. It does not dissolve ties but reinforces them. It makes for sobriety, veneration for the angels, fear of the demons, honor for men, love for the Master."[93]

Here is the converse of the Epiclesis. The descent of the Spirit conjoined with the words of consecration pronounced by the priest is essential for the bread and wine to become Christ's body and blood. Yet it is also true that drinking of the "immaculate cup of the Lord's own blood" fills the communing Christian with the Spirit. The presence of the Holy Spirit in the Christian produces sobriety and prudence so that he may do battle with the Devil. This new manner of drunkenness enables the Christian to be powerful and strong because God pours it forth from a spiritual rock. Drawing on Paul's designation of Christ as the spiritual rock (1 Cor 10:4), John seems to imply that partaking of Christ and his Spirit will make solid souls who are able to combat the attacks of the Devil. All this suggests that the weapons of spiritual warfare are the opposite of worldly armaments. Silence, tranquility, and inner strength are the instruments of engagement, all of which are fruits of holy communion.

✠ ✠ ✠

If the Christian rightly understood the heavenly gift of the Eucharist, he would not likely turn away from it, nor allow indifference to reign in the heart. In a real but higher metaphysical sense, the Christian at communion stands at the edge of eternity, at the portal of heaven, where God's life with all it entails can be mentally accessed and integrated into the entirety of one's life. This reality places the Christian in the paradoxical position of danger and safety at the same time. John seems very aware of this when he speaks about coming to the sacred table:

> I say this not so that we not come, but that we may not come simply in a perfunctory manner [ἁπλῶς]. As there is danger in just coming, so there is famine and death in not communing in those mystical suppers. This table is the sinews of the soul, the bond of the mind, the foundation of confidence,

93 *Homily against Those Who Are Drunk and on the Resurrection of Christ*, PG 50:436.

> our hope, our salvation, our light, our life. Leaving there after the sacrifice, in great confidence we will mount up through the sacred doors as fortified with golden weapons from every side. And what should I say about the future? Here this mystery makes earth a heaven for you.[94]

The reality of heaven entering the soul of the Christian has profound implications for coming to the Eucharist. It is a danger to come presumptuously and a greater danger not to come at all. The answer lies not in refraining from holy communion but in coming with proper dispositions. This may be best achieved by realizing the mysteries are the very "sinews of the soul" that are able to bind together the disparate aspects of a Christian's life. To partake of the mysteries is to receive that which can "make earth a heaven" for the soul and to experience "hope, salvation, light, and life."[95]

John Chrysostom's thoughts and preaching on holy communion flow naturally from his exalted view of the Church's liturgy. The uniqueness of the divine service among the institutions of this world is mirrored in the uniqueness of each Christian receiving the body and blood of Christ in holy communion. That singularity stands as both a warning against complacency and an invitation to the life-giving power of the Eucharist. The sacred mysteries enacted in the Church's celebration are the means by which virtues are increased, holiness grows, and the Christian is fortified for a life of service in the world. The battle in which the Christian engages is, as Paul said in Ephesians, not against flesh and blood but against principalities and powers of the spiritual world. The locus of that warfare is often *within* the soul of the Christian, and there is one particular challenge that John speaks about more than any other Father of the Church, the remembrance of evil (μνησικακία).

94 *Homily 24 on 1 Corinthians*, PG 61:204.

95 *Homily 24 on 1 Corinthians*, PG 61:204.

8

Mnesikakia: The Relentless Demon

All that John Chrysostom teaches about the Eucharist and holy communion circles back to the liturgy. It is the liturgy that calls the Christian away from the busyness and boredom of everyday life, and yet profitable participation in the liturgy can be marred by what the Christian brings to the experience, which no doubt explains why we encounter so many exhortations in John's homilies to put aside the cares of this world and to let go of those obstacles that can block proper involvement in the heavenly liturgy as it comes down to earth. Among these obstacles one stands out for the heavy emphasis John places on it as a significant barrier not only to communion but to salvation. *Mnesikakia* (μνησικακία) is literally "the remembrance of evil" and is sometimes translated "remembrance of injury," "nursing grudges," or "resentment." The word occurs more times in the Chrysostom corpus than in any other Greek Father of the Church.[1] This demon was John's greatest challenge in urging his people to live a virtuous life, because in this one vice he finds the greatest threat.

1 *Mnesikakia* or one of its congeners occurs 205 times in Chrysostom, 54 of which are nominal and 124 of which are verbal. The remainder are adjectival or adverbial. Of course, the forgiveness of enemies is discussed considerably more times even when the word *mnesikakia* is not used.

In one of the *Eclogues* constructed from Chrysostom's sermons around the tenth century, the anonymous author reflects Chrysostom's sentiments well when he speaks of the obstacle of *mnesikakia*, which can hinder the Christian's worthy participation. He singles it out as a formidable challenge to approaching the liturgy:

> Let us be attentive in partaking of the divine body. Let us not abandon the churches but gather and not just happen to engage in the activities in the church. Rather let us be fearful and trembling, casting our eyes below but our soul above. Let us sigh deeply in our heart. . . . When we enter the church, let us approach without having *mnesikakia* in our soul, as is fitting for God, lest we be condemned when we say, "Forgive us as we have forgiven."[2]

As we will see, Chrysostom views *mnesikakia* as perhaps the worst of all sins or vices because it can block God's forgiveness and without that forgiveness there can be no salvation. *Mnesikakia* is an extreme form of hate and one particularly hard to extricate from the human soul. It is, as it were, the equal and opposite of love because it destroys love. And of all the positive inner dispositions that John encourages, love stands head and shoulders above the rest. This he rightly sees in the letters of his favorite saint, Paul of Tarsus. In Col 3:14 Paul calls love "the bond of perfection," an idea that impressed itself deeply on John. He knew that having that perfect bond of love required the eradication of *mnesikakia*. As a curate of souls, John was ready to help excise this pernicious vice that would damage their love for humanity.

Earlier I noted that modern scholars studying Chrysostom's eucharistic passages had for a long time concentrated on finding evidence of John's belief in the real presence. The dynamics of previous eucharistic controversy help explain this focus, but the problem with this approach lies in posing questions to Chrysostom's texts that fail to capture his own emphases and concerns. I have no doubt that John cared more for the health of his people's souls than he did for defending the sacrament of the Eucharist. He mostly assumed the truths of the real presence and the true sacrifice of the cross held within it. The majority of his eucharistic teaching had to do with its moral

2 *Homily 47 (Approaching the Divine Mysteries Unworthily)*, PG 63:898. Although the *Eclogae* are not authentic, this quotation expresses something consistent with John's teaching. The first part is hard to identify with the exact wording of any known homily, but the second part seems to come from *On Repentance*, PG 49:346.

and spiritual implications.[3] Among the many vices John treats, he returns to *mnesikakia* more often than any other even when he does not name it as such. In a homily on Hebrews John minces no words as he declares that "*mnesikakia* is not a small sin but a great one."[4] Why is this vice more troublesome than others? Because it blocks forgiveness, God cannot countenance a person who will not forgive: "There is nothing, nothing that God hates and turns away from like a man of *mnesikakia* and holding on to anger."[5]

The subject of forgiveness has more relevance to secular society than one might think. Forgiveness in Chrysostom has recently been placed in conversation with modern treatments of the same subject that seem to be at odds with John's view. Certain philosophers have argued that it is not right to extend forgiveness to unapologetic and unrepentant offenders because to do so demeans the value of the victim and/or excuses the offense.[6] However, Samuel Kaldas has argued that Chrysostom did not in any way excuse the gravity of offense when he called for forgiving others. And John certainly did not think that forgiving an offender in any way demeaned a victim. Citing a couple of texts in Chrysostom, Kaldas claims that John's insistence on the necessity of forgiveness was grounded in an eschatological view of the human victim that affirmed his dignity.[7] A wider set of texts in Chrysostom treated below will reveal a richer ground in which the power of forgiveness grows.

In this chapter I will attempt to show how John Chrysostom counsels those afflicted by the demon of *mnesikakia*. In pursuing this course we will learn that *mnesikakia* not only destroys relationships among human beings but even destroys the one who holds on to grudges and past injuries. First, I will quickly survey some selected uses of *mnesikakia* before John and then try to define more closely how John viewed this vice. While this vice is worthy

3 These moral and spiritual aspects of Chrysostom's thought are explored at some length in Raymond J. Laird, "Mindset (γνώμη) in John Chrysostom," in *The Oxford Handbook of Maximus the Confessor*, ed. Pauline Allen and Bronwen Neil (Oxford: Oxford University Press, 2015), 194–211.

4 *Homily 27 on Hebrews*, PG 63:190.

5 *On the Debitor of Ten Thousand Talents*, PG 51:29. Though worded slightly differently, the same thought is expressed in his *Homilies on Genesis*, PG 53:248: "There is nothing, nothing that God so hates and turns away from like a man of *mnesikakia* and one who constantly keeps enmity against his neighbor in his soul."

6 For a discussion of the philosophical literature see Samuel Kaldas, "A Strange New Philosophy of Forgiveness: Insights from St. John Chrysostom on Forgiving the Unrepentant," *St. Vladimir's Theological Quarterly* 63, no. 3 (2019): 261–76.

7 Kaldas, "Strange New Philosophy," 273, 276.

of much greater exploration, here I show how John ties it to the Eucharist and the liturgy. As John then muses on various exemplars in Scripture (e.g., King David), he attempts to show the devastation that *mnesikakia* brings and the beauty of a forgiving heart. As a good pastoral philosopher, he desires the healing of the soul for his hearers who struggle with this vice. He fulfills that desire by offering the positive wisdom to be found in the virtue of forbearance. Releasing the hurt of past injuries, humility and forbearance soothe the wounded soul and liberate one to commune with God.

Retaining the memory of evils done and the resulting anger internalized also has an effect on the person himself. It closes that person off from grace and love. It can lead to despair or despondency. Although John sometimes states matters in a rather stark tone, his underlying motive is admirable. He is concerned that his hearers not do any greater harm to themselves than an enemy has already done by nursing resentments and harboring anger. Ridding one's soul of *mnesikakia* is an essential part of the prayer expressed in every eucharistic liturgy, "Forgive us our trespasses as we forgive those who trespass against us." Finding a way of cleansing one's soul of *mnesikakia* is very difficult, but John is certain of one thing in this regard. It takes an act of the will on the part of the person affected. This is why he sometimes uses forceful language, "Those who wish to approach the cross, hate slander. Loathe the remembrance of evil. Don't stop having mercy on the poor. Don't hesitate to care for the sick. Don't yearn for wealth. Don't stop visiting those in prison."[8] The fact that John would include "loathing *mnesikakia*" alongside caring for the poor and unfortunate suggests that he thought the substitution of virtues and acts of love would be an essential part of the eradication of vice. Fighting against *mnesikakia* became a centerpiece of John's exhortations to holiness.

MNESIKAKIA BEFORE JOHN CHRYSOSTOM

John Chrysostom was not the first Greek Father to use the word *mnesikakia* or expound its meaning.[9] Examples of its use prior to John in the late fourth

8 *The Adoration of the Cross*, PG 62:752.

9 *Mnesikakia* does not occur in the New Testament, but it appears as early as the Apostolic Fathers. See *Epistle of Barnabas* 2,8, "Let none of you hold a remembrance of evil against your neighbor in your heart."

century can be found in the three Cappadocian Fathers (Basil, Gregory Nazianzen, Gregory of Nyssa). The company that *mnesikakia* keeps in their minds can be seen in the lists of vices and virtues they give in which the word occurs. Basil, the elder statesman of the Cappadocian triumvirate, places this vice among all the other uncontrolled passions that destroy the soul, "anger and jealousy, and *mnesikakia*, lies, arrogance, mental disturbance, and nasty speech, laziness in prayers, the desire for things that can never be, fine clothing, beautifying one's face, social events and company beyond what is proper and necessary."[10] Gregory of Nyssa, Basil's younger brother who was given to mysticism much more than his practically minded sibling, includes *mnesikakia* in the list of vices that, he says, Paul had rejected and excised from his soul: "Neither pleasure, nor sorrow, nor rage, nor fear, nor guile, nor uncontrolled emotion, nor vanity, nor rashness. Not *mnesikakia*, not jealousy, not purposeful revenge, not greed or love of glory and honor, not any other thing that could stain the soul by some condition of the soul."[11] Gregory gives us a clue to his understanding of *mnesikakia* by its juxtaposition with jealousy (φθόνος) and purposeful revenge (ἀμυντική τις διάθεσις). Just as any of the vices listed here may poison the soul of a Christian, so this triad of hate presupposes the ill-will of someone against another. *Mnesikakia* seems to give rise to a deliberate choice and to acts of violence. Gregory Nazianzen, Basil's closest friend in his youth, also links *mnesikakia* to temper (θυμὸς) and anger (οργὴ) in one of his moral poems:

> Temper is the sudden seething of the mind
> Anger is the temper held within.
> *Mnesikakia* happens in recalling evil for an ambush.[12]

Here Gregory seems to consider *mnesikakia* a more extreme form of temper or anger inasmuch as it purposes to do harm to another. The Cappadocians all agree that *mnesikakia* is reprehensible, but they never appear to expound on the vice itself at any length.

10 Basil of Caesarea, *Sermo 13* (often called an ascetic sermon).

11 Gregory of Nyssa, *Homily 15 on the Song of Songs*, PG 44:1096. *Mnesikakia* occurs only fourteen times in Gregory's entire corpus.

12 Gregory Nazianzen, *Carmina Moralia*: Θυμὸς μέν ἐστιν ἀθρόος ζέσις φρενός· / Ὀργὴ δὲ θυμὸς ἐμμένων. Ὁ δ' εἰς κακὸν / Μνήμων, λοχῶν τε, μνησικακία τυγχάνει. *Mnesikakia* occurs only six times in Gregory's corpus.

Evagrius Ponticus (d. 399), an almost exact contemporary of John Chrysostom, invokes the concept more often than the Cappadocian Fathers and is more analytical of its meaning, perhaps due to his more overtly ascetic life.[13] Evagrius views *mnesikakia* as being as deadly as John does, and extricating it from one's mind is as crucial a task as Chrysostom believes: "Put great wrath and anger from you, and don't let remembrance of evil lodge in you."[14] The reason for his insistence lies in the pernicious effects that this vice has. *Mnesikakia* that is not driven from the soul darkens the mind of the one who seeks to pray and it blocks meaningful prayer. Conversely, prayer is really the only practice that can overcome *mnesikakia*: "A strong wind drives clouds away and remembrance of evil drives the mind away from knowledge. He who prays for his enemies is free from *mnesikakia*."[15] Evagrius was also the first writer to mention *mnesikakia* and love of money in the same breath, but he would not be the last: "The thought arises at the same time, and we fall prey to the demon of love of money and remembrance of evil."[16] As we will see, Chrysostom too sees a close link between these two vices. It is doubtful that John ever knew Evagrius or read his writings. It is more likely that they share some wisdom common to desert monks and urban ascetics like John.

Few, if any, of these instances of *mnesikakia* in earlier Fathers are connected explicitly to the Eucharist, but there is one case in which the remembrance of evil is mentioned in connection to the liturgy of the Church. Cyril of Jerusalem's *Mystagogical Lectures* have been translated numerous times and still stand today as a clear witness to the liturgy of Jerusalem in the mid-fourth century. In the fifth catechesis, Cyril recites the deacon's words "Let us receive and greet one another" and teaches that the kiss Christians give one another is different from "those in the marketplace." This kiss carries a far more meaningful significance: "this kiss unites souls to one another and weds all forgetfulness of evil [ἀμνησικακίαν] to them. So this kiss is a sign of their souls being mingled and all *mnesikakia* being banished."[17] This explains why the kiss or greeting of peace is integral to the liturgy and to the Christian life. It may not be an exaggeration to say that the whole purpose

13 Evagrius died in 399, eight years before John. *Mnesikakia* occurs thirty-five times in Evagrius's corpus.

14 Evagrius Ponticus, *Discourse to Virgins* 8,2.

15 Evagrius Ponticus, *Discourse to Monks*, 13,2.

16 Evagrius Ponticus (under the name of Nilus of Ancyra), *On Evil Thoughts*, 24,19.

17 Cyril of Jerusalem, *Mystagogical Lectures*, 5.

of participation in the liturgy is to rid the soul of *mnesikakia*. Certainly, John Chrysostom connected the two and hoped that the liturgy and the Eucharist would banish this evil from the Christian soul and community.

WHAT IS *MNESIKAKIA* FOR JOHN?

Since the liturgy was so important for John Chrysostom, it is not surprising that he would talk about serious moral deficiencies in connection with and in the context of the Eucharist. The very existence of the liturgy of the Church required that moral issues be dealt with every time one enters into liturgy, for it is there that the petition of the Lord's Prayer reminds us, "Forgive our debts as we forgive our debtors." As evidence of how important this fact is for John, he expands on it in a manner I have not found in any other Church Father:

> Upon entering the church, let us come, as is fitting for God, not recalling evils against us in our soul lest somehow we pray against ourselves. Rather let's pray, "Forgive us as we forgive our debtors." The saying is frightening and hard even to say. But he who says this cries out to God, "I have forgiven, Master. Forgive me! I have let them go. Let [my sins] go! I have made room [in my heart]. Make room [for me]! If I have held on to them [i.e., the offenses], hold on to mine. If I have not forgiven my neighbor, do not forgive my sins. In the measure I have used, measure it back to me.[18]

The intensity evident in this section shows how important the issue of forgiveness is for Chrysostom. Particularly striking is the spiritual effect that *mnesikakia* has on the person who prays at liturgy. Praying for God's forgiveness while retaining hatred for one's enemies is in effect to "pray against ourselves." There are several texts where John emphasizes that having *mnesikakia* leaves negative effects on the soul, but perhaps the most pernicious effect is that withholding forgiveness blocks God's forgiveness of sin.

The relation of this hidden vice to the liturgy comes out again in a passage from *Homily 20 to the People of Antioch*, in which John connects the problem of *mnesikakia* to holy communion on the one side and to God's lovingkindness on the other: "Just as it is impossible for an adulterer and a blasphemer to partake of this table, so too the one who has an enemy and

18 *Homily 9 on Repentance*, PG 49:346.

remembers evils [of the past] cannot enjoy holy communion."[19] This is all part of God's "holy laws" (ἱερῶν νόμων) because communion with God and *mnesikakia* are utterly incompatible. The law of forgiveness of one's enemies comes not from some arbitrarily designed decision but from the love of God for humanity: "How do you wish the gentle and meek Master to be to you if you become harsh and unforgiving to your fellow servant? But has your fellow servant insulted you? Haven't you insulted God many times?"[20] John weighs the relative evil of adultery and blasphemy with *mnesikakia* and finds the latter worse. But why is it worse?

> For the fornicator or adulterer has fulfilled his desire and the sin is over; although he may wish vigilantly to show great repentance after his fall, he has some comfort. But the one who remembers evil [*mnesikakia*] actively brings about sin on a daily basis and it is never over. In the first case, the fault comes into play and sin is committed. In this case sin is daring [to assert itself] daily. What pardon can we have if we give ourselves willingly to such an evil beast?[21]

John's assessment here turns on the difference between acts and habits. Adultery may occur because of a deep-seated internal disorder, but it may also be a temporary moral lapse out of weakness. Blasphemy may come from a sudden blast of anger or a deep hatred for God, but both sins are acts that are easily identified and renounced. *Mnesikakia* is more a persistent beast that dogs the Christian and destroys love and charity.

That *mnesikakia* constitutes a serious, even grave evil comes out clearly in John's handling of a parable that deals with the problem of unforgiveness. The parable of the Unforgiving Servant in Mt 18:21–35 is both natural and startling. It is natural insofar as forgiveness lies at the heart of the gospel of Christ. Jesus's command to repent because the kingdom of God is at hand brought with it the promise of forgiveness for those who turn back to God. It is also startling because of the seemingly impossible demand taught in the parable. I detect in John's treatment of this parable the surprise and even shock that may beset the Christian who seeks to live by its truth.

The radical nature of the forgiveness called for in the parable is underscored by John's introduction of Rom 11:29 ("The gifts and calling of God are

19 *Homily 20 to the People of Antioch*, PG 49:198.

20 *Homily 20 to the People of Antioch*, PG 49:199.

21 *Homily 20 to the People of Antioch*, PG 49:198.

irrevocable") into his explanation. The parable appears to teach that God can revoke forgiveness once given, and this seems to contradict Paul's definitive declaration that nothing God gives can be revoked. Here John asks, "What may be worse than *mnesikakia* when it calls up the love of God for humanity [already] shown and yet it cannot dispose him [the servant] to forgive sins? Will the anger against his neighbor prevail?"[22] The shock one senses comes from the lack of any spirit of forgiveness in the servant arising from his experience of the love of God. Why has the servant who owed so much retained such anger and hatred for his fellow servant? *Mnesikakia* is the one sinful disposition that rots away the soul and blocks God's forgiveness. And John heightens the evil latent in *mnesikakia* by juxtaposing the text from Romans:

> Although it is written that "the gifts of God are irrevocable," how can it be that an accounting is called for again after the gift [of forgiveness] is given, after love for humanity has been advanced? It is because of *mnesikakia*. It is so that should anyone sin in a manner that is not as harsh as this sin is in comparison to others, [we may know] that all the other [sins] can be forgiven. Not only could this one [sin] not find leniency, but also it brought the others back again. So *mnesikakia* is a twofold evil because it has no excuse with God and because the other sins, although forgiven, are again being brought up and counted against us. That is precisely what happened here.[23]

John sees an exception to the maxim of Rom 11:29, and the only sin/evil that can cause God to withdraw his forgiveness and mercy is the lack of the same in us toward our fellow servants. This is why I claimed earlier that John sees *mnesikakia* as perhaps the worst of all sins and why he proclaimed here what we noted earlier, "There is nothing, nothing that God hates and turns away from like a man of *mnesikakia* and holding on to anger."[24]

John's thoughts are sobering and arresting. As he works through various aspects of the parable he concentrates on the enormous difference between the debt the master forgave (10,000 talents) and the small amount owed to the unforgiving servant by his fellow servant (100 denarii). This prompts John to consider the unpayable debt that sinners owe to God, the Master of all. Forgetting the debt owed to God may be what causes the one who has *mnesikakia* to remember the debt owed to him. If the Christian thinks

22 *On the Debitor of Ten Thousand Talents*, PG 51:29.

23 *On the Debitor of Ten Thousand Talents*, PG 51:29.

24 *On the Debitor of Ten Thousand Talents*, PG 51:29.

of sin, it should be only his own sins he contemplates, not those of the one who hurt him. In case his hearers may be tempted to disagree with John, he reminds them, "Rather it is not I but Christ who showed this in the parable." From this he draws the broader but more important exhortation: "So let us be diligent in being purified of anger and reconciling with those who are disagreeable toward us, because we know that neither prayer, almsgiving, nor fasting nor partaking of the mysteries nor any other thing [can bring forgiveness] if we hold on to evil memories. Nothing will be able to advocate for us on that day."[25]

Considering the consequences of holding on to hurts, injuries, and sufferings that one has sustained at the hands of another is sobering. And Chrysostom meant it to be so. He wanted to stop the bitter Christian in his tracks and impress on him how remembrance of wrongs has to be eradicated from the soul in order to find salvation.

John not only denounces *mnesikakia* and warns against its harmful effects, he also sees the same vice latent in the moral examples of Scripture and praises those who overcome it. Quite naturally, we expect some discussion of forgiving enemies in connection with the account of Christ's crucifixion and his words, "Father, forgive them, for they know not what they do" (Lk 23:34). In his two homilies on the good thief on the cross, John employs imitation as the main mode of ridding oneself of *mnesikakia* and of acquiring the ability to forgive. He urges imitation of the Master (Christ) but also adduces moral examples from the New Testament (Stephen, Paul) to reinforce his plea for his flock to show mercy and grant forgiveness. Here John's appeal to imitation (μίμησις) means more than our modern English equivalent. As numerous patristic scholars have noted, *mimesis* in the Greek Fathers is more than bare imitation of behavior; *mimesis* means internalizing the attitudes and dispositions that the examples illustrate.[26] The affinity of Stephen the Deacon's stoning with Jesus's crucifixion, as clearly portrayed by the author of Acts, is not lost on Chrysostom, who uses Stephen and Paul to overcome the expected objection that the average Christian may not be able to imitate Christ himself.

John fortifies his appeal to forgive one's enemies by an appeal to Old Testament figures who display the same gracious desire for the salvation of

25 *On the Debitor of Ten Thousand Talents*, PG 51:30.

26 For more on *mimesis*, see Richard A. Layton, *Didymus the Blind and His Circle in Late-Antique Alexandria* (Urbana: University of Illinois Press, 2004).

others. They lived in a time of the *lex talionis* (an eye for an eye and a tooth for a tooth) but John's examples displayed a greater clemency that anticipated Christ's call to forgive even one's enemies. Moses prayed that he might be wiped out of the book of life if God would not forgive the sins of his people (Ex 32:32). David stands in John's mind as a stellar example of the willingness to forgive those who persecuted him. In *On the Cross and the Thief 1*, John cites the incident of Saul pursuing David in 1 Samuel 24, where David prefers to receive God's punishment for sin than to have it fall on those pursuing him. John again appeals to the story of Saul and David in the cave where the King was relieving himself. David was afforded the opportunity to take the life of one who hated him without cause and was urged to do so by his faithful men. David refused:

> David was the one who found him sleeping inside the cave, but he did not call him the son of Kish but instead used a name of honor. "I am not laying my hand on the Lord's Anointed [χριστὸν]." This shows he was free of anger and *mnesikakia*. David calls the one who injured him "the Anointed of the Lord." Saul is the one who thirsted for his blood, who set out to destroy him after he had received a myriad of benefits. But David had in view not what Saul deserved to suffer but only what was proper to do and to say. What does this mean? When someone seizes his enemy in prison, he does so with a threefold bond: the limited space of close quarters, his helplessness, and his need to rest. Would you not demand justice and punishment for him? You would not ever say, "I will not lay my hand on the Lord's Anointed," would you? But, yes, that is what David said.[27]

Noting that David was said to be a man "after God's own heart" (ἄνδρα κατὰ τὴν καρδίαν μου), John is anxious that every Christian should follow David's example and become "free from anger and *mnesikakia*." David did not brood over the injuries that Saul had inflicted on him because he did not view the king through the eyes of passion but rather saw that which he truly was, "the Lord's Anointed." There is an implicit truth that John would want for his people. *Mnesikakia* and the anger associated with it can only be expelled by taking a proper view of one's opponent. If someone views his enemy only as an enemy, then vindictive revenge seems the only path to follow. If the

27 *Eclogae 29*, PG 63:777. The Greek text has a rough correspondence with that in *If Your Enemy Is Thirsty*, PG 51:183. As I noted earlier, the *Eclogae*, while not authentic, are drawn from Chrysostom's bona fide homilies and often reflect his thinking.

injured party sees the person in question in his true status, then, like David, he can overcome the impulses of anger that arise from *mnesikakia*.

All these examples from the Old and New Testaments stand not only as encouragements to leniency and mercy but even function in Chrysostom as a standard of judgment. Yet these examples of the godly from both testaments are all faint reflections of Christ's person, his teachings, and his divine example:

> The more examples we have, the greater our judgment will be if we fail to imitate them. To pray for one's enemies is greater than to pray for one's friends. The latter will not profit you as much as the former. "If you love those who love you, you are doing nothing great," Christ says, "because tax collectors do the same." . . . Whenever we love our enemies, we become like God in proportion to our human strength because "he causes his sun to rise on the evil and the good and causes the rain to fall on the just and the unjust." Let us then become like the Father.[28]

The second homily on the good thief uses much the same material as the first and was probably preached on a similar occasion in a later year. Yet in this second homily we also see John's invocation of the love of God for humanity (*philanthropia*). Here John focuses on the crowd's mocking, "If you are the Son of God, come down from the cross." For Chrysostom these words reflect both ignorance and "shameless unbelief," for greater things than coming down from the cross were done by Christ (such as raising Lazarus). Yet Christ's concern was not to prove his divinity; it was to remain on the cross precisely to save those who mocked and derided him. This all is what prompted his prayer, "Father, forgive them, for they know not what they do." What could more show the love of God than such a petition? John brings out the love behind this request: "It is not only the cross but the words from the cross that show this ineffable love for humanity. Yet I ask that you attend carefully that you may see the greatness of God's love for humanity and how in their foolishness Christ uses the occasion for good."[29] Here we arrive at a crossroads, one side of which we take from our discussion in chapter 1, where I showed how central God's love of humanity was in John's preaching. The other is the human response to divine love. Will Christians embrace it and live according to it? The dissonance between divine love and the human

28 *Homily 1 on the Cross and the Thief*, PG 49:407.

29 *Homily 2 on the Cross and the Thief*, PG 49:414–15.

response helps us answer why *mnesikakia* is such a great evil. It is a mindset in direct opposition to God's philanthropic intentions. The one who was injured, ignored, despised, and rejected is also the one whose love remained undaunted in the face of human indifference or depravity. In this way, the Christian must be perfect like the heavenly Exemplar.

The close association of *mnesikakia* with anger, rage, and vindictiveness is not surprising, but there is one connection that we may not have ever suspected. John Chrysostom sees a link between wealth and *mnesikakia*. John became legendary for his rants against wealth and the wealthy. The wealthy took him to be their enemy because he never seemed to cease calling them out for their self-centeredness and neglect of the poor. However, what connection could there possibly be between wealth and *mnesikakia*? In a passage in *Homily 3 on 2 Thessalonians* we obtain some glimpse into John's thinking from what appears to be a passing use of *mnesikakia*:

> Wealth is indeed a thorn that has no fruit, ugly in appearance, distasteful to use, sorrowing those who touch it, not only bearing no fruit but even thwarting shoots. Such is wealth. Not only does it bear no eternal fruit but it holds back those wanting it. Thorns are the food of unreasoning camels. They are food for the fire and useful for nothing. Such is wealth, useful for nothing but to light the oven, for fixing on that day that burns like a pot, for feeding those irrational passions, that is, *mnesikakia* and anger. Such is the camel eating thorns. It is reported by knowledgeable people that there is nothing in their herds so wild, so sulky, and so *mnesikakon* as a camel. Such is wealth. Irrational passions feed the soul. They pierce and wound the rational faculties like thorns do.[30]

Wealth or the love of money can make one focus on oneself to the exclusion or even detriment of others. *Mnesikakia* can do the same. Remembering the injuries someone has inflicted can make one vengeful, or at least turn toward self-pity. John's comparison with the camel eating thorns underscores this truth. The love of wealth and the love of self that wealth can sometimes produce are subrational impulses (τὰ ἄλογα πάθη) that are similar to feelings of vengeance and anger. When John asks, as he occasionally does, why someone would injure himself more than he already has been injured by nursing *mnesikakia*, he is implicitly appealing to the use of reason to counter these

30 *Homily 3 on 2 Thessalonians*, PG 62:483.

subrational impulses. Giving in to anger and a vengeful spirit only reinforces the same self-centeredness that wealth also nurtures. That *mnesikakia* is a subrational or even irrational passion becomes clear in John's application of the term to camels. Even animals have memory or an analogue of memory and often respond to previous injuries with fear or aggression. *Mnesikakia* is not rational and therefore completely unfit for human beings.

Does wealth always produce *mnesikakia*? I doubt even John would have agreed with that conclusion. But there may have been a good reason why Paul said that "the love of money is the root of all evil" (1 Tim 6:10). Not only can the management of wealth require inordinate amounts of time, but the fear of losing one's wealth can drive a person to extreme measures of self-protection. And that is at the core of what *mnesikakia* entails. It is the thirst for vengeance arising from the impulse of self-protection.

MNESIKAKIA, SELF-HARM, AND VICTORY

John uses the natural impulse to protect oneself to counsel the eradication of *mnesikakia*. If protecting oneself were paramount, then the elimination of the vice of *mnesikakia* would also be of the utmost importance. There are a number of passages where Chrysostom makes important points on the self-harm that *mnesikakia* does. Retaining a bitter spirit consumes the heart of the one holding it inside and blocks the growth of charity. This leads us back to a homily we encountered earlier, *On Blessed Philogonius*. There we saw how John linked the Eucharist to the birth of Christ and the experience of the sacred table as extending the salvation of the Savior to the Church. Yet, as John approaches the consideration of the proper dispositions for holy communion, we hear him urging reconciliation and forgiveness.

John asks if any Christian is troubled by the lingering animosity of being wronged. That interior turmoil must be extricated in approaching holy communion, but another truth must also be considered. No matter how great the offense sustained, not forgiving the offender will be an even greater insult to God.[31] The solution for every Christian begins with having more regard

31 "Have you been greatly wronged and cannot bear to let go of your anger? What greater, more severe wrong will you do yourself? Those things that your enemy has done, however great they be, are not so bad as you do to yourself if you are not reconciled to him but rather trample on the law of God" (*On Blessed Philogonius*, PG 48:756).

for God's commands than hatred for the one who has hurt him.[32] Closely aligned with this moral consideration is a psychological fact that plays into the problem. By holding on to grudges and injuries, one endangers the health of one's soul. However deeply one has been injured, lack of forgiveness is an even deeper wound.[33] The reward in the final judgment will be great, and so Chrysostom urges his hearers to take the longer (and eternal) view of things.[34] Still, one does not have to wait for future peace and glory. The realities of heaven can begin to be experienced in this life through communion: "As the King enters your soul, there should be great tranquility, great silence, deep in your thoughts."[35]

John is clearly dealing with the same problem of *mnesikakia* even though the word itself does not occur in the homily *On Blessed Philogonius*. How seriously he views the issue shows itself by being at the very end of a homily that otherwise sounds a positive note. Recall that this homily was preached just a few days before Christmas/Epiphany, a time that surely qualified as a high feast day. John longs for the day to arrive as he equally longs for his flock to be liberated from the chains of unforgiveness and bitterness.

John seems very aware of the intense struggle one might experience with hatred and unforgiveness, as this feeling shows up in the way he begins the homily. A Christian can be so troubled, so disturbed by anger within, that he cannot see how communion could be possible or even desirable. *Mnesikakia* can dull the spiritual senses to the point of oblivion. Hate, anger, and rage can so block divine grace that one is tempted to believe that peace of heart will never be found. Yet it is precisely in this context that John reminds his hearers of the soothing effects of the King's presence in the soul. Choosing the word *king* to refer to Christ in this text seems more than accidental. In the cultural context of the day, John and his people knew that one does not dare to speak in the presence of a king without permission. However, he reminds

32 "Are you going to insult God? It is not so much a matter of the one who defends himself as it is of the one who insults God, who laid down these laws. So don't look at your fellow servant or at the greatness of his offenses. Rather, as you put God and respect for him in your mind, examine this" (*On Blessed Philogonius*, PG 48:756).

33 "The greater the act of violence you suffer in your soul in being reconciled to the one who has caused [you] pain after being troubled by a thousand evils, that much more will you enjoy a greater honor from the God who commanded these things" (*On Blessed Philogonius*, PG 48:756).

34 "And as you receive him here with much honor, so he will also receive you there with much glory, rewarding your obedience infinitely more greatly" (*On Blessed Philogonius*, PG 48:756).

35 *On Blessed Philogonius*, PG 48:756.

them that this is no earthly king. The King received in communion is the One himself who is tranquility, peace, contemplation. So Christ's presence in the Eucharist can be exactly what they need to overcome *mnesikakia* and its associated emotions.

Building on such a foundation, John makes his final argument for overcoming hate in the form of an appeal to self-protection. The problem of *mnesikakia* often arises from a person focusing on his or her own hurt. John here seems to counsel his people to look back at themselves with an attitude of protecting themselves from an even greater evil than the one inflicted upon them by others. John's advice brings to mind the proverbial line that the cure is often worse than the disease. If someone imagines that the cure for past injuries is to hate the one who inflicted the pain, if revenge seems to be the most satisfying course of thought and action, John asks his fellow believers to consider the effects of *mnesikakia* on their own souls. *Mnesikakia* and unforgiveness are a great enemy of the soul, even if not always visible and obvious. Revenge, like so many sins, may bring temporary satisfaction, but in the end it destroys the one who possesses it.[36] And John does not hesitate to put the matter in its most ultimate form. *Mnesikakia*, hate, and revenge are all offenses against God. The God who readily forgives the erring sinner upon repentance is the God who will reward the sinner who forgives another. The exercise of forgiveness toward others will make a person "enjoy a greater honor from the God who commanded these things."[37] In this way, John urges forgiveness and love because both the judgment for not forgiving and the reward for doing so will be extraordinary. So as John seeks to prepare his congregation for approaching the holy table properly, he asks them to look carefully at one of the most persistent and pernicious vices the human race has ever faced.

As with the parable of the Unforgiving Servant, we also expect Chrysostom to deal with *mnesikakia* and unforgiveness in his exposition of Paul's words in Rom 12:14–21. Wanting his hearers to overcome evil with good, John expands on Rom 12:14:

> Bless those who persecute you. He did not say, "Don't recall the evil or be revengeful." He was rather looking for something better. The first was

36 For an illuminating discussion of self-destructive effects of jealousy in Chrysostom see Laird, "Mindset (γνώμη) in John Chrysostom," 199.

37 *On Blessed Philogonius*, PG 48:756.

> characteristic of a wise man, but this latter [something better] belongs to angels. So he added, "Bless and do not curse," that we may do only that of the wise man. Those who persecute us are patrons of rewards. Assuming you are sober minded, you are preparing another reward for yourself after that one. The persecutor provides one reward from the persecution, but you do so for yourself from blessing him because it carries the greatest sign of love for Christ.[38]

By glossing *mnesikakia* with ἀμύνεσθε (to exact revenge, to defend oneself) he gives a sense of what it means to leave the remembrance of evil behind. Yet here John goes beyond just a negative command to appeal to love for Christ as a motive for treating the persecutor as a benefactor. How is possible for one who inflicts injury to be seen as a patron? Consider the converse. Self-harm is implied when one retains *mnesikakia* to the point to exacting revenge or dismissing the party that injures. John's is a vision beyond the natural realm because he sees both the persecutor and the blessing given to him as a twofold reward. Providence affords the injured a chance to gain a greater reward.

Later in the same homily John shows great prudence in counseling against *mnesikakia* and for a demonstration of love and grace toward those who have inflicted injury. He fully acknowledges the human tendency to return injury for injury and the desire to exact revenge, "hoping for punishment for the one who gave him pain because nothing is sweeter than seeing an enemy punished." Yet Paul's words call for a higher response to injury. He urged the Romans "to overcome evil with good" (Rom 12:21), to feed the enemy and give him something to drink, thereby heaping coals of fire on his head (Rom 12:20). John knew that "even if the enemy were a wild beast, he would not remain an enemy once he is fed." The corollary to such acts of kindness also has an effect on the injured party because "even if he were a thousand times more pusillanimous, he would not continue wanting punishment after feeding and giving drink." Such magnanimity is possible only when the injured person sees "the end [*telos*] of the problem," by which John seems to mean that God's plan for these situations is higher and better than human revenge. Engaging in acts that arise from *mnesikakia* means hanging on to the evil (τὸ γὰρ ἔτι μνησικακεῖν) and entails that the person would be diminished by evil. The reward that awaits the one who returns

38 *Homily 22 on Romans*, PG 60:609.

good for evil lies in becoming a better person, one who is better for others in this world and more pleasing to God, who arranged this order.[39]

Homily 50 on the Acts of the Apostles contains a lengthy treatment of the same theme of the self-harm that *mnesikakia* engenders and by contrast the victory contained in putting away anger and revenge. John appeals to the example of Paul before Felix the Governor (Acts 24). Paul did not reply to accusations tit for tat but answered only as was necessary for his defense. As John urges imitation of Paul, he explains the negative effects of *mnesikakia* and the positive benefits of responding to insult with grace and love:

> Let us imitate him [Paul] since he was an imitator of Christ. If he replied nothing to one who went to the extent of murder and slaughter, whose forgiveness may we be worthy of if we become like savages with ridicule and abuse, calling our enemies totally abominable and ugly things? What defense can we have if we retain such enemies? Aren't you listening? He who honors [another] honors himself. But we are abusing ourselves. Do you accuse others of abusing you? Why do you fall into [another] accusation? Why do you beat yourself up? Stay free of emotion. Don't let yourself be wounded more. Don't toss yourself into evil by wanting to strike another.[40]

John appeals to the natural inclination to protect oneself. The problem often lies in the offended party not knowing what will result in being hurt even more, so John lays down an axiom, "He who honors [another] honors himself." The wisdom of this preacher is remarkable. Responding to evil acts or words in kind is to fall into the same trap as the offender. Apparently, John felt the need to stress this truth because so few can recognize its value. So where does the strength come from to overcome *mnesikakia* and its associated anger? It derives from a readjustment of one's values, from a reassessment of what constitutes victory and defeat. John sees strength as the ability to overcome the demons lurking in the human soul, not as conquering an external source of aggravation. It is the person who injures another that is weak. The stronger person feels no need to do so:

> By abusing someone greater, he himself becomes weaker. Do you recognize when we have to grieve? It is when we engage in abuse but the other person remains silent. He then becomes stronger and we become weaker. But if the

39 All the quotations in this paragraph come from *Homily 22 on Romans*, PG 60:612.

40 *Homily 50 on the Acts of the Apostles*, PG 60:348.

> contrary is the case, you can rejoice. You are crowned and proclaimed victor without having ever entered the battle, without dealing with the hot sun, the heat, or the dust. You did it without wrestling or having a grip on him. All you did was stand or sit and wish it. For that you got a great crown. And not a great one but something even greater. For entering a match with your opponent is nothing equal to overcoming the flaming darts of anger. You have conquered without having to lock arms with him. You have dispelled your passionate emotion. You have destroyed the wild beast. You have bridled the raging madness just like the best herdsmen do.[41]

The victor's wreath, then, belongs to the Christian who conquers anger. The real beast to defeat is not the offending person but the passion that lurks in one's own soul, passion that is ready to devour love and thwart goodness. In the homilies on Acts John likens *mnesikakia* to madness (ἀπόνοια), an ailment worse than physical disease. While physical illness is often confined to one person, and even moral vices can be carried within the soul without detection, anger and madness are different. While it is theoretically possible to hold such passions within one's person, it rarely turns out that way in practice. Bitterness toward one's enemies often comes out if the opportunity affords. It may not be overt or obvious at first, but it comes out in any case. This is why John says that anger and madness are worse than sickness. And the converse is also true. Victory over anger, rage, and *mnesikakia* is a victory like no other. The greatest victory is the conquering of self.

THE ANTIDOTE TO *MNESIKAKIA* (REMEMBERING EVIL)

If *mnesikakia* is such a serious evil, if it is a vice that no Christian should toy with or ignore, what can be done to rid oneself of its grip? Does John the preacher offer any solid advice, any hope that such a persistent demon can be expelled? One thing is clear in John's preaching: customary, perfunctory, and legalistic solutions will not do.[42] Perhaps we are thrown back on the straightforward call of Jesus and other authors in the New Testament,

41 *Homily 50 on the Acts of the Apostles*, PG 60:348.

42 *Homily 20 to the People of Antioch*, PG 49:197: "Because the fasting of Lent is not sufficient to be able to commune, but it is also necessary and possible to not remember evil in the soul as a first virtue."

"Repent" (Mk 1:15). John would not disagree with that exhortation, but he knew that strong words alone were not sufficient to produce the desired change. The natural question from the person who is told to repent is how. Not knowing how to address the problem may become an excuse for not facing up to it, but John was not one to let that happen. In a similar instance, when John was urging his congregation to engage in good works, he heard this objection:

> How can I be in the world, some say, and in the midst of everyday affairs and still be saved? What is that, you say, O Man? Do you want me to show briefly that my being saved is a matter not of place but of the choice and manner of living? Adam was placed as a wreck in paradise as in a harbor. Lot was saved out of Sodom as on a sea. Job was justified on a dunghill. Saul, when he was in a cave, sent out [orders] as king from here and there. It is not a defense to say, "I cannot be in the world and in the midst of practical affairs and be saved."[43]

It is easy to imagine a similar objection in the case of *mnesikakia*. How could one even begin to eliminate this plague from the soul? Better just to give up and live with it. While not denying the difficulty involved, John insists that expelling *mnesikakia* is not optional. Paying heed to the exhortation to repent is a beginning, and John sees this as closely connected to *mnesikakia*:

> Move your accuser inside your conscience that you may not have an accuser at the Lord's judgment seat. One way of repentance is the best but there is another that is no less [important] than this. It is not to remember the evil your enemy did, not to hold on to anger, to forgive the sins of your fellow servants. And so your sins against the Master will be forgiven. Look, the second is to forgive sins: "You will forgive your debtors, your heavenly Father will forgive you."[44]

By having a resolute purpose to get rid of *mnesikakia*, one has taken the first step toward being free of its grip. The love of God that has forgiven much greater offenses of the offended party can function as a great impetus for that person to let go of the hurt and the hate that still plagues the soul. And perhaps the realization that one does more injury to one's own soul by not forgiving than the original offense inflicted will be a great boon

43 *Homily 9 on Repentance*, PG 49:344.

44 *Homily 2 on the Devil as Tempter*, PG 49:263.

to repentance. So, the willful determination to fight against *mnesikakia* is essential, but it still may not help cure the disease. What virtues must be substituted for this tendency to dwell on the hurt sustained from another? All growth in the highest virtue of love requires considerable labor, but even then one may not be up to the task without supernatural grace.

If growth in love and grace involves substituting a virtue for the vice of *mnesikakia*, what virtue is most important and effective in eliminating that evil? Recall that *mnesikakia* is not a sin consisting of discrete acts like robbery, adultery, or murder. It is more like greed or lust, an inner disposition that underlies many specific acts. *Mnesikakia*, like other vices, takes hold of its subject and dominates the mind and the heart where it is lodged. A powerful virtue is needed to overcome not only the discrete acts that may arise from *mnesikakia* but also the deeper motivations and patterns of thought that give rise to those acts. John is sure that humility is such a virtue. Without humility there is no hope for defeating *mnesikakia*. In that homily on Hebrews cited earlier John urges humility:

> So if we pray with humility, if we beat our chests with the tax collector, if we give voice to the same words as he, "Be merciful to me a sinner," we will obtain everything. Although we are not tax collectors, we still have other sins no less than his. Don't tell me that you have sinned only a little, for the substance of it is the same. Just as a man is called a murderer whether he murders a child or a man, so this is true of a greedy man whether he is greedy for much or for little. Remembrance of evil is not small but a great sin. For "remembering evil is a way to death" and "the one who is angry with his brother for no reason will be liable to Gehenna." So too for anyone who calls his brother a fool and an ignoramus and things like that. We also partake of the awesome mysteries unworthily and are malicious and abusive. Some of us often got drunk. Each one of these is by itself enough to get us expelled from the kingdom.[45]

Here is the fuller context of that powerful condemnation, "*mnesikakia* is not small but a great sin," and now we can see what the basis of those strong words is. The example of the tax collector in Lk 18:9–14 fits the bill for fighting *mnesikakia* perfectly. Why? Because remembering an evil done necessarily involves the opposite of humility—pride. Pride has many faces, which is perhaps the reason why it was designated a capital sin later in Christian history.

45 *Homily 27 on Hebrews*, PG 63:190.

Pride can manifest itself as boasting, vindictiveness, insistence on always being right, failure to listen to persons, intransigence, or simply selfishness. But no one can doubt that *mnesikakia* relies on pride as an instrument to grow its evil into vindictiveness. Pride rarely shows itself as pride; it more often masquerades behind some virtue twisted into evil. *Mnesikakia* doubtless masquerades as a desire for justice. One was wronged and another must pay. John unmasks *mnesikakia* to show what it is and how truly deadly it is.

With so formidable a foe as *mnesikakia* and its associated pride, how does the example of the tax collector help? What did John see in this man that could benefit the believer struggling with *mnesikakia*? One clear lesson is in John's mind. This man made no excuse, no calculating greater or lesser sins; his plea was "have mercy on me a sinner." And so John urges his hearers to beat their breast like him. In the end, whether the sin is social like extortion or private like *mnesikakia*, "the substance of it [all sin] is the same." John quotes from Proverbs that nursing grudges leads to death Then quoting Jesus in Mt 5:22, Chrysostom emphasizes that *mnesikakia* is worthy of the harshest judgment of God. Only a profound change in the inner disposition of the heart—only a move from hate to love—can prepare a person for God's judgment. And so too only these things will prepare a person to receive the Holy Eucharist. Abuse and malice will block God's grace in the mysteries as much as extortion or adultery.

Humility is inherently an inner disposition although it clearly affects all interactions with others. Yet humility may not be enough to silence the demon of *mnesikakia*. To understand the antidote to vindictiveness that arises from *mnesikakia*, John gives us the virtue of *anexikakia* (ἀνεξικακίᾳ).[46] Typically translated as "forbearance," ἀνεξικακίᾳ may have a wider significance. One cannot help noticing that both *mnesikakia* and *anexikakia* contain the root word κακία, meaning "evil" in the broadest and most general sense. Just as *mnesikakia* is the embedding of evils done in the memory, so *anexikakia* is the expulsion or excision of evil from the soul. That raises the question as to the proper translation of the latter term or at least what quality of soul is meant by *anexikakia*. In 2 Tim 2:24, the only verse of the New Testament where the word occurs, the word is aligned with gentleness and teachability and is contrasted with combativeness.[47] In John's usage, ἀνεξικακίᾳ shows

46 In the entire TLG corpus ἀνεξικακία and its congeners in all grammatical forms occur 1255 times, the majority of which occur in Christian authors. Ἀνεξικακία occurs 143 times (about 11%) in Chrysostom's corpus, most of which occur in the accusative (34) and genitive (57).

47 2 Tim 2:24: δοῦλον δὲ κυρίου οὐ δεῖ μάχεσθαι ἀλλ' ἤπιον εἶναι πρὸς πάντας, διδακτικόν, ἀνεξίκακον.

the meaning of forbearance as bearing with the evil done in a patient and understanding way. He even proclaims expelling *mnesikakia* as a victory when countered with forbearance: "You are thinking of conquering your enemy. Well, you will be conquered by evil, that is, by anger. So, if you want to conquer, be reconciled, and don't prosecute him. It is an illustrious victory when you conquer evil with the good, that is, with forbearance [ἀνεξικακίᾳ], when you have expelled anger and the remembrance of evil."[48] More precisely, forbearance in this context seems to mean resisting the urge to be vindictive. The victory that such forbearance affords lies in seeking reconciliation whereby an enemy becomes a friend. Given all that John has said about the evil of *mnesikakia* and its effects, is there any positive value in holding on to the memory of the afflictions others imposed? Is there any benefit to retaining and nursing the anger that resides in the injured party? The answer seems to be a clear negative. Surprisingly, John does in fact see something of value in expressing the anger that lies behind *mnesikakia*, but this positive use of anger requires a refocusing of one's emotions:

> If anyone has an enemy who has mistreated him, if he is angry, let him gather all his wrath, all his bitterness, and unload it on the head of the Devil. In this case, wrath is good, anger is useful, remembering evil is commendable. Just as bearing grudges against others is evil, the same thing is good in this case. So, if you have experienced a deep loss, in this case clear it away. But if you cannot remove it, even if you try with all your members . . . Has someone injured you? Bear the grudge against the Devil and never let your enmity against him be destroyed. Yet, did he not strike you? So remember the evil that he insulted your Master. He offended him, disgraced him, and made war with your brothers. Always be his enemy, always bitter, always savage.[49]

Wrath is good, anger is useful, remembering evil is commendable? In this exhortation from *Homily 22 on Ephesians* John seems to contradict all that he has said elsewhere about *mnesikakia*, but in fact this odd change of language only invites us to probe more deeply into the underlying problem. John recognizes that ridding oneself of anger and bitterness is easier said than done. Most people suffer from the residual effects of holding on to negative memories from past injuries. What can be done about this persistent problem?

John encourages us to acknowledge the hurt and pain caused by others. He calls it "a deep loss" (ἐλαττώματα) and knows that it is sometimes

48 *If Your Enemy Is Thirsty*, PG 5:182.

49 *Homily 22 on Ephesians*, PG 62:163.

profoundly impossible to extricate it from our memories ("if you cannot remove it, even if you try with all your members"). His mention of "members" (μετὰ τῶν μελῶν) suggests his awareness that sometimes Christians have exhausted their resources in trying to overcome this problem. Yet John has one more strategy that no other Greek Father seems to have thought of: begin a hate campaign against the Devil. Fight the Devil with his own medicine. It is the Devil who is the true source of the problem because he is not only the father of lies (cf. Jn 8:44); he is father of hate as well. In one sense hate is the one thing that the Devil understands. John does not mince words: "Always be his enemy, always bitter, always savage." But why this stratagem? Is it a last resort? John offers the ultimate motivation for hating the Devil. "So remember the evil that he insulted your Master. He offended him, disgraced him, and made war with your brothers." The evil treatment of Christ by the Devil will motivate the Christian to hate the Devil because he loves Christ. When the Christian turns his memory of past evils against the Evil One, it is like defending Christ against the attacks of that same evil power. However, is hating the Devil still not a form of hate and incompatible with love? How can the vice of *mnesikakia* be expelled unless all forms of hate are renounced? One explanation may lie in understanding that to love Christ means to hate his enemies, not in the sense of intense emotion but hate in the sense of what opposes Christ. In any case, love for Christ lies at the root of ridding oneself of *mnesikakia*.

It may not be too fanciful to say that for John the best and most effective answer to *mnesikakia* is love, for it is from love that humility, forbearance, and other virtues flow. In his commentary on 1 Corinthians 13, John hints at how the interaction of virtues works:

> Love thoroughly purifies everything. Look! A patient person is not completely kind. If he is not kind, the matter becomes evil and he is in danger of falling into *mnesikakia*. For this reason, love gave a medicine, which is kindness. Love keeps virtue pure. Again, the kind person is often easily content, but this love also sets the matter straight. For love, he says, "is not pompous, not puffed up." The kind and patient person often makes false pretensions. But such love takes away this evil.[50]

John implies a hierarchy of virtues in which kindness, though it be laudatory, is still inferior to love. Kindness and other virtues like generosity

50 *Homily 33 on 1 Corinthians*, PG 61:277.

or thoughtfulness may not necessarily fend off *mnesikakia*. Love, however, when perfected, expels the remembrance of evil. The perennial problem is that love is rarely perfected in the human soul in this world. If John is right in his insistence that God will not forgive those who refuse forgiveness to their fellow human beings, then salvation is in jeopardy, at least for those who fail to forgive. Can God's loving forgiveness be withheld? Why will God not forgive if we do not forgive our debtors? Doesn't God have the power to forgive even if we do not? Is he not merciful enough to forgive even those of us who cannot forgive others? And why has God tied our being forgiven to our willingness to forgive others? If we view this problem as an arbitrary law set by divine arrangement an answer may be lacking, but the answer may lie in something not about God but about us. The ability to forgive the sins of others does not lie in human strength, no matter how advanced a person may be in the pursuit of love. It requires divine grace, the very life of God in the human soul. If we think of this problem in purely legal terms, we miss something essential about the nature of salvation.

John took seriously Jesus's words in Mt 5:48, "Be perfect as your heavenly Father is perfect," as he understood the context of God allowing his goodness to fall upon the just and the unjust. Perfection in love means loving those who do not love in return, and "praying for those who persecute us." Final salvation means arriving at that perfection that comes from love, but human beings are incapable of that kind of love. Only an infusion of God's love into the human soul can bring a person to the place where he can love enough to forgive heinous offenses.

What happens in the case of an injured person being unable to forgive the offender? When someone refuses to forgive, he closes off the possibility of receiving that divine love. The soul shrinks in its spiritual capacity. Instead of magnanimity, the soul becomes pusillanimous, or "very-small-souled." Holding on to memories of past injuries drives love from our souls. If we are to reach God, we must love as God loves. God must be loved as he loves in a kind of parity of love. But such a goal is unreachable for us. We can never love God as he loves us. That is why we must have God's love in our souls to do so. Only God's love makes it possible to love as God does, and we must be filled with that love in order to forgive as God forgives. When God does not forgive us because we don't forgive others, it is not because of some arbitrary rule he established but because we are not capable of receiving his love, which alone can perfect us into the image of Christ his son (cf. Rom 8:29).

✠ ✠ ✠

It becomes clear that John Chrysostom sees *mnesikakia* as one of the worst vices afflicting the human soul. It gives rise to so many sinful attitudes and actions. From this it follows that eradicating *mnesikakia* should be one of the greatest goals of the spiritual life. Overcoming anger, bitterness, vindictiveness, brooding over past evils, and a myriad of other negative passions would indeed be one of the greatest victories that a Christian could ever have. That John felt this way is evident from his use of military language in describing King David's victory in conquering *mnesikakia*. David's dramatic victory over Goliath, the Philistine giant, is puny compared to his other victory: "David obtained a greater war trophy by sparing Saul's life than by cutting off Goliath's head. That victory was far more illustrious and the trophy more glorious."[51]

If the opposite of *mnesikakia* is to be filled with the love of God, then John's urgings can be understood as acts of love, because nothing could be more destructive of divine love in the soul than to withhold forgiveness of one's fellow sinner. Love of one's fellow human beings is a sure sign of goodness. Forgiveness of others is certainly one of the most difficult and yet important aspects of that love. It recognizes that others will sin and yet are not consigned to a hopeless state of loss. Forgiveness puts a sinner back on track and allows for second chances. Love also reaches out to another even when it is not convenient to do so. And that truth explains why John Chrysostom could not discuss the Eucharist without treating how it affected human relationships. The gift of Christ in the Eucharist is the supreme gift of self. It provides both model and impetus to give of oneself to others, especially to those who are less fortunate. Love that does not affect one's relations with others is not genuine love. Love that is not compassionate is not love. Love always reaches out to share and to embrace.

51 *Eclogae* 29, PG 63:780.

9

The Social Implications of the Eucharistic Liturgy

John Chrysostom believed that the Eucharist demands a love for one's neighbor that moves outside the comfort zone of every believer and reaches out to those who have been deprived of the world's goods. He viewed the Eucharist not only from the standpoint of the individual but from that of the community as well, because communion in the Eucharist is more than a private act of an individual Christian. Like marriage, it is an intensely personal participation, but it is never divorced from the moral duties one has toward others or from the obligations of love. No Greek Father of the Church seems to have been more aware of this than John Chrysostom. In chapters 7 and 8 we treated John's view of holy communion from the vantage point of the individual communicant. In this chapter, we examine communion in light of the relation of the Christian to his fellow members of the body of Christ and to the world at large. We already had that social standpoint in view when treating forgiveness and *mnesikakia*, but John is just as insistent that caring for the poor and downtrodden is incumbent on the person who consumes Christ in the Eucharist. The underlying question to be understood first is how the body of Christ can be best honored. John's answer is both clear and compelling. Christ is honored best in the poor. But who are the poor? Recent studies of the Chrysostom corpus have revealed that the answer is not so simple. Nevertheless, John does call Christians away from self-indulgence to consider the poor not as beneath the rich and powerful but as coheirs of God's largesse. Finally, we here examine how Chrysostom considers the obstacles to true generosity as he zeroes in on love of money and *mnesikakia*.

Scholars have long paid close attention to John Chrysostom's social teachings, and Christians in general with a bent toward social justice have also drawn on his writings to buttress their own program of social reform.[1] Recent analyses have revealed that the social situation in Chrysostom's day was more nuanced and complex than generic references to "the poor" might suggest.[2] We will return to this issue below but for now it is sufficient to recall that John Chrysostom was perhaps the greatest advocate of the poor among the Greek-speaking Fathers and possibly in the whole patristic tradition. This is partly due to Chrysostom's own framing of his life and partly due to what later Byzantine tradition ascribed to him. His homily *On Almsgiving* portrays him as an ambassador of the poor, while later writers summarized his life as "John the Almsgiver."[3] These ancient witnesses have echoed down to modern biographers, one of whom expresses a widely held view of John as "passionate champion of the poor."[4] Still, there has been little exploration of connections and implications between the Eucharist and the social obligations toward the poor in scholarly literature, but John's own words at times suggest those ties. Below I will suggest an explanation for such connections.

HONORING THE BODY OF CHRIST

Many Christians, moved by the social solidarity so evident in the Bible, have invoked John as one who clearly saw how oppressive the rich can be. They become advocates of radical social change in the interest of the weak and vulnerable with the confidence that John is their champion. Although the

1 Among the voluminous literature consult the more recent noteworthy volumes and articles. For a collection of early sources see Helen Rhee, ed., *Wealth and Poverty in Early Christianity*, Ad Fontes: Early Christian Sources (Minneapolis: Fortress Press, 2017).

2 For a thorough discussion of the scholarly literature see Wendy Mayer, "Poverty and Generosity toward the Poor in the Time of John Chrysostom," chapter 10 in *Wealth and Poverty in Early Church and Society*, ed. S. R. Holman (Brookline, MA: Holy Cross Orthodox Press, 2008), 193–215.

3 *On Almsgiving*, PG 51:261.

4 J. N. D. Kelly, *Golden Mouth: The Story of John Chrysostom; Ascetic, Preacher, Bishop* (London: Duckworth, 1995), 97.

concern for the poor and downtrodden is undoubtedly central to John's view of the role of the Church in society, the actions of social justice are not isolated from his view of the Eucharist, and that is what makes John's cry for social justice different from secularized views. In this connection there is a famous passage, quoted occasionally, which shows the tie between the altar of the Church and the needs of people in society:

> Do you want to honor Christ's body? Do not neglect him naked! Do not honor him here with silken garments but overlook him being destroyed by cold and nakedness. He who said, "This is my body" confirmed the matter with this word, "You saw me hungry but did not feed me" and "inasmuch as you did not do it to the least of these, you did not do it to me." He does not need coats but a pure soul. That thing demands much concern. Let us then learn wisdom and honor Christ as he wishes. The sweetest honor is for the one being honored to be honored as he wishes, not as we think it should be. Peter thought he was honoring Jesus by forbidding him to wash his feet, though what happened was not an honor but the contrary. So you too honor him with the honor that he commanded, namely, spending wealth on the poor. God does not need golden vessels but golden souls.[5]

This text has been noticed and read for a very long time, but its full significance has not always been appreciated. Above all, Chrysostom desires the Christian to respond to Jesus Christ in the way that Christ himself wants. In chapter 7 we noticed how John was concerned about the perfunctory performance of religious duties. He sought to elicit a deeper sincerity and authenticity than he sometimes noticed from Christians in worship. Here in *Homily 50 on Matthew* he seeks to show how showering gifts on the Church and its altar can be misplaced generosity if it means neglecting Christ's command. John quotes from the parable of the Sheep and Goats in Mt 25:31–46 and combines it with story of Jesus washing his disciples' feet in John chapter 13 to make the important point that Christians ought to honor Christ in the way that *he* wishes, not the way *they* imagine.

There is nothing hard to understand in this passage, but there are two noteworthy phrases that reveal John's mind. When he says that Christ "does not need coats but a pure soul" (Τοῦτο μὲν γὰρ οὐ δεῖται ἐπιβλημάτων, ἀλλὰ ψυχῆς καθαρᾶς), there is an identity between the indigent and Christ himself as the parable in Matthew makes clear. To minister to the needs of the poor

5 *Homily 50 on Matthew*, PG 58:508.

is to minister to Christ. However, there is more than meeting the temporal needs of those less fortunate. Clothing and feeding the needy can open a soul, both that of the donor and that of the recipient. It is not clear which John is thinking of, but both can be affected by true Christian charity. The giver loves Christ in the poor and thereby purifies his own soul as a gift to Christ. The recipient's soul too is drawn to Christ by the kindness coming from the Christian. Chrysostom also insists that "God does not need golden vessels but golden souls" (Οὐδὲ γὰρ σκευῶν χρείαν ἔχει χρυσῶν ὁ Θεὸς, ἀλλὰ ψυχῶν χρυσῶν). In this dictum, I think John is confronting a recurring mistake in the life of the Church, namely, to place priority and resources on things rather than people. God is in the business of saving souls, not precious metals. And so the Church should put its priorities on those who need salvation rather than on elaborate adornments. This focus on the poor is what honors Christ's sacred body, something that becomes even clearer in a section of the same homily that precedes the one quoted above:

> If you want to honor the sacrifice, bring your soul for which he was sacrificed. Make that kind of gold. Although a golden vessel may last longer than a lead or earthen vessel, what gain is there in that? So let us fix our eyes not on bringing golden vessels but on things arising from righteous works. Such things are more precious than gold, things devoid of greed. For the church is not forged in a gold or silver shop but in the festal assembly of angels. Souls are what we need. And God permits these things [gold and silver] for the sake of souls.[6]

These two passages not only follow closely on one another in the homily but manifest a certain symmetry of structure and thought. The passage quoted first actually follows the other in the homily itself, but both begin with very similar wording:

> If you want to honor the sacrifice,
> Εἰ γὰρ βούλει τιμῆσαι τὴν θυσίαν
> Do you want to honor Christ's body?
> Βούλει τιμῆσαι τοῦ Χριστοῦ τὸ σῶμα

Their similar wording introduces different ideas. How does a Christian honor Christ's body, which is the same as the sacrifice on the sacred table?

6 *Homily 50 on Matthew*, PG 58:508.

In the first passage (quoted second) one honors Christ by seeking pure gold, not the gold of chalices and ornaments but the gold of "righteous works or labors" (ἐκ δικαίων πόνων). Such pure desire will require vigilance against the vice of greed, and that vigilance can be strengthened by the knowledge of the true origin of the Church: "The church is not forged in a gold or silver shop but in the festal assembly of angels" (Οὐ γὰρ χρυσοχοεῖον, οὐδὲ ἀργυροκοπεῖόν ἐστιν ἡ Ἐκκλησία, ἀλλὰ πανήγυρις ἀγγέλων). Whatever else John may have meant by calling the Church "a festive assembly of angels," he clearly wants his hearers to see the heavenly origin and mystical reality of the Church. He alludes to Heb 12:22–23 over fifty times in speaking of the liturgy as the source of the Church's life.[7] Clearly, John sees in this biblical text not only the justification of his view of the Church but also a sanction for almsgiving because the Church is of divine origin, not human invention. The poor to whom he refers his fellow Christians are also members of the Church even if earthly appearance did not make it seem so. So the righteous labors that he views as golden are alms given to the poor and needy. And John leaves us in no doubt about the purpose. God is interested in saving people, not collecting expensive furniture. All the accoutrements of the Church are designed to lead people to heaven. Then in the second passage (quoted first) John sees God's Church as focused on "golden souls."[8] This all has significant implications for understanding the connection between the Eucharist and the social obligations of Christians.

The context around these two quotations enriches our understanding of how the Eucharist is the source and summit of service to the needy of the world. If a Christian desires to minister to the needs of those less fortunate, that Christian must be grounded in and nourished by the eucharistic mystery. John mentions that mystery as an agent of peace: "He [Christ] commands that this mystery always be pure from not only robbery but even enmity itself. For this mystery is a mystery of peace. It does not permit one to be repaid with money. If he did not spare himself for our sakes, then what may we be worthy of if we are stingy with money and lavish with our life,

7 The author of Hebrews says in 12:22–23, "But you have come to mount Zion, to the city of the living God, to the heavenly Jerusalem, to myriads of angels, to a festive assembly and to the church of the firstborn enrolled in heaven."

8 For an informative perspective on almsgiving as a way to heal the soul of the giver as well as the receiver, see Junghun Bae, *John Chrysostom on Almsgiving and the Therapy of the Soul* (Leiden: Brill, 2021).

that life for which he did not spare himself?"[9] John is partially quoting from Rom 8:32, in which Paul contends that God will not refuse any good to those for whom he did not spare even his own Son. What greater gifts could God give than those having to do with salvation? John answers summarily, "For he has given something even greater, that is, has set out himself."[10] Though this is a pithy saying, his verb choice, "set out" or "set up," for example a table for a meal (παρατίθημι), may be a direct pointer to the eucharistic table. That seems confirmed by what he says in the immediate context about the gift of Christ's flesh: "He gave us to be filled with his holy fleshes. He set himself out as sacrificed."[11] It is in this context of John's belief in a real communication of Christ's humanity to believers that he warns against an unholy reception because of mistreatment of others. What excuse can we Christians who commune in Christ give, "if eating a lamb, we become wolves"?[12] John is implicitly countering the rapacity that wealth can sometimes engender. He nowhere condemns riches per se, but only warns against the corrosive effect that wealth can have on a person. It can eat away at a person's soul, and one sure sign of that depletion is a lack of concern for the poor. John indicates the antidote in this same context when he reminds his hearers not to be ashamed of the cross and the mysteries that bear that cross. These solemn mysteries become the instruments of adorning and beautifying the soul so as to move it to care for the less fortunate.[13]

From these realities John draws out a number of social implications. In this arena of application, Chrysostom seems always to be addressing an underlying question: how do we best honor Christ? And the underlying assumption is that the answer lies in the parable of the Sheep and Goats in Matthew 25: the identity of Christ and the poor. To minister to the poor is to minister to Christ himself. While Chrysostom willingly concedes that material gifts for the Church are never unwelcome, he urges a better way to honor Christ. As he puts it, "with these" and even "before these" (μετὰ τούτων, καὶ πρὸ τούτων) visible donations, giving alms is better because

9 *Homily 50 on Matthew*, PG 58:508.

10 *Homily 50 on Matthew*, PG 58:508: Ὁ γὰρ τὸ μεῖζον δοὺς, τουτέστιν, ἑαυτὸν παραθεὶς.

11 *Homily 50 on Matthew*, PG 58:508.

12 *Homily 50 on Matthew*, PG 58:508.

13 *Homily 50 on Matthew*, PG 58:508: "Do not then be ashamed of the cross, for these are our solemn realities, these our mysteries. With this gift do we adorn ourselves, with this gift we are beautified"; Μὴ τοίνυν αἰσχύνου τὸν σταυρόν· ταῦτα γὰρ ἡμῶν ἐστι τὰ σεμνὰ, ταῦτα ἡμῶν τὰ μυστήρια· τούτῳ κοσμούμεθα τῷ δώρῳ, τούτῳ καλλωπιζόμεθα.

not only does the giver benefit but the receiver as well. And a danger lurks in limiting oneself to giving gifts of precious metal and ornate cloths. One may very well be feeding the "love of honor" (φιλοτιμία) whereas in giving alms "The whole matter is showing mercy and love of the human race."[14] Caring for the needy arises from the same motive we examined in chapter 1. God is himself a lover of humanity and seeks out the unlovely and those whom human beings turn from in disgust. God, on the other hand, shows his great love in condescending to those infinitely lower than himself. The moral implication seems clear enough. The Christian must reach out to those he may not be attracted to initially. In a section of the homily in which John contrasts these two ways, he insists on mercy and care for the needy:

> What profit is there when his table is filled with golden chalices but he is wasting away from hunger? First, give the hungry one his fill and then out of your excess adorn his table. Will you make a golden chalice and not give a cup of cold water? And what profit is there in preparing a gold embroidered cloth for the table but you do not provide the necessary shelter? What is the benefit of that? Tell me. If you surround the table with silver while you see one lacking the necessary food and do not relieve his hunger, would he thank you? Or would he not rather be very upset? And what about this? If you see a man clothed in rags and freezing cold, but you do not give him clothing, while you prepare golden columns [for the church], claiming to do this in his [Christ's] honor, would he not say that you pretended ignorance and think it an extreme insult?[15]

Some may wish to read John here as demeaning the formal worship of the Church, or as teaching that worship at the eucharistic table is an inferior form of service to God compared to caring for the needy. And such a reading may be a reason why some in history have focused on social programs as constituting the center of the Church's ministry. Yet, in light of all we have seen about the centrality of the Eucharist, it is a more judicious reading to see Chrysostom as trying to keep liturgy and the practice of alms together, to show how both are necessary and mutually imply each other. This latter reading is confirmed by John's reflection on Jesus's words about the poor always being with us.

14 *Homily 50 on Matthew*, PG 58:508.

15 *Homily 50 on Matthew*, PG 58:509.

If one wishes to make a lasting investment, one that cannot be lost or despoiled, attending to the needs of the hungry, the stranger, and the naked is a far better investment than adorning the walls of the Church. In this regard John quotes the fourth Gospel's version of Jesus's famous words, "The poor you always have with you, but me you do not always have" (Jn 12:8).[16] I think it significant that Chrysostom quotes this version and places it in a new context, for he firmly says that the hungry will not always be with us: "It is for this reason that it is necessary especially to be merciful because we do not always have the hungry person but only in the present life."[17] This reading holds two implications. By taking the opportunity to feed the hungry now, in this present life, we are ministering to Christ himself, who is hidden in the hungry. And such mercy for the less fortunate is an investment in the future life in a treasury that even the Devil cannot spoil because it resides "in an unassailable treasure box."[18]

Chrysostom's last words in *Homily 50 on Matthew* reinforce how almsgiving delivers from death and offers life. Noting the commands about almsgiving evident in the Old and New Testaments, John loosely quotes Lk 11:41, a text which has further roots in Tob 4:10 and 12:8, "This [giving alms] cleanses sins. Give alms and everything will be pure for you. This is greater than sacrifice. I desire mercy and not sacrifice. This opens the heavens. Prayers and alms rose up to be remembered in God's presence."[19] He conjoins this exhortation about almsgiving to prayer in a manner similar to Tob 12:8, "Prayer with fasting and almsgiving and righteous living is good." The phraseology around this verse also speaks of the superiority of almsgiving in contrast to gathering wealth. So John picks up on the biblical theme that the best way to store up treasure in heaven (cf. Mt 6:19–20) is to give away one's treasure on earth. Both the eucharistic liturgy and almsgiving "open the heavens" (τοῦτο τοὺς οὐρανοὺς ἀνοίγνυσιν), and therein lies the inseparable link between liturgy and life. Honoring Christ's body in the Eucharist is best done by honoring his body in the brethren.

16 Τοὺς πτωχοὺς πάντοτε ἔχετε μεθ' ἑαυτῶν, ἐμὲ δὲ οὐ πάντοτε ἔχετε. All three synoptic versions have the reverse order so that instead of Τοὺς πτωχοὺς πάντοτε, they have Πάντοτε τοὺς πτωχούς. If there is a slight shade of difference in meaning, the synoptics are stressing the "always," i.e., the perpetual presence of the poor, whereas in the Gospel of John the author stresses the contrast between the poor and Jesus himself.

17 *Homily 50 on Matthew*, PG 58:510.

18 *Homily 50 on Matthew*, PG 58:509.

19 *Homily 50 on Matthew*, PG 58:510. See also Acts 10:4.

The link between praying, almsgiving, and fasting is a common theme in the Church Fathers. Among the many examples we find two that are sufficiently illustrative: Gregory Nazianzen (Greek) and Peter Chrysologus (Latin). In his homily on the love of poverty Gregory insists that mercy is not optional if one wishes to follow Christ. As Gregory reflects on Jesus's teaching ("Blessed are the merciful, for they shall obtain mercy"), he urges two concomitant attitudes: promptness and joy. When reaching out in mercy to others, no delay should impede the act of generosity. Showing mercy begrudgingly betrays the very definition of mercy, which always flows from a generous heart. So Gregory urges, "Let us visit Christ whenever we may" and recounts the ways in which one can do so, all of which draw on the practical equation that serving the poor is serving Christ. And so like John Chrysostom, Gregory sees in the virtue of mercy a superior way to God, for "The Lord asks for mercy, not sacrifice, and mercy is greater than myriads of fattened lambs."[20] Almsgiving then leads one to Christ himself, because to minister to the poor is to minister to Christ. In Peter Chrysologus, the fifth-century bishop of Ravenna, we find an even more explicit explanation of the essential unity of these three penitential disciplines. *Sermon 43*, certainly preached during Lent, puts it boldly: "Prayer knocks at the door, fasting obtains, mercy receives. Prayer, fasting, mercy: these three are one, and they give life to each other."[21]

This tradition, shared widely across the ancient Church, begs for an explanation. In what way are these three the same or at least similar? Certainly for John, as for other Fathers of the Church, the Eucharist forgives sin since it is Christ himself. But how can prayer or fasting or especially almsgiving bring forgiveness? How can these practices "deliver from death" in the words of Tob 4:10? Are they parallel to and an alternative for the Eucharist? Are they alternatives for Christ himself? I believe that the objective/subjective distinction goes a long way to explaining John's views of the Eucharist and almsgiving. The liturgy of the Church, the body of Christ in the Eucharist, and the act of communion all have an objective quality about them that is not affected by the dispositions of the human subject. The liturgy opens heaven and unites it to earth, the Eucharist is the body and blood of Christ by virtue of Christ's own words of consecration and the presence of the Holy Spirit, and communion in that sacred body and blood has specific and definite

20 Gregory Nazianzen, *Oration 14: On the Love of the Poor*, PG 35:907–10.

21 Peter Chrysologus, *Sermon 43*.

meanings regardless of the attitudes and beliefs of the communicant or of the priest. One venerates the altar or table of the Church because Christ is truly there. And Christ is no less present in those who suffer in a myriad of ways. He is present in the hungry, the thirsty, the imprisoned, the naked, the homeless, the stranger. In some inexplicable manner, his presence in the needy is different from his mystical presence in the Eucharist, but Christ is still no less present in the poor than in the sacred elements.

Yet the subjective side is also of the highest importance. A Christian cannot truly have Christ in all his divine reality unless he is properly disposed. He must receive the body and blood with proper faith, with humble confession of sin, with love overflowing. The subjective side shows itself also in a willingness to live by Christ's command of love, and for John Chrysostom that desire must include those who are in the greatest need. If a Christian has the proper dispositions to receive the benefits of communion in Christ's body and blood, those same dispositions are present in prayer, in fasting, and in almsgiving. The heart that loves Christ and desires to receive him is the same heart that longs to pray, is willing to fast, and is loving enough to reach out to the needy. The common feature of the three penitential disciplines operates also in the act of sacramental communion. That feature is self-denial and sacrifice. Such a heart, filled with dispositions of grace, is able to receive forgiveness. Forgiveness in turn produces a life with righteous actions. Such a life makes death in spirit impossible. This explains why Chrysostom can say that almsgiving cleanses and why he approvingly quotes Lk 11:41 about all things becoming pure to the one with such a mind and heart. Such merciful actions as prayer and almsgiving rise up to plead forgiveness with God. In the end, John can embrace the saying "I desire mercy and not sacrifice" because the sacrifice brings forgiveness to a contrite heart. And almsgiving is a visible demonstration of such a contrite heart.

WHO ARE THE POOR?

Thus far we have spoken of the poor in very generic terms, but scholars have lately made some important discoveries in reading Chrysostom's discourses. Wendy Mayer has found some important differences in John's use of the category "the poor." She distinguishes, for example, between the voluntary poor (ascetics) and the economic poor (those deprived of money and goods).[22] While these and other distinctions are important for gaining a complete picture, our focus on the connections between poverty and the Eucharist allows us to see the broad trends in John's accent on the moral obligations toward the poor in a more theological light. Among the general lines of John's disquisitions on poverty that Mayer elucidates, several seem relevant to our theme. The instability of riches, for example, is often attributed by John to greed.[23] And poverty is not without some benefits in John's estimation. He even goes so far as to say that if there were no poverty, our common life might be endangered.[24] Poverty can help counter laziness by making work necessary—a fact especially important for the working poor (πένης). These are somewhat distinct from beggars (πτωχοί), who usually suffer worse than others. This latter category apparently evoked considerable disgust in John's contemporaries, as beggars were viewed as lazy or even fraudulent.[25] But John lays blame on those who neglect beggars rather than on the beggars themselves, because no one would voluntarily dishonor themselves or their families by begging. Hardheartedness toward beggars can only be overcome by almsgiving, which by its very nature gives indiscriminately to all.

One homily where cultural attitudes toward the poor show up in striking ways is his *Homily against Those Who Are Drunk and on the Resurrection of Christ.* Internal indications show that this homily must have been preached at the close of Lent and that John was concerned about riotous behavior in his flock, who had just completed the discipline of fasting. By using drunkenness as a metonym for a dissolute life, he proceeds to explain that there are many ways to be "drunk." Any form of undisciplined life counts as drunkenness. But there is one kind of inebriation that Chrysostom does commend, that urged by Paul in Eph 5:18, "Do not get drunk with wine, in which is excess, but be filled with the Spirit." Taking his cue from Paul's explicit reference to "wine," and leaving open other possible ways to get drunk, John exhorts his people to be drunk, that is, filled with the Holy Spirit. Such inebriation leads not to dissolution (παράλυσις) but to sobriety of the best kind. That kind

22 Wendy Mayer, "John Chrysostom on Poverty," in P. Allen, B. Neil, and W. Mayer, *Preaching Poverty in Late Antiquity: Perceptions and Realities*, Arbeiten zur Kirchen- und Theologiegeschichte 28 (Leipzig: Evangelische Verlagsanstalt, 2009), 69–117.

23 Mayer, "John Chrysostom on Poverty," 82.

24 Mayer, "John Chrysostom on Poverty," 85.

25 Mayer, "John Chrysostom on Poverty," 88.

of drunkenness is the only appropriate one for approaching the Eucharist. Any other will disgrace the feast. It is into this context that Chrysostom introduces the poor.

In Chrysostom's cultural landscape, the economically poor may have been considered the most likely to abuse the feast of Pascha with drunken behavior, especially as viewed by those in the upper classes. If so, then it would make sense of many of his subsequent statements about the poor and the rich. In this homily he places them side by side to proclaim their equality before the sacred table. The foundation for such a comparison lies in the nature of the eucharistic feast itself: "The present feast is not only of the earth but of heaven as well. Today there is joy on earth; there is joy in heaven." The celestial character of the Paschal feast does not go unnoticed: "Now the angels are skipping, now the archangels rejoice, now the Cherubim and the Seraphim celebrate the present feast."[26] And yet the angelic powers do not hesitate to lower themselves to human weakness. They have Christ himself as their leader:

> Their Master and ours is himself not ashamed to feast with us. And why should I say that he is not ashamed? He says, "I have strongly desired to eat this Passover with you" [Lk 22:15]. If he desired to celebrate the Passover feast with us, it is clear that the same is true of the resurrection. So when the angels and archangels rejoice, the Master of all the heavenly powers also celebrates the feast with us. What reason remains for despair?[27]

The mention of despair (ἀθυμία) is significant as John proceeds to encourage the poor, "Let no one be downcast because of his poverty."[28] Chrysostom then compares the rich and poor along several different lines, but his underlying contrast is between societal attitudes that both groups may have adopted and those attitudes proper to the Church. The difference could not be greater:

> The poor man is naturally downcast, the rich man in splendor. Why is this, then? Because the rich man sets the table with plenty and enjoys the delicacies. The poor man, because of his poverty, is forbidden from being

26 *Homily against Those Who Are Drunk and on the Resurrection of Christ*, PG 50:436.

27 *Homily against Those Who Are Drunk and on the Resurrection of Christ*, PG 50:436.

28 *Homily against Those Who Are Drunk and on the Resurrection of Christ*, PG 50:437. Anne-Marie Malingrey, interpreting John, says that ἀθυμίᾳ is "the great obstacle to the interior life." See *Jean Chrysostome: Lettres a Olympias*, SC 13 (Paris: Editions du Cerf, 1947), 50.

> shown the same distinction. Here [in the church] there is nothing like that. There is only one table for the rich and the poor. Even if someone is rich, he cannot add anything to the table. And if he is poor, he is served at table no less of communion because of his poverty. For grace is divine. And why are you amazed if there are rich and poor here? One and the same table is set for the king who has a crown and a purple robe and who exerts power—yes, for that king—and for the poor man who sits begging for alms. Such things are the Lord's gifts. He distributes communion not to those who are worthy but to those who come of their own free will and with understanding.[29]

John is insisting that the table of the Lord not be judged by the standards of worldly evaluation. Those secular standards would insist that the rich have a definite advantage over the poor. In any setting outside the Church, the rich would most probably be honored before and above the socially inferior. That is why John emphasizes the equality of both, but we should not make the mistake of thinking that he is advocating some kind economic equality. Encouraging the poor not to be downcast is because the Paschal celebration is a "spiritual feast" (ἑορτὴ αὕτη πνευματική) and because "grace is divine" (θεία γάρ ἐστιν ἡ χάρις). The equality here is one of access, not of outcomes.[30] Nor is it simply that both poor and rich have an equal share. No, they do not have equal tables but have "one and the same table" (μία τράπεζα πρόκειται). Both the rich and poor come on an equal basis because the only requirement is "their own free will and . . . understanding" (τῇ προαιρέσει καὶ τῇ διανοίᾳ).

John inculcates a clearer and deeper understanding of the power of the Eucharist to make all equal in the Church by reminding his listeners of the nature of the mysteries themselves. Quoting Paul that all who are baptized into Christ have put on Christ (Gal 3:27), Chrysostom draws out the implication, "Our Master honored the rich and poor alike, slaves and masters the same."[31] Because no one who is baptized need feel less important, he can

29 *Homily against Those Who Are Drunk and on the Resurrection of Christ*, PG 50:437.

30 In *Catechesis*, 2,13, John makes a similar point: "It is an amazing and paradoxical thing that every distinction and difference of social rank is out of place here. Even if one happens to possess worldly honors, even if he is conspicuously rich, even if he has high aims from his high birth, he stands here like the beggar and one clothed in rags, like one who has his eyes knocked out, or like one maimed in his leg and yet is not disgusted with the things happening. For he knows that in spiritual matters [realities] all these things are driven away and a good disposition of the soul is desired"; Antoine Wenger, *Huit catéchèses baptismales inédites*, SC 50 (Paris: Editions du Cerf, 1957), 140.

31 *Homily against Those Who Are Drunk and on the Resurrection of Christ*, PG 50:438.

and should reject any feelings of being inferior, "for whenever a poor man sees a rich man clad in a very expensive stole, he is smitten and calls himself the unhappiest of men. But here [in the Church] that deficiency is removed because one garment is for all, the washing of salvation."[32] Even the liturgy of the mysteries reflects this equality:

> What is the manner of the rich with the poor? Pay close attention! Often the rich and the poor stand side by side in church. The hour of the divine mysteries has embraced it, the rich one is thrust out like the uninitiated. The poor stands within the heavenly tabernacles and the rich is not irritated because he knew himself to be a foreigner to the divine mysteries. But O what divine grace! Not only is he [the poor man] of equal honor in the church because of God's grace, but whenever he stands, the poor man often comes before the rich in piety, and the rich man did nothing to help him who has nothing except piety. Nor does poverty deprive the believer who presents himself with confidence before the Holy Altar. Brothers, I say these things about those who are being instructed and not about those who are simply rich. Take note, brothers, how a master withdraws from the church and a faithful servant frequents the mysteries. The mistress of the house leaves but the servant girl remains. "God does not show partiality." In the church, then, there is no slave or free.[33]

Here we have hints even of the spiritual superiority of the slave, for "It [Scripture] also acknowledges him as free who has been liberated by divine grace."[34] And the poor in general, the socially lesser people, may have a distinct advantage over the rich and powerful. Michael Sherwin captures the exalted position of the poor in Chrysostom by characterizing them as "hidden emissaries of Christ."[35] What advantages do the poor have? Unlike the rich, they do not have to be as entangled in the affairs of daily life; "the king is entangled with a thousand affairs like a ship buffeted on every side and worn down by many sins. The poor man has only to think about the food he needs; he is free from business and can live a quiet life, peaceful,

32 *Homily against Those Who Are Drunk and on the Resurrection of Christ*, PG 50:437–38.

33 *Homily against Those Who Are Drunk and on the Resurrection of Christ*, PG 50:437.

34 *Homily against Those Who Are Drunk and on the Resurrection of Christ*, PG 50:437: ἐκεῖνον οἶδεν ἐλεύθερον τὸν ὑπὸ τῆς θείας χάριτος ἠλευθερωμένον.

35 Michael Sherwin, *On Love and Virtue: Theological Essays* (Steubenville, OH: Emmaus Press, 2018), 135.

sitting like a ship in a harbor in great safety as he approaches the table."[36] Chrysostom has no doubts about which goods are better and more desirable; the goods of heaven are far superior to the goods of earth. John himself knew both poverty in the solitude of the caves outside Antioch and the hustle and bustle of the city. I suspect that he much preferred the former but was forced to return to the latter for his own health. And in that he was able to see divine providence, but he still knew which life to treasure most. Spiritual wealth consists of being free from distractions, precisely those affairs foisted on people of influence and power. The distractions and temptations that accompany wealth can dull the spiritual senses and make one susceptible to sin. The wealth in which the poor share consists of "the hearing of the divine words, the prayer of the fathers, the blessings of the priests, concord, and peace and harmony—spiritual gifts and a spiritual reward."[37] Notice, then, that Chrysostom is not interested in economic equality as a goal in itself, but interested in reorienting the thoughts of his people to where true wealth lies.

We obtain a keener insight to Chrysostom's view of the poor in *Homily 27 on 1 Corinthians*. Here John picks up on Paul's rebuke in 11:22: "Or do you despise the church of God and shame those who have nothing?" He pays careful attention to the context and argument surrounding this text by noting that the Corinthians had turned the Lord's Supper into a private affair in which the social divisions of their culture had been reinforced. Paul even goes so far as to say that they were not eating the Lord's Supper but committing a travesty of that institution. Part of that distortion of the sacrament was that "one goes hungry and another gets drunk" (11:21). This callous disregard for the needs of others meant that they were in fact "despising the church" by neglecting those in need:

> Do you see how he transfers the accusation from the insult of the poor to the church? He does this to make the matter weightier. So look at the fourth accusation when [this behavior] insults not only the poor but the church also. Like making the Lord's Supper a private matter, so there is also the matter of location, like using your house as if it were a church. The church exists not for those who come together to be divided but for those divided to come together. Meeting together shows this. He did not say you starve those who have nothing but something much more shameful. "You

36 *Homily against Those Who Are Drunk and on the Resurrection of Christ*, PG 50:437.

37 *Homily against Those Who Are Drunk and on the Resurrection of Christ*, PG 50:438.

> shame them," he says, to show that it is not so much about food as about the insult against them.[38]

By focusing on the shaming (καταισχύνετε) of the poor John gets to the heart of the spiritual and moral issue about inequities in society. It is not simply that the Church should be a place where the less fortunate in this world are cared for. The very meaning and purpose of the Church is to bring together those who are separated and divided in society: "The church exists not for those who come together to be divided but for those divided to come together." A neglect of some in the Church means that the Church, the body of Christ, is being insulted. That is something a Christian should never desire or permit. Paul's and John's rebuke of such behavior has great relevance to the Eucharist, for the sacrament carries an inherent social meaning that cannot be ignored. When Paul says that "it is not the Lord's Supper" that the Corinthians are eating, John adds that the apostle is bringing them back to that evening on which "Christ delivered the awesome mysteries" (τὰ φρικτὰ μυστήρια παρέδωκεν ὁ Χριστός):

> For this reason, he called the earlier meal a supper. And that supper holds all those at the supper in common. There is not so much difference between the rich and the poor as there is between teacher and pupil. That difference is immense. What shall I say about teacher and pupil? Consider too the difference between the Teacher and the betrayer. But at the same time, he was at the supper with them and he [Christ] did not cast him out but gave him a share of his salt and made him a partaker of his mysteries.[39]

A genuine celebration of the Eucharist would not only follow whatever liturgical guidelines may have been in place in the apostolic period but, even more important, welcome all regardless of their social status. If Christ himself could allow the betrayer Judas to partake of the mysteries, how can Christians in John's day hold their brothers and sisters in contempt and shame them at the same meal ordained by Christ? Caring for the poor and needy is not about social engineering but about recognizing and enhancing the dignity of those who have been forgotten or overlooked by society, even a society that professes to be Christian such as Chrysostom lived in.

38 *Homily 27 on 1 Corinthians*, PG 61:228.

39 *Homily 27 on 1 Corinthians*, PG 61:227.

Human dignity is enhanced by being members of the Church and participants in the supper that Christ founded. But when Christians act as the Corinthians did, they end up insulting the most vulnerable and betraying the very meaning of the Church. The Church is supposed to be a place where class distinctions, so prominent in society around the Church, are no longer recognized. Yet the purpose of the Church is not to obliterate social classes; its purpose is to bring together those already divided from one another by society. And the greatest visible sign of that coming together is the Eucharist, which explains why Paul was so adamant about the liturgical abuses in the Corinthian church.

Why must the celebration of the Eucharist be a visible manifestation of a unity that suspends or even nullifies class distinctions? Because the very nature of the Church is also the nature of the Eucharist. Both sacrament and Church are one and catholic (καθολικός). To exclude certain members of the body of Christ from the celebration of the Eucharist on socioeconomic grounds is a betrayal of Christ's body. The very thing being celebrated is distorted, twisted, and betrayed. John makes this point vividly in the next section of the homily. Insisting that the Corinthian individualization of the Mass constitutes abuse of the Church, John asks:

> How and in what manner? Because it is the Lord's Supper, that is, the Master's, it ought to be common for all. The Master's things are not for one servant, and not for another. They are rather common to all. So, what is the Lord's is common for all. If he is your Master, which he surely is, then you ought not to separate it as your own but treat it as the Lord's and the Master's by setting it before all. This is what being the Lord's means. But now you are not permitting this to be the Lord's by its not being common for all but rather feasting by yourselves.[40]

The exclusion of certain members of the Church on the basis of class and/or social membership is tantamount to a denial of Christ's Lordship over the Church. What Christ gave to the Church as a whole is what the members of the Church must give to one another without distinctions based on secular thinking about social classes.

John's view of the poor and their condition, then, demands a great sacrifice on the part of Christians who have the goods of this world. Whatever the types and layers of poverty that can be discerned in the socioeconomic

40 *Homily 27 on 1 Corinthians*, PG 61:227.

situation in which John ministered, his ultimate concern was for the spiritual welfare of the rich and poor alike.[41] The problems were out there in the social structures but the solutions lay deep in the human heart. Only a generous heart, reborn in baptism and nourished by the Eucharist, could begin to answer the external social needs. Recognizing that truth, however, did not automatically engender giving and serving. There were many obstacles in the human heart. In John's mind the greatest barrier to compassionate giving was the love of money, or greed.

THE LOVE OF MONEY

In the last chapter we noted that wealth and *mnesikakia* have something in common in John's estimation. They can both feed irrational passions and end up destroying the soul. The problem of greed (πλεονεξία) or love of money (φιλαργυρία, φιλοχρηματία) resurfaces on many occasions and so one is not surprised to find John commenting on Paul's words in 1 Tim 6:5–10:

> They [people] imagine that gain is godliness, and indeed godliness with contentment is great gain, for we brought nothing into this world and we shall not take anything from it. If we have food and clothing, we shall be satisfied with these. Those who wish to be rich fall into the temptation and snare of the Devil and into many foolish and harmful desires that plunge men into punishment and destruction. For the love of money is the root of all evil. Desiring this, they have been drawn away from the faith and pierced themselves with many troubles.

This text provides John with an occasion to explain how and why the love of riches can be dangerous, but we must not understand "money" or "wealth" here in too narrow a sense for Chrysostom sees it metonymically, as representing a wider and larger scope of problems. Much like John knowing that there are many kinds of inebriation, so too he sees many kinds of riches and the many problems associated with them. This wider use of the words arises from his concern about the interior spiritual health of people. He is not addressing economic problems per se but addressing spiritual problems

41 Sherwin has emphasized another dimension of John's view of the poor at the Lord's table. Citing several homilies on Genesis and 1 Thessalonians, he points out how John sees *philoxenia* (usually translated "hospitality") as a high Christian duty. John again invokes the example of Abraham's hospitality to the three strangers. See Sherwin, *On Love and Virtue*, 134–35.

that have economic ramifications. As in other contexts, John is quick to point out that it is not money but the Christian's attitude toward money that can be a problem: "He did not say simply the rich but those who desire it. For it is true that someone may manage it well, thinking very lightly of it, and distributing it for the poor."[42] When one uses one's wealth for the benefit of others, he is following a Christlike path.

If wealth is not the problem, what is? John depends on Paul: "not those who are rich but those who wish to be." The reversal of values that Paul sees in those who "imagine that gain is godliness" results from not understanding that "godliness with contentment is great gain." This means that even the poor can enjoy a sense of gain:

> Godliness with contentment is great gain not when someone has wealth but when he doesn't. So that one may not fall into despair because of his poverty, [Paul] lifts him up and refreshes him by saying, "They imagine that there is gain." In fact, there is gain but not in the way he thinks but rather in a much greater way. At first, he lays it down only to take it up again. It is clear that this [kind of gain] is nothing because it remains here, it is not transferred or taken with us. How is it clear? Because we came into life with nothing and so we will depart with nothing. [Our] nature came naked and it departs naked. So superfluous things are useless. If we brought nothing in, we shall leave with nothing.[43]

Here we capture an insight into John's values. While wealth is not evil in and of itself, holding to superfluous things while not meeting the material needs of others engenders wrong thoughts and practices. When Paul says that "those who wish to be rich fall into the temptation and snare of the Devil," John asks what these temptations and snares are. Paul's description remains at a general and unspecified level, but John elaborates:

> What sort of temptation and snare do those who wish to be rich endure? They are enticed away from the faith. They are encompassed with dangers. It makes them more cowardly. He speaks of foolish desires. How is it not a foolish desire when they keep the mentally retarded and dwarfs, not because they love humanity, but for their own amusement, and when they have fish tanks in the halls, and when they feed wild beasts and play with their dogs and dress up their horses and are no less fond of them than their

42 *Homily 17 on 1 Timothy*, PG 62:592.

43 *Homily 17 on 1 Timothy*, PG 62:592.

> own children? All these things are foolish and superfluous. None of it is necessary or useful. He calls them foolish desires and harmful. What sort of harmful things? It is when they love inappropriate affections, when they yearn for their neighbor's things, when they indulge luxuries and desire drunkenness and wish for the ruin and destruction of one another.[44]

Such a catalogue of vices reminds us of Paul's own, of which he declares that "those who do such things will not inherit the kingdom of God" (Gal 5:19–21), but John's list has more of a focus on selfish pursuits that blind their practitioners to the higher and better values of God. By picking up on Paul's "many foolish and harmful desires" John adds that these people are also guilty of desiring superfluous things (τῶν περιττῶν). And that love of superfluous things has harmful effects on those who desire them by stripping them of any true love of humanity. It is God's own philanthropy that reaches out to the poor and so should impel the Christian to do likewise.

Luxuries (τρυφῇ) and superfluous things (τῶν περιττῶν) are part of the deception that riches can engender. John recounts Jesus's parable of the Sower (Mk 4:1–20) and hones in on the anxieties of this age and the deceptiveness of wealth in Mk 4:19.[45] Why would these things be a problem in the spiritual life? Because the anxieties associated with riches tend to weaken a person's resolve to live a life of sacrifice and love, a tendency arising from the fact that the virtues are all interconnected:

> When he spoke of the anxieties of this age and the deceptiveness of riches he was in fact laying down everything. It also implied empty glory and all the other things. The deceptiveness of wealth encompasses all this too. So, for example, sensual pleasure, gluttony, maliciousness, and empty honors, and such things. He added the road and the rock by showing that it is not enough to give up money but also [one should] pursue other virtues with discipline. So, what if you are free from money but are unmanly, and soft? . . . One part [of virtue] is not enough for salvation but we must begin with careful listening, a continual recollection. Then we must add manly courage, then contempt of riches and letting go of the things of daily life.[46]

Here is John in a different context emphasizing that all virtues and vices are wrapped up in the one person. The nurture of vice softens one's

44 *Homily 17 on 1 Timothy*, PG 62:593.

45 *Homily 44 on Matthew*, PG 57:469.

46 *Homily 44 on Matthew*, PG 57:469.

determination to live a disciplined (ascetic) life while one virtue can be a way of strengthening all the other virtues the Christian is seeking. The deception resident in wealth lies in its ability to lead its owner into the illusory belief of self-importance. It is not an accident that John would name "empty honor" (κενοδοξία), because this vice is fostered in the soul of one who imagines his own importance. And empty honor can give rise to other vices. The false security afforded by wealth can lead a person to "sensual pleasure, gluttony, maliciousness."

John's criticisms of wealth arise partly from his relative evaluation of the goods of this world versus the goods of heaven. And to adopt a heavenly perspective is one of the main effects of the Eucharist on the Christian. Showing kindness to those less fortunate than ourselves is part and parcel of a life centered on the Eucharist. Conversely, neglecting the poor is a sure sign of sharing the heart of Judas. John has no doubt that the vice of greed was at the root of Judas's betrayal of Jesus. Chrysostom links Judas's love of money to the Eucharist in *Homily 47 on the Gospel of John*, in which he is commenting on Jn 6:53–71. This last part of the bread of life discourse deals with the difficult teaching that "unless you eat the flesh of the Son of Man and drink his blood, you shall not have life in you. He who eats my flesh and drinks my blood has life in himself" (6:53–54). As Chrysostom expounds this text, he hopes to do what Jesus himself did, "to attract them [hearers] by the greatness of his teachings and by their fullness,"[47] but understanding Jesus's words will require a radical change in perspective. No longer can one have "an earthly view" but only "a mystical and spiritual sense" will suffice. Into this context John again inserts Judas as the archetype of an earthly-minded man:

> Since Judas was seized with the dreaded sickness of the evil love of money, even before he betrayed his own Master ... let us fear too lest we ever imitate Judas by love of money. You do not betray Christ, do you? When you see the poor man around wasting away with hunger, or destroyed by cold, you accrue to yourself the same judgment. When we share in the mysteries unworthily, we perish like the Christ-killers. And quite rightly so. How long will the love of present things, things superfluous and foolish, hold you captive? Wealth is among those superfluous things in which there is nothing profitable. How long shall we be transfixed by vain things? How

47 *Homily 47 on the Gospel of John*; Sr. Thomas Aquinas Goggin, SCH, *Homilies on Saint John the Apostle and Evangelist: Homilies 1-47*, FC 33 (Washington, DC: The Catholic University of America Press, 1957), 476.

> long will we not fix our eyes on heaven, not live soberly, and not take our fill of earthly and transitory things?[48]

We saw in an earlier chapter how Chrysostom, in his homilies on Judas's betrayal, used the occasion to call on his hearers to exercise forgiveness against those who had wronged them. He strenuously warned against a hardened heart and took Judas as his example because he had so many opportunities to allow his heart to be softened by Jesus's presence and actions. Judas, however, also becomes the archetype of a greedy man since he held the purse for Jesus's disciples. And it is this greed that lies behind any neglect of the poor or refusal to help them. In John's mind, both unworthy communion in the mysteries and neglect of the needy are as reprehensible as Judas's avarice. John speaks of a "dreaded sickness" that afflicted Judas. That sickness clouded his vision of who Christ was, and that is the same deficiency that can affect the communicant who does not see clearly who Christ is in the mystery of the Eucharist. When someone fails to see Christ in the poor and downtrodden, one is falling into the same trap as Judas. As with Christ's betrayer, nothing Christ does profits the communicant whose vision is obscured when seeing the needy. And John does not hesitate to warn his people of impending doom if they neglect the needy, because not clothing the naked is tantamount to refusing Christ himself since "Christ has not even had the necessary clothing." Here again Chrysostom is drawing on the practical equation of Christ and the needy.

John gives an insightful hint as to the root of greed. Both then as now some may see that they are indeed afflicted with the love of money (cf. 1 Tim 6:10), but they don't know how to rid themselves of it. Greed or holding on to material things results from a lack of vision, of seeing things in their proper perspective. To be "transfixed by vain things" is to lose sight of the heavenly reward, and that was Judas's fundamental flaw, a fixation with the present at the expense of faith in the future. And that is why, according to John, Judas could profit from none of the marvelous things he had witnessed with the Son of God: "Nothing profited him, not good works, not gifts, not being with him [Christ], not worship, not having their feet washed, not communing at the table, not holding on to the money bag; these things became the instruments of punishment."[49] Being fixated on material things, then, narrows one's

48 *Homily 47 on the Gospel of John*, PG 59:268. See also Goggin, 483–84.

49 *Homily 47 on the Gospel of John*, PG 59:268.

vision of life so as to push out the greater vision of heaven and its goods. Greed blinds one to the debilitating effects of obsession with material goods and to the higher goods of spiritual goodness.

What is true wealth? John Chrysostom had no doubt that the goods of heaven made one far wealthier than the greatest and most abundant goods of earth. Therein lies Judas's betrayal, not the betrayal of Christ but the betrayal of his own true self. He traded the goods of eternity for the goods of this world, and it was a deadly trade according to John. Contrary to all expectations John sometimes says that the rich and the poor are equal, not in the sense of access to the mysteries of salvation that we saw above, but in an even more profound manner. Recognizing how his claim may be startling to his hearers, John asks:

> How are the poor and the wealthy the same? The statement uttered is true. The poor because they lack money; the rich because of [their lack of] the storehouses of faith. It is better to be poor in the daily needs of life and to be rich in spiritual things. The end of the first is corruption; the profit of the second cannot be taken away. This is why the Son says, "Do not store up treasures on earth," calling us to store up heavenly [treasures]. This is by supporting the poor, visiting the sick, looking out for those passed over, releasing debtors without the ability to pay, demanding a loan from God. "For the one who is merciful to the poor lends to God" [Prov 19:17]. The angels who contemplate the Judge of all offer these things up. The one who says [this] commands the one who brings about the good. "Your prayers and your alms rise up as a remembrance before God" [Acts 10:4]. To him be glory and power, now and forever and unto the ages of ages. Amen.[50]

Here is an exchange of visions, the acknowledgment that wealth in the daily affairs of this life pales into insignificance compared to the spiritual goods of heaven. Though John does not quote it here, one is reminded of Jam 2:5, where the author asks, "Has not God chosen those who are poor in the world to be rich in faith and heirs of the kingdom, which he has promised to those who love him?" Using other language, John concurs that seeking spiritual wealth engenders a vision of life in direct contradiction to the mindset of Judas. This mindset turns wealth and poverty on their heads. Following Jesus's command to store up treasures in heaven must be the Christian's greatest goal. But John also answers the question of how. It is by engaging

50 *On the Assembly of Archangels*, PG 59:756.

in works of mercy. Quoting the words spoken to the centurion Cornelius in Acts 10:4, John sums up the importance of alms and prayer as the way to have one's vision of life clarified and one's goals reoriented to the true goods of the life to come.

EXPLAINING GREED AND THE REMEMBRANCE OF EVIL

In this last chapter and the previous one we have seen two vices that John Chrysostom deplores: greed and *mnesikakia*. His recognition of these two was born no doubt from a combination of his meditations on Scripture and his observations of human behavior. The combination of these two certainly shaped his vision of the world and the Christian's place within it. I have contended that John's advocacy of almsgiving and his pointing out the evils of greed were motivated not by social justice concerns in the modern sense but by a pastoral concern for the souls of his hearers. John seems to have known as well as anyone that these vices can destroy the spiritual life of a Christian. But what do these two vices have in common and how does exposing their evils promote Christian spirituality? Is there perhaps a deeper explanation for John's opposition to these two vices? Generosity toward those who cannot repay is a cure for greed and forgiveness of past wrongs and the release of the desire for revenge is a cure for the remembrance of evil (μνησικακία). But what does either of them have to do with the Eucharist? Greed and the remembrance of evil have in common the desire and intention of holding on to something that a person considers essential to his well-being but in the end destroys the person. *Mnesikakia* holds on to memories and the desire for revenge. People who indulge *mnesikakia* probably consider such revenge the only available response to the evil done them. Greed holds on to material possessions and fears that letting them go will result in self-ruin.

Why are such attachments bad? From a slightly different angle we notice that both vices allow a person to consider himself superior to others. The acquisition of material objects motivated by greed tends to buttress the self-image of the one who possesses them. He compares himself to others and may feel a sense of self-importance. Clinging to the evils one has suffered at the hands of another allows the person to view himself as better than the offender. Both arise from pride, that evil hydra whose many heads, once severed, grow again to bigger proportion under different guises. Pride is always enlivened by the desire to maintain and exalt oneself.

How can almsgiving aid the greedy or vengeful person? Caring for the needs of others can take a person out of himself by focusing on the needs of another. If one encounters people who are less fortunate, it can evoke two opposite responses. One is to ignore or neglect the needy, a response that will only further reinforce the self-absorption of the greedy. The other is a desire to help better the plight of the less fortunate, a response that will draw out the best in those tempted by greed. A vengeful person also faces two possible responses to the image of the offender in his mind. He can continue hating the offender, a response that will surely deplete him further of the virtue of love. Or he can seek to forgive the offender by prayer and spiritual sacrifice. Only the latter response affords the opportunity to be free of the grip of hate.

A person who reaches out to others in almsgiving or who forgives the offender of the past is grasping the opportunity for his inner self-image to be transformed from self-centered to other-centered. And this is the essence of love that Paul names as the binding power of all the other virtues: "Above all put on love, which is the bond of perfection" (Col 3:14). John Chrysostom's focus on the inward nature of virtue certainly builds on Paul's emphasis on freedom in Christ as emanating from an inner transformation that proceeds from the inside out (2 Cor 3:18; Gal 4:19). Almsgiving fosters freedom from self-absorption; forgiveness of past wrongs fosters freedom from bitterness and rancor.

Growth in virtue and the elimination of vice is certainly a worthy goal for everyone in John's view of the Christian life. Yet the question remains: what do these have to do with the Eucharist? Might one not view the liturgy and the Eucharist as a major component of the average Christian's life while the growth in virtue remains in another compartment? Is there a connection? What we have seen in John's theology of the Eucharist suggests a closer connection in three ways. The first is that the external liturgy stands as a visible reminder of God's condescension and grace. The union of heaven and earth that we outlined in chapter 1 comes about only because "he has brought down this [heavenly] melody to us" and because the theandric presence of Christ is a vivid reminder of the gift of self that everything in his earthly life proclaimed. Closely allied is the reality of *anamnesis*, not as a mental act of recall on the part of priest or people but as a divinely ordained presence of celestial realities in material reality. Yet that presence of the spiritual in the physical can impel the struggling Christian to cleanse his own memory of past hurts and to love so deeply that even the most despised in his world can be loved. And the final truth is that Christ's gift of self empowers the Christian to give himself to others in the imitation of the Redeemer himself, not imitation in the modern sense of aping a prototype but in the most profound sense of possessing inwardly the same virtue as Christ himself.

✠ ✠ ✠

The social implications of the gospel, so clearly articulated by Jesus himself in passages like Mt 25:31–46, passes into the sacramental life of the Church. The Eucharist then is as much a call to service as the words of Christ himself. One may rightly wonder how participation in the eucharistic sacrifice is related to compassionate care for the less fortunate. Are sacramental mysticism and social action simply parallel but essentially unconnected pursuits? Do the good works required of Christian living only provide evidence of a true faith or is there a more intrinsic connection? What we observed in *Homily 50 on Matthew* answers the questions rather definitively. The body of Christ lies on the table and is clothed in the poor. This identification of Christ with the poor, expressed in different ways in other homilies, means that the command to good works is not a fundamentally extrinsic addition to an otherwise nonsocial ritual. The Eucharist naturally and inexorably leads to love of others because it imparts love to the Christian. Christ himself is the preeminent Lover of the human race. That love, lodged deeply in the heart, means that the Christian is no mere social justice warrior. He is and should be always motivated by love for Christ and the salvation of others. As John says elsewhere, a Christian not concerned about the salvation of others is no Christian at all. The Christian is not a social worker attempting to make society better or a zealot for social change. He is a human agent on fire with a sacrificial love for others concerned for their temporal welfare and their eternal destiny. There is no tension between concern for the salvation of souls and social justice. They fit hand in glove.

Conclusion
The Eucharist and Salvation

Our exploration of John Chrysostom's theology of the Eucharist has insisted that the sacrament of the sacred table cannot be adequately understood apart from its home in the divine liturgy. Although this understanding was the case for the whole Church in ancient Christianity, it was perhaps emphasized more in the Greek-speaking East and by none more completely than John himself. The straightforward but dynamic idea that the Church's liturgy is a union of heaven and earth functions as the backdrop for the salvific notion of deification. In the past, some scholars have contended that no Antiochene writer had any doctrine of deification, in contrast to the Alexandrians like Cyril or the Cappadocians like Gregory of Nyssa.[51] Their contention is based on a paucity of vocabulary of deification in John and other Antiochenes. It is true that John does not employ the standard terminology of deification, but from the

51 See Norman Russell, *The Doctrine of Deification in the Greek Patristic Tradition* (Oxford: Oxford University Press, 2004), 237. Russell later acknowledged a needed modification of his early view. See his essay "A Common Christian Tradition: Deification in the Greek and Latin Fathers," in *Deification in the Latin Patristic Tradition*, ed. Jared Ortiz (Washington, DC: The Catholic University of America Press, 2019), 272–93. The collected essays in this volume show that the Latins possessed a vibrant doctrine of deification, though its language may vary with the author and vary from the Greek East's.

passages I have adduced here such a judgment seems precipitous. Other scholars have reached similar conclusions. Brian Dunkle maintains that Chrysostom used the adage of "What Christ is by nature, we become by grace" to underscore the notion of deification.[52] Pak-Wah Lai goes even further and argues that John's thought constituted "nothing less than a doctrine of deification."[53] John's use of the vocabulary of mingling, mixing, union, and participation seems to be very much like deification. The question certainly warrants further investigation. Yet the groundwork for deification has already been laid in the idea that the liturgy constitutes a union of heaven and earth. The union contemplated is not only of two distinct realms, the natural and the supernatural, but of the persons who inhabit those realms. And ultimately that union is about the Christ present in the Eucharist and in the communicant. This preeminent insight announces that the Christian faith is about Christ died and risen even though there were multiple registers in which this central truth came to expression. For John Chrysostom the register that he emphasized most was the liturgical reality of the Word-Made-Flesh.

The importance of liturgy arises again in the context of biblical typology. Once we clear away confusion about the subject, we observe the diverse expressions of types among the Church Fathers, but they still a had common core shared by all. Noting a deep theological exegesis already evident in John the Evangelist, we see that this became the common possession of the mystagogical-catechetical tradition. The sacraments, especially the Eucharist, had become a focal point of instruction from Alexandria to Antioch; it was not "the prerogative of any one school. One finds it in both East and West, in the Antiochenes as well as in the Alexandrians. It is precisely this unanimity of the tradition which allows us to recognize it with such certainty and to distinguish it from the other trends which come to be comingled with it."[54] The relative uniformity of mystagogical catechesis across the ancient Church testifies to a unity centered on the eucharistic celebration. It seems that the later language of calling the Eucharist "the source and summit of the Christian life" was already woven into the fabric of ancient Christian faith.

52 Brian Dunkle, "The Twofold Affection: The Background of John Chrysostom's Use of Φύσις and Χάρις," *Vigiliae Christianae* 75, no. 4 (2021): 374.

53 Pak-Wah Lai, "John Chrysostom and the Hermeneutics of Exemplar Portraits" (PhD diss., University of Durham, 2010), 133.

54 Jean Daniélou, "What Is Typology?" *Antiphon* 25, no. 3 (2021): 336.

The liturgy is the proper context for understanding the Eucharist, but in saying so we are in danger of reversing an essential order. The liturgy does not make the Eucharist, but the Eucharist makes the liturgy. Immediately one can object that it is through the forms and sequence of the liturgy as well as through the priest's ministry that the Eucharist is accomplished. Have not the texts and ideas adduced in earlier chapters on the presence of the sacrifice in the liturgy and the priesthood adequately demonstrated that it is the liturgy that produces the Eucharist? While these are rightly stressed as necessary concomitants of the Eucharist, the facts and teachings adduced still stand in need of explanation, because the liturgical forms and sequence are still only external expressions rather than the inner core of the eucharistic reality. The ministry of the Church with its ordained priests is in fact a necessary condition of making the Eucharist available to the people of God, but the inner core of the sacrament is not dependent on the liturgy; rather the liturgy is dependent on the inner core. That inner core of the Eucharist is Christ himself. The numerous passages adduced in the course of this investigation show clearly that it is not Christ in some vague manner that makes the liturgy what it is in the sense that he commanded it, but that it is Christ's presence that emanates out from the sacrament and fills the entire liturgy with meaning and mystery. Nor is this mystery the *idea* of Christ present; it is the concrete reality of the Word-Made-Flesh, a presence resulting from the Incarnation. This is why the notion of actualization is so important. God's salvific plan was actualized in the Incarnation of Christ and its continuation is actualized in every liturgy.

Actualization is only one of the central ideas in the constellation of meanings that has run through this book. The twofold meaning of actualization is inextricably tied to the *oikonomia* of salvation history, to the *sugkatabasis* (condescension) that is the center of that *oikonomia*, and to the essence of the Church's liturgy. I argued in chapter 1 that John sees the liturgy of the Church as the privileged moment, the divinely appointed *kairos*, in which heaven meets earth and the worship of this world is caught up into the already active worship of the heavenly powers. That worship is connected ever so intimately to the acts of redemption accomplished by God, acts that climaxed in the Paschal Mystery of Christ. In other words, when the realities of heaven are actualized in the worship of the Church, the entire life of Christ is present too.

Here is the twofold meaning of actualization. Heaven is actualized in the earthly liturgy (vertical, mystical) and the life of Christ is actualized in the present worship of the Church, even though centuries separate the two periods (horizontal, historical). As for the historical, we observed at several points that the notion of actualization was already present in the life of the ancient people of God (Israel). To my satisfaction, Brevard Childs showed Israel's worship "as a means of actualizing the past." As the great events of Israel's redemption are recounted in its liturgy (cult), "actualization occurs when the worshiper experiences an identification with the original events. He bridges the gap of historical time and participates in the original history."[55] Childs rendered a great service not only to biblical studies but also to patristics, because the very same process and acts of actualization that he observed in the Hebrew text are operative in many of the Church Fathers. The very history of redemption (*oikonomia*) is what the liturgy is all about.

Yet there are profound differences between what Israel experienced and what the Church of the new covenant experiences. These differences reach to the very core of the superiority of the new covenant. We understand the beginnings of those differences in John's Gospel, in Paul's letters, and especially in the Letter to the Hebrews. They are developed even further in certain Fathers of the Church, particularly Chrysostom. For him and many other Fathers, the Old Testament types were mere signs pointing forward to greater fulfillments that contained mystic realities. This contrast between the new and the old is expressed in multifaceted ways in the New Testament but none more clearly than that in John 1:17, "The law was given through Moses, but grace and truth through Jesus Christ." For John Chrysostom the institutions and customs of the old covenant served a proleptic but limited function. In the new covenant there is the fullness of heavenly realities embodied in the signs.

Numerous liturgical studies in the patristic literature only reinforce this idea of actualization. The concept of *anamnesis* was such a prominent part of the patristic conception of the Eucharist because it constituted more than mental recollection.[56] *Anamnesis* meant making present the salvific work of Christ so that the worshiping community may be drawn into that work and enjoy its benefits.[57] This pattern was already present in the personalized

55 Brevard S. Childs, *Memory and Tradition in Israel* (London: SCM Press, 1962), 82.

56 See R. J. Halliburton, "The Patristic Theology of the Eucharist," in *The Study of Liturgy*, ed. Cheslyn Jones, Geoffrey Wainwright, and Edward Yarnold (New York: Oxford University Press, 1978), 201–8.

57 J. D. Crichton put it succinctly: "Every sacramental and liturgical act is a participation in the

tone of Exodus 13:8, "You shall tell your son in that day saying, this is because the LORD did this for me in my coming out of Egypt." And it was present in the subsequent Jewish traditions as well: "In every generation a man must so regard himself as if he came forth himself out of Egypt."[58] So too, Chrysostom and other Fathers see the Church at worship as experiencing the redemption of Christ as much as when it was accomplished. Chapter 3 abundantly demonstrated that John viewed the Eucharist as part and parcel of the *oikonomia*. The liturgy of the Church was not an addition, an addendum to God's *oikonomia*. It was an essential element in it. This is how John could say so poignantly in his homily *On Blessed Philogonius*, "This table [of the Eucharist] fulfills the order of the manger." The order of the manger is the arrangement of *sugkatabasis* that issues from the *philanthropia* of God. The life of Christ lives in the liturgy and the Eucharist!

If there were no link or connection between the historic Jesus and the present-day liturgy, the latter would become a mere ritual without power or significance. Some decades ago, there was a burning question posed by some New Testament scholars: the Jesus of history or the Christ of faith? The very posing of the question suggested a disjunction between the real person of history and the faith proclaimed by the Church. The further implication sometimes lingered around these discussions that the doctrines of the Church about Christ (e.g., two natures) were divorced from the historical Jesus. The theological task was to overcome this barrier and somehow find the relevance of the "real" Jesus for the Church today. This episode in the history of modern theology serves to show how often the dynamics of an inquiry are framed by the way in which the question is posed. I firmly believe that such a question would never have arisen in the mind of John Chrysostom. And in all my reading of patristic literature I have never seen such a question seriously considered. When Chrysostom in the East or figures like Augustine and Leo in the West preached on the life of Christ, the prevailing sentiment reigned that the Jesus reported in Scripture was the same as the one present in the Church through preaching and especially in

paschal mystery of Christ" ("A Theology of Worship," in *The Study of Liturgy*, ed. Cheslyn Jones, Geoffrey Wainwright, and Edward Yarnold [New York: Oxford University Press, 1978], 25).

58 *Mishnah Pesahim*, 10, 5. See Herbert Danby, *The Mishnah: Translated from the Hebrew with Introduction and Brief Explanatory Notes* (Oxford: Oxford University Press, 1933), 151.

the sacrament of the Eucharist. As Leo the Great put it so succinctly, "What was visible in the life of our Redeemer has passed into the sacraments."[59]

Leo's words are John's thoughts too. I would suggest that these two giants of ancient Christianity shared so much because they both lived in a sacramental worldview. For them, the natural world was never only natural. They considered it filled with divine presence.[60] Even more, they shared a common vision of the Church and its liturgy as a *kairos* of God meeting with the human race in order to lift up that race to the heights of heaven. For John as well as for thousands of other pastors in ancient Christianity, life and liturgy always circled back to Jesus Christ. And the surest way to reach back (and up) to Christ was to share in his body and blood in the sacrament of the Eucharist. For both John and a host of other Church Fathers, the Jesus of history is the Christ of the sacraments and liturgy.

The one great mystery of Christ died and risen is diffused across the ages of history and at the same time encapsulated in the sacrament of his body and blood. John's preaching telescoped the wide horizon of redemptive history into a microscopic moment of the *kairos* of liturgical worship. In the sacramental encounter with Christ, the earthly Church accesses the eternal and infinite reality of Christ's salvific grace. That is the glory of the Eucharist. If John never uses our modern term "real presence," he leaves us in no doubt about his belief in it. His use of language is in fact what provides the historic foundation of what was later affirmed in the medieval debates about Christ's presence in the Eucharist. John's vocabulary is not philosophically recondite, but he affirms in a myriad of ways that the same Jesus who lived, died, and rose again is present in that same humanity in the sacrament. It cannot be overstated how this straightforward fact set the groundwork for later medieval disputes. Beginning in about the tenth century, the medievals in the West posed the question of the *kind* or *mode* of presence based on the assumption of the Fathers that Jesus's humanity was truly present in the Eucharist. And that question arose not necessarily from an aura of skepticism but from an amazement in the face of the mystery. John Chrysostom never posed those questions, but he did affirm vigorously the reality of Christ's humanity in the sacrament. Among the many texts that attest to it, we can

59 Leo the Great, Sermon 74,2, PL 54:398; *Quod itaque Redemptoris nostri conspicuum fuit, in sacramenta transivit.*

60 This theme is explored in Hans Boersma, *Heavenly Participation: The Weaving of a Sacramental Tapestry* (Grand Rapids MI: Eerdmans Publishing Company, 2011).

recall his words in *Homily 46* on John 6, "When for your sake I had assumed flesh and blood, I gave you back again the very Flesh and Blood through which I had become your kinsman."[61] The continuity of the historic body of Jesus and the eucharistic body of Christ in his thinking is undeniable. That explains why John can at times choose vivid verbs to capture this reality: "Christ . . . showed the great longing . . . not only to provide for those who desired to see him but also to touch, eat, and sink their teeth into his flesh, to be entwined with him and to be filled with all desire."[62] These expressions of his eucharistic faith stand among many others to show that while John never argued for the real presence, he assumed it for what was to him a more important reason, namely, to show the reality of true communion in Christ's body and blood for the Christian in his own day. So when he takes on the voice of Christ, John heightens the mystery even more: "I don't give food in the way others do. Rather, I feed you with my own fleshes; I furnish myself to you and want all of you to be noble. . . . I shared in flesh and blood for your sake. I distribute again the same flesh and blood by which I become your kinsman."[63] These comments on the text of the fourth Gospel reflect what we have seen in a wider range of Chrysostom's homilies. The vivid and graphic language functions more powerfully than the modern term *real presence*, since the latter term is a summarizing abstraction. For John, the real presence of Christ in the Eucharist meant a genuine and captivating presence of the human Jesus in the lives of Christians no matter when they lived. It was Christ who was John's everything.

LITURGY AND INCARNATION

It is impossible to understand the Eucharist in John's preaching apart from the liturgy, but it is equally impossible to understand the liturgy apart from the Incarnation as mystery of Christ. His humanity and the particulars of his life on earth form the inner core of the liturgy and the eucharistic mystery. If we insisted on defining what John Chrysostom meant by the real presence of

61 *Homily 46 on the Gospel of John*, Sr. Thomas Aquinas Goggin, SCH, *Homilies on Saint John the Apostle and Evangelist: Homilies 1-47*, FC 33 (Washington, DC: The Catholic University of America Press, 1957), 469; PG 59:261.

62 *Homily 46 on the Gospel of John*, PG 59:260–61.

63 *Homily 46 on the Gospel of John*, PG 59:261.

Christ in the Eucharist, we could do no better than to affirm the sacramental reality of the earthly life of Christ extended in space and time. This was expressed admirably in a Western key by Jean Corbon:

> The economy of salvation that emerges from the Father through his Christ in the Holy Spirit expands to become the divinized life that Christians live in the Holy Spirit, through the name of Jesus, the Christ and Lord, in movement toward the Father. But the celebration of the liturgy is the place and moment in which the river of life, hidden in the economy, penetrates the life of the baptized in order to divinize it. It is there that everything that the Word experiences for the sake of man becomes Spirit and life.[64]

It is an ongoing life of Christ in the Church that the liturgy affords. Conversely, the liturgy makes no sense apart from the reality of Christ's life in the Eucharist. The Eucharist is a supreme demonstration of God's *philanthropia* in that it perfects human aspirations of worship and union with the divine, a perfection that arises from the nature of the gift. John's many eucharistic affirmations showed God's *philanthropia* by emphasizing Christ's self-gift: "This very thing again arose from his ineffable affection. Here in a much greater way he transformed it into the more awesome and more glorious sacrificial liturgy when he changed the sacrifice itself and instead of the slaughter of irrational animals he commanded himself as the offering."[65] The language of self-offering suggests two directions at once. Christ offered his body (and life) back to the Father on the cross, but he also offers himself to the faithful in the Eucharist. And these are not two unrelated offerings. In simultaneously offering himself to both, Christ unites the faithful to the Father in heaven.

The Incarnation of the Logos ought not to be thought of as limited to the initial appearance of Christ on earth. Understanding a current that runs deep in patristic thought, Andrew Hofer aptly observed, "The incarnation, then, should not be thought of as only the particular act of the Word's taking flesh from a virgin in Nazareth. It is rather that one's life in the flesh, whose actions and sufferings lead us to contemplate and praise the most holy Trinity."[66]

64 Jean Corbon, *The Wellspring of Worship*, trans. Matthew J. O'Connell (San Francisco: Ignatius Press, 2005), 221. For further discussion see Matthew Levering, *Engaging the Doctrine of Revelation: The Mediation of the Gospel through Church and Scripture* (Grand Rapids, MI: Baker Academic, 2014), 59–85.

65 *Homily 24 on 1 Corinthians*, PG 61:200.

66 Andrew Hofer, *The Power of Patristic Preaching: The Word in Our Flesh* (Washington, DC: The Catholic University of America Press, 2023), 15.

The Scriptures themselves represent a type of incarnation, as a number of scholars have pointed out. The Bible is replete with instances of *sugkatabasis* understood as accommodation. The link between Chrysostom's Christology and his exegesis is an area still to be explored more fully.[67] The link between the Incarnation and the liturgy is even more evident. The Church and its liturgy is a kind of ongoing incarnation much like the body of Christ in the Eucharist is an ongoing incarnation of the physical body of Jesus, who walked the earth. Just as Christ's presence lives in the world through his Church and its members, so the Church is itself created and sustained by that same body.

We noted earlier how the eminent Old Testament scholar Brevard Childs had laid bare the implicit meanings of remembrance in the experience of ancient Israel because those events of the past continue to exert an influence on the worshiper.[68] The text of Exodus 12 is itself enough to show that *zikaron* meant more than simply "remembrance." Such remembrance presupposed a living presence of the past. The liturgical experience of Israel as participating in the original salvific event of the Exodus provided the rich background for the *anamnesis* of the Lord's Supper. The Church continues to experience the historical Jesus in its celebration. It is this material reality of Christ that stands front and center in the divine *oikonomia* taught in the New Testament. Considered in the abstract, God could have arranged salvation history such that the material could be absorbed into the spiritual, and such a plan would have been very successful in winning converts, as the rise and spread of Gnosticism subsequently showed. This ordering, however, would have constituted a betrayal of the divine intention. God's plan was not absorption but condescension. Given the limitations of the present-day meaning of *condescension*, I preferred to invoke John's favorite term *sugkatabasis* or a "coming-down-to-be-with" in order to capture the pungent but wide-reaching significance of John's theology. And this is why the Eucharist is so much more than an afterthought in John's theology.

The Logos becoming flesh remained for John not an abstract doctrinal truth that had to be affirmed because he was a Christian but a mental and metaphysical reality that lived loudly in his soul. Several times in quite

67 For a fuller explanation, see Bradley Nassif, "John Chrysostom on the Nature of Revelation and the Task of Exegesis," in *What Is the Bible? The Patristic Doctrine of Scripture*, ed. Matthew Baker and Mark Mourachian (Minneapolis: Fortress Press, 2016), 54–57.

68 Childs, *Memory and Tradition in Israel*, 63.

different homilies he erupts into vivid descriptions of Christ's sufferings and pain that seem to emerge from a more profound level of his consciousness. We have cited *Homily 24 on 1 Corinthians* several times, but it also contains one of these vivid passages:

> Death did not bear the body that was nailed and whipped. This is the body that the sun saw crucified and turned back its rays. This is why the veil was torn in half and rocks crumbled and the whole earth shaken. This is that body that was bloodied, pierced with a sword, and gushed forth saving fountains of blood and water for the whole world. Do you want to learn its power from a different source? Ask the woman with the hemorrhage who did not touch him but the garment around him. Or rather not the entire garment but the hem.[69]

John here asks a question we saw him asking in his baptismal catechesis. What is the origin of the power of Christ's body? Why could final death itself not overcome that body bludgeoned beyond recognition and nailed to a tree? Why was veil of the temple split in two (Mt 27:51)? Why did the earth shake? The woman healed of her twelve-year hemorrhage knows. And the answer to that question reflects the logic of the Incarnation, a logic of hiddenness. Christ's life contained a power veiled by his humanity. The Eucharist too contains a power veiled by the simple elements that carry that same power. This conviction is what allows John to apply to himself and others the words that immediately precede those already quoted:

> I emphasize that we should not slaughter ourselves by rashness but with all awe and purity let us approach. Whenever you see what lies before you, say to yourself, "Because of this I am no longer a body of dust and ashes, no longer a prisoner but free. This is why I have hope of heaven and to receive good things in them [the mysteries], life without death, the end of angels, intercourse with Christ.[70]

The dignity of being a child of God is enhanced greatly by seeing "what lies before you" (i.e., the bread and wine of the Eucharist). This sacramental reality contains the very hope of heaven and sets the captive free from slavery to sin. And perhaps the greatest benefit of all is that communion with Christ when united to him (τὴν μετὰ Χριστοῦ ὁμιλίαν).

69 *Homily 24 on 1 Corinthians*, PG 61:203.

70 *Homily 24 on 1 Corinthians*, PG 61:203.

THE CROSS OF CHRIST AND SALVATION

Recall the laudatory language John used of the cross of Christ and the blood shed on that cross. In chapter 3 we laid out John's encomium of the cross in a poetic scheme to underscore how the cross was the triumph over evil. John employed vocabulary that is never used in the New Testament, but which has clear applications and implications among the canonical authors, especially Paul. Perhaps the most compelling was the cross as a war memorial (*tropaion*), for this term signaled the triumphant nature of the crucifixion, an increasingly important theme in both the Eastern and Western Church. The same is true for the panegyric on the blood of Christ. In chapter 5 we noted that Chrysostom's commentary on the Eucharist in John chapter 6 seemed to know no bounds in its praise of Christ's blood. It is the source of all that is good because it beautifies the soul of the communicant beyond natural limits. John has employed his rhetorical training in the service of his most valued treasure, the cross of Jesus Christ.

The war memorial metaphor begins to form a part of the theology of the cross in the Latin church in about the same period as John Chrysostom. Among other instances, it appears in the famous poem of Venantius Fortunatus, *Pange Lingua*. The standard translation by Edward Caswall downplays the military language that Venantius used, but the triumphant nature of the poetic celebration can hardly be missed: "Sing with a glorious tongue / the battle of war / and on the war memorial [*trophaeo*] of the cross / tell the noble triumph / how the world's redeemer / conquered by being immolated."[71] And in the thirteenth century we hear Thomas Aquinas referring to Augustine as invoking the same metaphor when describing the triumphal entry into Jerusalem in John 12. For Aquinas, as for his fifth-century predecessor, the branches of the crowds signified their praises "because he [Christ] was about to conquer death by his dying and to triumph over the Devil in the war memorial [*trophaeo*] of the cross."

This emphasis on the cross in the Chrysostom corpus aligns well with the recent exposition of Khaled Anatolios, who sought to characterize an Eastern theology of salvation with a focus on the cross of Christ. Anatolios tried to capture this theology under the rubric of "doxological contrition," a

71 "Pange Lingua," in F. A. March, *Liturgia Horarum and Latin Hymns*, trans. Edward Caswall (1894).

multifaceted concept with tentacles stretching out in various directions.[72] Most noteworthy for our purposes is that the cross, or Paschal Mystery, functions as both the source and goal of repentance (*metanoia*). In this certain way, Anatolios corrects Western misconceptions that have sometimes seen the Eastern view of salvation as focused on overcoming death rather than sin primarily. Even Eastern theologians, perhaps in reaction to Western views, have sometimes seen deification as participation in the divine nature with little attention to sin and expiation. By placing the cross at the center of his Eastern theology of salvation, Anatolios attempts to show that Christ is not only the one who perfectly glorifies the Father (Jn 17:1, 4, 22) but also the one who perfectly repents of sin as the vicarious representative of humanity.

Doxological contrition then is an inherently paradoxical juxtaposition which simultaneously emphasizes both the expiatory nature of Christ's death and the triumph of the cross as the means by which the glory of God is opened up to believers. This formulation accords well with John's acclamations of the cross and the blood of Christ poured out as "the salvation of souls" that washed away sins. John sometimes views the cross as both expiation and triumph in the same breath, "It is the blood that wiped away the written condemnation of our sins. This is the blood that cleansed your soul, that washed away the stain, that triumphed over the evil rulers and authorities."[73] John's partial quotation of Col 2:14 makes it clear that he interprets the apostle's text as a combining of the expiatory and triumphal aspects of the work of the cross. And it is possible that further analysis of John's view of the cross would confirm Anatolios's contention that contrition and repentance serve the end of doxology. In other words, contrition and doxology are not symmetrical concepts. Repentance is not an end but a means provided by God's mercy in the movement toward doxology.

Thus when Chrysostom calls the cross "a war memorial" and "the will of the Father," it is so because it reopens the human race to sharing in the glory of the Father. This is no doubt why John can boldly call the cross "the glory of the Only Begotten Son," not only in the sense of honor but in the ontological sense of that glorious life that the Son shares with the Father and the Spirit. The cross is the portal to trinitarian glory. And so the cross can become "the safety of your church," "the wall of the Saints," and "the light of the whole

72 Khaled Anatolios, *Deification through the Cross: An Eastern Christian Theology of Salvation* (Grand Rapids, MI: Eerdmans, 2020).

73 *The Cemetery and the Cross*, PG 49:398.

earth." It would seem that for John there is no other path to eternal glory than through the cross. Similar expressions arise in his encomium of the blood shed on the cross. He naturally speaks of those blessings that the blood of Christ brings on those objects and institutions that transcend the individual. This blood "sanctified the golden altar" of Israel's worship, "ordained priests," and "cleansed the sanctuary." That same blood "makes demons flee" and "calls angels to our side." If the blood applied to the doorposts could protect the children of Israel—and it was only a type of the true blood—then surely the blood of Christ shed on Calvary could "drive away demons." Yet Chrysostom seems to reserve the highest praise for the effects of Christ's blood on the individual communicant. This blood can "imprint the royal image on us" and "give birth to an irresistible beauty." By becoming "the salvation of souls," the blood of Christ "makes them beautiful, enflames them, and makes our mind brighter than fire." All this praise for the blood of Christ amounts to "making heaven accessible" by communion in the very divine nature of Christ.

I have no doubt that John Chrysostom thought of salvation as a participation in Christ, a union with the Crucified, a sharing in the redemption of the cross. When John thought of participation in the mysteries and communion with Christ, he may have often visualized Christ's intense sufferings. *Homily 15 on 1 Timothy* certainly suggests this. The mention of a love-charm (φίλτρον) in connection with Christ's sufferings in this homily provides a perspective that one will find later in the medieval West, where intense meditation on the wounds of Jesus became widespread, but it is no less important for Chrysostom:

> I will display this love-charm not only with these but also with the things I suffered. It was for your sake I was spit on. I was beaten with a cudgel. I emptied myself of glory. I left my Father and came to you who hated me and turned away and who cannot bear to hear my name. I pursued and ran after you that I might take hold of you. I united and joined you together with myself. Eat me, drink me. I hold you above and below I am mingled with you. Is this not enough for you that I hold your first fruit above? Does not this satisfy your desire? I came down again below and I am not simply mingled with you. I am chewed, I am digested little by little that great mixing and mingling and union may come about. Things united still stand in their own limits, but I am interwoven with you. I don't want to be separate. I want

> both to be one. So, knowing these things and his solicitude for us, let us do everything that can show us not unworthy of his great gifts.[74]

Overwhelmed by the love of God for humanity that would not only send Christ into the world but allow him to be mistreated so cruelly for the sake of union with the human race, John sees the condescending Incarnation as a love-charm dangled before the eyes of believers. That divine love came down not only to mingle among the human family but to be united with it completely. As John sometimes does, he takes on the voice of Christ himself to express the depths of his own emotion at the condescending love of God. Three features of this passage point to the Eucharist. There is the obvious reference in the words "Eat me, drink me," which by the first-person object pronoun ("me") evokes John 6:57, "He who eats me will live because of me." And the word "eat" (τρώγω) is taken up by Chrysostom's use of τρώγομαι, "I am eaten or chewed." But the last feature is hidden in the phrase "I hold your first fruit above." According to Paul, Christ himself is the first fruit of the eschatological harvest, and the hope of future resurrection lies in Christ himself but is also given to the faithful in the Eucharist.

In this eucharistic context John can now use a host of verbs with both a wide semantic range and a graphic depiction of Jesus's earthly passion. There are verbs indicating the active pursuit of humanity by Christ: "I pursued" (κατεδίωξα), "I took hold" (κατάσχω), "I emptied myself of glory" (τὴν δόξαν ἐκένωσα), and "I left the Father" (τὸν Πατέρα εἴασα). These expressions give more solid content to John's belief in the love of God for humanity. Taken together, they suggest a loving intention combined with tenacious perseverance. The self-emptying of the Son of God (cf. Phil 2:7) is in pursuit of something even greater, union with his creatures. And John chooses verbs of union to emphasize this reality: "I became one with you" (ἥνωσά σε) and "I joined you to myself" (συνῆψα ἐμαυτῷ). And yet these last two verbs could still be understood as an external union, much like gears of a motor interlocking, but John seems to say more and so uses verbs that indicate mixing and intermingling (οὐχ ἁπλῶς μίγνυμαί σοι, ἀλλὰ συμπλέκομαι).

The first verb (μίγνυμαί) is a metaphorical extension from usage regarding liquids whereas the second (συμπλέκομαι) is properly used of humans inseparably engaged with one another. This may be why he sees "intermingling or being engaged" as stronger semantically than "mixing." Chrysostom

74 *Homily 15 on 1 Timothy*, PG 62:586.

then elaborates with another set of verbs and nouns that is nothing short of breathtaking. As all the verbs are in the first person, John again is taking on the voice of Christ himself: "I am chewed" (τρώγομαι), "I am digested little by little" (λεπτύνομαι κατὰ μικρὸν), "I am interwoven with you" (ἐγὼ δὲ συνυφαίνομαί σοι). These last verbs help reinforce the nouns John chooses, "joining, mixing, and union" (πολλὴ ἡ ἀνάκρασις γένηται καὶ ἡ μίξις καὶ ἡ ἕνωσις). And if there could be any doubt about John's desire to express the unity of Christ and the believer, he adds, "I have united myself to you. I want both to be one" (ἥνωσά σε, ἓν εἶναι βούλομαι τὰ ἀμφότερα).

Now it is this theology of union that explains the graphic language of John in the opening sentences of this paragraph from *Homily 15*, "These things I suffered. It was for your sake I was spit on. I was beaten with a cudgel." Surely a man so despised and humiliated could not act as a love-charm to draw human beings into himself! And yet that is exactly what John affirms. Perhaps John saw here something that only the eyes of faith can appreciate. The self-sacrifice of Jesus on the cross, reiterating the self-emptying of the Incarnation, functioned as a magnet to draw a lost humanity to himself. This is what the Eucharist and its accompanying liturgy make possible many centuries after Jesus's earthly life. This is in fact a better way to see the reality of Jesus in the Eucharist than with a catchphrase like "the real presence." It is not a generalized human presence that Chrysostom sees in the Eucharist but the presence of a man broken, emaciated, and wonderfully philanthropic in the very act of dying. The divine irony is that such a death destroys death and results in a triumph unparalleled in all of human history. In the words of a communion prayer in the Western liturgy this death gives life to the world (*per mortem tuam, mundum vivificasti*). And it is this death that is communicated to the faithful in the sacrament of the mystical table.

THE EUCHARIST AND THE HEALING OF THE SOUL

I have claimed that John Chrysostom was first and foremost a curate of the soul whose pastoral concern always fell on the moral and spiritual dimensions of the faith he professed. This is evident in his advice about preparing for communion (chap. 7), in his pronouncements on forgiveness and *mnesikakia* (chap. 8), and in his warnings against wealth (chap. 9). At the same time, the means by which the soul of the believer is healed lies primarily in the liturgy, for it is there that one encounters the glory of God in a unique manner. Yet as long as the liturgy remains something external to the believer it cannot effect a transformation of the soul. The Eucharist is what enables the Christian to live a Christ-like and Christ-filled life. The Eucharist is the most personal communion imaginable in this life, but one is never alone in communing with Christ because human beings are inextricably bound up with others. This reality is what makes sense of John's heavy emphasis on forgiving others.

To see the significance of Chrysostom's answers to human need, we must step back once again and take into account the context into which he spoke. In the introduction I cited the work of Pierre Hadot on the nature of Hellenistic philosophy being about the healing of the soul. Epicurus's memorable saying "Vain is the word of that philosopher that does not heal the sufferings of man" is reflected in many ways throughout Hellenistic philosophy and is highly relevant for the time of Chrysostom. In earlier generations the philosophers of late antiquity like the Stoics were viewed as turning toward more practical ethical concerns and abandoning the theoretical aims we see in someone like Aristotle. Hadot corrected this picture by insisting that the Stoic Epictetus, for example, insisted on both the theoretical and the practical in all three areas of philosophy: physics, logic, ethics. Epictetus's distinction was rather between discourse *about* philosophy (theoretical) versus the *practice of* philosophy (practical).[75] This distinction operates in all contexts whether one is in the realm of natural knowledge (physics), correct reasoning (logic), or moral choice (ethics). All this becomes relevant to John Chrysostom when we hear Epictetus say, "Gentlemen, the philosopher's lecture hall is a hospital,"[76] and supposedly the inscription over a great library in Alexandria was "hospital for souls" (ἰατρεῖον τῆς ψυχῆς).

John Chrysostom's preaching was geared toward the cure of souls like these philosophers, and this is why his exhortations about the Eucharist were primarily about moral and spiritual transformation. In his homilies on the Gospel of John, Chrysostom seems to understand that "the condition of his listeners requires a kind of medical care" that can transform their lives

75 Pierre Hadot, *Philosophy as a Way of Life: Spiritual Exercises from Socrates to Foucault*, ed. Arnold I. Davidson, trans. Michael Chase (Oxford: Blackwell Publishing, 1995), 191.

76 Arrian, *Discourses of Epictetus* 3, 23, 30; ἰατρεῖόν ἐστιν, ἄνδρες, τὸ τοῦ φιλοσόφου σχολεῖον.

into a better art of living.[77] That *ars vivendi* corresponds to the practice of philosophy that Epictetus urged. John's preaching constituted the theoretical part while the living out the faith of the Eucharist was the practical. While the temptation to engage in flowery rhetoric no doubt plagued John in his pursuit of healing of the soul, he ultimately knew that it was truth that had the power of transformation, not rhetorical power or persuasive finesse.

What were those truths that John's hearers needed to know? Preeminent was the necessity of forgiveness, the lack of which leaves the soul in a debilitated state. Yet virtues and vices come in groups. *Mnesikakia* is never alone. We noted earlier that holding grudges and vindictiveness is closely aligned with the love of money. We explained the relation between the two as rooted in a self-orientation. Now it is possible to widen the scope to any vice, material or otherwise. At root, greed, unhealthy attachment to relationships or the pursuit of knowledge, or even tenaciously holding to one's opinions can be vices that are centered on self. So it is not surprising that Chrysostom piles up vices and virtues in lists that contain *mnesikakia*. We quoted as an example his homily on the cross:

> "Those who wish to approach the cross,
> Hate slander.
> Loathe the remembrance of evil.
> Don't stop having mercy on the poor.
> Don't hesitate to care for the sick.
> Don't yearn for wealth.
> Don't stop visiting those in prison.[78]

Here John offers six imperatives: three positive and three negative. Among the negative are *mnesikakia*, slander, and love of money. The commonality among the vices is clearly the desire to hurt other human beings, and although money does not have to be such a tool, the love of money can sometimes drive people to hurt others in the pursuit of wealth. The positive commands all center on those less fortunate (the poor, the sick, prisoners).

77 Athanasios Despotis, "The Philosophical-Religious Hybridity in John 6 and Its Reception in the Commentaries of Origen and Chrysostom," in *Drawing and Transcending Boundaries in the New Testament and Early Christianity*, ed. Jacobus Kok, Martin Webber, and Jermo van Nes (Münster: LIT Verlag, 2020), 59–60.

78 *The Adoration of the Cross*, PG 62:752.

Doing good to them suggests an orientation toward others, a spirit of service and love.

What does this tell us about *mnesikakia*? It certainly means that our relationship with God affects and is affected by relationships with others. And it suggests that being oriented to others instills a desire for reconciliation while an orientation to self holds on to open wounds. The pain of being injured by another is no small matter. Such pain can be so intense at times that forgiveness of another seems impossible. St. John Chrysostom knew this problem well, perhaps from observing others but certainly from his own experience. He calls on the injured party to place faith in God's wisdom above one's own emotional pain. That is why he asks Christians to do no more harm to themselves by not forgiving; giving forgiveness brings with it a kind of liberation from the chains of bitterness. The answer to *mnesikakia* is the cross. To internalize the cross of Christ is to love others, to repent vicariously for them, to give them the gift of forgiveness. To forgive others genuinely requires a kind of repentance because forgiveness can never be real unless one looks at one's own faults and sees in them a need for God's forgiveness. This recognition of one's need of forgiveness induces the repentant to give the same to others. To abandon *mnesikakia* requires more than facilely imitating Christ on the cross. It requires internalizing the cross. It is only when the cross triumphs in the soul that forgiving one's offenders and loving one's enemies becomes possible. And the cross cannot be accessed through mental magic. Only the Eucharist has the fullness of the cross!

Earlier, in chapter 9, I argued that the vices of greed and *mnesikakia* share a self-orientation that can be overcome only by focusing on the other party as needy and worthy of love. Almsgiving was a key to that process, which explains Chrysostom's strong insistence on its importance for the Christian. I was only able to provide limited textual evidence for my explanation, but there is an abundance of evidence in the wider Chrysostom corpus. Claire Salem produced this evidence from a systematic study of John's homilies on Matthew.[79] Even though Chrysostom's preaching on Matthew is his largest body of biblical exposition, it is still only a moderate portion of total preaching. What she revealed by her assemblage of texts was that at the heart of his conception of man as man Chrysostom saw virtue as a natural pursuit for

79 Claire Elayne Salem, "Sanity, Insanity, and Man's Being as Understood by St. John Chrysostom" (doctoral diss., Durham University, 2010).

all Christians.[80] And at the heart of virtue was a refocus of human attention away from human praise and approval to seeking approval from God. We have seen the figure of Judas invoked many times by Chrysostom but here again he becomes the model of greed and covetousness as John broadens out the application to all: "Nothing so makes us subject to the Devil like wanting more and loving greed."[81] By contrast, growth in virtue frees the Christian to serve as a light to the world: "Quite rightly did he [Christ] speak of the light, because nothing makes a man so remarkable as the display of virtue, even if he would prefer to be inconspicuous."[82] And one of the greatest virtues is concern for the welfare of others and especially the "poor."

Helping the less fortunate turns out to be as profitable for the one who helps as for the one being helped. We noticed something similar in treating the vice of *mnesikakia*. John urged forgiveness not only because the Lord commanded it but also because exercising forgiveness would boomerang back to the forgiver with grace. Showing mercy and goodness to others cannot help having beneficial repercussions for the merciful.[83] And showing mercy is one of the chief ways in which human beings distinguish themselves from brute animals. Mercy is an essential element of being human.[84] And it is the common humanity of giver and receiver that Chrysostom often appeals to in urging compassion for others:

> Inasmuch as you did it for one of these, you did it for me. And the converse he speaks about the same persons. Even though there was nothing holding him [the poor man] up, he is still a man inhabiting the same world as you, seeing the same sun, having the same soul, the same Master, having partaken of the same mysteries as you, called to the same heaven as you, having a great claim, that is, poverty, and needing necessary food.[85]

This common humanity not only functions as a natural spur to compassion, mercy, and forgiveness but also explains why these separate virtues reinforce one another. Or consider the converse question. What then is the

80 Salem, "Sanity," cites *Homily 23 on Matthew*, 5, PG 57:314.

81 *Homily 13 on Matthew*, 4, PG 57:212.

82 *Homily 15 on Matthew*, 7, PG 57:233. See Salem, "Sanity," 79–80.

83 *Homily 77 on Matthew*, 6, PG 58:710: "It is not possible for the one who seeks the good of the rest to overlook his own." Quoted in Salem, "Sanity," 81.

84 Salem, "Sanity," 81, citing *Homily 52 on Matthew*, 5, PG 58:524.

85 *Homily 35 on Matthew*, 3, PG 57:409.

connection between greed, unforgiveness, and lack of compassion for the less fortunate? This question can be approached from at least three perspectives: a system of priorities, a lack of proper vision, and ultimately a failure to imitate Christ himself.

One might read Chrysostom's exhortations as attempting to correct a mistaken system of priorities. And certainly, moving from vices to virtues always entails a reordering of one's priorities. Often conscious decisions to reposition one's life require a strong will because doing so can be difficult but necessary in order to correct the past. How can one find the strength or wisdom? By envisioning others in a different manner. Lack of compassion, the absence of mercy, and the unwillingness to forgive always see other human beings as outside the scope of humanity and therefore unworthy of love. The only way to greater compassion, mercy, and forgiveness is an empathy for those with whom one is not inclined to identify. John is ultimately calling for growth in a sense of common humanity.

It is Christ's life that serves as a model of charity. That love of Christ forgives by recalling his words with regard to the penitent thief, "Father, forgive them, for they know not what they do" (Lk 23:34). It is the compassion of Christ as he looked upon the crowds as "sheep without a shepherd" (Mt 9:36) that must enflame the heart of the believer. And it is the mercy of Christ, who said about the woman anointing his feet, "Her sins, which are many, are forgiven because she loved much" (Lk 7:47). This imitation of Christ is no mere external aping but an internal change that reflects the heart of Christ.

If the Eucharist is to be a healing sacrament, one of the most potent obstacles to its efficacy must be defeated: indifference. Earlier, in chapter 7, I noted how subtle indifference to spiritual goods could be. Unlike sinful acts such as adultery, stealing, or even sins of omission like not caring for the poor, indifference is a condition more like *mnesikakia*. Both are ongoing conditions of the inner person, who is either unaware or negligent. For Christians like those in earshot of John's preaching, indifference could take several forms. We saw him speaking against those who exited the church before the celebration of the mysteries and those whose communion in the mysteries was perfunctory.[86] Neglecting the sacrament entirely would be the more obvious instance of indifference, but communion without thought or fervor could also be a more subtle form of the same vice. However, is indifference a vice? Blake Leyerle studied *rathumia* in the Chrysostom corpus and

86 See *Homily 3 on the Incomprehensibility of God*, SC 28, 216.

found a range of meaning associated with the term.[87] Typically translated "laziness," she found that John can use the word with a signification stretching from indifference through acquiescence, or inertia to lethargy or sloth. In its being roughly equivalent to our "indifference" we discover John using the term in some unexpected contexts. The ancestral sin of Adam and Eve, for example, displays a "great indifference," and the murder of Abel by Cain shows the same vice.[88] These and many other examples show that John meant something more than an occasional apathy. *Rathumia* indicated a persistent and conscious neglect of spiritual truths and realities. It may have even implied a rejection of a spiritual quest that ends in complete apathy.

John's preaching was based on the need to have goads and stimulants to holiness. Leyerle has done a significant service in laying bare a variety of ways in which Chrysostom sought to stimulate his hearers to devotion and action.[89] The one that is closest to our purpose here is that which involves the Eucharist. We have already seen John attempting to entice his congregants to fervor by pointing to the unique place of the sacrament. One text we did not cite is from a *Homily on Repentance* where he again appeals to the eucharistic table as a goad to devotion:

> The mystical table is prepared, the Lamb has been slaughtered for you, the priest is agonizing for you. The spiritual fire is bursting out from the immaculate table, the Cherubim are attending, and the Seraphim are flying with their six wings covering their faces and all the incorporeal powers interceding along with the priest in your behalf. Spiritual fire is descending and the blood from that immaculate side [of Christ] is being emptied into the bowl for your cleansing. Are you not afraid, are you not embarrassed to be found a liar at this fearful hour?[90]

The lie that John is referencing is the inconsistency between the active engagements of the world that take up almost all of the Christian's time and the one hour asked by God for worship in the Church. That holy hour may bring fear or at least awe, but sin is no reason to shun this table. It was to remove sin in the lives of believers that the table was given. All one need do

87 Some form of the noun ῥαθυμία occurs 792 times in the Chrysostom corpus.

88 Blake Leyerle, *The Narrative Shape of Emotion in the Preaching of John Chrysostom*, Christianity in Late Antiquity 10 (Berkeley: University of California Press, 2020), 151–52.

89 Leyerle, *The Narrative Shape of Emotion*, 154–82.

90 *Homily 9 on Repentance*, PG 49:345.

is be as devoted to the eucharistic table as one is to his business or to other worldly affairs. John sees the Eucharist and the mystical table on which the sacrament is celebrated as what is needed to awaken the soul.

The healing of the soul may have been the main part of the philosophic wisdom of Chrysostom's day, but I think one would be mistaken to attribute to him only a desire to offer Christianity as a remedy like the other medico-philosophical gurus of late antiquity. His vision stretches out longer and wider than simply helping his flock to learn how to be happy in this life. Christ was more than a medicine for the soul. He was for John the Son of God made flesh, and the Eucharist was that human Jesus communicated to the faithful. For John that was the healing for the soul and the gateway to heaven.

✠ ✠ ✠

If Christ was the center of John Chrysostom's view of the world, the outer boundaries of that worldview were infinite. And they were infinite because John fully recognized the mystery that lay at the core of his worldview. The greatest part of that mystery was that all God's dealings with the human race grew out of an infinite love in the heart of the Trinity and were directed by an arrangement (*oikonomia*) leading to salvation. God's incomprehensible greatness demanded that divine condescension or *sugkatabasis* be at the heart of the plan of salvation. Man could not reach God if God did not first reach down to man. The common link between the Incarnation and the liturgy lay in *sugkatabasis*. Both entail God coming down to meet human need, but that coming down is for the purpose of lifting up. Thus to be in the eucharistic presence of Christ is to be exalted into the heavens with the angels, and therein lies one of the most prominent emphases of the Christian East. John's vision, like that of other Eastern Fathers, is an upward spiral mounted on the wings of angels.

The fact that Chrysostom viewed Christ and his saving work as central to his own conception of the Eucharist draws our minds back to the deepest motivation for the divine sacramental arrangement. *Philanthropia*, or the love of humanity, underlies and enlivens every aspect of John's preaching and colors his whole view of the liturgy. In a fresh way Michael Sherwin has shown that this conception of love is part and parcel of Chrysostom's idea of divine friendship.[91] John repeatedly singles out Abraham as a "friend of God" (cf. Jam 2:23) because of his hospitality to strangers, and he urges his fellow Christians to follow Abraham's example. Being a "friend of God" is more than is suggested by our modern meaning of the term; it connotes a profound love of a superior for an inferior. Sherwin draws on previous studies of patron-client friendship in late antiquity to see in Chrysostom a view of God pursuing a loving friendship with the human race. The Eucharist represents a banquet given by the patron that "reveals his network of friends" and functions as the place where Christ enters into friendship with us. Yet Christ does more than throw a great feast for his people; "He himself becomes the food they eat and the clothes they wear."[92] The conclusion is straightforward but far-reaching. The Eucharist manifests God's infinite love for humanity, and salvation consists of participation in that sacrament that communicates divine love for humanity.

91 Michael Sherwin, *On Love and Virtue: Theological Essays* (Steubenville, OH: Emmaus Press, 2018), 129–30.

92 Sherwin, *On Love and Virtue*, 133.

Epilogue
The Broader Significance of John Chrysostom

Our journey through a portion of the writings of John Chrysostom has revealed a rich and multifaceted perspective on the Eucharist. It has shown John to be a more profound and caring pastor than some have imagined him to be. So that these insights do not remain hidden in the confines of detailed chapters, I would like to offer some final reflections that revolve around three trajectories: continuities across space and time, the presence of the human Jesus in the Eucharist, and the Eucharist as gift.

Continuities are of greater importance than simple scholarly fascination because Christianity is a historical religion that implies that the past has important implications for the present. The major communions of East and West recognize this fact and consciously seek to base their practices and doctrines on those historical continuities. John himself sought to maintain and foster continuity between East and West when he sent a delegation to Pope Siricius at the time of his ordination as Bishop of Constantinople to ask for help in ending the schism that had occurred between Antioch and Rome. And later John again appealed to Pope Innocent and other Western bishops for help in unifying a divided church in Constantinople.[1] At various points I have compared John Chrysostom

1 Benedict XVI mentions these efforts at unity in his speech on Chrysostom in 2007, "Letter of His Holiness Benedict XVI on the Occasion of the 16th Centenary of the Death of St. John Chrysostom."

with other Eastern Fathers outside of the Antiochene orbit such as Gregory of Nyssa and Cyril of Jerusalem. These Fathers, who were roughly contemporary with John, have their own distinctive emphases, but they share with the Golden Mouth a faith in the Eucharist and the centrality of the liturgy. At times I have also cited later Greek luminaries such as John Damascene and Nicholas Cabasilas, who supply evidence of major continuity of eucharistic faith in the East over the centuries. A better understanding of continuity in the Greek-speaking Fathers across both space and time seems a fruitful path of future investigation. John Chrysostom is considered one of the three great hierarchs of the East along with Basil (the Great) of Caesarea and Gregory Nazianzen, and yet there are significant differences between them. Not contradictions, but divergences. A doctrine of deification has long been considered one of those differences but, in previous chapters, I pointed to texts and ideas in Chrysostom that give credence to his espousing deification, even if he does not use the same language as an Alexandrian or a Cappadocian.

Continuity between East and West is also an important challenge in our contemporary world, and occasionally I have indicated instances of both continuity and discontinuity in the previous pages. One of those challenges had to do with the relation of the consecratory words of Christ to the Epiclesis of the Holy Spirit. In a widespread and popular narrative, people in the East and West have sought to differentiate themselves from one another in this matter. Those in the West have emphasized the consecratory words of Christ as sufficient for the transformation of the bread and wine into the body and blood of Christ. Those in the East have stressed the Epiclesis, or calling down of the Holy Spirit, as the key ingredient in that change. But we have seen in chapter 4 that John Chrysostom in fact did stress the importance of Christ's words when he insisted, "This utterance transforms the gifts." And in the fourteenth century Nicholas Cabasilas also spoke very strongly about the power of Christ's words while at the same time insisting on the role of the Holy Spirit in transforming the gifts. Subsequent eucharistic theology in the West has strongly emphasized the power of Christ's words to effect that change. We have already seen Ambrose of Milan underlining the power of the divine word in the eucharistic liturgy. Both the words of Christ and the Holy Spirit are essential to the transformation of the bread and wine into the body and blood of Christ in both the Eastern and Western Church. Why has there been this ongoing tension?[2]

2 The relative emphases on the words of institution and the Epiclesis are not a simple division between East and West. For further discussion see Bernard Blankenhorn, *Bread from Heaven: An*

I aver that one of the reasons why Western theologians may emphasize the spoken word has to do with the order of the liturgy. Some Eastern theologians have probably thought that the West emphasized the words of Christ because it was too fixated on being overly rationalistic when in fact it may have been simply a function of the Epiclesis *preceding* the consecratory words of Christ. Unlike in the East where the Epiclesis *follows* the words of consecration, most, if not all, the Western liturgies have the Epiclesis first. So, if the Holy Spirit has been seen as descending upon the gifts first, then the words of consecration would complete the process of transmutation. Then the gifts would indeed be sanctified and transformed. But if the Epiclesis follows the words of consecration spoken by the priest—as it does in the Liturgy of St. John Chrysostom—then it would make sense to deny that the words are the definitive moment of transformation since the Holy Spirit has not yet been invoked to make that change. What can be easily missed is the common faith of both East and West. Both are affirming that the Holy Spirit and the words of Christ are necessary to bring the body and blood of Christ to the people of God. That liturgical reality reflects the original moment of Incarnation of the Eternal Son. When the angel Gabriel announced to Mary that she would bear the Savior, he promised that it would be the Spirit who would descend to bring about the Incarnation (Lk 1:35). In a similar way the consecratory words are necessary to proclaim but it is the Spirit who is the effective agent of transformation. In the later vocabulary of the medieval West, the words of consecration are the formal cause and the Holy Spirit is the efficient cause of the Eucharist. Daniel Cardo summarized an important point that word and gesture can also indicate the Spirit's descent: "We can find here a beautiful fruit of the new Eucharistic Prayers, in which the Sign of the Cross over the offerings is always the conclusion of the epiclesis, forming, therefore, one act of blessing in which the Holy Trinity seals the bread and the wine that will become the body and blood of Jesus Christ."[3]

The greatest liturgical commonality between East and West is one that may not be immediately obvious in reading John Chrysostom or any number of Western Fathers. It is the one commonality that most makes sense of the liturgy and the Christian faith as a whole, but it is submerged just below the

Introduction to the Theology of the Eucharist (Washington, DC: The Catholic University of America Press, 2021), 218–43.

3 Daniel Cardo, *The Cross and the Eucharist in Early Christianity: A Theological and Liturgical Investigation* (Cambridge: Cambridge University Press, 2019), 149.

surface in their writings. It is the presence of the human Jesus and his sacrifice in the Eucharist. This common faith was more assumed than argued. It was so deeply embedded in the consciousness of ancient Christians that figures like Irenaeus could argue from the Eucharist to the resurrection of the flesh.[4] Hilary of Poitiers too argued from the gift of God's nature in the Eucharist to the interpersonal communion of the three-personed God.[5] These examples reflect what we find in John Chrysostom. What later was called the real presence and the sacrifice of the cross was the assumed faith in John's preaching. It did not need to be argued because few if any questioned it.

The presence of the human Jesus comes to its highest expression in the cross. If the cross is central in Eastern thought and in Chrysostom, it is no less important in the Western Fathers. Anyone with even a cursory acquaintance with Augustine's theology of grace knows that the Bishop of Hippo insisted on the cross and the Paschal Mystery as the true source of all grace. His insistence on the primacy of grace includes the grace of repentance, the same emphasis found in the Byzantine liturgy of the East. This commonality makes sense when one is prepared to look at a deeper level for a unified conception of salvation in the ancient Church. Emphases between East and West may differ, the use of language and metaphor may vary, and misunderstandings have certainly arisen, but the centrality of the Paschal Mystery cannot be denied. If we ask what other source of grace there could be in the patristic conception of salvation, we must conclude that only in the Paschal Mystery, only in the cross and resurrection of Christ, can there be the answer. While the accent falls less on the triumph of the cross in the West, the Passion of Christ is no less seen as the source of all grace. When Thomas Aquinas spoke centuries later of Christ's Paschal Mystery as the cause of the efficacy of the sacraments, he was not articulating a new idea, a theological novum as it were.

Given what we have discovered about the centrality of the cross in Chrysostom it is not surprising that his homilies would be invoked in the connection between the cross and the Eucharist. Thomas Aquinas marshals Chrysostom in support for his contention that the Eucharist truly conveys grace and does not seem to be shy about recruiting Chrysostom's graphic language of the participation in the Passion of Christ. In posing the question of whether the Eucharist conveys grace, Aquinas sees the water and blood

4 Irenaeus, *Against Heresies*, 4,18,5.

5 Hilary of Poitiers, *De Trinitate*, 8.

flowing from Jesus's side (Jn 19:34) through a Chrysostomic lens as John sees the believer drinking from the Savior's side.[6] And Aquinas is not afraid of quoting Chrysostom's very physical language of "handling, eating, embracing" the flesh of Christ to indicate participation in the Eucharist.[7]

Aquinas is self-consciously affirming what he knows to be the united tradition of the Church before him, in which the humanity of Christ was seen to be the instrument of divinization. He asks the question whether the power (*virtus*) of the sacraments derives from the Passion of Christ. In answer, Thomas distinguishes between two types of instruments, an *instrumentum separatum* and an *instrumentum conjunctum*. As is often the case in the *Summa Theologiae*, Aquinas offers simple examples. A separate instrument would be a stick whereas a conjoined instrument would be the hand, the latter being more inherent to the organism than the former. He identifies the sacraments as separated instruments but the humanity of Christ as a conjoined instrument and declares, "The principle efficient cause of grace is God himself, to whom the humanity of Christ is joined like an *instrumentum conjunctum*. . . . The salvific power of the sacrament is derived from the divinity of Christ through his humanity into the sacraments themselves."[8] The sacraments have no power apart from the humanity of Christ. That humanity is preeminently present in the sacrament of the altar. That humanity whose agony John Chrysostom described in such graphic detail, the humanity that hung on the cross, is what carries the divinizing nature of God into the soul of the believer through the Eucharist.

Quite independently of our research, Brian Dunkle has outlined how Thomas Aquinas also observed Chrysostom dwelling on the earthly life of Christ and connected it to the Eucharist. Recall that for John the Eucharist is an extension Christ's human life. The textual evidence amassed in chapter 3 could be expanded even more to show how the linkage between the two played a key role in John's thinking. Chrysostom's works hold an honored

6 *ST* III Q. 79 a. 1. Aquinas quotes from John's *Homily 85 on the Gospel of John* on John 19:34 (PG 59:463).

7 *ST* III Q. 79 a. 1 (3rd reason); the quotation comes from *Homily 46 on the Gospel of John* (PG 59:260), where John says, "Christ . . . showed the great longing . . . not only to provide for those who desired to see him but also to touch, eat, and sink their teeth into his flesh, to be entwined with him and to be filled with all desire." For further exploration of Aquinas's use of Chrysostom see Joseph Wawrykow, "The Greek Fathers and the Eucharistic Theology of Thomas Aquinas," in *Thomas Aquinas and the Greek Fathers*, ed. Michael Dauphinais and Andrew Hofer (Ave Maria, FL: Sapientia Press, 2019), 274–302.

8 *ST* III Q. 62 a. 5.

place in Aquinas's *Catena Aurea*, which some scholars have argued was a central and enduring work by Thomas's side after he constructed it. John's exegetical works, however, also show up prominently in the *Tertia Pars* of the *Summa Theologiae*. In this regard, Aquinas seems to be innovative in that previous *Summae* and *Sentences* concentrated on broad theological principles in dealing with Christology. Thomas also dealt with the specifics of Christ's life (*acta et passa*) as portrayed in the Gospels. Thus in *ST* III QQ. 27–59, he follows John's example in handling major events in Jesus's life, and he quotes Chrysostom approvingly the majority of the time although he does so critically because he does occasionally disagree with the Patriarch of Constantinople. As Dunkle notes, the broader significance of Aquinas's treatment of Christ's life (the *dispensatio*) is that "Chrysostom is not a decorative afterthought, but rather a sure guide in leading the reader to grasp the motive of the Incarnation."[9] All this implies that Thomas Aquinas may well be John Chrysostom's theological heir as much as Maximus the Confessor or Nicholas Cabasilas is.

Continuity with the ancient Fathers extends down to today. The patristic and liturgical renewal in the twentieth-century West was ample evidence of the desire to mine deeply the sources of faith.[10] One of those was the unparalleled *Sources Chretiennes* founded by Jean Daniélou, Henri de Lubac, and others in the 1940s. I know of no other project so extensive and so academically sound that still endures to this day. One great fruit of all that patristic research was to show that the Fathers of the Church provided the vision to see the centrality of the death and resurrection of Christ as the center point of all Christianity. The accuracy and beauty of that truth captured succinctly what was so evident in Chrysostom and in Western figures like Ambrose, Augustine, and Aquinas. The centrality of Christ's death and resurrection as forming the core of the liturgy endures to this day in the East, as one might expect, but these same truths are also abundantly attested

9 Brian Dunkle, "Thomas Aquinas's Use of John Chrysostom in the *Catena Aurea* and the *Tertia Pars*," in Dauphinais and Hofer, *Thomas Aquinas and the Greek Fathers*, 163.

10 While the patristic movement of the twentieth century has been well documented, the groundwork for it laid in the nineteenth century has been largely overlooked. Aside from the Oxford Movement in the Anglican Church and John Hnery Newman's appropriation of the Fathers, the lacuna is only now being filled in with works like Joseph Carola *Engaging the Church Fathers in Nineteenth-Century Catholic Theology: The Patristic Legacy of the Scuola Romana*. (Steubenville, OH: Emmaus Road Publishing, 2023).

in the modern West. The liturgical continuities across spatial and cultural landscapes are really quite remarkable. The only reason for the lack of appreciation is neglect. The Second Vatican Council in its teachings on the liturgy reverberates with the same underlying message that we have seen in John Chrysostom:

> When the fullness of time had come [God] sent His Son, the Word made flesh, anointed by the Holy Spirit, to preach the gospel to the poor, to heal the contrite of heart, to be a "bodily and spiritual medicine," the Mediator between God and man. For His humanity, united with the person of the Word, was the instrument of our salvation. Therefore, in Christ "the perfect achievement of our reconciliation came forth, and the fullness of divine worship was given to us." The wonderful works of God among the people of the Old Testament were but a prelude to the work of Christ the Lord in redeeming mankind and giving perfect glory to God. He achieved His task principally by the paschal mystery of His blessed passion, resurrection from the dead, and the glorious ascension, whereby "dying, he destroyed our death and, rising, he restored our life." For it was from the side of Christ as He slept the sleep of death upon the cross that there came forth "the wondrous sacrament of the whole Church."[11]

The liturgy has always been about Jesus Christ in both East and West. Almost every sentence in this summary from *Sacrosanctum Concilium* can be matched with something from John's homilies. When the Council speaks of "the wondrous sacrament of the whole Church," it is drawing on prayers taken from the Western liturgies, but they could just have easily been taken from the homilies of John Chrysostom. That phrase, for example, reminds us of John's most frequent adjectives in characterizing the mysteries. John sees them as "awesome and awe-inspiring" (φρικτός καὶ φρικώδης) because in those mysteries he sees the heavens come down to earth and the realities of the metaphysical world embodied in the physical. John's awareness of how awesome the mysteries are leads him to focus on silence as the most appropriate response to these realities. While he sometimes urges silence as a preparation for participation in the mysteries, he more often emphasizes it as a result of encountering those mysteries. I have several times cited those beautiful words from his homily *On Blessed Philogonius*. "You are about to receive the King under your roof in communion. As the King enters

11 Vatican Council II, *Sacrosanctum Concilium*, December 4, 1963, 1,5.

your soul, you should be in much tranquility, much silence, deep peace of thoughts."[12] These words could have as easily been spoken by a Western Father. John's allusion to the words of the centurion in Matthew chapter 8 was in fact incorporated into the Western communion rite and therefore owned by Westerners as well as by those in the East.

I have maintained that John Chrysostom was a curate of souls first and last. His preaching was motivated not by a desire for rhetorical flair but by a love for his flock. That same motivation lay behind his many exclamations on the Eucharist. The vivid imagery he used in talking about the cross and the Eucharist are all directed to the same goal, that of building up the spiritual lives of his hearers. Part and parcel of his thought was the realization that the Eucharist was a gift, gratuitous but demanding. While God was under no obligation whatsoever to give the Eucharist, he freely did so because he wanted to communicate the life of his Son to the people of God. Receiving the Eucharist, however, demanded much from those same people. John especially called his communicants to forgiveness of their enemies and to charity toward the less fortunate. This practical emphasis perdures down to our own time. In 2005 Benedict XVI (Joseph Ratzinger) issued his first encyclical, entitled *Deus Caritas Est*, in which he discussed the meaning of the Eucharist in the practice of the Christian faith. Like many other theologians, Ratzinger connected the sacrifice of the cross, the Eucharist, and a life of charity in an explicit way: "Jesus gave this act of oblation an enduring presence through his institution of the Eucharist at the Last Supper. . . . The Eucharist draws us into Jesus' act of self-oblation. More than just statically receiving the incarnate Logos, we enter into the very dynamic of his self-giving."[13] John Chrysostom would have been very pleased that one of his spiritual sons had perceived the inseparable link between the Eucharist and the gift of self. Both John and Benedict would emphasize how the union with God through the sacrament moves us beyond a static reception into the dynamic of self-giving love: "The sacramental mysticism, grounded in God's condescension towards us, operates at a radically different level and lifts us to far greater heights than anything that any human mystical elevation could ever accomplish."[14] Benedict's words here seem to echo Chrysostom's belief that the Christian life must be lived from a supernatural stance.

12 *On Blessed Philogonius*, PG 48:756.

13 Benedict XVI, Encyclical Letter *Deus Caritas Est* (December 25, 2005), 13.

14 Benedict XVI, *Deus Caritas Est*, 13.

✠ ✠ ✠

Like the Eucharist itself, John's preaching about it seems to defy explanation. It is so varied in expression and rich in content that summaries seem to do it violence. Yet, long contact and intimacy with his preaching does emit some light. What is striking is how he believes and teaches so much more than appears on the surface. Many in the past have read his commentaries on the Bible as being rather prosaic and pedestrian, and in reading some of those homilies one can see how one might arrive at such a conclusion. I have contended, however, that John's preaching is much richer than once thought. Wendy Mayer arrived at essentially the same conclusion when she maintained, "For John perhaps more than for any other preacher of his time, the *telos* of exegetical preaching is to effect, through repeated exposure to the oral interpretation of scripture, the transformation of the listener into a living embodied hermeneutic exemplar."[15]

The depth of John's preaching lies in the connections he makes between the sacramental life of the Church and the saving events of Christ's life, especially those between the Paschal Mystery and the Eucharist. The inner connection between the cross and the ongoing life of the Church lies at the heart of the gospel. What Chrysostom, Augustine, and many other Church Fathers had said in a more ancient vocabulary was what Thomas Aquinas emphasized so strongly, namely, that the Paschal Mystery is the ultimate source from which all grace and mercy flows. This emphasis on a unique mystery subsisting under different modes seems to suggest a constant identity underneath changing appearances. The several registers (historical, liturgical, mystical) and multidimensional symbolism evident in John and other Fathers all refer back to the unique reality of Christ died and risen.

Today, sustained contact and exploration of the Church Fathers can aid the Church in bringing to expression the way in which Christ's presence in history, in the Church, and in the Eucharist provides meaning and engenders integration in the lives of those attached to him. Being in Christ means becoming what Christ was in the world. His humanity mediated the divine within him. His will was to give his life as a gift to those he would redeem

15 Wendy Mayer, "The Homiletic Audience as Embodied Hermeneutic: Scripture and Its Interpretation in the Exegetical Preaching of John Chrysostom," in *Hymns, Homilies, and Hermeneutics in Byzantium*, ed. Sarah Gador-White and Andrew Mellas, Byzantina Australiensia 25 (Leiden: Brill, 2021), 13.

(Mk 10:45). His sacrifice was to endure in the life of the Church through its sacramental economy. The Christian who participates in that economy is united to Christ and becomes what he is. Most of all, as Christ the Son was the recipient of the Father's *philanthropia,* so the Christian lives out of and conveys this profound love of God for humanity. Living the Paschal Mystery is the engine that drives that life; the Eucharist is the fuel that drives the engine.

Bibliography

Allen, P., B. Neil, and W. Mayer, eds. *Preaching Poverty in Late Antiquity: Perceptions and Realities*. Arbeiten zur Kirchen- und Theologiegeschichte 28. Leipzig: Evangelische Verlagsanstalt, 2009.

Ambrose of Milan. *On the Mysteries*.

Anatolios, Khaled. *Deification through the Cross: An Eastern Christian Theology of Salvation*. Grand Rapids, MI: Eerdmans, 2020.

Aquilina, Mike. *The Eucharist Foretold: The Lost Prophecy of Malachi*. Steubenville, OH: Emmaus Road Press, 2019.

Arrian. *Discourses of Epictetus*.

Artemi, Eirini. "The Fulfillment of the Church through the Sacrament of the Holy Eucharist according to Nicholas Cabasilas." *Roda da Fortuna Revista Eletrônica sobre Antiguidade e Medievo* 5, no. 2 (2016): 65–179.

Augustine. *Commentary on John*. Available at http://www.augustinus.it/latino/index.htm.

Bady, Guillaume. *Trop occupé pour t'occuper de ta vie? Le guide au quotidien d'un père de l'église textes présenté and choisi*. Paris: Editions du Cerf, 2015.

———. *La Source sans fin: La Bible chez Jean Chrysostome*. Cahiers de Biblia Patristica 23. Turnhout: Brepols, 2021.

Bae, Junghun. *John Chrysostom on Almsgiving and the Therapy of the Soul*. Leiden: Brill, 2021.

Bareille, J. *Oeuvres Complètes de Saint Jean Chrysostome*. 21 vols. Paris: Libraire de Louis Vives, 1865.

Barkhuizen, J. H. "John Chrysostom, *Homily 50* on Matthew 14:23–36 (PG 58,503–510): A Perspective on His Homiletic Art." *Acta Classica* 38 (1995): 43–56.

Basil of Caesarea. *Sermo 13*.

Batiffol, Pierre. *L'Eucharistie: La Presence Réele et la Transubstantiation*. 10th ed. Études d'histoire et de théologie positive. Paris: Libraire Victor Lecoffre, 1930.

Baur, Chrysostomos, OSB. *S. Jean Chrysostome et ses oeuvres dans l'histoire littéraire: Essai présenté à l'occasion de XV centenaire*. Louvain: Bureaux de recueil, 1907.

———, trans. *Kommentar zum Evangelium des heiligen Matthaus*. Bibliothek der Kirchenvaeter. Muenchen: Verlag der Jos Koesel, 1915.

———. *John Chrysostom and His Time*. Translated by Sr. M. Gonzaga, RSM. 2 vols. Westminster, MD: Newman Press, 1959.

Benedict XVI (Joseph Ratzinger). "Letter of His Holiness Benedict XVI on the Occasion of the 16th Centenary of the Death of St. John Chrysostom." https://www.vatican.va/content/benedict-xvi/en/letters/2007/documents/hf_ben-xvi_let_20070810_giovanni-crisostomo.html.

Betz, Johannes Eucharistie in der Schrift und Patristik Handbuch der Dogmengeschichte vol 4 Freiburg: Herder, 1979.

Blankenhorn, Bernard. *Bread from Heaven: An Introduction to the Theology of the Eucharist*. Washington, DC: The Catholic University of America Press, 2021.

Blass, F., and A. Debrunner. *A Grammar of the Greek New Testament and Other Early Christian Literature*. Chicago: University of Chicago Press, 1961.

Boersma, Hans. *Heavenly Participation: The Weaving of a Sacramental Tapestry*. Grand Rapids MI: Eerdmans Publishing Company, 2011.

Boersma, Hans. *Scripture as Real Presence: Sacramental Exegesis in the Early Church*. Grand Rapids, MI: Baker Academic, 2017.

Bornert, René. *Les Commentaires byzantines de la divine liturgie de VIIe au XVe siècle*. Archives de l'Orient chrétien 9. Paris: Institut francais d'Etudes byzantines, 1966.

Bradshaw, Paul. *Eucharistic Origins*. Oxford: Oxford University Press, 2004

Brändle, Rudolf . "Eucharistie und christliches Leben" in D. Hellholm and D. Sänger (eds.), *The Eucharist – Its Origins and Contexts: Sacred Meal, Communal Meal, Table Fellowship in Late Antiquity, Early Judaism, and Early Christianity* (Tubingen: Mohr Siebeck. 2017), 1191-1215.

Brottier, Laurence. "L'Appel des demi-Chrétiens à la vie angélique." In *Jean Chrysotome predicateur: Entre idéal monastique et realité mondaine*. Paris: Editions du Cerf, 2005.

———. *Les Propos sur la contrition de Jean Chrysostome: Le destin d'écrits de jeunesse méconnus*. Paris: Editions du Cerf, 2010.

Cabasilas, Nicholas. *A Commentary on the Divine Liturgy*. Translated by J. M. Hussey and P. A. McNulty. Crestwood, NY: St. Vladimir's Seminary Press, 2002.

Cabrol, F., and H. LeClercq. *Reliquiae liturgicae vetustissimae*. Monumenta Ecclesiae Liturgica 1. Paris, 1913.

Cardo, Daniel. *The Cross and the Eucharist in Early Christianity: A Theological and Liturgical Investigation*. Cambridge: Cambridge University Press, 2019.

Carola, Joseph S.J. *Engaging the Church Fathers in Nineteenth-Century Catholic Theology: The Patristic Legacy of the Scuola Romana*. Steubenville, OH: Emmaus Road Publishing, 2023.

Childs, Brevard S. *Memory and Tradition in Israel*. London: SCM Press, 1962.

Christo, Gus George. *Martyrdom according to John Chrysostom: To Live Is Christ, to Die Is Gain*. Lewiston, NY: Mellen Press, 1997.

Corbon, Jean. *The Wellspring of Worship*. Translated by Matthew J. O'Connell. San Francisco: Ignatius Press, 2005.

Crichton, J. D. "A Theology of Worship." In *The Study of Liturgy*, edited by Cheslyn Jones, Geoffrey Wainwright, and Edward Yarnold, 3–29. New York: Oxford University Press, 1978.

Cyril of Jerusalem. *Mystagogical Lectures*.

D'Ales, A. "Incomprehensibili chez Jean Chrysostome." *Recherches de science religieuse* 23 (1933): 302–20.

———. "Un Texte Eucharistique de Saint Jean Chrysostome." *Recherches de science religieuse* 23 (1933): 451–62.

Danby, Herbert. *The Mishnah: Translated from the Hebrew with Introduction and Brief Explanatory Notes*. Oxford: Oxford University Press, 1933.

Daniélou, Jean. "Le symbolisme des rites baptismaux." *Dieu vivant* 1 (1945): 15–43.

———. *The Bible and Liturgy*. Notre Dame, IN: University of Notre Dame Press, 1956.

———. *Sur l'incompréhensibilité de Dieu*. SC 28 (bis). Paris: Editions du Cerf, 1970.

———. "What Is Typology?" *Antiphon* 25, no. 3 (2021): 336–38.

Dauphinais, Michael, and Andrew Hofer, eds. *Thomas Aquinas and the Greek Fathers*. Ave Maria, FL: Sapientia Press, 2019.

Dauphinais, Michael, and Matthew Levering, eds. *Reading John with St. Thomas Aquinas: Theological Exegesis and Speculative Theology*. Washington, DC: The Catholic University of America Press, 2005.

De Aldama, J. A. *Repetorium Pseudochrysostomicum*. Paris: CNR, 1965.

de Lubac, Henri. *Corpus Mysticum l'Eucharistie et l'Eglise au Moyen Age Etude historique*. Paris: Editions du Cerf, 2009. Originally published 1944.

Despotis, Athanasios. "The Philosophical-Religious Hybridity in John 6 and Its Reception in the Commentaries of Origen and Chrysostom." In *Drawing and Transcending Boundaries in the New Testament and Early Christianity*, edited by Jacobus Kok, Martin Webber, and Jermo van Nes, 47–67 (Münster: LIT Verlag, 2020).

De Wet, Chris L. "John Chrysostom on Envy." *Studia Patristica* 47 (2010): 255–60.

———. "The Priestly Body: Power-Discourse and Identity in John Chrysostom's *De Sacerdotio*." *Religion and Theology* 18 (2011): 1–29.

di Nola, Gerardo, ed. *Cristo, Eucaristia, la Vergine Madre del Signore*. Vatican: Libreria Editrice Vaticana, 1997.

———. *La Dottrina Eucharistica de Giovanni Crisostomo*. Vol. 3 of *Bibliotheca Patristica Eucharistica*. Vatican City: Libreria Editrice Vaticana, 1997.

———. *La Dottrina Eucharistica dei Secoli I-IV*. Vol. 4 of *Bibliotheca Patristica Eucharistica*. Vatican City: Libreria Editrice Vaticana, 2000.

Dragas, George D. "Perceptions of John Chrysostom in Contemporary Greek Orthodoxy." In *Chrysostomosbilder in 1600 Jahren Facetten der Wirkungsgeschichte eines Kirchenvaters*, edited by Martin Wallraff and Rudolf Braendle, 373–409. Berlin: Walter de Gruyter, 2008.

Dumortier, Jean. *Jean Chrysostome: Homélies sur Ozias*. SC 277. Paris: Editions du Cerf, 1981.

Dunkle, Brian. "Thomas Aquinas's Use of John Chrysostom in the *Catena Aurea* and the *Tertia Pars*." In *Thomas Aquinas and the Greek Fathers*, edited by Michael Dauphinais and Andrew Hofer, 151–64. Ave Maria, FL: Sapientia Press, 2019.

———. "The Twofold Affection: The Background of John Chrysostom's Use of Φύσις and Χάρις." *Vigiliae Christianae* 75, no. 4 (2021): 355–74.

Elm, Susanna. *Sons of Hellenism, Fathers of the Church: Emperor Julian, Gregory Nazianzen, and the Vision of Rome*. Berkeley: University of California Press, 2012.

Evagrius Ponticus. *Discourse to Virgins*.

Fabricius, Cajus. *Zu den Jugendschriften des Johannes Chrysostomos: Untersuchungen zum klassizismus des Vierten Jahrhunderts*. Lund, Sweden: Hakan Ohlssons Boktryckeri, 1962.

Fagerberg, David W. *Theologia Prima: What Is Liturgical Theology?* 2nd ed. Chicago: Hillenbrand Books, 2004.

Feingold, Lawrence. *The Eucharist: Mystery of Presence, Sacrifice, and Communion*. Steubenville, OH: Emmaus Press, 2018.

———. *Touched by Christ: The Sacramental Economy*. Steubenville, OH: Emmaus Press, 2021.

Finn, Thomas M. *The Liturgy of Baptism in the Baptismal Instructions of St. John Chrysostom*. Catholic University of America Studies in Christian Antiquity. Washington, DC: The Catholic University of America Press, 1967.

Gavrilyuk, Paul, Andrew Hofer OP, and Matthew Levering. *The Oxford Handbook of Deification*. Oxford: Oxford University Press, forthcoming.

Goggin, Sr. Thomas Aquinas, SCH. *Homilies on Saint John the Apostle and Evangelist: Homilies 1-47* FC 33. Washington, DC: The Catholic University of America Press, 1957.

———. *Homilies on Saint John the Apostle and Evangelist: Homilies 48-88*. FC 41 Washington, DC: The Catholic University of America Press, 1959.

Grace, Madeline. "The Ponderings of Ignatius of Antioch and John Chrysostom on the Great Gift of the Eucharist." *Diakonia* 34 (2001): 97–107.

Gregory Nazianzen. *Carmina Moralia.*

———. *Oration 14: On the Love of the Poor.*

Gregory of Nyssa. *Against Eunomius.*

———. *Homily 15 on the Song of Songs.*

Gross, Jules. *The Divinization of the Christian according to the Greek Fathers.* Translated by Paul A. Onica. Anaheim, CA: A&C Press, 2002.

Hadot, Pierre. *Philosophy as a Way of Life: Spiritual Exercises from Socrates to Foucault. Edited by Arnold I. Davidson,* translated by Michael Chase. Oxford: Blackwell Publishing, 1995.

Halliburton, R. J. "The Patristic Theology of the Eucharist." In *The Study of Liturgy,* edited by Cheslyn Jones, Geoffrey Wainwright, and Edward Yarnold, 201–8. New York: Oxford University Press, 1978.

Halton, Thomas. "Some Images of the Church in St. John Chrysostom." *American Ecclesiastical Review* 153, no. 2 (1965): 96–106.

Hammond, Carolyn, trans. *Augustine: Confessions.* LCL 26–27. Cambridge, MA: Harvard University Press, 2014, 2016.

Harkins, Paul W. *Discourses against Judaizing Christians by St. John Chrysostom.* FC 68. Washington, DC: The Catholic University of America Press, 1979.

———. *Homilies on the Incomprehensible Nature of God by St. John Chrysostom.* FC 72. Washington, DC: The Catholic University of America Press, 1984.

Hay, Camillus. "St. John Chrysostom and the Integrity of the Human Nature of Christ." *Franciscan Studies* 19, nos. 3–4 (1959): 298–317.

Heintz, Michael. Review of *Church, World, and Kingdom: The Eucharistic Foundations of Alexander Schmemann's Pastoral Theology,* by William C. Mills. *Antiphon* 21, no. 1 (2017): 72–74.

Hellholm, David and Dieter Sänger (eds.), *The Eucharist – Its Origins and Contexts: Sacred Meal, Communal Meal, Table Fellowship in Late Antiquity, Early Judaism, and Early Christianity* 3 vols. Tubingen: Mohr Siebeck, 2017.

Hilary of Poitiers. *De Trinitate.*

Hill, Robert C. *St. John Chrysostom: Homilies on Genesis.* FC 74. Washington, DC: The Catholic University of America Press, 1986.

———. *Commentary on the Psalms.* Brookline, MA: Holy Cross Orthodox Press, 1998.

———. *Old Testament Homilies.* Vol. 1. Brookline, MA: Holy Cross Orthodox Press, 2003.

Hofer, Andrew. *The Power of Patristic Preaching: The Word in Our Flesh.* Washington, DC: The Catholic University of America Press, 2023.

Howell, Kenneth J. "Natural Knowledge and Textual Meaning in Augustine's Interpretation of Genesis: The Three Functions of Natural Philosophy." In *Interpreting Nature and Scripture: History of a Dialogue in the Abrahamic Religions,* edited by Jitse M. van der Meer and Scott M. Mandelbrote, 117–45. Leiden: Brill. 2008.

———. *Clement of Rome and the Didache: A New Translation and Theological Commentary.* Zanesville, OH: CHN Resources, 2012.

———. "The Eucharist as a Hermeneutical Lens in the Preaching of Peter Chrysologus." *Toronto Journal of Theology* 35, no. 2 (2020): 199–207.

———. "The Eucharist and the Life of Christ in the Preaching of John Chrysostom." *Nova et Vetera* 19, no. 3 (2021): 791–824.

Hunter, David G. *A Comparison between a King and a Monk/Against the Opponents of the Monastic Life: Two Treatises by John Chrysostom.* Lewiston, NY: Edwin Mellen Press, 1988.

Ignatius of Antioch. *Letter to the Ephesians.*

Irenaeus of Lyons. *Against Heresies.*

John Damascene. *On the Orthodox Faith.* In *Die Schriften des Johannes von Damaskos,* vol. 2, edited by P. B. Kotter, 3–239. Patristische Texte und Studien 12. Berlin: De Gruyter, 1973.

Kaldas, Samuel. "A Strange New Philosophy of Forgiveness: Insights from St. John Chrysostom on Forgiving the Unrepentant." *St. Vladimir's Theological Quarterly* 63, no. 3 (2019): 261–76.

Keating, Daniel A. *The Appropriation of Divine Life in Cyril of Alexandria* Oxford: Oxford University Press, 2003).

Kelly, J. N. D. *Golden Mouth: The Story of John Chrysostom; Ascetic, Preacher, Bishop.* London: Duckworth, 1995.

Kilmartin, Edward J. "John Chrysostom's Influence on Gabriel Qatraya's Theology of Eucharistic Consecration." *Theological Studies* 42, no. 3 (1981): 444–57.

———. "The Active Role of Christ and the Holy Spirit in the Divine Liturgy." *Diakonia* 17 (1982): 95–108.

Krupp, Robert. *Shepherding the Flock of God: The Pastoral Theology of John Chrysostom.* American University Studies. New York: Peter Lange Press, 1992.

Kwasniewski, Peter. "Aquinas on Eucharistic Ecstasy: From Self-Alienation to Gift of Self." *Nova et Vetera* 6 (2008): 157–204.

Lai, Pak-Wah. "John Chrysostom and the Hermeneutics of Exemplar Portraits." PhD diss., University of Durham, 2010.

Laird, Raymond J. "Mindset (γνώμη) in John Chrysostom." In *The Oxford Handbook of Maximus the Confessor.* Edited by Pauline Allen and Bronwen Neil, 194–211. Oxford: Oxford University Press, 2015.

Lampe, G. W. *Patristic Greek Lexicon.* Oxford: Oxford University Press, 1961.

Lawrence, Melvin E. *The Christology of John Chrysostom.* Lewiston, NY: Mellen University Press, 1996.

Layton, Richard A. *Didymus the Blind and His Circle in Late-Antique Alexandria.* Urbana: University of Illinois Press, 2004.

Leo the Great. *Sermon 74*.

Levering, Matthew. *Engaging the Doctrine of Revelation: The Mediation of the Gospel through Church and Scripture*. Grand Rapids, MI: Baker Academic, 2014.

———. "Liturgy and Trinity." *Antiphon* 23, no. 3 (2019): 226–60.

Leyerle, Blake. *The Narrative Shape of Emotion in the Preaching of John Chrysostom*. Christianity in Late Antiquity 10. Berkeley: University of California Press, 2020.

Libanius. *Libanius: Autobiography and Selected Letters*. Translated and edited by A. F. Norman. LCL 478. Cambridge, MA: Harvard University Press, 1992.

Malingrey, Anne-Marie, trans. *Jean Chrysostome: Lettres a Olympias*. SC 13. Paris: Editions du Cerf, 1947.

———. *Jean Chrysostome: Sur le sacerdoce*. SC 272. Paris: Editions du Cerf, 1980.

March, F. A. *Liturgia Horarum and Latin Hymns*. Translated by Edward Caswall. 1894.

Margerie, Bertrand de. *Introduction à l'histoire de l'exégèse les pères grecque et orientaux*. Paris: Editions du Cerf, 1980.

Markschies, Christoph. "Current Research on the Eucharist in Ancient Christianity" *Early Christianity* 7 (2016) 417-446.

Markschies, Christoph. God's Body: Jewish, Christian, and Pagan Images of God Waco, TX: Baylor University Press, 2019.

Marriott, Charles, trans. *Homilies on Saint John the Apostle and Evangelist*. Reprinted in *Nicene and Post-Nicene Fathers*, edited by Philip Schaff, vol. 14. Buffalo, NY: Christian Literature, 1889. Available online at http://www.newadvent.org/fathers/240146.htm.

Marsaux, Jacky. "Pour une nouvelle approche de l'eucharistie chez Jean Chrysostome à partir de la pragmatique." *Studia Patristica* 37 (2001): 565–70.

———. "La Théologie de l'Eucharistie selon Jean Chrysostome: Étude du schéma sacrificiel." Doctoral diss., Université Paris-IV et Institut Catholique de Paris, 2008.

———. *L'eucharistie, école de vie*. Les Peres dans la foi 99. Paris: Editions du Cerf, 2009.

———. *Jean Chrysostome, lecteur de l'Ecriture*. Cahiers Evangile Supplement 188. Paris: Editions du Cerf, 2019.

Maxwell, Jaclyn. *Christianization and Communication in Late Antiquity: John Chrysostom and His Congregation in Antioch*. Cambridge: Cambridge University Press, 2006.

Mayer, Wendy. "Chrysostomica: An Online Bibliography of Scholarship on John Chrysostom and Attributed Writings." PDF available at https://www.academia.edu/6448870/Chrysostomica.

———. "Poverty and Society in the World of John Chrysostom." In *Social and Political Life in Late Antiquity*, edited by W. Bowden, A. Gutteridge, and C. Machado, 465–84. Leiden: Brill, 2006.

———. "Poverty and Generosity toward the Poor in the Time of John Chrysostom." In *Wealth and Poverty in Early Church and Society*, edited by S. R. Holman, 193–215. Brookline, MA: Holy Cross Orthodox Press, 2008.

———. "John Chrysostom on Poverty." In *Preaching Poverty in Late Antiquity: Perceptions and Realities*, edited by P. Allen, B. Neil, and W. Mayer, 69–117. Leipzig: Evangelische Verlagsanstalt, 2009.

———. "Shaping the Sick Soul: Reshaping the Identity of John Chrysostom." In *Christians Shaping Identity from the Roman Empire to Byzantium*, edited by Geoffrey D. Dunn and Wendy Mayer, 140–64. Leiden: Brill, 2015.

———. "John Chrysostom: Moral Philosopher and Physician of the Soul." In *John Chrysostom Past, Present, Future*, edited by Doru Costache and Merio Baghos, 193–215. Sydney: AIOOS Press, 2017.

———. "The Homiletic Audience as Embodied Hermeneutic: Scripture and Its Interpretation in the Exegetical Preaching of John Chrysostom." In *Hymns, Homilies, and Hermeneutics in Byzantium*, edited by Sarah Gador-White and Andrew Mellas, 11–29. Byzantina Australiensia 25. Leiden: Brill, 2021.

Mayer, Wendy, and Pauline Allen. *John Chrysostom*. The Early Church Fathers. New York: Routledge, 2000.

Meconi, David Vincent, SJ. *Peter Chrysologus*. The Early Church Fathers. New York: Routledge, 2021.

Meredith, Anthony. Review of *Jean Chrysostome: Sermons sur la Genèse*, edited by Laurence Brottier. *Journal of Theological Studies* 51 (2000): 732–33.

Meyendorff, Paul. *On the Divine Liturgy: Germanus of Constantinople*. Crestwood, NY: St. Vladimir's Press, 1999.

Meyer, Louis. *Saint Jean Chrysostome: Maitre de Perfection Chrétienne*. Paris: Gabriel Beauchesne, 1933.

Mikloshazy, Attila. *Benedicamus Domino: Let Us Bless the Lord*. Ottawa: Novalis, 2001.

Mills, William C. *Church, World, and Kingdom: The Eucharistic Foundations of Alexander Schmemann's Pastoral Theology*. Mundelein, IL: Hildebrand Books, 2011.

Mitchell, Margaret. "The Archetypal Image: John Chrysostom's Portraits of Paul." *Journal of Religion* 75 (1995): 15–43.

———. "A Patristic Perspective on Pauline Periautologia." *New Testament Studies* 47 (2001): 354–71.

———. *The Heavenly Trumpet: John Chrysostom and the Art of Pauline Interpretation*. London: Westminster John Knox Press, 2002.

Mohler, Johann Adam. *Symbolism*. New York: Crossroads, 1997.

Molinié, Pierre. *Jean Chrysostome, exégète: Le commentaire de la deuxième épître aux Corinthiens*. Orientalia Christiana Analecta 305. Rome: Pontificio Istituto Orientale, 2019.

Monk Moses. *On the Providence of God*. Platina, CA: St. Herman of Alaska Brotherhood, 2015.

Naegle, August. *Die Eucharistielehre des Heiligen Johannes Chrysostomus*. Freiburg, Germany, 1900.

Nairn, J. Arbuthnot. *Περὶ ἱερωσύνης (De Sacerdotio) of St. John Chrysostom*. Cambridge: Cambridge University Press, 1906.

Nassif, Bradley. "Theoria in St. John Chrysostom's Exegesis: A Study in Biblical Hermeneutics and the Spiritual Life." PhD diss., Fordham University, 1991.

———, ed. *New Perspectives on Historical Theology: Essays in Honor of John Meyendorff*. Grand Rapids, MI: Eerdmans Publishing, 1996.

———. "Antiochene θεωρία in John's Chrysostom's Exegesis." In *Exegesis and Hermeneutics in the Churches of the East*, edited by Vahan S. Hovhanessian, 51–66. New York: Peter Lang, 2009.

———. "John Chrysostom on the Nature of Revelation and the Task of Exegesis." In *What Is the Bible? The Patristic Doctrine of Scripture*, edited by Matthew Baker and Mark Mourachian, 49–66. Minneapolis: Fortress Press, 2016.

Neville, Graham, trans. *Six Books on the Priesthood*. Crestwood, NY: St. Vladimir's Press, 2002.

Nilus of Ancyra. *On Evil Thoughts*.

Norris, Thomas J. *Cardinal Newman for Today*. New York: New City Press, 2010.

Nowak, Edward. *Le Chrétien Devant la Souffrance: Étude sur la Pensée de Jean Chrysostome*. Paris: Beauchesne, 1972.

Ortiz, Jared. ed. *Deification in the Latin Patristic Tradition*. Washington, DC: The Catholic University of America Press, 2019.

Ottosson, Krister. "The Love of God in St. John Chrysostom's Commentary on the Fourth Gospel." *The Church Quarterly Review* 100 (1965): 315–23.

Palardy, William B. "The Church and the Synagogue in the Sermons of St. Peter Chrysologus." PhD diss., Catholic University of America, 1992.

Papavassiliou, Vassilios. *Journey to the Kingdom: An Insider's Look at the Liturgy and Beliefs of the Eastern Orthodox Church*. Brewster, MA: Paraclete Press, 2012.

Ratzinger, Joseph. *The Feast of Faith*. San Francisco: Ignatius Press, 1980.

Raya, Joseph. *The Face of God*. Denville, NJ: Dimension Books, 1976.

Rhee, Helen, ed. *Wealth and Poverty in Early Christianity*. Ad Fontes: Early Christian Sources. Minneapolis: Fortress Press, 2017.

Rordorf, Willy. *La Doctrine des Douze Apotres*. SC 248. Paris: Editions du Cerf, 1998.

Russell, Norman. *The Doctrine of Deification in the Greek Patristic Tradition*. Oxford: Oxford University Press, 2004.

Rylaarsdam, David. *John Chrysostom on Divine Pedagogy: The Coherence of His Theology and Preaching*. Oxford: Oxford University Press, 2014.

Salem, Claire Elayne. "Sanity, Insanity, and Man's Being as Understood by St. John Chrysostom." PhD diss., Durham University, 2010.

Satterlee, Craig Alan. *Ambrose of Milan's Method of Mystagogical Preaching*. Collegeville, MN: Liturgical Press, 2002.

Scaglioni, Carlo. *Synkatabasis: La Condescendenza Divina in Giovanni Crisostomo*. Naples: Il Pozzo di Giabcobbe, 2011.

Scheeben, Matthias. *The Mysteries of Christianity*. St. Louis: B. Herder, 1951.

Schmemann, Alexander. *Introduction to Liturgical Theology*. London: Faith Press, 1966.

———. *For the Life of the World*. Crestwood, NY: St. Vladimir's Press, 1973.

———. *The Eucharist: Sacrament of the Kingdom*. Crestwood, NY: St. Vladimir's Press, 1987.

Sherwin, Michael. *On Love and Virtue: Theological Essays*. Steubenville, OH: Emmaus Press, 2018.

Solano, Jesus. *Textos Eucaristicos Primitivos, edicion bilingue de los contenidos en la Sagrada Escritura y los Santos Padres*. Vol. 1, *Hasta fines del siglo IV*. Madrid: Biblioteca de Autores Cristianos, 1952.

———. *Textos Eucaristicos Primitivos, edicion bilingue de los contenidos en la Sagrada Escritura y los Santos Padres*. Vol. 2, *Hasta el fin de la epoca patristica (s. VII-VIII)*. Madrid: Biblioteca de Autores Cristianos, 1954.

Souter, Alexander. *The Earliest Latin Commentators on the Epistles of St. Paul*. Oxford: Oxford University Press, 1927.

Stone, Darwell. *A History of the Doctrine of the Holy Eucharist*. London: Longmans, Green, 1909.

Taft, Robert. *The Great Entrance: a History of the Transfer of Gifts and Other Pre-anaphoral Rites of the Liturgy of St. John Chrysostom*. Rome: Pontificium Institutum Studiorum Orientalium, 1975.

———. "The Authenticity of the Chrysostom Anaphora Revisited: Determining the Authorship of Liturgical Texts by Computer." *Orientalia Christiana Periodica* 56 (1990): 5–51.

———. "The Epiclesis Question in the Light of Orthodox and Catholic Lex Orandi Traditions." In *New Perspectives on Historical Theology: Essays in Honor of John Meyendorff*, edited by Bradley Nassif, 210–37. Grand Rapids, MI: Eerdmans Publishing, 1996.

———. "The Spirit of Eastern Christian Worship." In *Beyond East and West: Problems in Liturgical Understanding*, 143–60. 2nd ed. Rome: Edizioni Orientalia Christiana, 2001.

———. "Toward a Theology of the Christian Feast." In *Beyond East and West: Problems in Liturgical Understanding*, 15–29. 2nd ed. Rome: Edizioni Orientalia Christiana, 2001.

Thurén, L. "John Chrysostom as a Rhetorical Critic: The Hermeneutics of an Early Father." *Biblical Interpretation: A Journal of Contemporary Approaches* 9 (2001): 180–218.

Tillard, Jean-Marie. *Flesh of the Church, Flesh of Christ: At the Source of the Ecclesiology of Communion*. Collegeville, MN: Liturgical Press, 2001. French original published in 1992.

Tolton, Caroline. "From Memory to Topology: The Architecture of Persuasion in the Sermons of Peter Chrysologus." PhD diss., University of Chicago Divinity School, 2005.

van de Paverd, Frans *Zur Geschichte der Meßliturgie in Antiocheia und Konstantinopel gegen Ende des vierten Jahrhunderts - Analyse der Quellen bei Johannes Chrysostomos* Orientalia Christiana Analecta 187 Rome, 1970.

Vatican Council II. *Sacrosanctum Concilium*. December 4, 1963.

Veniamin, Christopher. *The Orthodox Understanding of Salvation: Theosis in Scripture and Tradition*. Dalton, PA: Mount Tabor Publishing, 2016.

Verosta, Stephan. *Johannes Chrysostomus: Staatsphilosoph und Geschichtstheologe*. Graz, Austria: Verlag Styria, 1960.

von Hildebrand, Dietrich. *Liturgy and Personality*. Manchester, NH: Sophia Institute Press, 1993.

von Saxon, M. *La doctrine de St. Jean Chrysostome sur la divine Eucharistie*. Report of the XIX Eucharistic Congress, London, 1909.

Wawrykow, Joseph. "The Greek Fathers and the Eucharistic Theology of Thomas Aquinas." In *Thomas Aquinas and the Greek Fathers*, edited by Michael Dauphinais and Andrew Hofer, 274–302. Ave Maria, FL: Sapientia Press, 2019.

Wenger, Antoine, trans. *Huit catéchèses baptismales inédites*. SC 50. Paris: Editions du Cerf, 1957.

Wiles, Maurice F. *The Divine Apostle*. Cambridge: Cambridge University Press, 1967.

Wilken, Robert. *John Chrysostom and the Jews: Rhetoric and Reality in the Late 4th Century*. Eugene, OR: Wipf and Stock, 1983.

Wylie, Amanda Lee Berry. "John Chrysostom and His Homilies on the Acts of the Apostles: Reclaiming Ancestral Models for the Christian People." PhD diss., Princeton Theological Seminary, 1992.

Young, Frances. *Biblical Exegesis and the Formation of Christian Culture*. Cambridge: Cambridge University Press, 1997. Reprint, Peabody, MA: Hendrickson, 2002.

Zizioulas, John. *Eucharist, Bishop, Church: The Unity of the Church in the Divine Eucharist and the Bishop during the First Three Centuries*. Brookline, MA: Holy Cross Orthodox Press, 2001.

General Index

The Homilies and Writings of St. John Chrysostom Cited

PG *Patrologia Graeca* (ed) J.P. Migne (Paris, 1858) vols 48–64.

SC *Sources Chretiennes* (Paris: Editions du Cerf)

(note: some of the homilies listed below have been considered spurious by the editors of the *Patrologia Graeca*).

HOMILIES ON BIBLICAL BOOKS

Old Testament

New Testament

OTHER VOLUMES IN THE PATRISTIC THEOLOGY SERIES

The Power of Patristic Preaching: The Word in Our Flesh
by Andrew Hofer, OP

Bede the Theologian: History, Rhetoric, and Spirituality
by John P. Bequette

Cross and Creation: A Theological Introduction to Origen of Alexandria
by Mark E. Therrien